Study Guide

Basic Psychology

Fourth Edition

Study Guide

GLEITMAN
Basic Psychology
Fourth Edition

JOHN JONIDES
UNIVERSITY OF MICHIGAN

PAUL ROZIN
UNIVERSITY OF PENNSYLVANIA

W • W • NORTON & COMPANY • NEW YORK • LONDON

Permission and credits, constituting an extension of the copyright page, are located on pages 277–78.

Printed in the United States of America

Composition and layout by Roberta Flechner Graphics

Fourth Edition

ISBN 0-393-96918-5 (Pbk.)

W. W. Norton & Company, Inc., 500 Fifth Avenue, New York, N.Y. 10110
W. W. Norton & Company Ltd., 10 Coptic Street, London WC1A 1PU

2 3 4 5 6 7 8 9 0

CONTENTS

Acknowledgments vi
To the Student vii

Chapter 1 Introduction 1

Part 1 Action

Chapter 2 Biological Bases of Behavior 6
Chapter 3 Motivation 22
Chapter 4 Learning 33

Part 2 Cognition

Chapter 5 Sensory Processes 56
Chapter 6 Perception 69
Chapter 7 Memory 84
Chapter 8 Thought and Knowledge 96
Chapter 9 Language 108

Part 3 Social Behavior

Chapter 10 The Biological Basis of Social Behavior 119
Chapter 11 Social Cognition and Emotion 133
Chapter 12 Social Interaction 147

Part 4 Development

Chapter 13 Physical and Cognitive Development 157
Chapter 14 Social Development 168

Part 5 Individual Differences

Chapter 15 Intelligence: Its Nature and Measurement 187
Chapter 16 Personality I: Assessment, Trait Theory, and the Behavioral-Cognitive Approach 201
Chapter 17 Personality II: Psychodynamic, Humanistic, and Sociocultural Approaches 212
Chapter 18 Psychopathology 226
Chapter 19 Treatment of Psychopathology 245

Appendix A Statistics: The Collection, Organization, and Interpretation of Data 254
Appendix B Report Sheets 265

Copyrights and Acknowledgments 277

ACKNOWLEDGMENTS

The authors would like to thank Caroline Arnold, Jason Fabozzi, Elizabeth Gross, Georgia Larounis, Jennifer Lerner, Laura Lowery, Maureen Markwith, Linda Millman, Deborah Reyher, Nathan Witthoft, and Barbara Zeeff for their contributions and valuable suggestions.

In the course of developing the sections entitled "Investigating Psychological Phenomena" for each chapter, we have had occasion to seek the advice of colleagues and students who have particular expertise in the areas in question. We would like to acknowledge the help of Lyn Abramson, Henry Gleitman, Aaron Katcher, Charles G. Morris, Lorraine Nadelman, Harriet Oster, Christopher Peterson, Martin E. P. Seligman, W. John Smith, Marjorie Speers, and Edward Stricker. We also thank Walter Love and Jeannie Morrow for special assistance in field testing a number of the activities that we have included.

Finally, we thank Cathy Wick for her encouragement and advice throughout the development of the text. We are also extremely grateful to Margaret Farley who reviewed the entire manuscript with great care.

The authors of this guide are listed in alphabetical order on the title page.

TO THE STUDENT

This study guide is designed to help you to understand and apply the material presented in *Basic Psychology*, Fourth Edition, by Henry Gleitman. Each chapter in the study guide corresponds to one in the textbook. There are four sections in each study guide chapter: Learning Objectives, Programmed Exercises, Self Test, and Investigating Psychological Phenomena. The first three sections will help you determine the essential ideas of the chapter, as well as give you experience with possible test questions. The fourth section, Investigating Psychological Phenomena, allows you to extend your knowledge of some issues raised in the text. This section will also give you a feeling for how the data used by psychologists are collected, and how theories are tested in psychology. Let us briefly review the function of each of these sections.

LEARNING OBJECTIVES

We have provided an outline of the key issues discussed in each chapter. Each entry in the outline refers to a basic fact, theory, or relationship that you should have learned from the chapter. These entries are listed in order of occurrence in the chapter and are arranged under the same headings used in the chapter. It may be useful to read the learning objectives before reading the chapter, as well as after. They will help to orient you to the major issues, or the "big picture," of the chapter.

PROGRAMMED EXERCISES

For each chapter of the text, we have provided fill-in-the-blank questions. These questions test your basic knowledge of the key words and concepts of the chapter. These questions are very straightforward and can be looked up and verified in the text. So that you will know whether you are correct, the answer has been provided on the right side of the page. Be sure to cover that side of the page with your hand or a piece of paper as you do the exercises.

To facilitate locating the answers in the text, the programmed exercises are also arranged under the major headings of the textbook, and they follow the order of presentation in the text. This allows you to see which fact or theory pertains to which major point of the chapter.

SELF TEST

For each chapter in the text, we have prepared a self test composed of multiple-choice questions. They also follow the order of the text. In general, these questions are more difficult than the fill-ins, though both types of questions cover the range of materials presented in the text. The multiple choices sometimes highlight subtle distinctions, ask for some amount of integration, or test your ability to apply some of the material in the text.

Since multiple-choice questions are commonly used in examinations, and since they can also be very instructive, we will spend some time in this section discussing how to answer them. We will also describe and illustrate some different types of multiple-choice questions used in this study guide.

First, some basic strategies. Most multiple-choice questions on examinations, and in this study guide, have four or five choices. On most examinations there is a penalty of –1/3 point for wrong answers of four-choice questions, and –1/4 point for wrong answers on five-choice questions. This would mean that wild guessing should net a score of zero. But if you can eliminate even one choice, it pays to guess among the remaining alternatives.

Read each question carefully. Try to understand the *point* of the question. Read through the alternatives. The answer may be obvious to you. If not, try to eliminate some of the choices. You may be able to eliminate choices on the following grounds:

1. The choice is inherently inconsistent, illogical, or actual nonsense (e.g., word salad: a bunch of usually relevant terms combined in a meaningless way).

2. The choice makes sense and may even be true, but it is not an *answer* to the question.

3. On the basis of your knowledge, the choice is just the wrong answer to the question.

Get used to sorting out sense from nonsense and relevant from irrelevant answers. These skills will stand you in good stead in many of your activities outside of this course. Work with the remaining choices (if more than one choice remains), and do the best you can to determine the best fit between the question and the answer.

We will illustrate a number of different types of multiple-choice questions, all represented in this study guide. For each example we will indicate the correct answer and add comments on some of the incorrect choices.

Straight factual questions. Many multiple-choice questions simply ask for your knowledge of facts: names, definitions, and basic concepts.

1. The Prime Minister of Great Britain at the end of World War II was:
   a. Neville Chamberlain
   b. Winston Churchill
   c. Harold Wilson
   d. Sir D. Winter
   e. Anthony Eden

Comment: This is a very straightforward question. You know it or you don't. The answer is *b*, Winston Churchill. The other names were selected to make the question somewhat difficult: Three of the other choices were prime ministers of Great Britain at the beginning of or after the war, and one, Sir D. Winter, is a fictitious name.

2. The best way to describe inflation is:
   a. increase in the gross domestic product not accompanied by increased unemployment
   b. a general increase in prices
   c. a decrease in the money supply
   d. a decrease in the value of the monetary system, when associated with a gross domestic product
   e. another form of recession

Comment: This question is more difficult than 1. This is in part because the choices are more difficult. The correct answer is *b*. Answers *a*, *c*, and *e* are just wrong. Though *a* is consistent with inflation, it does not define it. Item *d* is inherently wrong, that is, it is sort of nonsense. What does it mean to decrease the value of the monetary *system* as opposed to money? And everything is associated with some gross domestic product. Keep your eyes open for nonsense. There is a lot of it in the world.

Evaluating evidence for a theory. In this type of question you are asked to judge whether particular results (real or hypothetical) support a particular theory (or which theory would be supported or opposed by a particular result). The theory and/or results may have been presented in the text, or they may be introduced in the question. The question tests both your knowledge of the materials, and your progress in understanding how to evaluate evidence. This type of question is often formulated in the negative—"Which of the following would be evidence against theory X?"—simply because it is usually easier to come up with results supporting major theories than results opposing them. We will assume, for the next sample question, that you have read in some text or other that Yentzel claimed that the crime rate increases as population mass and density increase. (Yentzel is a fictitious name.)

3. Which of the following would be evidence against Yentzel's theory? (Note: We assume that New York is larger than Philadelphia, which is larger than Tucson.)
   a. Philadelphia has a crime rate higher than Tucson
   b. a few cities with increasing population also have increasing crime rates
   c. a few cities with decreasing population have an increase in crime rate
   d. Philadelphia has a lower crime rate than New York
   e. the ratio of murder to robberies is lower in New York than in Tucson

Comment: The correct answer is *c*, because this result is opposite to what would be predicted by Yentzel's theory. Answers *a*, *b*, and *c* are supporting evidence for the theory. Answer *e* is irrelevant: The theory says nothing about the types of crime, and *e* says nothing about the overall crime rate. (Note another clue to the right answer: *b* and *c* are opposites, so it is likely that one is evidence against the theory. However, clever exam writers know about this and sometimes put in opposites that are irrelevant to the question, to keep you on your toes.)

Extending a principle or theory to a new situation. This type of question tests your understanding of a principle, theory, or concept by asking you to apply it to a situation other than those presented in the text.

4. If the saying "a stitch in time saves nine" were applied to medicine, one would recommend:
   a. reducing the amount of sewing in surgery
   b. increasing the cost of medical insurance
   c. increasing the frequency of checkups
   d. increasing the number of physicians
   e. making prescription drugs available over the counter

Comments: The correct answer is *c*. To answer the question, one must understand the saying and translate it into medical terms. This translation would be something like: Medical precautions can lead to avoidance of major illnesses. Alternative *a* is irrelevant to the *real* meaning of the saying and simply follows the *literal* meaning. Answer *b* would not lead, in any direct way, to avoidance of illness. But *b* is a sort of correct answer, since one might assume that increasing the cost of medical insurance would lead to increased coverage. The answer says increasing the *cost*, not the *amount* of insurance. Answer *c* relates directly to the saying: More checkups should lead to early discovery of illnesses that might prove harmful if allowed to develop. While *d* might well cut down the rate of illnesses, it is not a direct way of arriving at prevention. Lastly, *e* is irrelevant to the issue raised in the saying.

Relating different ideas or facts, or integrating materials. This type of question often involves materials from different sections of a chapter, or perhaps from different chapters (we have refrained from the latter, since we don't know the order in which you will be reading the chapters in the book).

5. The President of the United States is related to the electoral college as a U.S. Senator is related to:*
   a. his own college faculty
   b. the voters of his state
   c. the members of the House of Representatives
   d. the state of his electors
   e. the state of his voters

Comment: The correct answer is *b*. The electoral college is the group of people who actually elect the president. The voters of a senator's state are the people who elect the senator. Item *a* is totally wrong and simply a play on the word college. Item *c* is factually wrong. Item *d* is wrong and doesn't make too much sense, and item *e* is a reversal of the correct answer and has no relation to the question.

*This type of relation is often stated as "President of the U.S.: electoral college::U.S. Senator: ___________."

INVESTIGATING PSYCHOLOGICAL PHENOMENA

For each chapter of the text, we have presented one or two activities or experiments. These activities build upon concepts or theories presented in the chapter and extend and deepen your knowledge and understanding of these concepts or theories.

The activities give you an opportunity to understand something about the progress of psychology as a science. While the text emphasizes our current understanding of psychology, the activities emphasize the process through which we arrive at this understanding. How is the theory tested? How do psychologists get data to describe basic relations or test theories? How do they analyze the data? We hope to give you a feeling for how progress is made, while at the same time indicating the problems and difficulties associated with the serious study of something as complex as the human mind.

We have attempted to provide you with a variety of activities. Some emphasize the generation or testing of theories, others data collection or analysis. We have tried to cover the major methods of data collection used by psychologists: Among all the activities are included examples of the experiment, the questionnaire, direct observation, and the interview. In many cases we provide data from studies we have done with introductory psychology students as a base for comparison with the data you collect. In each activity in which you collect data, we guide you through some analysis of the data and get you to try to interpret the data and relate it to issues raised in the text. If your instructor wishes to include the activities as part of the course, he or she may ask you to tear out the report (data) sheet pages, and hand them in. These sheets are duplicated at the end of the book in Appendix B. Otherwise, you may consider these activities as a less formal extension of your education in psychology.

We have tried out all of these activities on undergraduate students like yourselves. We have only included studies that work out for the great majority of students. Of course, with people as variable as they are, all the studies that you do on one of a few students will not show the same results. But we expect that most of you will get most of the predicted results.

Many of the most important phenomena in psychology cannot be included in these activities because they must be measured under controlled conditions, which you could not easily arrange. Some involve expensive equipment, like timers that can time thousandths of a second, or panels of lights and switches. Some important relations are not striking enough to be seen in one or a few subjects. We have tried to find, for each chapter, at least one activity that can be appreciated within the limits that you will be working under. We require no equipment other than pencil, paper, some sort of second indicator (stopwatch, digital watch with second indicator, or a watch with a second hand), and materials presented within this study guide. We have limited the time demands on you for any activity to less than one hour. In all but a few cases, we have limited the number of subjects to a very few. At the beginning of each activity, we indicate the equipment involved and the time demands it will make on you and the subjects.

These activities are designed to be both educational and entertaining. We hope that you find that they meet these goals.

CHAPTER 1

Introduction

Learning Objectives

THE SCOPE OF PSYCHOLOGY

1. What are examples of psychological phenomena?

Electrically triggered images

2. What do experiments on electrical stimulation of the brain tell us about the relationship between psychology and physiology?

Ambiguous sights and sounds

3. What determines the interpretation of an ambiguous stimulus?

The perceptual world of infants

4. How does the study of infants suggest that some abilities may be innate?

Displays

5. How is social interaction in animals mediated by displays? How do displays differ from one animal to another? Give examples.

Complex social behavior in humans

6. How are humans more complex in their social behavior than other animals?

A SCIENCE OF MANY FACES

7. What fields have contributed to the development of psychology?

THE TASK OF PSYCHOLOGY

8. What is, and what is not, the main purpose of psychology?

Programmed Exercises

THE SCOPE OF PSYCHOLOGY

1. Psychology involves not only the study of the mind, but also the study of ____________.	behavior
2. Electrical stimulation of the brain sometimes results in reports of ____________.	sensations
3. ____________ is an important determinant of how we perceive an ambiguous figure.	Context
4. The study of perceptual skills in infants using the visual cliff shows us that some skills are ____________ while others are ____________.	learned, innate
5. In animals, any social interactions depend largely on ____________ forms of communication.	innate
6. Many types of animal communication are based on signals called ____________.	displays

7. The behavior of panicky crowds is determined not only by each individual, but also by individuals' ____________ interactions. social (group)

A SCIENCE OF MANY FACES

8. Psychology can be studied from perspectives emphasizing ____________ (overt behavior), ____________ (human knowledge), ____________ ____________ (the influence of others on individual action), ____________ (growth), and ____________ differences (how people are alike or different). action cognition, social interaction development, individual

THE TASK OF PSYCHOLOGY

9. Psychology, like other sciences, seeks ____________ principles to explain its phenomena, rather than concentrating on individual events. general

Self Test

1. Psychology is the:
   a. science of the mind
   b. science of behavior
   c. both of the above
   d. none of the above

2. When the brain is stimulated electrically:
   a. visual experience may occur
   b. previous memories may be blocked
   c. new memories are blocked
   d. none of the above

3. If we are first shown a picture of a rat, and then the ambiguous figure below, we will most likely see:

   a. the man
   b. the rat
   c. the rat or the man, depending on other factors
   d. neither the rat nor the man

4. The visual cliff results suggest that:
   a. perceptual skills are learned
   b. perceptual skills are innate
   c. perceptual skills could be innate
   d. none of the above

5. Psychology consists of the study of
   a. action
   b. cognition
   c. social processes
   d. all of the above

Answer Key for Self Test

1. c p. 1
2. a p. 1
3. b p. 2
4. c p. 3
5. d p. 5

Investigating Psychological Phenomena

THE CONSISTENCY OF DREAMS

Equipment: None
Number of subjects: One, yourself
Time per subject: Ten or twenty minutes
Time for experimenter: Ten to twenty minutes

Although Chapter 1 is meant as a general introduction to psychology, its examples also provide insight into how psychological phenomenon are studied experimentally. Here we offer yet another example of an experimental approach to a psychological phenomenon. You will be asked to study a series of dream reports from three different dreamers, and to determine which reports should be categorized with each dreamer. Here are the specifics:

One of the fundamental issues in dream research concerns the extent to which dreams represent the realization of basic problems, wishes, needs, or areas of concern to the dreamer. Are the dreams of any one dreamer identifiably more similar to one another than the dreams of several dreamers? Is there consistency in a dreamer's dreams?

To test this idea, nine dream reports have been transcribed below. These reports were collected from three individuals, with three reports collected per individual. Your task is to select which three dreams were produced by each of the three individuals who were sampled.

There are several criteria that you could use to classify the dreams. One caution: You might think to use the language characteristics, that is, the use of certain consistent phrases, but don't be led astray by such a strategy. Language characteristics would not be appropriate criteria, since the purpose is to assess whether there is evidence of consistency in dream *content*. So you should concentrate on the content of the dreams as a basis for classification.

DREAM 1

A girl and I were being chased through a woods. We entered a log cabin. We were hiding when two people came in after us. One of the men who entered was tall with a thick dark beard. He looked like a typical backwoodsman. His assistant, by contrast, was short and fat. I decided to outsmart them. I crawled into a back room and began to make some noise. I stood on a box holding a milk bottle in my hand. The man entered, I hit him over the head several times, but the bottle did not break and he only laughed. The next thing I knew, the man was pointing a two-barrelled shotgun at me. I noticed that the ends of the barrels seemed magnified. He shot me in the lower right stomach. I looked down at the hole, saw the blood, and felt very weak. Then I was driving in my car by some railroad tracks. The wheels of my car became stuck on the tracks; my car would only move backward. I saw a train approaching rapidly and somehow managed to move off the tracks. I watched a huge train go past. My car continued moving in reverse. I had to keep the car moving perfectly straight, which was a very difficult task, and the train only missed me by inches. As I sped backward, I noticed a fence alongside the tracks, I saw a spot where the fence had been pushed down. I got out, picked up my car, and climbed over the fence. As I did this, I noticed two wounds, the one from the shotgun and a similar mark on the other side of my body, I began to look for a girl, not sure if I was looking for the one who had been with me in the cabin. I searched through a series of backyards, hiding behind bushes. I felt guilty about something. I found the girl I was looking for; she helped me attempt an escape. She led me back over to the fence, which was on a hill above the tracks. I started to climb the fence, which resembled a baseball backstop, but I was too weak from my wounds to be successful. The girl climbed on ahead and offered to hold my shirt as I climbed. Suddenly, two men on the railroad tracks below caught my eye. They were shooting at me with a bow and arrow. I told the girl not to worry; I thought I would be safe because the wind would deflect the arrows. Three or four of the arrows missed, but I was finally hit on my left front pocket. Luckily, the arrow had pierced my wallet instead of going into my leg. (In real life I keep my wallet in another pocket.)

DREAM 2

New York was being attacked by Germans. My mother told me not to worry. She told me that the last time the Germans attacked, only three persons who were in a cemetery had been killed. I went to warn my grandmother, who was at my uncle's basement apartment. My aunt was standing outside of the building. She also told me not to worry; she said she would wait outside for me. I walked down two flights of stairs. Strangely, the walls were made of dirt. I saw several of my relatives. Suddenly, I heard a loud noise. Water poured out of one of the walls. My uncle and cousin were covered with dirt. I dug them out just before they would have suffocated. I left with my grandmother. Then, things changed to a cemetery; I saw people walking behind a coffin. I was looking down from an aerial view. (I have had this kind of dream once before, several years ago.)

DREAM 3

I was with a group of people in the church I attended as a child. I knew most of the people there. I saw Paul Newman among the group. Guns appeared from somewhere; everyone grabbed one. Two groups formed; shooting started. I watched Newman fight a burly man. It seemed I became Newman—I could hear and feel everything he felt and heard. We threw "ourself" out into the open to try for a clear shot, but had no time to shoot before we were shot by the burly man. We felt the searing pain; I was sure death was imminent. Suddenly, the pain cleared. We shot the burly man, killing him. The fighting ended. We went inside, once again having our own identities. I saw Newman shaking his head, saying that it was only supposed to have been a game.

DREAM 4

I was on a highway, walking instead of driving. There were no cars, and everyone was walking, but I felt as if I were in a car. I saw someone I knew; we started talking. I got off at the exit to the beach. I walked up a circular ramp. The end of the ramp resembled a manhole. I had a bathing suit on under my clothes, but I had no towel. I started looking for one. I found two that looked as if they did not belong to anyone, so I took them. A woman approached me while I was lying on the sand. She said they were her towels. I told her I had taken them by mistake; she said she was going to call the police. I stayed; the police never came.

DREAM 5

I was in a restaurant or a cafeteria. I picked up some food. I thought it was a dessert and expected it to be sweet and delicious. Instead, I found that it tasted terrible. I thought someone had substituted salt for sugar in the recipe. I felt as though the salty taste grew and grew; I was now alone in a vast, dry wasteland with no relief in sight. (I woke up with the taste of salt still parching my mouth.)

DREAM 6

First, I was seated on the top bunk of my bed. I was with some friends. Then I found myself walking around piles of boards. My house had been destroyed—either it had collapsed or burned down—and my belongings were covered with rubble. Then I was outside the house digging a ditch longer than it was deep. Building materials lay nearby. While I dug, I got dirt in my hair. I wanted a hat, so I went to the part of the house where the boards were. After finding a hat, I started out of the rubble. Some of the boards fell out of place; they knocked my father's car, our dog, and a chair over a steep cliff. I did not look over the cliff. I could hear my father's car smash into pieces. Then I saw a large field below the cliff. The dog and the chair also broke into pieces. The pieces began moving end over end to the other side of the field. When they stopped rolling, they were reassembled. I felt very unhappy about all this. I returned to the ditch and saw my father. I told him not to worry as he would soon be getting a company car. Then things changed and I was driving in my convertible with three friends. We had a case of beer with us. The road was covered with snow, although it was only snowing lightly at that moment. We stopped at a house where I walked around to the yard. It was twenty-three minutes to six, and I had to be home at five, but I felt that I could not tell my friends this. I saw my roommate swinging on a pole in the backyard. He said he wanted to swing up onto a window ledge. I offered to help; he refused my offer. Eventually we both got up on the ledge. I looked in through the window. A lady was in the kitchen. By now it was almost six, so I jumped down from the ledge, saying I had to go. I was alone.

DREAM 7

I was in a room I am familiar with but cannot now identify. A girl I work with was also there. The room made me think of Patricia Hearst; perhaps she had lived there. I thought she might be close by. I searched for clues. I wanted to find the clue that would solve the kidnapping case. I found something small lying on the floor; it was thin and cylindrical with screwlike threads at one end. I felt that this might be the clue to the kidnapping that I was looking for, but when I showed it to the girl she said it was something of hers. She took it.

DREAM 8

My brother and I were standing on a patio waiting for something. Four or five large jet planes passed the yard. The planes were a few feet above the ground. As my brother went to get a better look, another plane came by and snatched him up. He was strapped into a seat like a baby's car seat. Next, I was inside a house. I was handed a tube about a foot long. The tube was clear; it had white caps at either end. Something was inside—something red and jellylike.

It reminded me of lobster. I was shocked when they told me it was my brother. I wanted to let him out of the tube; I was also afraid of what might happen. The organism was fighting violently; it was my brother. A strange-looking person entered the room then. He said he was my brother. I thought the person was wearing a disguise. I grabbed him; we started to fight. Somehow I was convinced it was my brother. I said, "I hate to do this, but it's for your own good." Next I found myself walking with two friends towards a building. I had books in my hand. I then noticed that all of the lights in the town were off, so that there was no sense in continuing to go where I had intended. I crossed the bridge and left my friends, telling them I was going back for something. I returned to the patio. People were coming towards me. My brother was standing beside me. A group of girls I knew walked out of the building; I then recognized it to be a movie theater. I walked over to one of the girls, who said that she had seen an "awfully strange movie." I was very relieved that everything that had just happened to me was only a movie, and that my brother was safe beside me.

DREAM 9

I was going to school in Paris. I did not feel that I was really in Paris, however. I received a letter from a friend. He had just spent two weeks in Lorraine. He thought I should also travel. I decided to go to Geneva.

Write your answers in the spaces below:

Dreamer A ________ ________ ________

Dreamer B ________ ________ ________

Dreamer C ________ ________ ________

After you have made your judgments, check the correct answers on the bottom of this page. How correct were you? Based on your results, what would you conclude about the consistency of people's dreams? What is the implication of these conclusions for a theory of dreams? You may want to come back to these results after you have read Chapter 17, which provides much more detail about the topic of dreams. In this chapter you will discover that certain theories of dreams claim that the overt content of a dream may be different from its true (but hidden) meaning. Certain events in dreams are supposed to symbolize other events that are not directly present. Once you have read this section, you should return to these nine dreams to check whether you might be able to discover some "latent" content in them that could provide a new basis for your judgments.

ANSWERS TO DREAM EXPERIMENT

Dreamer A ________ 8,6,1

Dreamer B ________ 9,4,2

Dreamer C ________ 7,5,3

CHAPTER 2

Biological Bases of Behavior

Learning Objectives

THE ORGANISM AS MACHINE

Descartes and the reflex concept

1. Be familiar with Descartes' conception of the reflex, and how, in part, it still forms the basis of animal and human action.

The basic nervous functions: reception, integration, reaction

2. Be able to describe fully the action sequence: reception, integration, reaction.
3. What functions do the following serve: receptors, afferent nerves, efferent nerves, effectors, interneurons?

NERVE CELL AND NERVE IMPULSE

The neuron

4. What are dendrites, the axon, the myelin sheath, and the nodes of Ranvier?
5. What purpose do the sensory neurons and motor neurons serve?

The electrical activity of the neuron

6. Be able to describe the electrical activity of the neuron; know the difference between resting potential and action potential.
7. What is the all-or-none law?
8. What effect does stimulus intensity have on the number of neurons stimulated and on the frequency of impulses?

INTERACTION AMONG NERVE CELLS

The reflex

9. Describe the reflex.

Inferring synaptic function

10. How did Sherrington infer the existence of the synapse? Describe temporal summation.
11. Be able to explain central excitatory state and inhibition.

The synaptic mechanism

12. Describe Loewi's classic demonstration of the existence of neurotransmitters.
13. Know the anatomy of the synaptic mechanism (pre- and postsynaptic neurons, synaptic gaps, synaptic vesicles, and neurotransmitters), and the way that neural excitation (the nerve impulse) is transmitted across the synapse.
14. Be able to explain how inhibition and excitation occur at synapses, and how the postsynaptic neuron integrates the various inhibitory and excitatory effects on it.
15. What are the basic differences between action potentials and synaptic transmission?

16. What is a neurotransmitter? What is the lock-and-key model?
17. What are drugs called agonists and antagonists, and what are the different ways in which they can exert their effects?
18. What are the effects of some major neurotransmitters (acetylcholine, dopamine, and norepinephrine), and how are these effects modified by (respectively) the drugs curare, chlorpromazine, and amphetamines?
19. Indicate the opposing ways in which dopamine has been proposed to be involved in schizophrenia and Parkinson's disease.

INTERACTION THROUGH THE BLOODSTREAM: THE ENDOCRINE SYSTEM

20. Explain the mode of action of the endocrine system, and know the similarities and differences between the types of interaction and transmission in the nervous and endocrine systems.

THE MAIN STRUCTURES OF THE NERVOUS SYSTEM

The evolution of central control

21. Describe the tendency toward increasing centralization in the evolution of the nervous system.
22. Describe disinhibition, and explain how it reveals the hierarchical organization of the nervous system.

The peripheral and central nervous systems

23. Be able to distinguish the peripheral and the central nervous system, and the somatic and autonomic nervous system.
24. Describe the basic anatomy of the brain: what functions do the hindbrain, midbrain, and forebrain serve?

THE CEREBRAL CORTEX

25. Know the structure of the cerebral cortex, including the four lobes.

Projection areas

26. Describe the function of projection areas of the brain, and indicate what determines how much space in these areas is devoted to different parts of the body.

Association areas

27. What are association areas?
28. Explain how PET, MRI, and CAT scans operate.
29. What are apraxia and agnosia?
30. Distinguish receptive and expressive aphasias in terms of site of brain damage and type of symptoms.

How neat is the hierarchy?

31. Discuss the idea of multiple hierarchies in the nervous system.

ONE BRAIN OR TWO?

32. Explain the meaning of lateralization, and how the brain organization of left-handers differs from that of right-handers.

Evidence from split brains

33. What does research on people with split brains tell us about the differences between the cerebral hemispheres?

Lateralization in normal subjects

34. Be able to explain how measures of reaction time indicate which hemisphere of normal people is more activated.

Two modes of mental functioning

35. What are the two modes of mental functioning that some believe are associated with the right and left hemispheres? How has this notion been distorted in the process of popularization?

What the brain can tell us about the mind

36. Explain the aim of cognitive neuropsychology, and indicate how use of the dissociation technique serves this end.

SOME FINAL COMMENTS

37. Discuss the differences between psychological and physiological explanation, and when each is appropriate.

Programmed Exercises

THE ORGANISM AS MACHINE

1. The conception of humans as machines can be traced to the great French philosopher ____________.
   Descartes

2. According to Descartes, excitation from the senses leads to muscle contraction in what we now call a ____________.
   reflex

3. The three basic components of an action sequence are ____________, ____________, and ____________.
   reception
   integration, reaction

4. Nerves that connect receptors to the central nervous system are called ____________ nerves.
   afferent (sensory)

5. Nerves carrying excitation from the central nervous system to muscles and glands are called ____________ nerves.
   efferent (motor)

6. Afferent neurons usually produce effects in efferent neurons via ______neurons.
   inter-

NERVE CELL AND NERVE IMPULSE

7. The basic building block of the nervous system is the nerve cell, or __________.
   neuron

8. The basic unit of nervous function is the ____________ ____________.
   nerve impulse

9. Label the following diagram of the neuron.

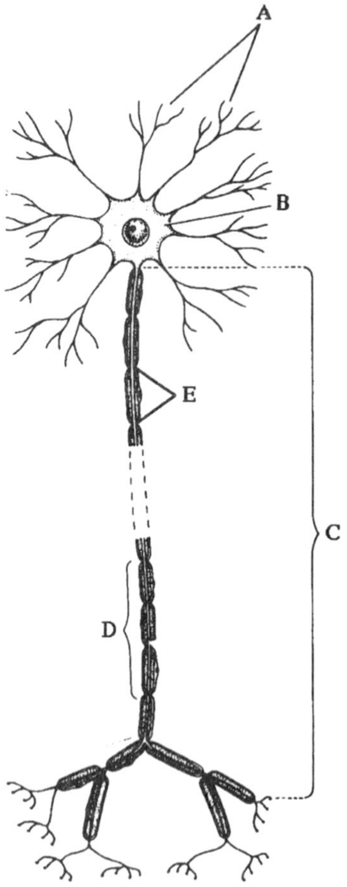

   A. __________ B. __________
   dendrites, cell body

   C. __________
   axon

   D. __________ __________
   myelin sheath

   E. __________ ___ __________
   nodes of Ranvier

10. Receptor cells ____________ stimulus energy into nerve impulses.

transduce

11. The axons of ____________ ____________ terminate in effector cells and activate the ____________ ____________.

motor neurons
skeletal musculature (muscles)

12. In complex organisms, the vast majority of neurons are neither sensory nor motor, but rather ____________.

interneurons

13. The fine wire or tube that allows investigators to record electrical activity in neurons is called a ____________.

microelectrode

14. The ____________ ____________ of the neuron is about –70 millivolts.

resting potential

15. The reversal of polarization that passes along a nerve fiber when it is stimulated is called the ____________ ____________.

action potential

16. When the cell membrane is depolarized past a certain ____________ value, the ____________ ____________ results.

threshold
action potential
(or nerve impulse)

17. The ____________-____________-____________ law states that the size of the action potential and its speed are independent of the intensity of the stimulus, provided the stimulus is above threshold intensity.

all-or-none

18. The above-mentioned law does not apply to the stimulation of nerves since there is much variation in the ____________ of the neurons in the nerve.

thresholds

19. Stimulus ____________ is conveyed by both increases in the number of neurons firing and by increases in individual neurons' ____________ of firing.

intensity
frequency

INTERACTION AMONG NERVE CELLS

20. The fact that a chicken may run around for a while after its head has been cut off shows that some movements and reflexes are controlled by the ____________ ____________.

spinal cord

21. The ____________ is an elementary built-in response pattern, executed automatically when stimulated.

reflex

22. The gap between the axon terminals of one neuron and the dendritic processes of another is called the ____________.

synapse

23. The existence of the synapse was inferred from evidence at the level of ____________ by the great English physiologist ____________.

behavior, (Sir Charles) Sherrington

24. Subthreshold stimulation, when applied a few times in rapid succession, may lead to a response. This illustrates the phenomenon of ____________ ____________.

temporal
summation

25. According to Sherrington, temporal summation occurs because of integration at the ____________, which is accomplished by "storage" of excitation from previous stimulation. This results in an increase in the ____________ ____________ ____________.

synapse
central
excitatory state

26. Sherrington observed that when a flexor muscle contracts, the corresponding extensor relaxes. This is an example of ____________ ____________.

reciprocal inhibition

27. Whether a neuron fires or not is determined by the net result of its integration of ____________ and ____________ stimulation.

excitatory, inhibitory

28. Loewi's classic experiment showed that stimulation of the vagus nerve to the heart caused release of a ___________, which we now call ___________. — neurotransmitter, acetylcholine

29. Electrical activity is transmitted across the synapse by neurotransmitters, from the ___________ neuron to the ___________ neuron. — presynaptic, postsynaptic

30. The synaptic vesicles contain chemical substances called ___________. — neurotransmitters

31. Label this diagram of a synapse.

C
D
A
E
B

A. presynaptic membrane
B. postsynaptic membrane
C. synaptic vesicle
D. neurotransmitter
E. synaptic gap (or synapse)

32. The activity of the postsynaptic neuron results from the summation of ___________ and ___________ postsynaptic potentials. These are produced by ___________ liberated by firing of the presynaptic neuron. — inhibitory, excitatory neurotransmitters

33. While action potentials are all-or-none, synaptic potentials are ___________. — graded

34. Inhibitory neurotransmitters ___________ the nerve's resting potential, while excitatory neurotransmitters ___________ it. — increase decrease

35. Excitatory neurotransmitters open ___________ channels in the postsynaptic membrane. — ion (sodium)

36. The idea that neurotransmitters only affect the postsynaptic membrane if their shape fits the shape of certain receptor sites on that membrane is called the ___________-___________-___________ model. — lock-and-key

37. Acetylcholine, dopamine, and norepinephrine are all ___________. — neurotransmitters

38. Drugs that enhance a transmitter's activity are called ___________. Drugs that impede a transmitter's activity are called ___________. — agonists antagonists

39. Some drugs enhance synaptic function by interfering with ___________ by the presynaptic cell. Some drugs act by altering the levels of substances called ___________, which are required for the synthesis of particular neurotransmitters. — reuptake precursors

40. Curare, chlorpromazine, and amphetamines are ___________ that affect synaptic transmission. — drugs

41. The action of the neurotransmitter ____________, which causes muscles to contract, is blocked by the drug ____________. — acetylcholine, curare

42. The arousing effects of the neurotransmitter ____________ are enhanced by the group of drugs called ____________. — norepinephrine, amphetamines

43. The arousing effects of the neurotransmitter ____________ are blocked by the drug ____________, which is used to treat the major mental disorder ____________. — dopamine, thorazine, schizophrenia

44. ____________ and ____________ disease may be "opposites" in the sense that the former may result from dopamine excess and the latter from dopamine deficiency. — Schizophrenia, Parkinson's

INTERACTION THROUGH THE BLOODSTREAM: THE ENDOCRINE SYSTEM

45. The ____________ glands secrete ____________ into the bloodstream. — endocrine, hormones

46. ____________ are chemical messengers that are distributed indiscriminately throughout the body, while ____________ exert their effects in a very limited area. — Hormones, neurotransmitters

THE MAIN STRUCTURES OF THE NERVOUS SYSTEM

47. Early in evolutionary history the cell bodies of many interneurons began to clump together to form ____________. This is an early stage in the evolution of ____________ control. — ganglia, central

48. An increase in the strength of a reflex when higher brain centers are removed is called ____________. — disinhibition

49. The brain and spinal cord together comprise the ____________ ____________ ____________. — central nervous system

50. The two divisions of the peripheral nervous system are the ____________ and the ____________. — somatic, autonomic

51. The portion of the hindbrain concerned with controlling some critical body processes, such as respiration and heartbeat, is called the ____________. — medulla

52. The portion of the hindbrain that controls bodily balance and motor coordination is called the ____________. — cerebellum

53. In the brain anatomy, and in the hierarchical organization of action, the part of the brain that comes between the hindbrain and forebrain is called the ____________. — midbrain

54. The ____________ is a part of the forebrain involved in the control of behavior patterns that stem from basic biological urges such as feeding. — hypothalamus

55. An older portion of the cerebral hemispheres with particular importance in the mediation of emotional and motivational activities is called the ____________ ____________. — limbic system

56. Label the four major lobes of the human cerebral cortex.

A. ____________ C. ____________

B. ____________ D. ____________

A. frontal
B. parietal
C. occipital
D. temporal

57. Label the following structures on the sketch of the human brain.

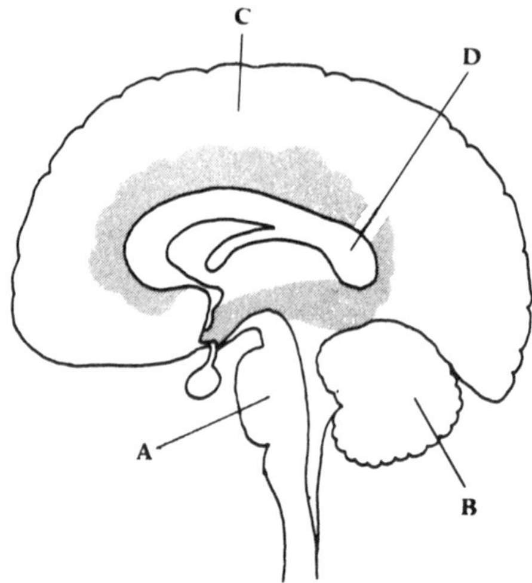

A. ____________
B. ____________
C. ____________
D. ____________

A. hindbrain (medulla)
B. cerebellum
C. cerebral cortex
D. corpus callosum

THE CEREBRAL CORTEX

58. Excitation of the left ____________ ____________ ____________ will lead to movements of the right side of the body.

motor projection area (motor homunculus)

59. In humans, the greatest amount of cortical space for motor functions is assigned to the ____________ and the ____________.

fingers, tongue

60. Each portion of the body surface is represented in the sensory homunculus, located in the ____________ ____________ of the ____________ lobes.

somatosensory area, parietal

61. The projection areas for vision and hearing are located in the ____________ and the ____________ lobes, respectively.

occipital
temporal

62. The portion of the cerebral cortex that is part of neither the motor nor the sensory areas is described as the ____________ ____________. association area

63. When there is damage to neural tissue, we describe it, technically, as a _________. lesion

64. It is now possible to make precise representations of brain structure with the aim of localizing lesions. When this technique involves computer reconstruction of brain structures based on multiple X-ray exposures, it is called a ________ scan. CAT

65. The most widely used neurodiagnostic technique is based on the principle of nuclear magnetic resonance, and is called an ____________ scan. MRI

66. When the picture of the brain is based on representation of the level of metabolic activity in different areas of the brain, it is called a ____________ scan. PET

67. ____________ is a serious disturbance in the organization of voluntary action. Apraxia

68. A disorganization of aspects of the sensory world, without loss of basic sensory capacities, is termed ____________. agnosia

69. A patient with a primary disorder in the expression of speech can be described as suffering from language apraxia, or an ____________ ____________. This disorder is commonly caused by lesions in ____________ ____________. expressive aphasia Broca's area

70. In right-handed persons, aphasia usually results from lesions in the ____________ hemisphere. left

71. A language defect reflected primarily by an inability to comprehend language, or a language agnosia, is described as a ____________ ____________. The lesions responsible for this disorder commonly occur in ____________ ____________. receptive aphasia Wernicke's area

ONE BRAIN OR TWO?

72. The asymmetry of function in the human cerebral hemispheres is described as ____________. lateralization (of function)

73. In terms of differences in function between left and right cerebral hemispheres, left-handers are generally less ____________ than right-handers. lateralized

74. A right-hander who, following a stroke, has great difficulty with spatial representation, maps, and the perception of complex forms, probably has a lesion in the ____________ hemisphere. right

75. A split-brain patient is someone whose ____________ ____________ has been surgically severed. corpus callosum

76. A right-handed split-brain patient would probably not be able to name a common object placed in his ____________ hand. left

77. Lateralization can be demonstrated in normal subjects by showing that right-handers show a longer ____________ ____________ to name objects flashed to their left as opposed to their right visual field. reaction time

78. Many psychologists believe that ____________ and ____________ processes represent radically different modes of thought, which reflect different clusters of intellectual functioning. verbal, spatial

SOME FINAL COMMENTS

79. For explanations of certain types of events, such as why a particular person opposes legalization of drugs, a ____________ level of explanation is more appropriate than a ____________ level. psychological physiological

Self Test

1. Which of the following commonly observed characteristics of human or animal behavior goes counter to Descartes' reflex notion?
   a. the withdrawal response upon touching a hot object
   b. the appearance of a behavior (e.g., running) in the absence of any obvious stimulus
   c. the existence of nerves connecting receptors and effectors to the brain
   d. the repeatability of reflexes
   e. none of the above

2. By viewing animal behavior as the result of a machine's responding to external stimuli, Descartes made the claim that:
   a. animal behavior is governed by physical laws and is therefore predictable
   b. animal behavior can only be understood in terms of the hierarchical organization of the nervous system
   c. animals must have souls
   d. neither humans nor animals have free will
   e. introductory psychology is *the* fundamental science

3. The course of excitation through the nervous system following a stimulus is:
   a. interneuron, efferent nerve, afferent nerve
   b. efferent nerve, interneuron, afferent nerve
   c. afferent nerve, interneuron, efferent nerve
   d. integration, reception, reaction
   e. action reaction, integration

4. The tripartite view of an action sequence—reception, conduction and integration, reaction—is clearly represented by the sequence of:
   a. afferent nerve, efferent nerve, interneuron
   b. axon, cell body, dendrites
   c. push, fall, hurt
   d. axon, interneuron, dendrite
   e. none of the above

5. Under normal circumstances the path of excitation in the neuron would follow which of the following sequences?
   a. dendrite → cell body → axon → synapse
   b. axon → dendrite → synapse → cell body
   c. dendrite → cell body → synapse → axon
   d. dendrite → axon → cell body → synapse
   e. synapse → dendrite → axon → cell body

6. Which of the following is *not* part of an individual neuron?
   a. axon
   b. myelin sheath
   c. synapse
   d. dendrite
   e. cell body

7. Receptor cells:
   a. are always a specialized part of sensory neurons
   b. transduce physical stimuli into neural impulses
   c. are responsible for the conduction of optic stimuli
   d. a and b
   e. b and c

8. Which of the following properties are characteristic of interneurons?
   a. they usually show much branching of dendrites
   b. they perform the integration function of the action sequence
   c. they comprise the majority of neurons
   d. all of the above
   e. none of the above

9. When graphed over time, the complex electrical event known as the action potential looks something like:

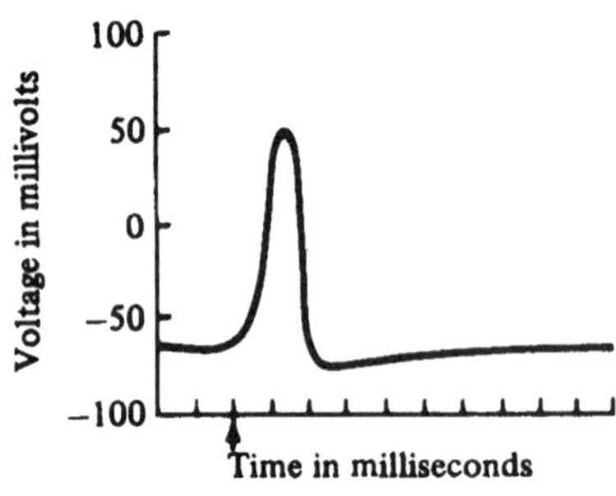

A

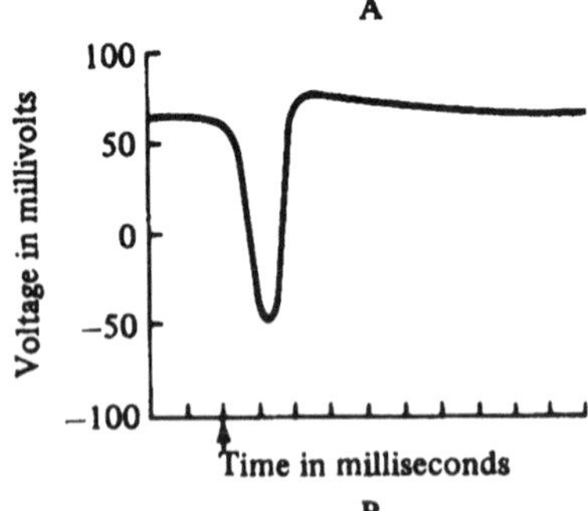

B

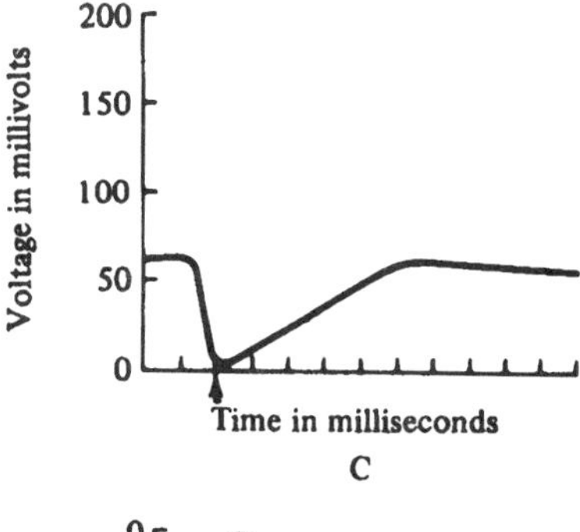

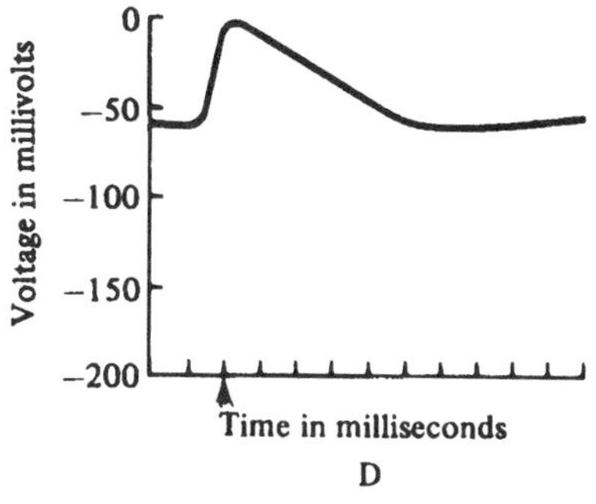

e. none of the above

10. The all-or-none law states that
    a. the threshold of a single neuron is a property which alternates between two extreme values but never has any of the values in between
    b. reflexes cannot involve just the spinal cord; the entire nervous system must respond by generating a central excitatory state
    c. an axon terminal releases a chemical substance, called a neurotransmitter, when an action potential arrives
    d. the frequency of spikes in an individual nerve fiber increases with the number of action potentials per unit time
    e. once a stimulus exceeds the threshold of an individual neuron, further increases in stimulation intensity make no difference in the height and form of the action potential generated

11. The all-or-none action potential is:
    a. accompanied by depolarization of the nerve membrane
    b. preceded by a resting potential
    c. propagated from one part of the membrane
    d. all of the above
    e. none of the above

12. How can the nervous system represent increase in the intensity of a *stimulus*?
    a. by an increase in the size of the action potential in every neuron fired by the stimulus
    b. by an increase in the number of neurons being fired by the stimulus
    c. by an increase in the frequency of firing in the neurons fired by the stimulus
    d. b and c
    e. a and c

13. Sherrington used a spinal animal in order to:
    a. eliminate inhibition
    b. simplify the system he was studying
    c. take advantage of brain modulation in neural activity in the spinal cord
    d. study the irreversibility of conduction
    e. cut expenses

14. From his observations of temporal summation in reflexes, Sherrington inferred the existence of:
    a. receptors
    b. inhibition
    c. the synapse
    d. disinhibition
    e. the simple reflex

15. A subthreshold stimulus will evoke a spinal reflex if it is repeated within a reasonable interval, say 1/2 second. This temporal summation is caused by:
    a. increased frequency of neural firing
    b. enhanced central excitatory state
    c. the spinal cord
    d. the release of neurotransmitters from motor neurons to interneurons
    e. inhibition

16. Consider this example: Brief strong stimulation of a receptor produces no movement, but a longer period of stimulation causes a particular muscle to stop contracting. These results could most easily be explained by the principles of:
    a. excitation and inhibition
    b. inhibition and spatial summation
    c. all-or-none law and inhibition
    d. temporal summation and the all-or-none law
    e. inhibition and temporal summation

17. Sherrington reported that the time (reflex latency) between stimulation of a reflex and the reflex response was much longer than the time it would take for an action potential to go from the receptor to the muscle. This "delay" could be accounted for in terms of:
    a. inhibition
    b. excitation
    c. the all-or-none law
    d. the time for depolarization of the axon membrane
    e. the time for the neurotransmitter to cross the synaptic gap and stimulate the postsynaptic neuron

18. Axon conduction resembles synaptic transmission in that:
    a. both involve neurotransmitters
    b. both are about the same speed
    c. both are all-or-none
    d. all of the above
    e. none of the above

19. Many neurons fire action potentials at a moderate rate even when they are not receiving synaptic excitation from presynaptic neurons. This is called spontaneous activity. Which plot indicates what would happen to the firing rate of such a neuron if it was first exposed to synaptic inhibition and then synaptic excitation?

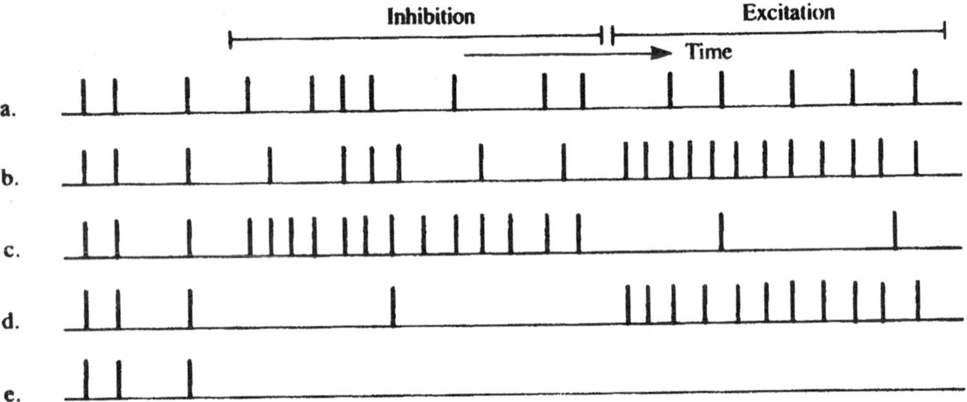

20. The lock-and-key model accounts for:
    a. the existence of neurotransmitters
    b. the summation of excitation and inhibition in postsynaptic neurons
    c. the fact that specific neurotransmitters stimulate specific postsynaptic neurons
    d. the release of neurotransmitters from synaptic vesicles
    e. the all-or-none law

21. Thorazine and curare have in common the fact that they:
    a. block the action of specific neurotransmitters
    b. enhance the action of specific neurotransmitters
    c. produce postsynaptic inhibition
    d. produce postsynaptic excitation
    e. relieve the symptoms of schizophrenia

22. Many researchers now believe that in at least some cases of depression, the cause is low levels of dopamine or norepinephrine in the brain. If this were true, then we would expect chlorpromazine to ________ depression, and amphetamines to ________ depression.
    a. increase, decrease
    b. decrease, increase
    c. increase, increase
    d. decrease, decrease
    e. have no effect on, have no effect on

23. A new drug is found to increase arousal. All but one of the following are possible modes of action of that drug. Which is *not*?
    a. blocks reuptake of dopamine
    b. increases availability of norepinephrine
    c. blocks the enzyme that breaks down dopamine at the synapse
    d. mimics the effect of norepinephrine
    e. blocks the postsynaptic receptor for norepinephrine

24. Hormones and neurotransmitters are both:
    a. secreted only by endocrine glands
    b. secreted into the bloodstream
    c. chemical messengers
    d. all of the above
    e. none of the above

25. Neuron is to ganglion as
    a. brain is to spinal cord
    b. ganglion is to brain
    c. excitation is to inhibition
    d. synapse is to neurotransmitter
    e. dentist is to pain

26. The phenomenon of disinhibition:
    a. exists only in insects
    b. depends on reflex interaction, especially in the spinal cord
    c. reveals the presence of inhibition
    d. takes place entirely within a single neuron
    e. all of the above

27. In which of the following sequences are the main divisions of the central nervous system arranged in ascending order?
    a. peripheral, somatic, autonomic
    b. cerebellum, integration centers, transmission tracts
    c. spinal cord, autonomic system, brain
    d. spinal cord, motor areas, sensory areas
    e. spinal cord, brain stem, cerebral hemispheres

28. Match the structure on the left with its associated function on the right

i. medulla	a. respiration and heartbeat
ii. cerebellum	b. basic biological urges
iii. hypothalamus	c. balance and motor coordination

    i. ________
    ii. ________
    iii. ________

29. Which of the following statements is *not* true of the limbic system?
    a. it is a subcortical structure
    b. it is anatomically associated with the hypothalamus
    c. it is present on both sides of the brain
    d. it is involved in the control of emotional and motivational activities
    e. it integrates the functions of the cerebral hemispheres

30. The lobes of the cerebral hemisphere are:
    a. frontal, parietal, occipital, temporal
    b. hindbrain, midbrain, forebrain
    c. limbic system, corpus callosum, cerebral cortex
    d. each cerebral hemisphere is a single lobe of the cerebral cortex
    e. none of the above

31. What part of an elephant might you expect to have a particularly large representation in the motor homunculus?
    a. the ears
    b. the front legs
    c. the back legs
    d. the trunk
    e. the eyes

32. Following a stroke, a patient shows grossly diminishing sensitivity to touch and other stimulation in the right hand and arm. The probable site of the lesion is:
    a. the motor homunculus
    b. the left somatosensory area
    c. the right somatosensory area
    d. the left frontal area
    e. the right frontal area

33. You think a person has brain damage, and want to find out where. All but one of the following approaches would be very helpful. Which would *not* be very helpful?
    a. MRI scan
    b. determination of particular behavioral and mental symptoms
    c. CAT scan
    d. analysis of blood chemistry
    e. PET scan

34. A disorder in the organization of voluntary movement is called:
    a. agnosia
    b. aphasia
    c. apraxia
    d. amenorrhea
    e. none of the above

35. A person exhibiting an inability to coordinate the separate details of the visual world into a whole suffers from:
    a. visual agnosia
    b. receptive aphasia
    c. a lesion in Broca's area
    d. a lesion in Wernicke's area
    e. visual apraxia

36. Apraxia and expressive and receptive aphasia have in common:
    a. lesions in the same brain area
    b. basic sensory and motor functions are intact
    c. some deficit in voluntary motor function
    d. a and b
    e. a and c

37. Damage in a left-handed person in the language center often has less drastic consequences than in a right-handed person because:
    a. left-handers are slower to develop language functions
    b. recovery is more rapid in the left hemisphere in left-handers
    c. the hemispheres are not as functionally lateralized in left-handers
    d. highly developed visual-spatial abilities compensate for language loss
    e. a and d

38. Afferent input from the right hand projects primarily to the left hemisphere while the left hand projects primarily to the right hemisphere. In an average right-handed, split-brain patient, which hand would the subject have to use to handle an unseen object in order to name it?
    a. the left hand
    b. the right hand
    c. neither hand could do it
    d. both hands could do it equally well
    e. a split-brian patient cannot name any objects

39. A right-handed subject has lost the entire projection area of his left occipital cortex, as shown below, but is otherwise normal. Which of the following deficits would you expect?

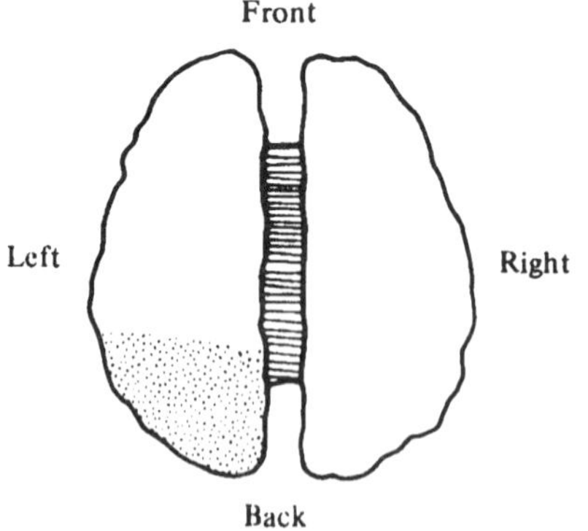

    a. loss of the right side of his visual field
    b. loss of the left side of his visual field
    c. inability to produce speech despite ability to understand it
    d. inability to understand speech despite the ability to produce it
    e. inability to read

40. The same subject referred to in the previous question suffers an additional defect: His corpus callosum is completely cut. What is the extent of his deficit?
    a. inability to produce or understand speech
    b. inability to produce speech despite understanding it
    c. inability to understand speech despite the ability to produce it
    d. inability to read
    e. visual agnosia

41. For a normal right-handed subject, which of the following findings would be expected?
    a. a shorter reaction time to respond to a spatial problem presented in the left visual field
    b. better vision in the right visual field
    c. longer reaction time to respond to a verbal problem presented in the right visual field
    d. all of the above
    e. b and c

42. In which of the following tasks would you expect superior performance from the left hemisphere of a right-hander?
    a. matching paint colors
    b. recognizing faces
    c. remembering a series of movements to be performed in a specific order
    d. drawing the floor plan of a familiar house
    e. all of the above

43. Theories of lateralization hold that, for right-handers, the left hemisphere is more involved with ________, and the right hemisphere is more involved with __________.
    a. verbal material, spatial material
    b. sensory function, motor function
    c. PET scans, CAT scans
    d. visual perception, auditory perception
    e. a and d

Answer Key for Self Test

1. b p. 11
2. a p. 11
3. c p. 12
4. e p. 12
5. a pp. 13, 21
6. c pp. 13, 21
7. b p. 13
8. d p. 14
9. a p. 15
10. e p. 16
11. d pp. 15–16
12. d p. 16
13. b p. 18
14. c p. 18
15. b p. 18
16. e pp. 18–19
17. e p. 21
18. e p. 22
19. d pp. 16–21
20. c p. 22
21. a pp. 23–24
22. a pp. 23–24
23. e pp. 23–24
24. c p. 22
25. b pp. 26–27
26. c pp. 26–27
27. e pp. 27–28
28. i. a, ii. c, iii. b pp. 28–30
29. e p. 30
30. a p. 32
31. d p. 32
32. b p. 32
33. d pp. 33–35
34. c p. 35
35. a p. 35
36. b pp. 35–36
37. c pp. 37–38
38. b pp. 38–39
39. a p. 38
40. d pp. 38–39
41. a p. 39
42. c p. 40
43. a p. 40

Investigating Psychological Phenomena

SPEED OF THE NERVE IMPULSE: THE USE OF REACTION TIME IN THE MEASUREMENT OF A PSYCHOLOGICAL PROCESS

Equipment: A stopwatch that indicates seconds
Number of subjects: Five
Time per subject: Fifteen minutes (all subjects are involved at the same time)
Time for experimenter: Twenty-five minutes

One of the great stumbling blocks to advances in theory about psychological processes was the belief that thought, and hence nervous impulses, occurred instantaneously or nearly so. In fact, the German physiologist Johannes P. Müller (1801–1858) once estimated that the speed of the nerve impulse was eleven million miles per second. Naturally, this claim that nerve impulses travel at an immeasurably fast rate discouraged scientific research on the physiology of the nervous system and encouraged mystical or dualistic interpretations of mind. It also discouraged study of the speed of various mental activities, research that is today an important cornerstone of the field of cognitive psychology.

In 1850, Herman Ludwig Ferdinand von Helmholtz (1821–1894) succeeded in measuring the speed of the nerve impulse and found it to be much slower than previously believed, between fifty and one hundred meters per second in humans. This finding was followed by intensive investigation of the nervous system within the framework of the physical and biological sciences. It also opened the door to the use of reaction time as a tool in the study of thought processes. This experiment is an attempt to familiarize you with the general logic used by a psychologist who is interested in measuring the speed of a psychological event that cannot be directly observed. To accomplish this, you must first understand the experiment that Helmholtz performed and also how his experimental technique can be applied to the measurement of the speed of the nerve impulse in humans.

Helmholtz's technique was quite simple. He first dissected out a muscle and an attached nerve fiber from a frog's leg. The experiment then consisted of stimulating the nerve at various distances from the muscle and measuring the length of time between nerve stimulation and muscle contraction. First, he electrically stimulated the nerve close to the point at which it was attached to the muscle, then he stimulated the nerve farther from this point of attachment. He found that the second reaction time (that is, the time between stimulation and contraction) was longer than the first. To obtain an estimate of nerve impulse speed, he used a simple bit of reasoning: The difference in time between the two measurements must correspond to the time it takes the impulse to travel the distance between the two points of stimulation (see figure). Hence, the distance between the points of stimulation divided by the time *difference* between the conditions of stimulating close to the muscle versus stimulating farther away should yield an estimate of nerve impulse speed. This is how he obtained his estimate of fifty to one hundred meters per second. Let A and B be two points of stimulation, M be the point at which the nerve connects to the muscle, t_A be the time to contraction from stimulation at A, and t_B, the time to contraction from stimulation at B.

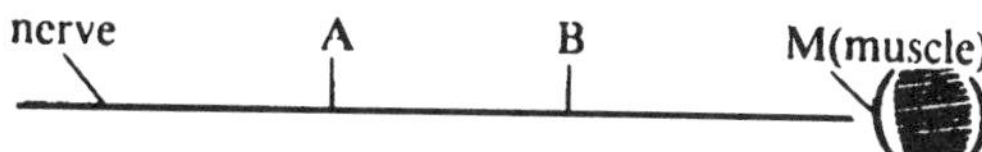

Then $\frac{(A \text{ to } M) - (B \text{ to } M)}{t_A - t_B}$ = speed of nerve impulse.

Happily, Helmholtz's estimate can be demonstrated in humans without resorting to dissection. You might suppose that the simplest way to do this would be to perform the following sort of experiment: Stimulate someone on the ankle (by pinching him, for example) and have him respond by pushing a button as soon as he feels the stimulation. With a good timer, you could then measure the time between stimulation and depression of the button. To estimate nerve conduction time, you would then measure the total distance between ankle and brain, and between brain and finger and divide this number by the subject's reaction time. But there are complications which make this procedure unsuitable. Part of the reaction time, for example, would be due to the length of time it took the subject to decide to press the button, a figure which is obviously more than simply nerve impulse time. From the point of view of processes in the nervous system, the reaction time includes the time to cross synapses as well as axon conduction time. In short, total reaction time is a confounded measure.

Thus, the experiment must be made more complicated. Using Helmholtz's logic, one could measure not only the time between ankle stimulation and response, but also between, say, upper arm stimulation and response. The ankle condition should result in a longer reaction time than the upper arm condition. The difference between these reaction times corresponds to the time it takes for the nerve impulse to travel a distance equal to the difference between the ankle and the finger, and the upper arm and the finger. Notice that this difference excludes any time due to such things as decision-making processes. So the nerve conduction time can be estimated by subtracting the distance of the upper arm to the brain from the distance of the ankle to the brain (the distance from the brain to the finger is constant) and dividing by the reaction time difference.

In practice, the reaction time for either stimulating the ankle or stimulating the upper arm is quite small, and hence a clock that measures time in hundredths of a second would be needed to measure it. This problem can be solved by adding together the reaction time of several people; after obtaining the total time, simply dividing this by the number of people would give the average individual time. This general mass reaction time technique will be used to measure the speed of the nerve impulse. Perform the nerve impulse speed experiment in the following way:

Get five people to participate. Have them form a circle with each person very loosely clasping the ankle of his neighbor to the right. Tell each person to squeeze the ankle he is holding when he feels his ankle squeezed. Be sure the subjects' eyes are closed during all trials. You can then start the experiment by squeezing one person's ankle and simultaneously noting the time on a second hand of a watch. Now watch the ankle that you squeezed. When you see it squeezed for the fifth time (excluding your initial squeeze) note the time that elapsed. Repeat this procedure for a total of five times, each time recording the time in the spaces provided in part I of the answer sheet on the next page (record results to an accuracy of .1 second).

Next have each person in the circle release the ankle he is holding and grasp the upper arm, *just below the shoulder* of the person to his right. You run another five trials exactly as you did for the ankle trials, each time recording the time in part II of the answer sheet.

You will probably note that the total reaction time dropped within each set of five trials. Why? Hopefully, the last two to three trials yielded about the same values.

These ten trials serve as practice: The group of five subjects and the measurer "learn" in some general way, to do this task efficiently. Having completed practice, you are now ready to begin the measurement of the speed of the nerve impulse. Run four more trials as before, the first and fourth with ankle stimulation, the second and third with upper arm. This will generate two ankle and two upper arm mass reaction times (record these in part III of the data sheet).

Each reaction time represents the sum of twenty-five reaction times (five subjects, five times each). Obtain the average individual reaction time by dividing the total reaction times by twenty-five.

Now average the two ankle reaction times and, separately, the two upper arm reaction times. Subtract the average arm time from the average ankle time. This is the amount of time it takes the impulse to go the extra distance from the ankle to the level of the shoulder. To calculate the speed of the nerve impulse, you must estimate the magnitude of this distance (in meters).

Measure the distance for the third tallest person in your group of five subjects. Measure the distance from the ankle to the base of the neck and from the upper arm to the base of the neck. Take the difference between the numbers, divide by the time difference, and you will have an estimate of the speed of the nerve impulse. How does it compare with Helmholtz's estimate? (Helmholtz estimated a speed of from 50 to 100 meters per second. Modern measurements range from 6 to 122 meters per second, depending on the type of nerve fiber). *(If your instructor collects the data, fill out the report sheet in Appendix B.)*

FURTHER EXPERIMENTS

Now that you have calculated an estimate of the speed of the nerve impulse, you might want to test whether some fairly common variables will affect this speed. Consider fatigue for instance. If a person is tired, does her nerve impulse speed slow down? To test this, design your own experiment, using the same measurement technique you used to get your main estimate of nerve impulse speed. To test whether fatigue has an effect, measure the speed both at a time when subjects are well rested and at a time when the same subjects are tired (for example, in the morning and at night, or before and after exercise). Does fatigue affect nerve impulse speed? Note, by the way, that given the way the estimate is obtained, it is possible to find that fatigue may well slow down reaction time in general, yet have no effect on the speed of the nerve impulse.

Can you think of other variables that might affect (speed up or slow down) nerve impulse speed? If so, design experiments to test your hypotheses.

Report Sheet

Practice — Time in seconds*

Part I
Trial 1 ankle = ____________
Trial 2 ankle = ____________
Trial 3 ankle = ____________
Trial 4 ankle = ____________
Trial 5 ankle = ____________

Part II
Trial 1 upper arm = ____________
Trial 2 upper arm = ____________
Trial 3 upper arm = ____________
Trial 4 upper arm = ____________
Trial 5 upper arm = ____________

Test

Part III
Trial 1 ankle time = __________
÷ 25 = ________ (a)
Trial 2 upper arm time = __________
÷ 25 = ________ (b)
Trial 3 upper arm time = __________
÷ 25 = ________ (c)
Trial 4 ankle time = __________
÷ 25 = ________ (d)

$\frac{a+d}{2}$ = _____ (average ankle time)

$\frac{b+c}{2}$ = _____ (average upper arm time)

Average ankle time − average upper arm time = _____ (difference 1)

(1) Distance of ankle to base of neck (for third tallest person) = _____

(2) Distance of upper arm to base of neck (for third tallest person) = _____

Distance 1 − distance 2 = _____ (difference 2)

$\frac{\text{difference 2}}{\text{difference 1}}$ = (speed of nerve impulse)

*Record time accurate to .1 second.

CHAPTER 3

Motivation

Learning Objectives

MOTIVATION AS DIRECTION

1. Describe the organization of individual motives into those that serve self-regulation, self-preservation, and self-restoration.
2. Indicate the relation between potentiation and motivation.
3. Can directed action be reconciled with Descartes' notion of humans and animals as reflex machines?

Control systems

4. Describe the action of negative and positive feedback systems. Give examples of negative and positive feedback systems from modern technology.

Homeostasis

5. What is homeostasis?

TEMPERATURE REGULATION

6. Know how reflexes and behavior function to maintain body temperature. Define setpoint.
7. Describe the way the two branches of the autonomic nervous system function in temperature regulation, and the role of the hypothalamus.

THIRST

8. Describe how the brain is informed about the body's need for water.

HUNGER

The signals for feeding

9. What is the evidence indicating that animals regulate calorie (energy) intake?
10. Indicate the internal and external signals that influence hunger and satiety.

Hypothalamic control centers

11. Describe the role of the hypothalamus in feeding.
12. What is the dual-center theory? How do the phenomena of aphagia and hyperphagia support this theory?
13. How does the idea of setpoint help account for the regulation of temperature and food intake, and how does it account for the behavior of hyperphagic rats?

Obesity

14. Indicate bodily factors that may contribute to obesity, and review genetic evidence that establishes a role for bodily factors.
15. What behavioral factors may be involved in obesity?
16. What aspects of obesity can the setpoint hypothesis explain?
17. Review the success of treatments for obesity. What are some factors that interfere with treatment success?

Anorexia and bulimia

18. Describe the symptoms and possible causes of anorexia nervosa and bulimia.

FEAR AND RAGE

19. Evaluate the relevance of homeostasis and potentiation to fear and rage.

Threat and the autonomic nervous system

20. What are the functions of the parasympathetic and sympathetic systems?
21. Describe the emergency reaction. What role does the sympathetic arousal system play in the flight-or-fight response? Understand the biological survival value of the emergency reaction.
22. Discuss the polygraph approach to lie detection, and the advantages and shortcomings of this technique.

Central controls

23. How are fear, rage, and predatory attack responses organized in the central nervous system? What is the role of the limbic system?

Disruptive effects of autonomic arousal

24. Describe the immediate disruptive effects of sympathetic arousal, and possible long-term effects on health.

Pain and the endorphin system

25. Describe adaptive and maladaptive aspects of pain.
26. Indicate the evidence for nervous system mechanisms to modulate pain. What stimulates them, and what is the role of the endorphins in producing analgesia?

SLEEP AND WAKING

27. Distinguish the activating from the directing effects of motivation.

Waking

28. Describe the role of subcortical and cortical areas in wakefulness.

The stages of sleep

29. Be able to describe the stages of sleep.
30. What are the two kinds of sleep?

The functions of sleep

31. What are the effects of sleep deprivation? What is known about the functions of sleep and the determinants of the sleep cycle?

Dreams

32. What is the relation between REM sleep and dreaming?
33. Discuss whether dreaming has a function, and if so, what it might be. What is the activation-synthesis hypothesis?

WHAT DIFFERENT MOTIVES HAVE IN COMMON

The psychology of reward and the arousal level

34. What is meant by optimal arousal level? What is the evidence for an optimal arousal level above zero?
35. Explain how drugs can be used to manipulate arousal. Give examples of depressant and stimulant drugs, and contrast the effects of these two types of drugs.
36. Describe drug addiction and the phenomena of tolerance and withdrawal.
37. Describe the opponent process theory of motivation. How do studies of drug addiction support this theory?

The biology of reward

38. What do studies of electrical stimulation of the brain tell us about motivation? Are there both general and motivation-specific pleasure centers in the brain?

THE NATURE OF MOTIVES

39. What might all motives have in common?
40. Indicate how the biological basis for motives interacts with individual experience (learning).

Programmed Exercises

1. Temperature maintenance, hunger, and thirst involve motives aimed at self-__________. Fear and rage are associated with motives of self-__________, whereas sleep is directed at self-__________.

   regulation
   preservation
   restoration

2. Motives increase the tendency to perform specific groups of behaviors. This tendency is sometimes called __________.

   potentiation

MOTIVATION AS DIRECTION

3. In __________ __________ systems, the feedback strengthens the initial behavior.

   positive feedback

4. In a __________ __________ system, the feedback stops, or even reverses, the original behavior.

   negative feedback

5. The maintenance of a stable equilibrium in the body is called __________.

   homeostasis

TEMPERATURE REGULATION

6. Vasoconstrictionis a form of __________ response to __________ in body temperature.

   reflexive, decreases

7. Voluntary and reflexive heat-loss responses are brought into play when the body temperature drops below a temperature standard determined internally, which is called the __________.

   setpoint

8. The autonomic nervous system sends its commands to __________ and __________ __________.

   glands
   smooth muscles

9. The __________ and __________ divisions of the autonomic nervous system work in opposite directions to control temperature. The __________ division acts to generate heat, to counteract low temperatures.

   sympathetic,
   parasympathetic
   sympathetic

10. The activation of the divisions of the autonomic nervous system is determined by __________ located in the part of the brain that controls these divisions, the __________.

    (thermo)receptors
    hypothalamus

THIRST

11. The brain detects the body's need for water from different receptors that are sensitive to either body fluid __________ or __________.

    volume,
    concentration

HUNGER

12. The fact that animals increase intake of foods that are diluted with nonnutritive substances suggests that they regulate __________.

    calories (energy)

13. Receptors sensitive to the metabolic state (energy need) of the organism have been postulated to exist in the __________ and __________.

    liver, brain

14. Satiety signals also originate in the gastrointestinal system, from nutrient receptors in the __________.

    stomach

15. __________ stimuli, like the attractiveness of food, can influence the amount ingested, but their effectiveness depends in part on the __________ state of the organism.

    External
    internal (metabolic)

16. The dual-center theory is supported by the fact that lesions in the lateral hypothalamus produce __________, while lesions in the ventromedial hypothalamus produce __________.

    aphagia
    hyperphagia

17. According to dual-center theory, "on" and "off" feeding centers in the hypothalamus are mutually ____________.
    inhibitory

18. The fact that hyperphagic rats gain weight and then maintain themselves at the new, higher weight suggests that they are regulating their body weight around an elevated ____________.
    setpoint

19. One nonpsychological difference among people that can affect obesity involves ____________ "efficiency."
    metabolic (digestive)

20. The high resemblance in obesity and body distribution of fat in ____________ argues for a ____________ determinant of obesity.
    twins
    genetic

21. Restrained eaters and obese people may have, on the average, higher ____________ than the rest of the population.
    setpoints

22. A justification of getting treatment for obesity is that thinner people are more attractive, and hence are more ____________ successful. There are also ____________ benefits for not being very obese.
    socially
    health (medical)

23. ____________ ____________ is an eating disorder characterized by extreme and self-imposed underweight.
    Anorexia nervosa

24. ____________ is an eating disorder characterized by repeated binge and purge bouts.
    Bulimia

FEAR AND RAGE

25. The parasympathetic system handles the ____________ functions of the body.
    vegetative

26. The sympathetic system has an ____________ function.
    activating

27. Sympathetic action is supported or amplified by the secretion of the hormone ____________ (or ____________).
    adrenaline,
    epinephrine

28. The emergency reaction results from activation of the ____________ nervous system.
    sympathetic

29. Decreased electrical resistance of the skin, or the ____________ ____________ ____________, is sometimes used as an index of autonomic arousal, as in lie detector tests.
    galvanic skin
    response

30. The portion of the brain that governs the autonomic system and is responsible for the control of emotional reactions is called the ____________ system.
    limbic

31. Evidence indicates that there are different brain control centers for ____________ attack and ____________.
    predatory, rage
    (counterattack)

32. ____________ arousal can have disruptive effects, which, if maintained, can compromise health.
    Autonomic

33. ____________ can trigger fear and rage, and serves as an indicator that something is wrong or damaged.
    Pain

34. Reduced feeling of pain, or ____________, is produced by secretion of opiate-like substances in the brain called ____________.
    analgesia
    endorphins

SLEEP AND WAKING

35. The sleep-waking cycle emphasizes the ____________ function of motives, as opposed to the ____________ function.
    activating
    directing

36. The record of the voltage changes occurring in the brain over time is called the ____________ ( ).
    electroencephalogram
    (EEG)

37. An EEG associated with waking relaxation shows ___________ waves.	alpha
38. Rapid eye movements (REM), a waking EEG, relaxed muscles, and low sensitivity to external stimulation all characterize ___________ (also called ___________) sleep.	active REM
39. Sleep deprivation studies suggest that sleep is a ___________ process.	restorative
40. The tendency to sleep varies across any 24-hour period, suggesting that sleep is ___________-___________ or ___________.	clock-driven, circadian
41. Dreaming typically occurs during ___________ sleep.	active (REM)
42. The average person dreams (exhibits REM sleep) for about ___________ hour(s) each night.	1–2
43. According to ___________, dreams have a function of allowing expression of unacceptable wishes in a disguised form.	Freud
44. According to the ___________- ___________ hypothesis, the dream is simply a reflection of the brain's aroused state during active sleep.	activation-synthesis

WHAT DIFFERENT MOTIVES HAVE IN COMMON

45. The fact that animals will learn to press a lever to engage in sexually arousing behavior argues for an ___________ ___________ of ___________ that is greater than zero.	optimal level, arousal
46. Alcohol, barbiturates, and opiates are examples of ___________ drugs.	depressant
47. Amphetamines and cocaine are examples of ___________ drugs.	stimulant
48. Addiction is associated with decreased sensitivity to a drug. This effect is called ___________.	tolerance
49. Addiction is also characterized by effects opposite to a drug's effects when the drug is discontinued. This is called ___________.	withdrawal
50. According to ___________-___________ theory, withdrawal symptoms can be explained as a result of action by the nervous system to neutralize the effects of the drug.	opponent-process
51. Hot peppers produce unpleasant pain in people who try them for the first time. Yet many come to like the "burn" after many experiences. This could be accounted for by ___________-___________ ___________, which might hold that the body counteracts this pain by generating pleasure internally.	opponent-process theory
52. Rats will learn to press a lever if it is followed by ___________ ___________ of certain ___________ ___________ in the brain.	electrical stimulation pleasure centers
53. There is evidence that brain stimulation reward mimics ___________ rewards, and also produces a ___________ reward.	specific nonspecific

Self Test

1. Potentiation is:
   a. electrical in nature
   b. selective facilitation of certain responses
   c. hunger and thirst
   d. self-restorative
   e. the shift from one motive-state to another

2. Motivated behavior presents a serious problem to some machine models of behavior, because:
   a. motivated behavior involves a whole set of different reactions, any of which may lead toward the same goal
   b. motivated behavior involves direction, and this assumes a type of feedback that cannot be incorporated into machines
   c. motivated behavior assumes the operation of at least one type of servomechanism
   d. all of the above
   e. none of the above

3. In human sexual behavior, sexual foreplay seems gradually to increase sexual arousal of the partners. This would be an example of:
   a. homeostasis
   b. negative feedback
   c. a servomechanism
   d. positive feedback
   e. none of the above

4. Which of the following is a reflexive thermoregulatory response to high temperature?
   a. shivering
   b. constriction of the blood vessels in the skin
   c. sweating
   d. piloerection (ruffling of fur)
   e. moving to a colder place

5. The word pair *reflexive-voluntary* represents a relationship paralleled by which of the following pairs?
   a. homeostasis-whole organism
   b. vasoconstriction-vasodilation
   c. sweating-panting
   d. vasoconstriction-building a shelter
   e. none of the above

6. A dog is in a room comfortably heated to 75°F. His hypothalamus is cooled experimentally. The result will be:
   a. he will shiver and his body temperature will go up
   b. he will shiver and his body temperature will go down
   c. he will pant and his body temperature will go up
   d. he will pant and his body temperature will go down
   e. no change in temperature, because his skin temperature remains unchanged

7. A rat's hypothalamus is cooled, and it learns to settle down over a warm air current in one part of its cage. This behavior illustrates:
   a. the operation of hypothalamic thermoreceptors
   b. the mobilization of voluntary behavior by the hypothalamic thermoregulatory system
   c. that directly manipulating hypothalamic temperature can cause an animal to make a response that is inappropriate to its actual body temperature
   d. all of the above
   e. none of the above

8. Maintenance of the body's water supply is affected by all except:
   a. regulation of the volume of body fluids
   b. changes in reabsorption of water and minerals by the kidneys
   c. drinking in response to signals from internal receptors
   d. regulation of the concentration of body fluids
   e. extent of piloerection (ruffling of fur)

9. In both thermoregulation and thirst:
   a. receptors in the hypothalamus sense important aspects of bodily needs
   b. homeostasis occurs
   c. there is both reflexive and voluntary control
   d. all of the above
   e. none of the above

10. When rats are given a great deal of exercise, their intake of food increases, that is, they eat a larger amount of food. Rats also decrease their intake of a food if it is enriched, so that it contains more calories per gram. These findings suggest that:
    a. stomach fullness must be critical in regulating the rat's food intake
    b. the rat is regulating the volume of food consumed
    c. the rat is regulating the caloric or energy value of the food consumed
    d. all of the above
    e. a and c

11. Which of the following statements best summarizes the way that internal and external signals influence food intake?
    a. Signals from various internal structures (brain receptors, liver, etc.) determine the amount eaten; external factors have almost no effect.
    b. Metabolic information from receptors in the brain controls about half of food intake, and external stimulation the other half.
    c. Metabolic information from receptors in the liver, brain, and possibly other locations interacts with external stimulation to determine the amount eaten.
    d. Palatability is the main determinant of amount eaten, as shown by the experiments in which ice cream was diluted with quinine.
    e. Hypothalamic receptors for internal and external events have a dual role in maintaining caloric intake.

12. Initiation of eating is most likely to be associated with:
    a. high blood glucose
    b. excitation of the lateral hypothalamus
    c. inhibition of the lateral hypothalamus
    d. high liver glycogen
    e. excitation of the ventromedial hypothalamus

13. Dual-center theory makes all but one of the following assumptions or predictions. Which assumption is not a necessary part of the theory?
    a. Information from internal and external receptors is integrated in the hypothalamus.
    b. The relation between the two hypothalamic feeding centers is one of mutual inhibition.
    c. The liver is the primary source of information concerning the metabolic state of the organism.
    d. Damage to the "on" center should produce aphagia.
    e. Damage to the "off" center should produce hyperphagia.

14. Two rats (or people) differ greatly in weight and fatness, but each of them holds its weight rather constant over a period of months. These results suggest that the two differ in:
    a. setpoint
    b. stomach size
    c. ability to regulate body weight
    d. ability to regulate food intake
    e. size of hypothalamus

15. Which one of the following has *not* been suggested as a cause of obesity in humans?
    a. damage to the lateral region of the hypothalamus
    b. high digestive efficiency
    c. a high setpoint
    d. overresponsiveness to the palatability of food
    e. high metabolic efficiency

16. The results in this figure can be explained by the restrained-eating hypothesis, since:

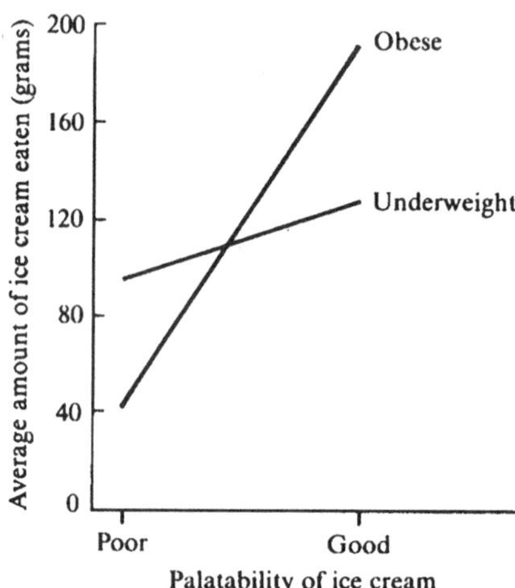

    a. not eating is disinhibited because of the high palatability of the food
    b. highly palatable ice cream is not restrained
    c. highly palatable ice cream is more fattening than ice cream of poor palatability
    d. ice cream is external to the eater
    e. obese subjects have a higher setpoint than underweight subjects only when ice cream is palatable

17. When dieters break their diets, they often go on an eating binge. This can be accounted for as:
    a. dropping of setpoint
    b. raising of setpoint
    c. negative feedback
    d. activation of the ventromedial hypothalamus
    e. disinhibition

18. Which of the following best describes the relation between restrained eating and setpoint?
    a. People with higher setpoints are likely to be restrained eaters.
    b. Anyone with a high setpoint will be a restrained eater.
    c. Restrained eating probably causes a higher setpoint.
    d. a and c
    e. all of the above

19. A major distinction between anorexia nervosa and bulimia is that:
    a. females predominate only in anorexia nervosa
    b. only anorexics are well below normal weight
    c. only bulimia is commonly found in people in the 15–25-year age range
    d. all of the above
    e. none of the above

20. The sympathetic branch of the autonomic nervous system is responsible for which of the following?
    a. decreased heart rate
    b. crying after a sad movie
    c. vegetative functions, such as digestion
    d. emptying of the colon and bladder
    e. none of the above

21. The responses of a cat about to do battle with a dog are mediated by:
    a. the parasympathetic system
    b. the sympathetic system
    c. vegetative functions
    d. the galvanic skin response
    e. b and c

22. Which of the following is *not* associated with activity of the sympathetic system?
    a. the emergency reaction
    b. epinephrine
    c. secretion by the adrenal medulla
    d. increased heart rate
    e. secretion of digestive enzymes

23. Imagine a person who has an unusual amount of voluntary control over her autonomic nervous system. Such a person should be able to:
    a. markedly reduce her weight
    b. successfully "beat" lie detector tests
    c. never experience fear
    d. get along without sleeping
    e. a and d

24. The shaded area of this cross-section of the brain represents a part of the brain that is involved in motivation and emotion. It is called the:
    a. hypothalamus
    b. limbic system
    c. cerebellum
    d. pituitary gland
    e. corpus callosum

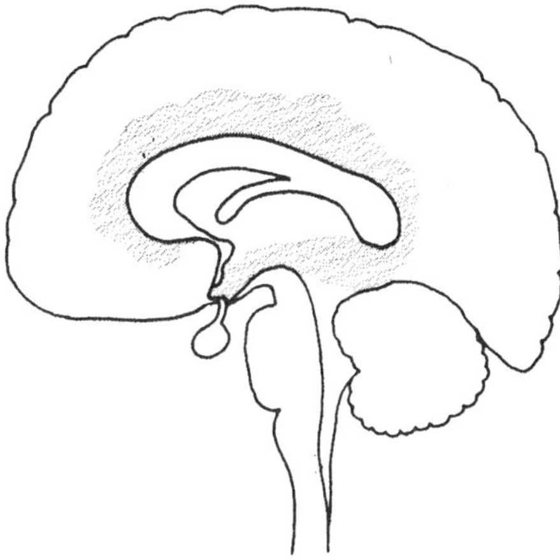

25. Which of the following statements about pain is false?
    a. experience of chronic pain is adaptive
    b. experience of acute pain is adaptive
    c. acupuncture can reduce pain
    d. pain in one location can reduce pain in another
    e. a and b

26. Active sleep is sometimes called paradoxical sleep because:
    a. behaviorally the person seems to be sleeping, but his brain waves show a pattern of activity usually associated with a waking EEG
    b. it occurs at unexpected times, e.g., in a noisy environment or during the day
    c. the person is easily roused, yet his EEG consists of slow, large amplitude, synchronous waves
    d. all of the above
    e. a and b

27. Which of the following pairings represents a contrast between active sleep and quiet sleep?
    a. rapid eye movements—no rapid eye movements
    b. dreaming—lack of dreaming
    c. EEG waking activity—EEG slow waves
    d. all of the above
    e. a and c

28. Restorative functions for sleep are suggested by:
    a. increased duration of sleep after sleep deprivation
    b. linkage of sleep to subcortical centers
    c. increased duration of sleep after bodily exhaustion
    d. the existence of active sleep
    e. a and c

29. When subjects are awakened after fifteen minutes of REM they relate longer dreams than when they are awakened after five minutes of REM. This result is evidence that:
    a. dreams are not only better remembered during REM, but actually unfold during REM
    b. dreams are rarely influenced by external sensory stimulation
    c. as dreams progress, they are related to memories of waking life
    d. dreams are mediated by the cerebral cortex and subcortical centers
    e. all of the above

30. Suppose a person is drowsy and inactive much of the time. Which of the following drugs is most likely to reverse these effects?
    a. alcohol
    b. barbiturates
    c. opiates
    d. cocaine
    e. heroin

31. A person addicted to a specific euphoria-producing drug suddenly stops using this drug. He goes into a deep depression. This reaction is an example of:
    a. the effects of tolerance
    b. the effects of addiction
    c. a withdrawal symptom
    d. inhibition
    e. a and c

32. Withdrawal results from the same forces that produce tolerance to drugs, according to:
    a. opponent-process theory
    b. optimal arousal theory
    c. studies on electrical stimulation of the brain
    d. restraint theory
    e. b and d

33. According to the opponent-process theory account of tolerance and withdrawal, the effects of opiate withdrawal should be most like the effect of:
    a. alcohol
    b. barbiturates
    c. amphetamines
    d. cocaine
    e. c and d

34. Studies on electrical stimulation of the brain have indicated:
    a. the existence of motivation-specific "pleasure centers" in the brain
    b. the possible presence of general "pleasure centers"
    c. priming, a positive feedback of stimulation on responding for further stimulation
    d. all of the above
    e. none of the above

35. Food sometimes tastes better after the first few bites, and then gradually becomes less tasty as we consume substantial amounts. This sequence can be accounted for as:
    a. an effect of brain stimulation
    b. increasing levels of all neurotransmitters
    c. positive feedback followed by negative feedback
    d. opponent processes, in which endorphins are secreted more and more during a meal
    e. an instance of lateralization

36. Which of the following can be considered a homeostatic motive?
    a. hunger
    b. sex
    c. curiosity
    d. a and b
    e. none of the above

37. Animals and humans continue to experience hunger after stomach removal, although the stomach clearly contributes to the hunger experience. This type of finding suggests that a basic feature of many motivation systems is:
    a. arousal
    b. potentiation
    c. redundancy
    d. opponent processes
    e. a and b

Answer Key for Self Test

1. b p. 45
2. a pp. 45–46
3. d p. 46
4. c p. 48
5. d pp. 48–49
6. a p. 50
7. d p. 50
8. e p. 51
9. d pp. 48–51
10. c p. 53
11. c pp. 53–54
12. b p. 55
13. c p. 55
14. a p. 55
15. a pp. 56–57
16. a p. 57
17. e p. 57
18. a p. 57
19. b p. 59
20. e pp. 60–61
21. b p. 61
22. e pp. 60–61
23. b p. 62
24. b p. 63
25. a pp. 64–65
26. a p. 68
27. d p. 68
28. e pp. 68–69
20. a p. 71
30. d p. 75
31. c p. 75
32. a pp. 75–76
33. e pp. 75–76
34. d pp. 76–77
35. c pp. 75–76
36. a p. 77
37. c p. 77

Investigating Psychological Phenomena

EFFECTS OF MENTAL PROCESSES ON AUTONOMIC ACTIVITY

Equipment: Stopwatch or watch with second indicator
Number of subjects: Three
Time per subject: Ten minutes
Time for experimenter: Forty minutes

As part of its role in the control of bodily functions, the autonomic nervous system (ANS) controls heart rate. In this way it can influence the rate of delivery of oxygen and nutrients to the cells of the body. In times when the body is stressed, increased heart rate (and other changes) increases the delivery of nutrients to cells, as well as increasing the rate of disposal of waste products. The changes in heart rate are produced directly by nerve impulses sent to the heart. They are also produced indirectly by stimulation, through autonomic pathways, of the release of epinephrine (adrenaline) and related substances from the adrenal glands.

Arousal of the sympathetic system, and hence increased heart rate, occurs when the organism is undergoing physical exertion. But it can also be produced by mental events. Such a pathway would allow an organism to mobilize its physiological resources in anticipation of a physical stress. On the other hand, it also allows for high and ultimately damaging levels of sympathetic arousal based on chronic anxiety or mental tension.

In this study we will demonstrate the effectiveness of the sympathetic nervous system link between mental activity and heart rate. Subjects will be asked to increase their heart rate by thinking about either strenuous physical activity or something that is mentally exciting.

Make sure that your subject is seated comfortably, has been relaxing for at least ten minutes, and did not engage in any strenuous activity in the last half hour. Before reading the instructions make sure you can find the subject's pulse on his or her wrist. The unit of recording for heart rate will be a thirty-second interval. You will record the number of beats every thirty seconds on the data sheet below. Allow fifteen seconds to pass between each thirty-second interval or recording so that you will have enough time to record the pulse and give the instruction. If you have an instruction to give the subject (e.g., "Relax," "Increase Mental"), give the instruction as soon as you have recorded the pulse rate, but wait the full fifteen seconds before counting heartbeats.

Instructions to read to the subject:

This is a short, ten-minute experiment to determine whether you can control the rate of beating of your heart. When I say "Begin," you should close your eyes and relax while I take your pulse. After a minute I will say "Increase physical activity," and you should try to increase your heart rate by thinking about some physical activity in which you are personally engaged and which requires a lot of exertion. After I record your pulse I will say, "Relax," and you should stop trying to increase your heart rate and relax again. I will take your pulse for another minute and then I will say "Increase mental activity." This time you should try to increase your heart rate by thinking of something that is exciting but that does not involve a lot of physical activity. This could be a fearful experience that you have had, the excitement from watching a sports event, preexamination anxiety, and so on. Following this one-minute episode I will say, "Relax," and you should stop trying to increase your heart rate and relax. I will take your pulse for one final minute. Before you begin the experiment decide on each image you will think about for the physical activity and the mental activity. After you have decided, stop thinking about the images until I give you the instruction during the actual experiment.

Give the subject a few minutes to decide on images and then to stop thinking about them before you begin the experiment. Wait one minute after the subject has selected the two images, to allow any excitation that this may have produced to go away.

DATA FROM THREE SUBJECTS (A, B, AND C)

Instruction and time	A	B	C
"Begin and Relax"			
00:00–0:30			
0:45–1:15			
"Increase physical activity"			
1:30–2:00			
2:15–2:45			
"Relax"			
3:00–3:30			
3:45–4:15			
"Increase mental activity"			
4:30–5:00			
5:15–5:45			
"Relax"			
6:00–6:30			
6:45–7:15			

List for each subject the basic situation that they imagined in the "increase" minutes.

	Physical	Mental
A	____________	____________
B	____________	____________
C	____________	____________

Plot the data for each subject on the graph below.

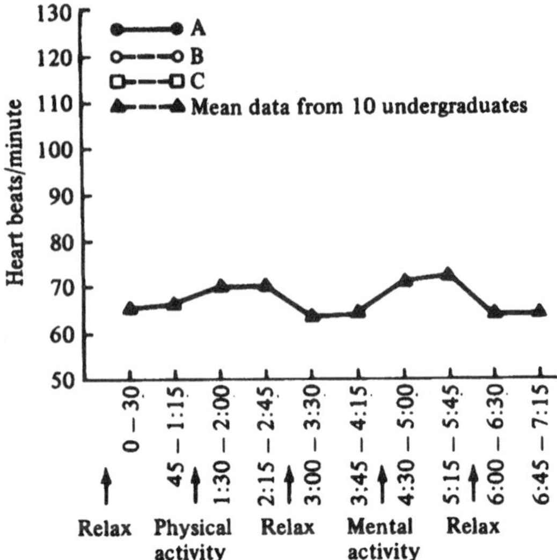

Use a different symbol for each subject, and connect the symbols for each subject by lines. Since heart rate is usually expressed as beats per minute, double each of the numbers you have recorded (since you recorded beats per thirty seconds) before plotting. We have plotted the results from ten undergraduates (mean). In our study nine of the ten undergraduates showed the increased heart rate effect.

Do all of your subjects show an ability to increase heart rate by mental activity? Which procedure, thinking of physical activity or of something mentally exciting, is more effective? *(If your instructor collects the data, fill out the report sheet in Appendix B.)*

FURTHER PROJECTS

Lowering heart rate is much more difficult than raising it. You might see if you can get some subjects to do that.

Some people have great difficulty in raising their heart rate. If one of your subjects is such a person, you could try to get an increase by having the subject *talk* about physical activity or something exciting during a one-minute period.

You could also explore whether certain kinds of "exciting thoughts" (e.g., fear, excitement of a spectator at a sports event) are more effective in raising heart rate.

CHAPTER 4

Learning

Learning Objectives

1. Describe the point of view of behavior theorists, their fit with American values and the way behavior theory is built on the idea of hardwired behaviors and their modification.

HABITUATION

2. Define habituation and discuss its adaptive significance.
3. Distinguish between short-term and long-term habituation.

CLASSICAL CONDITIONING

Pavlov and the conditioned reflex

4. Explain the basic procedure (paradigm) of classical conditioning, and define conditioned and unconditioned stimuli and responses.
5. Distinguish between conditioned and unconditioned reflexes (associations) and habituation.

The major phenomena of classical conditioning

6. Draw a curve to represent the acquisition and extinction of a conditioned response.
7. Be able to define: reinforcement, second-order conditioning, extinction, and spontaneous recovery.
8. Describe generalization and discrimination, and contrast the two processes.

Extensions of classical conditioning

9. Indicate how classical conditioning can account for acquired fears and phobias, and describe how conditioned fear is measured.

INSTRUMENTAL CONDITIONING

10. Review the major similarities and differences between classical conditioning and instrumental conditioning.

Thorndike and the law of effect

11. Explain the law of effect and indicate the evidence that supports it.
12. What is the relation between the law of effect and the evolutionary principle of survival of the fittest?

Skinner and operant behavior

13. What additions and modifications did Skinner propose to Thorndike's view of instrumental conditioning?

The major phenomena of instrumental conditioning

14. How do the phenomena of instrumental conditioning parallel those of classical conditioning?
15. Define negative and positive reinforcers, and indicate their relation to appetitive and aversive stimuli.
16. Describe the processes of generalization, discrimination, and shaping in instrumental conditioning.
17. Give examples of conditioned and primary reinforcers, and describe how a conditioned reinforcer can be produced or eliminated.
18. Describe the effect of delay of reinforcement.
19. Define and describe schedules of reinforcement and their properties, and indicate the effect of the schedules on resistance to extinction.

20. Indicate the ways in which aversive stimuli influence learning, by describing punishment, escape, and avoidance learning.
21. Why is avoidance learning often hard to extinguish?

COGNITIVE LEARNING

22. Compare behavior theory with cognitive learning theory, contrasting learning of responses to learning of cognitions (representations).

A cognitive view of classical conditioning

23. Discuss the effects of different times of onset of the conditioned and unconditioned stimulus. What is the most effective CS–US interval, and why is this adaptive?
24. Distinguish contiguity and contingency, and explain the studies that indicate that contingency is a critical factor in the formation of conditioned responses.
25. Explain the analogy between scientific thinking (the amateur scientist) and classical conditioning.

A cognitive view of instrumental conditioning

26. Review the evidence supporting the position that what is learned in instrumental conditioning is act-outcome associations, as opposed to the strengthening of specific responses. Describe latent learning.
27. Explain the role of contingency in instrumental conditioning, and its relation to learned helplessness.
28. How has learned helplessness been used to explain some types of depression in humans? What is the proposed relation between learned helplessness and function of the immune system?

VARIETIES OF LEARNING

Biological constraints on associative learning: belongingness

29. What is the basic criticism of behavior theory that is described as biological constraints? In what sense can animals and humans learn arbitrary relationships?
30. What is the equipotentiality principle, and what is the evidence against it? Describe belongingness or preparedness.
31. Describe the phenomenon of taste aversion learning, and indicate why it illustrates biological constraints.
32. Discuss belongingness in response–outcome relations in instrumental conditioning.

Adaptive specializations of learning

33. Summarize the argument that there are specialized types of learning in particular species and ecological niches. Provide an illustration.
34. Indicate some similarities across situations and species in properties of learning. How do these relate to environmental "universals" and convergent evolution?

COMPLEX COGNITION IN ANIMALS

Cognitive maps

35. What are cognitive maps and what is the evidence that animals have them?

Insightful behavior

36. Describe the phenomenon of insight in animals, and indicate why it presents problems for behavior theory.
37. How do we determine whether insight or trial and error is a better way of describing a particular learned behavior?
38. Explain what a higher-order relationship is, and illustrate this with results from matching to sample and same-different symbol studies.
39. What is meant by "access" to intellectual operations?

TAKING STOCK

40. Evaluate the strengths and shortcomings of behavior theory.

Programmed Exercises

1. ____________ ____________ believe that a few simple laws of learning can account for most of human and animal behavior.	Behavior theorists
2. Behavior theorists argue that the organism's ____________ repertory of behaviors is supplemented by continual ____________.	hardwired rewirings

HABITUATION

3. ____________ is a decline in the tendency to respond to stimuli that have become familiar due to repeated exposure.	Habituation
4. ____________-____________ habituation occurs over minutes. Another variety, ____________-____________ habituation, lasts for a few days.	Short-term long-term
5. The reinstatement of a habituated response after a period of no exposure to the habituated stimulus is called ____________ ____________.	spontaneous recovery

CLASSICAL CONDITIONING

6. Unlike habituation, classical conditioning involves the formation of ____________ between events.	associations
7. ____________ ____________ was first demonstrated in the laboratory by Ivan Pavlov.	Classical conditioning
8. After classical conditioning, the salivation of a dog upon presentation of a previously neutral bell would be called a(n) ____________ ____________. The previously neutral bell is now called a(n) ____________ ____________.	conditioned response (CR) conditioned stimulus (CS)
9. In Pavlov's laboratory, food in the mouth was a(n) ____________ ____________, and the salivation it produced was a(n) ____________ ____________.	unconditioned stimulus (US), unconditioned response (UR)
10. Salivation to meat powder in the mouth is a(n) ____________ ____________. Salivation to a tone paired with meat powder in the mouth is a(n) ____________ ____________.	unconditioned reflex (response) conditioned reflex (response)
11. According to Pavlov, when the CS is followed by the US, the connection between them is ____________.	reinforced

12.

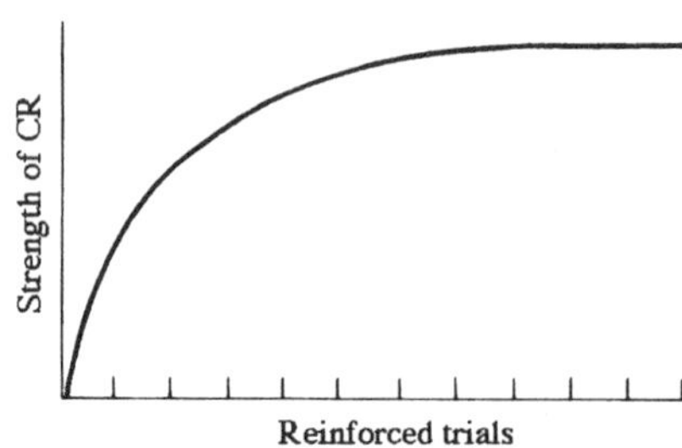

This graph is an example of an idealized ___________ ___________. | learning curve

13. A light is paired with shock. Subsequently, a tone paired with the light comes to elicit fear. This is an example of ___________-___________ ___________. | second-order conditioning

14. If after a CR has been established, the CS is presented but is not followed by the US, the result will be ___________ of the CR. | extinction

15. If time is allowed to pass, the CR will reappear when the CS is presented. This is the phenomenon of ___________ ___________. | spontaneous recovery

16. Horizontal stripes on a card (CS) are paired with a puff of air to the eye (US), resulting in a conditioned eye blink response. Now, the first time vertical stripes are presented, a conditioned eye blink is observed. This is an example of ___________ ___________. | stimulus generalization

17. The greater the difference between a CS and another test stimulus, the weaker the CR to this test stimulus. This relationship is described as a ___________ ___________. | generalization gradient

18. Reinforcement (US presentation) after CS^+, and nonreinforcement (no US) after CS^- leads to ___________. | discrimination

19. Animals show ___________ ___________ when a stimulus paired with shock is presented to them. This is called the ___________ ___________ ___________. | response suppression; conditioned emotional response

20. According to a classical conditioning analysis, the object of a phobia or fetish can be considered a ___________ ___________. | conditioned stimulus

INSTRUMENTAL CONDITIONING

21. In classical conditioning, a relation between two stimuli is learned. In instrumental conditioning, however, the relation that is learned exists between a ___________ and a ___________. | response, reward

22. The experimental study of instrumental learning was begun by ___________ in the context of a debate over the mental continuity of man and animals, which was stimulated by the evolutionary theories of ___________. | (Edward L.) Thorndike; (Charles) Darwin

23. Thorndike's ___________ ___________ ___________ states that the consequences of a response determine whether it becomes strengthened or weakened. | law of effect

24. The most prominent figure in modern behavior theory was ________.	(B. F.) Skinner
25. Skinner emphasized distinctions between classical conditioning and instrumental learning. In the former, responses are ________, while in instrumental learning they are ________.	elicited, emitted
26. Skinner used the term "________" to describe the "voluntary" or "emitted" responses that are studied in instrumental learning. He preferred to measure ________ ________ as a measure of response strength.	operants response rate
27. In instrumental conditioning, the delivery of an ________ stimulus (some preferred situation or substance, e.g., food) following a particular response is called positive ________.	appetitive reinforcement
28. In instrumental conditioning, the situation in which an instrumental response eliminates or prevents an ________ stimulus is described as ________ ________.	aversive negative reinforcement
29. Although operants are not elicited by external stimuli, the stimuli can control behavior as ________ ________.	discriminative stimuli
30. Animals can be trained to perform difficult responses by the process of ________, using the method of ________ ________.	shaping, successive approximation
31. After a neutral stimulus is paired with a reinforcer such as food, the neutral stimulus acquires reinforcement properties. This is called ________ ________.	conditioned reinforcement
32. Conditioned reinforcement is established by a procedure that seems to be the same as ________ conditioning.	classical
33. Reinforcements become less effective the longer the ________ between the response and the reinforcement.	delay (time)
34. The rule set up by the experimenter (or society) that determines the occasions on which a response is reinforced is called a ________ ________ ________.	schedule of reinforcement
35. An animal that is reinforced for every five responses is on a ________ ________ schedule.	fixed ratio
36. Responses acquired with intermittent reinforcement exhibit greater resistance to extinction. This is termed the ________ ________ ________.	partial reinforcement effect
37. Loud noises, painful stimuli, bitter tastes, and social rejection are examples of ________ stimuli.	aversive
38. In ________ training, an aversive stimulus follows a particular response.	punishment
39. ________ learning is a type of instrumental learning in which the organism is required to perform a response which terminates or reduces an aversive stimulus.	Escape

40. Avoidance responses are particularly resistant to ___________. This may account for the persistence in humans of certain intense fears, or _________. — extinction; phobias

41.

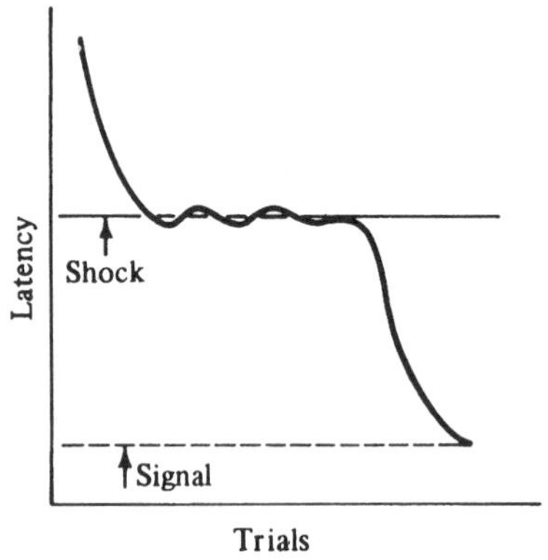

This graph illustrates the transition from __________ to _________ learning. — escape, avoidance

COGNITIVE LEARNING

42. Behavior theorists emphasize that learning modifies ___________. In contrast, cognitive theorists argue that learning involves acquisition of ___________. — responses (action); knowledge (cognitions, representations)

43. According to the most modern dominant view, in classical conditioning organisms acquire ___________ of the relation between two stimulus events. — representations

44. Learning of a conditioned response (CR) occurs most efficiently when the ___________ precedes the ___________ by a small time interval. This is called ___________ pairing. — CS, US; forward

45. Pavlov and others claimed that togetherness in time, pairing, or ___________ forms the basis for classical conditioning. — contiguity

46. Later research suggests that what is critical for conditioning is that the CS predicts the US, so that there is a __________ between CS and US. — contingency

47.

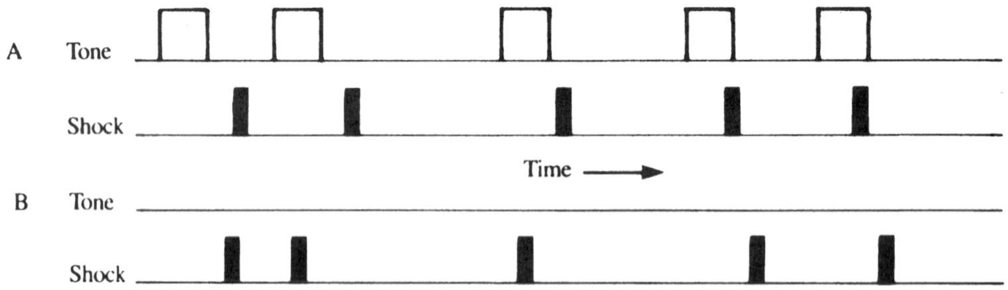

The pattern of shock and signals shown in A above is most likely to give rise to the state of ____________, whereas the — fear

____________ shock shown in B is likely to give rise to the state of ____________. — unsignaled (uncontingent); anxiety

48. Evidence indicates that rather than strengthening specific responses, instrumental reinforcement creates __________-____________ associations. — act-outcome

49. Learning in the absence of reward indicates that responses need not occur for learning to occur. This is called ____________ learning. — latent

50. Just as is the case with classical conditioning, what is learned in instrumental learning is a ____________. — contingency

51. Dogs given inescapable shocks are then placed in an avoidance situation shuttlebox where they could learn a jumping response to escape and avoid shock. Instead, they lie quietly and take the shocks. Their behavior has been interpreted as learning that the presence or absence of shocks is not contingent on their behavior, a state called ____________ ____________. — learned helplessness

52. The symptoms shown by helpless dogs resemble those seen in the human disorder of ____________. — depression

53. Helplessness training seems to increase susceptibility to cancer. This may be because this training suppresses the ____________ system. — immune

VARIETIES OF LEARNING

54. Behavior theory assumes that the relation between stimuli in classical conditioning, or between response and outcome in instrumental learning, is ____________. This assumption is known as the ____________ principle. — arbitrary; equipotentiality

55. One criticism of behavior theory holds that there are certain built-in limitations called ____________ ____________ that determine what a given animal can easily learn. — biological constraints

56. Belongingness in animal learning, as illustrated by taste aversion learning, seems to fit well with the survival needs of animals. Thus, rats, who rely heavily on ___________ in feeding, tend to associate that with the aftereffects of eating, while birds, who rely on ___________ in feeding, tend to associate this type of stimulus with the aftereffects of eating. — taste; vision (sight)

57. The fact that it is easier to train a pigeon to flap its wings to escape shock than to receive food is an instance of ____________ in ____________-____________ relations in instrumental learning. — belongingness (preparedness); response (act)-outcome

58. The fact that rats learn to associate the taste, but not the sight of food with illness is an instance of ____________ learning. — prepared

59. Acquisition of bird song, navigational abilities, and memories for sites where food has been stored all represent ___________ ____________ of learning. — adaptive specializations

60. Similarities in properties of learning across species and situations suggest ____________ features of the world across environments. The similarities can be accounted for through the process of ____________ evolution. — common (universal); convergent

COMPLEX COGNITION IN ANIMALS

61. Tolman's original work, later work on the radial-arm maze with rats, and food retrieval by chimpanzees suggest that animals have __________ __________. — cognitive maps

62. Köhler claimed that animals can acquire ____________, as well as responses. — cognitions

63. The figure below represents a situation studied by Köhler in which he demonstrated the phenomenon of ____________. — insight

64. An animal is shown one stimulus and, below it, two other stimuli. One of these two is identical to the upper stimulus. The correct response is to indicate this stimulus. This procedure is called ____________ ____________ ____________. — matching to sample

65. The idea of "sameness" developed by Sarah, the chimpanzee, is an example of a ____________-____________ relationship. — higher-order

66. A creature that knows what it knows, or can use specific capacities in new situations, is said to have ____________ to its own intellectual operations. This can be considered an aspect of ____________. — access, intelligence

67. A major criticism of behavior theory that emerges from recent work is that we must explore not only what animals (and humans) *do*, but also what they ____________. — know

Self-Test

1. Behavioral theorists share with Descartes the conviction that:
   a. one must study the nervous system to understand behavior
   b. learning is the most important aspect of animal behavior
   c. complex behavior can be analyzed into simpler, more elementary processes
   d. almost all behavior can be described as hardwired
   e. c and d

2. An animal startles when it is exposed to the sound of either a door slamming or a gong ringing. It is then exposed, about ten times, to the gong ringing followed by the door slamming. Now, when the gong rings, the animal does *not* show startle. This is an example of
   a. habituation
   b. classical conditioning
   c. extinction
   d. associations
   e. a learning curve

3. Classical conditioning and habituation have in common the fact that both:
   a. involve associations
   b. require a conditioned stimulus
   c. are built-in responses that animals show in laboratory situations
   d. involve a change in response to a stimulus
   e. occur primarily in dogs, though they may occur in some other species

4. In a classical conditioning experiment in which a tone is paired with meat in the mouth, a dog comes to salivate to the sound of the tone. The tone is called the:
   a. conditioned stimulus
   b. unconditioned stimulus
   c. unconditioned response
   d. stimulus generalization
   e. reinforcer

5. Ivan Pilaff developed a fear of German shepherds because, on a few occasions, he was bitten by them. Some weeks later, he became friendly with someone who had a German shepherd as a pet. After a few visits to this friend plus shepherd, he became fearful of the friend, even though this particular German shepherd never bit him. This is an example of:
   a. discrimination
   b. extinction
   c. reinforcement
   d. learning with a long delay
   e. second-order conditioning

6. A dog is first classically conditioned to seven stimuli (A–G) until he responds equally to all. He then gets some further training. At the end he produces the unusual generalization curve shown below. What was the further training the dog received?

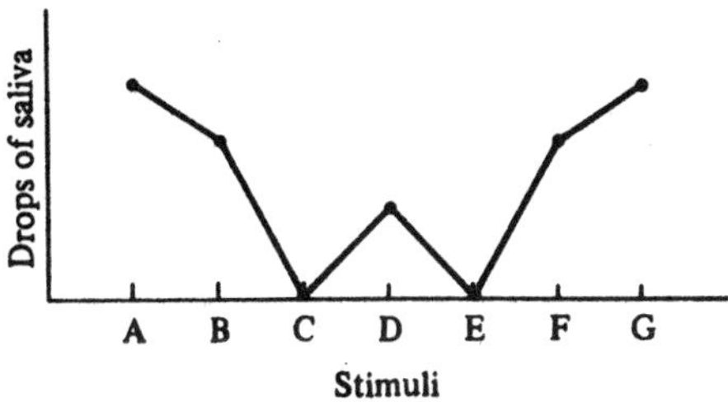

   a. extinguished stimuli A, B, D, F, and G
   b. extinguish B, D, and F; further condition A and G
   c. extinguish C and E
   d. extinguish C, D, and E
   e. further condition A and G

7. This figure illustrates the phenomenon of:

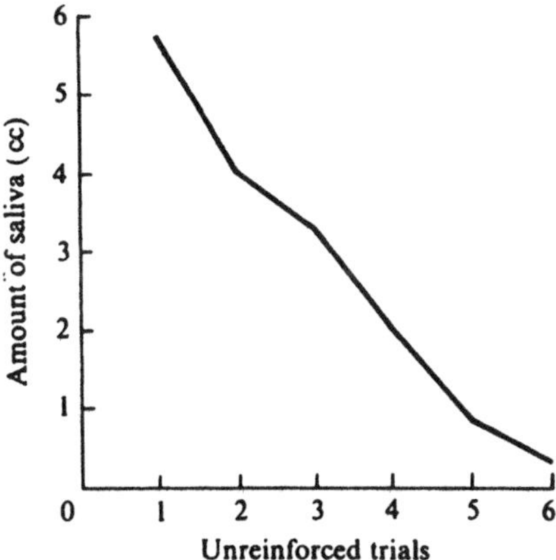

   a. conditioning
   b. generalization
   c. extinction
   d. reconditioning
   e. spontaneous recovery

8. Classical conditioning has been:
   a. shown to occur only with salivation
   b. used to explain responses to music, in conjunction with Romantic conditioning
   c. demonstrated only in vertebrates
   d. suggested as an explanation for phobias
   e. a and c

9. During World War II, air raid sirens preceded bombing raids. A person who, as a result of fear, stopped her ongoing activity (e.g., eating, working) when sirens sounded showed:
   a. response suppression
   b. a siren phobia
   c. extinction
   d. spontaneous recovery
   e. a generalization gradient

10. Instrumental learning differs from classical conditioning in that:
    a. in instrumental learning, a response-reward association is learned, while in classical conditioning, a relation between stimuli is learned
    b. associations are formed only in classical conditioning
    c. responses are never involved in classical conditioning
    d. instrumental learning always occurs gradually, in trial-and-error fashion, whereas classical conditioning occurs very rapidly
    e. a and c

11. According to the law of effect, responses followed by reward:
    a. increase in latency
    b. are not always reinforced
    c. become trials or errors
    d. are strengthened
    e. all of the above

12. The parallel between Darwin's theory of evolution and instrumental conditioning is between:
    a. mental continuity and trial-and-error learning
    b. learning and extinction
    c. survival of the fittest and the law of effect
    d. a and b
    e. all of the above

13. As described by Thorndike, instrumental learning:
    a. is gradual
    b. involves no complex, uniquely human processes
    c. is accomplished on a trial-and-error basis
    d. is a means of strengthening particular responses
    e. all of the above

14. Skinner added to Thorndike's conception(s) the idea that the responses conditioned in instrumental learning were:
    a. emitted or voluntary, as opposed to elicited as in classical conditioning
    b. increased in strength by the process of reinforcement
    c. selected from all responses emitted on the basis of the law of effect
    d. a and c
    e. all of the above

15. The desire for goods grades illustrates the phenomenon of:
    a. stimulus generalization
    b. simultaneous discrimination
    c. conditioned reinforcement
    d. successive approximation
    e. a and d

16. A rat is placed in a chamber and is given a number of pellets of food, each preceded by a clicking sound. It is later trained to lever press, with the reinforcement only the sounding of the click, but no food. Every other day the rat receives pairings of click and food, and on the alternate days, it presses only for the click. Eventually, it stops pressing the lever on the "click" days. This cessation could be explained as:
    a. generalization
    b. loss of conditioned reinforcement properties by the click
    c. discrimination between clicks in two different situations
    d. an illustration of the importance of delay of reinforcement
    e. spontaneous recovery

17. In order to shape an animal to perform a difficult response, all but one of the following procedures should be followed. Which procedure is *not* appropriate?
    a. Provide a clear signal for the arrival of reinforcement.
    b. Present the reinforcement immediately after the response is performed.
    c. Initially reinforce approximations to the desired response.
    d. At first, reinforce those parts of the desired response sequence that come at the end of the sequence.
    e. Work with the most difficult component in the response sequence first.

18. Skinner and Thorndike share in common a belief in:
    a. the importance of schedules of reinforcement
    b. the law of effect
    c. the idea that instrumental behavior is emitted
    d. the superiority of instrumental training with discrete trials
    e. all of the above

19. A hippopotamus is placed in a puzzle box. On the first trial he performs a series of responses: R1 (ramming at the doors), R2 (bellowing), R3 (stamping on the floor), and finally, R4 (stepping on a pedal which opens a door and lets him out and gives him access to mountains of hippopotamus food). According to the law of effect, any response that is followed by reinforcement will be connected to the stimulus situation. This being so, there should be a strengthening of R1, R2, and R3, but, in fact, we notice that these responses decline in probability. How would Thorndike explain this?
    a. by referring to the importance of conditioned reinforcement
    b. by invoking schedules of reinforcement
    c. by referring to the role of delay of reinforcement
    d. by referring to disinhibition
    e. by referring to generalization

20. Consider each swing by a baseball player as an operant response, and every successful hit (single, double, etc.) as a reinforced swing. What schedule of reinforcement is a baseball batter on?
    a. continuous reinforcement (fixed ratio 1)
    b. fixed ratio
    c. variable ratio
    d. extinction
    e. a or d

21. Paradoxically, when an operant is reinforced on a schedule (e.g., every third response is reinforced), the response shows a greater resistance to extinction than when it received an equal number of reinforced responses on *every trial.* This effect (partial reinforcement effect) is paradoxical because:
    a. the nonreinforced trials in partial reinforcement training are extinction trials and should weaken the response
    b. CS-US contingencies must be precisely controlled in order for good conditioning to occur
    c. the animal on partial reinforcement performs more responses in training
    d. the organism is learning a discrimination during training
    e. all of the above

22. In a classic experiment (appropriately) on classical conditioning, it was shown that classical conditioning could occur when animals were temporarily paralyzed with a drug, so that they could not respond. (Of course, when testing for conditioning with a CS, the animals were no longer paralyzed.) Which position does this result support?
    a. the cognitive learning view
    b. the behavior theory view
    c. Pavlov's position
    d. Skinner's position
    e. b and c

23. This figure demonstrates that it is very difficult to produce conditioning with:

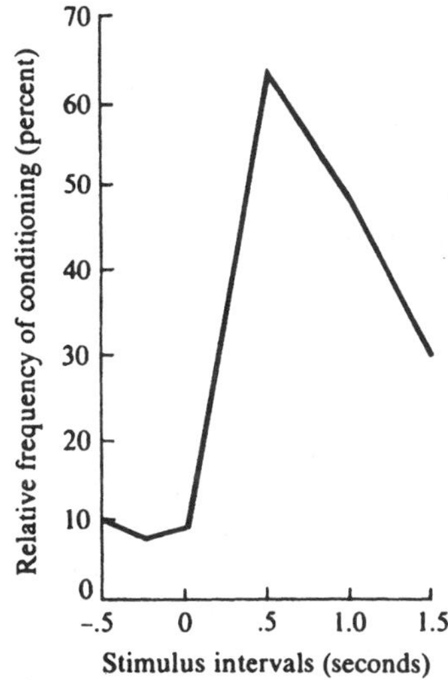

    a. forward pairing
    b. second-order conditioning
    c. extinction
    d. simultaneous pairing
    e. all of the above

24. Consider the following table of occurrences of CS and US. What predictions would the contiguity and contingency accounts make of whether conditioning would occur in this case?

	US	No US
CS	9	1
No CS	9	1

a. both predict conditioning
b. both predict no conditioning
c. only contingency predicts conditioning
d. only contiguity predicts conditioning
e. neither predicts conditioning

25. Consider the following table of occurrences of CS and US. What predictions would the contiguity and contingency accounts make of whether conditioning would occur in this case?

	US	No US
CS	7	3
No CS	3	7

a. both predict conditioning
b. both predict no conditioning
c. only contingency predicts conditioning
d. only contiguity predicts conditioning
e. neither predicts conditioning

26. In the case of unsignaled shock (a random relation between a signal and shock), the relation between a signal and the shock is one of:
a. anxiety
b. absence of contingency
c. contingency
d. contiguity
e. blocking

27. Some properties of classical conditioning suggest that it functions to make predictions about events in the world, somewhat like a scientist makes. Which feature(s) of classical conditioning suggests(s) this property?
a. sensitivity to contingency
b. forward pairing
c. spontaneous recovery
d. all of the above
e. a and b

28. A rat learns to run down a runway when reinforced with a sugar solution in the end box. After learning this, it is then fed a bitter (negatively reinforcing) solution in this same end box. When put back in the start box of the runway, it runs to the end less quickly than before. This illustrates:
a. second-order conditioning
b. generalization
c. learned helplessness
d. the law of effect
e. cognitive learning

29. Studies on learned helplessness in dogs and infants' responses to mobiles that they could or could not control are evidence for the importance of:
a. the law of effect
b. contiguity
c. contingency
d. belongingness
e. none of the above

30. Animals exposed to lights randomly paired with shock (hence, unsignaled shock) sometimes develop pathologies related to stress. The relation of this finding to learned helplessness is the same as the relationship of:
a. conditioning to extinction
b. the optimum CS-US interval to contingency
c. generalization in classical conditioning to generalization in instrumental conditioning
d. behavior therapy to the partial reinforcement effect
e. extinction of instrumental conditioning to establishment of classical conditioning

31. There is evidence that learned helplessness depresses the function of the immune system, resulting in greater susceptibility to cancer. What experience other than learned helplessness would also be likely to have these effects?
a. avoidance learning
b. unsignaled shock
c. escape learning
d. punishment training
e. punishment

32. A simplified version of John Garcia's belongingness experiment would present bright-noisy tasty water to rats, followed by X-ray produced illness. The rats would show an aversion only to the taste (one of the groups in the experiment

described in the text). However, without the use of a second group in which shock is the US, this experiment could be criticized by a behavior theorist, because:
a. bright-noisy type of stimuli don't associate well with US's like those induced by X-rays
b. the bright-noisy stimuli might have been generally less effective as CS's than the taste stimulus
c. this result would contradict the bird studies, showing selective association of visual stimuli and gastrointestinal effects
d. the selective association could have been previously learned by the rats
e. all of the above

33. Rats have a special ability to associate tastes with illness. Pigeons learn to peck a key for food, but have difficulty learning to peck a key to avoid shock. Both of these phenomena demonstrate belongingness. However, they differ in that the belongingness in the case of learned taste aversions occurs between __________ while in the pigeon example it occurs between __________.
a. species-specific stimuli, general stimuli
b. stimuli, responses
c. responses, stimuli
d. stimuli, responses and outcomes
e. stimulus and response, responses

34. Which of the following instances of human learning most clearly represents arbitrary, as opposed to biologically specialized or prepared, learning?
a. acquisition of grammar
b. learning to catch a ball
c. learning the rules of chess
d. learning to judge distance
e. a and b

35. Which of the following phenomena presents a serious problem to behavior theory?
a. learning without performing a response or without getting a reward
b. taste aversion learning
c. insight learning
d. cognitive maps
e. all of the above

36. Which of the following statements describes a fundamental difference between behavior and cognitive theorists?
a. Behavior theorists think a response is necessary for learning, while cognitive theorists think responses may be merely an index of learning.
b. Behavior theorists believe in reinforcement, and cognitive theorists believe in belongingness.
c. Behavior theorists believe in belongingness, while cognitive theorists believe in preparedness.
d. all of the above
e. none of the above

37. Differences in types of learning in different species or situations are referred to as:
a. convergent evolution
b. insight learning
c. adaptive specializations of learning
d. a and b
e. all of the above

38. Some similarities in the properties of learning across species and situations result from:
a. universal properties of environments
b. convergent evolution
c. adaptive specializations of learning
d. a and b
e. all of the above

39. In his attempts to demonstrate higher mental processes in animals, Köhler's experiments differed from those of Thorndike in that:
a. Köhler used an animal that might have greater reasoning power
b. Köhler used situations in which it was possible to "reason" a solution
c. Köhler used problems that could be gradually understood
d. a and c
e. a and b

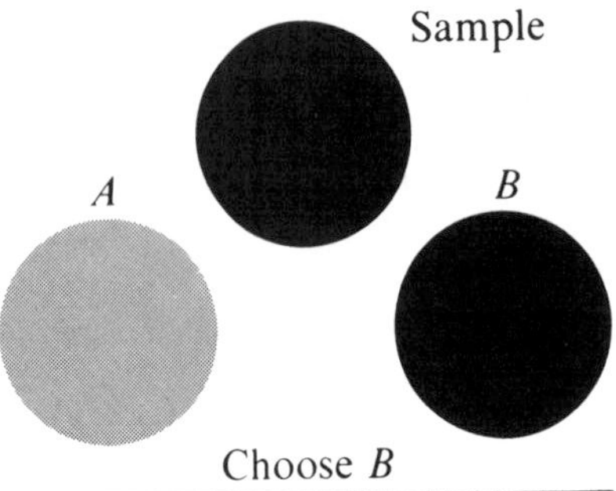

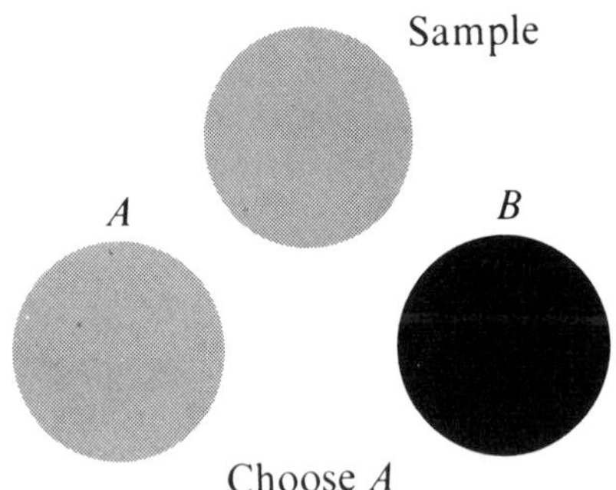

The figure sets out a problem used frequently in studies with primates. The problem is called:
a. discrimination
b. symbol manipulation
c. learning to learn
d. matching to sample
e. generalization

41. Critical evidence for a concept of "sameness" in chimpanzees comes from the demonstration of:
a. discrimination
b. generalization
c. belongingness
d. matching to sample
e. transfer of training

42. A relationship like "same," which holds regardless of the specific objects that are used to illustrate it, can be described as:
a. a good relationship
b. a higher-order relationship
c. an excellent relationship
d. insightful
e. matching to sample

43. Which of the following pairs best expresses a distinction between behavior theory and cognitive theory?
a. discrimination versus generalization
b. same versus different
c. biological constraints versus higher-order relationships
d. insight versus out of sight
e. doing versus knowing

44. Cognitive theorists criticize behavior theorists on the grounds that behavior theorists:
a. assume animals are able to learn any arbitrary relationship
b. underestimate the ability of some animals to show sophisticated learning in some specific situations
c. rely too much on the response as a necessary part of learning
d. a and c
e. all of the above

45. Transfer of training and access have in common:
a. extension of an ability or performance beyond a specific domain
b. the presence of adaptive specializations of learning
c. presence only in humans
d. great resistance to extinction
e. a and c

For the following three questions, (46–48) the same set of answer alternatives are relevant.

Each question describes a major principle of behavior theory. For each one, choose the answer that describes a finding that casts doubt on this principle. The possible answers are listed below.
a. learning sets
b. random pairing of CS and US leads to no conditioning
c. insight learning
d. learned helplessness
e. taste-aversion learning

46. Contiguity in time of two stimuli is sufficient grounds for conditioning.

47. Any CS can be associated equally well with any US.

48. Learning occurs gradually.

Answer Key for Self-Test

1.	c p. 81	25.	a pp. 100–2
2.	a p. 82	26.	b p. 102
3.	d p. 82	27.	e pp. 100–1
4.	a p. 85	28.	e p. 103
5.	e p. 86	29.	c pp. 104–5
6.	c p. 86	30.	c p. 105
7.	c p. 86	31.	b p. 105
8.	d p. 88	32.	b pp. 108–9
9.	a p. 88	33.	d pp. 108–9
10.	a p. 89	34.	c p. 111
11.	d p. 90	35.	e pp. 113–15
12.	c pp. 89–90	36.	a p. 99
13.	e pp. 90–91	37.	c p. 111
14.	a p. 92	38.	d pp. 111–12
15.	c p. 95	39.	e pp. 114–15
16.	c p. 93	40.	d pp. 115
17.	e pp. 94–95	41.	e pp. 115–16
18.	b pp. 90–92	42.	b p. 116
19.	c p. 95	43.	e p. 117
20.	c p. 96	44.	e pp. 116–17
21.	a p. 97	45.	a p. 116
22.	a pp. 99–100	46.	b p. 100
23.	d p. 100	47.	e p. 108
24.	d pp. 100–1	48.	c p. 114

Investigating Psychological Phenomena

MAZE LEARNING

Equipment: Stopwatch or watch with second indicator
Number of subjects: One (yourself)
Time per subject: Twenty to thirty-five minutes
Time for experimenter: Twenty to thirty-five minutes

This experiment illustrates a basic feature of learning: the acquisition curve, or the gradual acquisition of a skill or task. It employs a technique that was commonly used with animals in the earlier part of this century. The task is to find a way through a maze, presumably through learning a series of correct choices at the various choice-points. In the experiment you will proceed through the same maze four times: each time, a record will be kept of both your total time to completion and the number of errors (false entries). Learning would be demonstrated by a drop in either time to completion or the number of errors, as the number of trials increases.

Beginning on page 49, a maze is reprinted 4 times. In each case, using the second indicator on a wrist watch or a stopwatch, time yourself from the time you begin with a pencil at the starting point to the time you leave the maze. You should never pick your pencil off the paper until the maze is completed. If you make an error, simply retrace your steps with the pencil. Upon completion of the maze, record the total time taken at the bottom of the page. Do not record the number of errors until you have finished all the mazes, since calculation of errors would be like another trial (you would have to work through the maze again).

Finish all four trials and then calculate errors for each trial. An error is defined as the crossing of the imaginary line at the mouth of an "alley" that leads to a dead end. One such entry can only count for one error, no matter how far you go up the blind alley before realizing that it is blind. In other words, once you have entered an alley which will ultimately be blind, you can only score one error, even if there is a further choice-point along this path (both of these choices would of course have to be blind alleys). The only way you can score two errors for the same blind alley is if you enter it twice.

Plot the time/trial and errors/trial on the two graphs provided on the next page. Do you show evidence for gradual mastery of the maze? Compare your results with those from a group of undergraduate students that we have plotted on the same graph. We have plotted the mean (the average) scores. Individuals vary a lot; not all individuals show smooth curves like these averaged curves. In the graph, •———• represents the mean for eight subjects. H and L represent the range. H is the highest value of eight subjects; L is the lowest score of eight subjects.

In the earlier part of this century, psychologists speculated about what exactly is learned when a rat or human learns a maze. Some, like John B. Watson, took a "molecular" position and claimed that a sequence of responses is learned. The most critical responses would be those at the choice-points: From this point of view, the learning would be represented as a series of turning instructions (e.g., left, right, right), one for each successive choice-point. Others, such as Edward Chace Tolman, argued that the subject, rat or human, developed a spatial representation of the maze in his head, a "cognitive map," rather than a sequence of responses. What do you think you actually learned in this task?

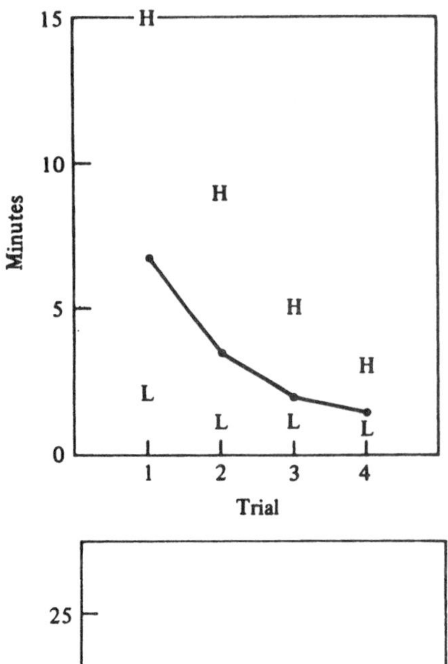

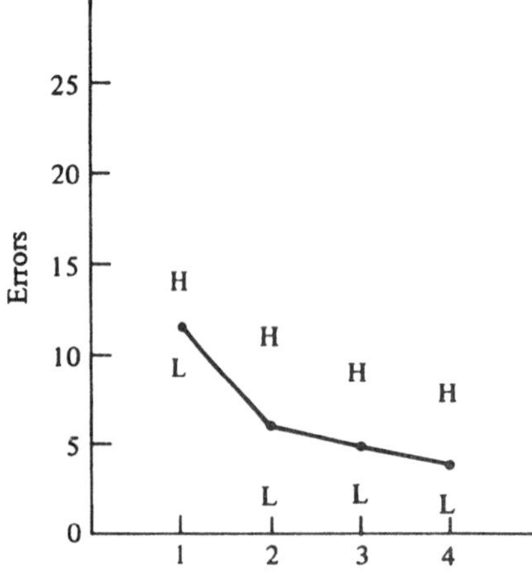

You should realize that this type of maze differs markedly from the mazes used for rats, or the life-size mazes for humans. In these cases, the subject does not get a direct picture of the whole layout; rather, the subject can only see the part of the maze in the immediate vicinity of the choice-point. This, of course, would make it much harder for the subject to build up a map of the maze. To get a feeling for the difference, cut out a hole about 1/2" square from the center of a full-sized piece of paper. Place it at the beginning of the fifth duplication of the maze, and attempt to move through the maze with the pencil again, moving the hole along as you move the pencil. If you had learned a series of turns or choices, this procedure should not seriously affect your performance. On the other hand, insofar as you used a "map," or some sort of larger view of the shape of the maze and your path through it, this procedure would seriously affect your performance. *(If your instructor collects the data, fill out the report sheet in Appendix B.)*

FURTHER ACTIVITIES

We have included one extra copy of the maze. You can use this copy for further experiments: If you need more than one maze, you can make a copy of this unused maze.

You might wish to test the idea of a map of the maze versus a set of turning responses, by trying to run the maze backward (start at finish and end at start). What predictions would you make? A cognitive map view would hold that the backward run would be a lot easier than the first run in the "proper" direction, since the same maze map would work in both directions. But a response-learning view would not predict that having learned the maze in the original order would aid in the learning of the reversed maze. The sequence of turns (e.g., left, left, right, left, etc.) would be entirely different when running the maze backward.

Of course, there is a problem here. How do you know how long it would have taken to run the maze backward if you did that on your first trial? You don't. One possibility would be to run a few people on one trial forward and a few others on one trial backward. One could then see if one direction was harder than the other. Another possibility, not as satisfying, is just to assume that it should be about as easy forward as backward, since it wasn't designed to be more difficult one way than the other.

Another activity would be to look at forgetting. Do the final maze in a few days or a week and compare your time and errors to your performance today. Would you expect you performance to be about the same as trial 4? Better than trial 1?

On the following three pages, cover the top (completed) maze while doing the bottom one.

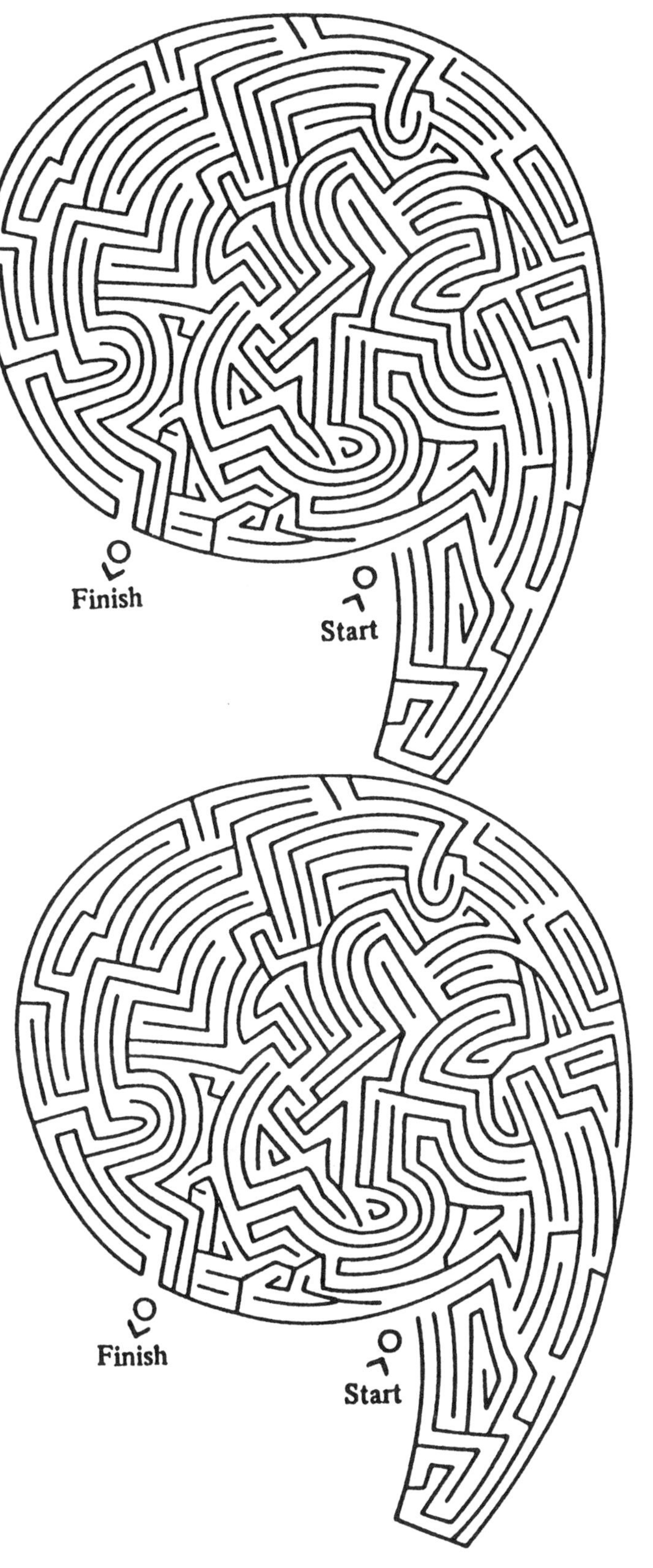
Finish
Start
Finish
Start

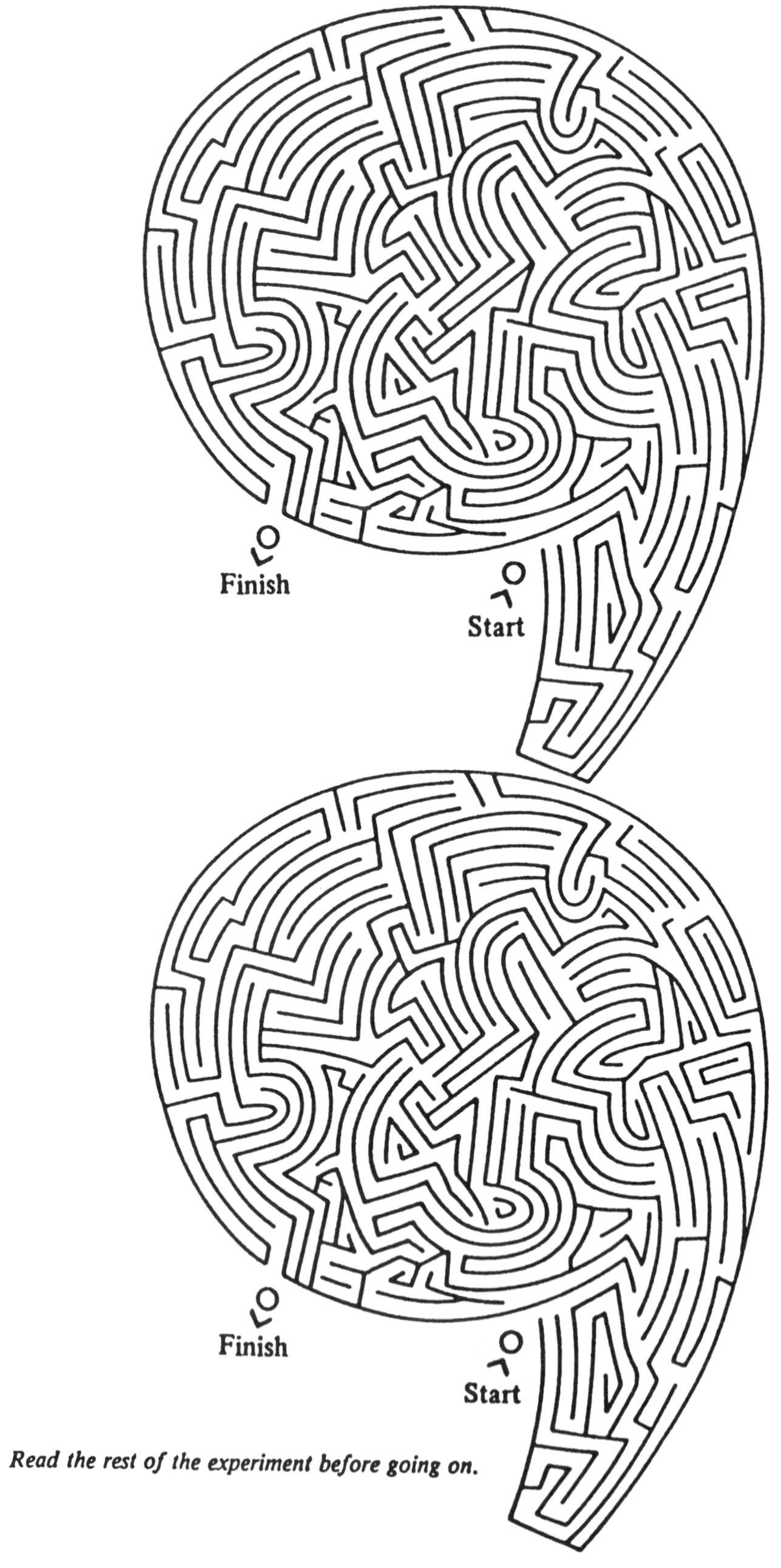

Read the rest of the experiment before going on.

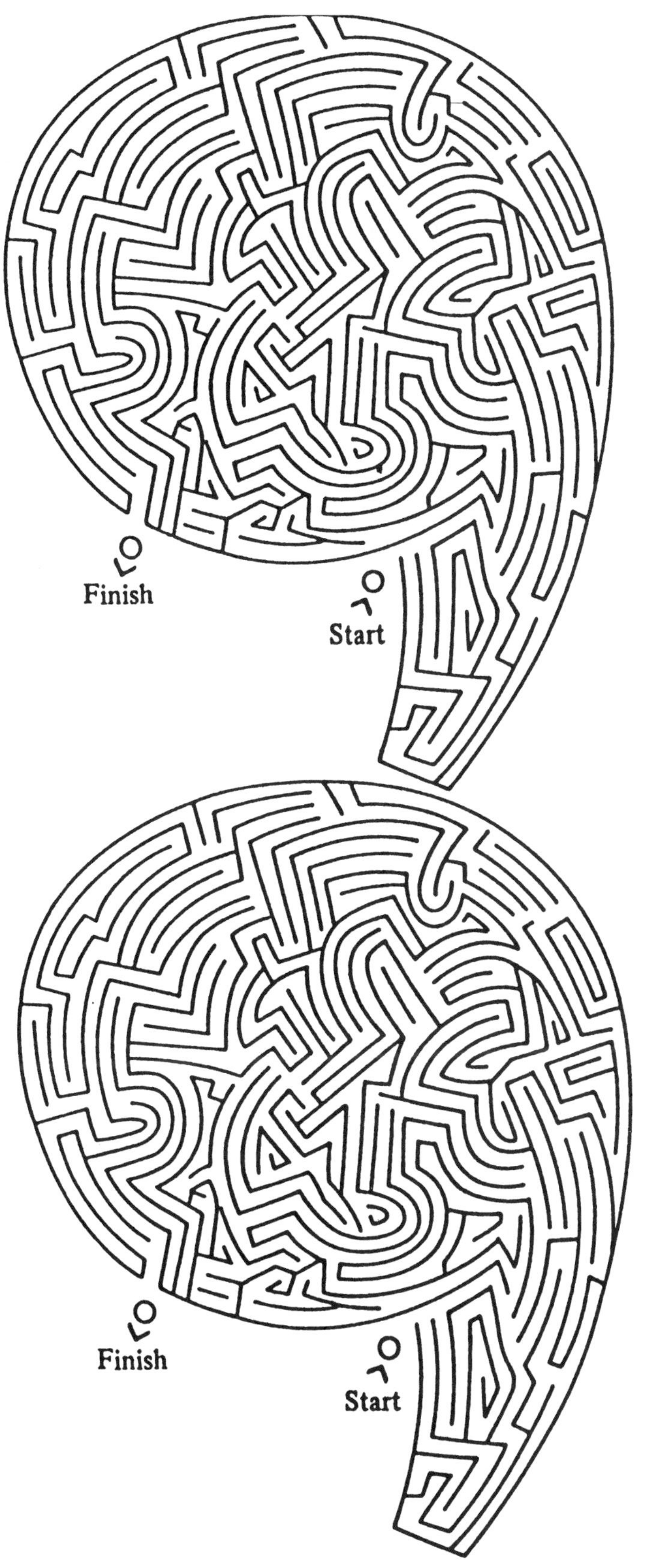
Finish
Start
Finish
Start

LEARNED TASTE AVERSIONS

Equipment: None
Number of subjects: Five to eight
Time per subject: Five minutes
Time for experimenter: Sixty minutes

One of the basic assumptions of behavior theory is that any conditioned stimulus (CS) could become associated with any unconditioned stimulus (US). That is, it is assumed that the relation of the CS to the US is arbitrary. This assumption has been seriously challenged by the discovery of the phenomenon of learned taste aversions in rats. As first documented by John Garcia and his colleagues, rats can learn in one trial to associate a taste (CS) with illness (US). They will subsequently avoid the taste. This learned taste aversion was of particular importance because Garcia and his colleagues showed that this rapid learning would only occur with tastes as the CS and certain types of illness as the US. This specificity of association between tastes and illness is an illustration of belongingness, the nonarbitrariness of associations.

Because learned taste aversions differ from most of the frequently studied types of learning, they were investigated in some detail. We now know that:

1. The specificity (belongingness) is between tastes and specific types of illness: symptoms from the upper gastrointestinal system, especially nausea, seem by far the most effective.

2. The learning typically occurs in one trial (thus allowing rats to avoid poisons without too many life-threatening trials).

3. The rat can accomplish this learning even if the illness follows the taste by more than one hour. This challenges the view that two stimuli must occur close together in time in order to be associated. CS-US intervals of more than an hour rarely, if ever, support conditioning in traditional classical conditioning, using salivation or startle responses, and tones, bells, and lights.

4. Novel tastes show much more conditioning than familiar ones. This makes sense: if eating of the familiar food has not been followed by illness, it is reasonable to associate the illness with the new food. This is true in other types of classical conditioning as well: there is generally more conditioning to novel stimuli.

It often happens that after a new phenomenon is described, it is found to be common, and one wonders how it could have escaped notice before. So it was with learned taste aversions. A phenomenon similar to that described by Garcia in the rat seems to occur in humans. Most commonly, someone eats a (usually new) food and gets ill within a few hours. Nausea and vomiting are particularly common symptoms. After this one experience, a person finds the food distasteful. Garb and Stunkard (1974) distributed a questionnaire about such experiences to about 700 people. They found that somewhat over one-third of people have had at least one such experience. The analysis of the results of their questionnaire confirmed the presence of the basic properties of learned taste aversions in humans:

1. Belongingness. Aversions were almost always limited to the food and its taste. Rarely were there reports of aversion to the restaurant, tablecloth, accompanying people or other stimuli that were also associated, in time, with the illness. Furthermore, the illness in question almost always (87 percent of the time) involved the gastrointestinal system.

2. One-trial learning. The aversions usually occurred after one food-illness pairing.

3. Long CS-US intervals. There was often an interval measured in hours between food ingestion and illness.

4. Novelty. Novel foods (tastes) seem more effective. In spite of the fact that almost everything eaten on any given day would be familiar, 45 percent of the aversions involved foods that had been eaten no more than twice before the pairing with illness.

5. "Irrationality." In many cases, a subject knew that the food did not cause the illness (e.g., other people eating the same food did not get ill, and/or other friends not at the meal came down with the same viral illness at about the same time). Yet, this knowledge that the food did not cause the illness did not weaken the aversion.

We will attempt to confirm the phenomenon of learned taste aversion in humans and highlight its unusual properties. Since, according to Garb and Stunkard, about one-third of people show this phenomenon, we will ask you to interview five to eight people, in the hope that you will find one to four subjects with aversions. We will use an interview protocol that asks many of the same questions covered in Garb and Stunkard's questionnaire. Read the introduction, below, to each subject. If the subject has an aversion, ask each of the questions indicated and record the answers.

LEARNED TASTE AVERSIONS: INTERVIEW PROTOCOL

If a person becomes sick after eating a particular food, he may develop an intense dislike, called an aversion, for that food, whether or not it was responsible for the illness. For example, one person developed a high fever after eating pizza in a restaurant, and found that he did not like pizza any more. Another person became very nauseous after eating a breakfast with hash-brown potatoes, and found the potatoes distasteful after this experience. She also found she did not want to eat from the plate that the potatoes were on. Have you ever come to dislike a food because you became ill after eating it? If so, please answer the following questions:

1. Your current age.
   (Subject A) ________ (B) ________
   (C) ________ (D) ________
2. Age when the aversion experience occurred.
   (A) ________ (B) ________ (C) ________
   (D) ________
3. What is the food? (A) ____________
   (B) ____________ (C) ____________
   (D) ____________
4. Describe the experience in terms of what and where you were eating, and the symptoms of the illness. *(Use extra sheet of paper if necessary.)*
   (A) ______________________________________
   ____
   ____
   (B) ______________________________________
   ____
   ____
   (C) ______________________________________
   ____
   ____
   (D) ______________________________________
   ____
   ____
5. Did this happen only once? If more than once, how many times? (A) ________, ________
   (B) ________, ________ (C) ________,
   ________ (D) ________, ________
6. What was the most important symptom you had?
   (A) ____________ (B) ____________
   (C) ____________ (D) ____________
7. Were you nauseous? Did you vomit (if not mentioned in answer above)? (A) ________,
   ________ (B) ________, ________
   (C) ________, ________ (D) ________,
   ____
8. About how long after you ate the food did the symptoms appear? (A) ________
   (B) ________ (C) ________ (D) ________
9. Do you believe that the food actually caused your illness? (A) ________ (B) ________
   (C) ________ (D) ________
10. List all the foods that you can remember at the meal before you got sick. Indicate for each food whether it was relatively unfamiliar (you ate it no more than three times in your life). Indicate if you developed an aversion to any of these foods:

	Food	Unfamiliar	Aversion
(A)			
	____________	________	_____
	____________	________	_____
	____________	________	_____
	____________	________	_____
(B)			
	____________	________	_____
	____________	________	_____
	____________	________	_____
	____________	________	_____
(C)			
	____________	________	_____
	____________	________	_____
	____________	________	_____
	____________	________	_____
(D)			
	____________	________	_____
	____________	________	_____
	____________	________	_____
	____________	________	_____

11. List all the other things or events that you can remember at this same meal and in the time after the meal and before the illness (e.g., the restaurant, table settings, people with you, books read, and so on). Indicate if you acquired an aversion to any of these items.
    (A) ______________________________________
    ____
    (B) ______________________________________
    ____
    (C) ______________________________________
    ____
    (D) ______________________________________
    ____
12. Do you still have this aversion? (A) ________
    (B) ________ (C) ________ (D) ________

13. Was (Is) the aversion to the taste, smell, and/or sight of the food?

Taste	Smell	Sight
(A) ______	(A) ______	(A) ______
(B) ______	(B) ______	(B) ______
(C) ______	(C) ______	(C) ______
(D) ______	(D) ______	(D) ______

Summarize the results from all of your subjects below. You decide which questions are relevant to each feature of learned taste aversion, and summarize your results with respect to each of the features listed below.

BELONGINGNESS Relevant questions (Nos.)

____

____

____

ONE-TRIAL LEARNING Relevant questions (Nos.)

____

____

____

LONG CS-US INTERVAL Relevant questions (Nos.)

____

____

____

NOVELTY EFFECT Relevant questions (Nos.)

____

____

____

"IRRATIONALITY" Relevant questions (Nos.)

____

____

____

OTHER INTERESTING RESULTS

____

____

____

Do your data confirm the basic properties of learned taste aversion?

Comment: Interview protocols like this are quite common in psychological research. They are essentially questionnaires, but they are administered by a researcher or someone on his or her staff. In a way they are more subjective than questionnaires because the interviewer could influence the answers of the subject, especially if there is embarrassing material in the protocol. On the other hand, the interview allows for an interaction between the researcher and the subject: If a subject misunderstands a question, he or she can be corrected. If the subject says something that is ambiguous, it can be expanded. Similarly, if the subject says something of unusual interest, it can be followed up.

The introductory statement in the interview is critical. We tried to write it so as not to guarantee that subjects would only describe specific food aversions based on gastrointestinal illness. Note that we gave one example of another sort of illness and also suggested the possibility of an aversion to items other than tastes. This certainly does not guarantee an "unbiased" sample of aversions, but it allows for exceptions to the phenomena as described by Garcia and, later, by Garb and Stunkard. Garb and Stunkard's introductory paragraph was more suggestive of gastrointestinal illness than is the paragraph we use here. *(If your instructor collects the data, fill out the report sheet in Appendix B.)*

PROBLEMS AND FURTHER ACTIVITIES

Garb and Stunkard's questionnaire and our interview are not experiments. They can demonstrate that one-trial taste-illness aversions occur in humans. But by themselves they cannot demonstrate belongingness. Remember that Garcia's experiments with rats showed that although lights and tastes were equally paired with both illness and electric shock, the taste was much more strongly associated with illness and the lights with shock. Our introduction for the subjects (and more so Garb and Stunkard's) pointed the subject toward taste-illness associations. We did not ask the subjects if they ever got to dislike a restaurant or a person because they were "followed by" illness or whether they ever got to dislike a food because it was followed by pain or a variety of other unpleasant events. On the contrary, we could ask whether, as a consequence of a very unpleasant event such as a death in the family or painful injury, a subject developed an aversion to any object, event, or food. Such questions have not been asked systematically. Do you have any such aversion? Do any of your friends? If there are many aversions linking food with unpleasant events "outside of the body" or outside of the gastrointestinal system, or if there are aversions to visual or other objects paired with illness, then there is little evidence for the belongingness effects in humans. We don't think there *are* many such effects, but we are not sure at this time.

We have suggested that nausea and vomiting are especially important in generating taste aversion. See if you can get evidence for this. If you know anyone (including yourself) with a food allergy, interview him, using a protocol like the one we have used for aversions. (You will have to make a few modifications.) The critical question is whether people with food allergies develop aversions to these foods. In particular, if the allergy produces no symptoms in the gastrointestinal system, is there an aversion? There is some recent data (Pelchat and Rozin, 1982) that suggest that people with food allergies outside of the gastrointestinal system do not have aversions to these foods—that is, they don't dislike these allergenic foods.

References

Garb, F., and Stunkard, A. Taste aversions in man. *American Journal of Psychiatry*, 1974, *131*, 1204–1207.

Logue, A. W., Ophir, I., and Strauss, K. E. The acquisition of taste aversion in humans. *Behavior Research and Therapy*, 1981, *19*, 319–33.

Pelchat, M. L., and Rozin, P. The special role of nausea in the acquisition of food dislikes by humans. *Appetite*, 1982, *3*, 341–51.

CHAPTER 5

Sensory Processes

Learning Objectives

THE ORIGINS OF KNOWLEDGE

The empiricist view

1. Be familiar with the viewpoint of the British empiricists.
2. What is the distinction between proximal and distal stimuli?
3. What are sensations?
4. Understand the role of association in the empiricists' view of perception.

The nativist rejoinder

5. How does nativism differ from empiricism?
6. What is the sequence of events leading from the stimulus to the reported sensation?
7. Why is the just noticeable difference (j.n.d.) important in measuring sensory intensity?
8. What is Weber's law?

Detection and decision

9. What are the various types of errors possible in a detection experiment? How do payoff manipulations affect response bias?
10. How is signal-detection theory applicable to problems other than the detection of weak stimuli?

A SURVEY OF THE SENSES

Kinesthesis and the vestibular senses

11. Define kinesthesis.
12. Describe the function of the semicircular canals.

The skin senses

13. Be familiar with the four basic skin sensations. What is known about the receptors that correspond to these sensations?

The sense of taste

14. What are the four basic taste qualities?

The sense of smell

15. How do smell and taste combine?
16. As a distance sense, why is olfaction a minor sense in humans? Of what importance is smell to humans?
17. Be familiar with the various functions of pheromones in humans and other animals.

Hearing

18. What is the stimulus for hearing? How do sound waves vary?
19. Know how the amplitude and frequency of sound stimuli are measured. How do these relate to loudness and pitch?
20. Describe the structure of the ear as it collects the auditory stimulus. How does this structure help in the perception of sounds?
21. How is the cochlea designed?
22. Describe the place and firing frequency theories of pitch perception. Why does each seem important to perception, and what triggers each?

The senses in overview

23. How does evolution shape the sensory apparatus that different animals have? Give an example.
24. What are four principles that govern the structure of all sensory systems?

VISION

The stimulus: light

25. What are the characteristics of light, and what are their visual consequences?

Gathering the stimulus: the eye

26. How is the eye like a camera?

The visual receptors

27. Describe the retina.
28. Be familiar with the following terms: rods, cones, bipolar cells, ganglion cells, optic nerve, and blind spot.
29. Where is visual acuity greatest and why?
30. Understand the duplex theory of vision.
31. How are visual pigments similar to and different from the emulsions on film?

Interaction in time: adaptation

32. What is sensory adaptation? What does the organism gain by sensory adaptation?

Interaction in space: contrast

33. Recall that brightness contrast increases with progressive intensity difference between two regions and with decreasing distance between them. How is this phenomenon important to visual perception?
34. Be familiar with the characteristics of receptive fields and the effects of lateral inhibition.

Color

35. What are the dimensions of color?
36. Describe the color solid. How are different dimensions of color represented in it? What is its relationship to the color circle?
37. Differentiate between additive and subtractive mixture of colors. Give examples illustrating each.
38. What are complementary colors? How do their complementary characters account for simultaneous color contrast and negative afterimages?

The physiological basis of color vision

39. Explain the difference among the three cone types in human color vision.
40. It is important to understand the opponent-process theory thoroughly. Be aware of the relevance of primary colors, color antagonists, and inhibition.
41. What is the physiological evidence for the opponent-process theory?
42. Describe different types of color blindness.

Feature detectors

43. How do electrophysiological studies of the action of single neural cells tell us about perception and feature detection?
44. How can adaptation studies inform us about the perception of complex attributes of forms?
45. Be familiar with the aftereffect of visual movement.
46. Understand how the perception of complex forms such as faces might be related to the use of feature detectors.

Programmed Exercises

THE ORIGINS OF KNOWLEDGE

1. John Locke postulated that all knowledge comes by way of experience. This school of thought is known as ____________.	empiricism
2. Locke used the metaphor of a ____________ ____________ in describing the human mind at birth.	tabula rasa (blank slate)
3. An object in the real world is known as a ____________ stimulus.	distal
4. When the energy from an object impinges on a sensory surface, we say that this pattern of energy has become a ____________ stimulus.	proximal
5. Empiricists assumed that the raw materials of knowledge are ____________.	sensations
6. According to the empiricists, complex ideas are perceived by the linking together, or ____________, of two or more sensations.	association
7. Two identical objects have different retinal sizes. This clue that one object is closer than the other is known as ____________ ____________.	linear perspective
8. Kant believed that a number of aspects of perception are innate. This view has since been labeled ____________.	nativism

9. The study of the relationship between properties of the stimulus and sensory experience is known as ____________. — psychophysics

10. The study of the neural consequences of a stimulus is ____________. — psychophysiology

11. The ____________ ____________ is the minimal stimulus energy needed to produce a sensation. — absolute threshold

12. You find that you are unable to tell the difference between a 25-lb. weight and a 28-lb. weight, but you can differentiate the 25-lb. weight from any other weight over 28 lbs. Something slightly over 3 lbs. is your ____________ ____________. It will produce a ____________ ____________ ____________ in this weight range. — difference threshold, just noticeable difference (j.n.d.)

13. A difference threshold is 2 lbs. when the standard is 40 lbs. ____________ law predicts that the difference threshold with a 20-lb. standard would be ____________ lb(s). — Weber's; 1

14. Imagine that we toss a coin 100 times, each time asking a subject to predict the outcome (heads or tails). We find that 73 times he predicts heads. We also find that he knows that on the average, 100 tosses will result in approximately 50 heads. We can then attribute his deviation from this figure to a ____________ ____________. — response bias

15. One duty of an air traffic controller is to watch a radar screen and determine what planes are in the area. There are two kinds of errors she might make in this task. First, she may not see a small dot on the screen, thus committing a ____________, as it is often called in signal-detection theory. On the other hand, she may report a plane when there is none there. This is called a ____________ ____________. Considering the costs of these two errors, the ____________ ____________ error is probably more common than the ____________. — miss; false alarm, false alarm, miss

16. Corresponding to the two types of errors, there are also two kinds of correct responses. When an event occurs in the world and we say that the event occurred, that is known as a ____________. When an event hasn't occurred in the world and we say that it hasn't, we have given a ____________ ____________. — hit; correct negative

17. We have looked at response bias that is caused by the costs of making various types of errors and response bias due to unspecified internal preferences. In a detection experiment, response bias can be altered by varying the ____________ ____________. — payoff matrix

18. Imagine the following payoff matrix.

Subject says:	yes	no
stimulus present	+$5.00	–$1.00
stimulus absent	–$10.00	+$5.00

Assuming that the subject would have no response bias if a payoff matrix was used which rewarded "yes" and "no" responses equally, it is most likely that the subject will produce more ____________ responses with the above matrix. — no

19. If you make a selection error during the admission of a student to medical school that results in a student who cannot complete his degree, you have made a ____________ ____________ error . — false alarm

A SURVEY OF THE SENSES

20. The ____________ ____________ indicate rotation of the head. They are located in the ____________ ____________. — semicircular canals, inner ear

21. The four basic skin sensations are: ____________, ____________, ____________, and ____________. — pressure, warmth, cold, pain

22. It is believed that pressure sensations are produced by specialized ____________ in the skin that sense movement and vibration of skin and hair. — receptors

23. Sensations of ____________ and ____________ are probably signaled by free nerve endings in the skin. — temperature, pain

24. The four basic taste qualities are: ____________, ____________, ____________, and ____________. — sour, sweet, salty, bitter

25. The technical term for smell is ____________. — olfaction

26. The sense of smell can be valuable in communication for organisms employing ____________. — pheromones

27. One line of evidence suggesting that pheromones are important to humans comes from the study of ____________ synchrony. — menstrual

28. Light intensity is to vision as ____________ is to hearing. — amplitude

29. Hue is to vision as ____________ is to audition. — pitch

30. The purpose of the middle ear, oval window, and inner ear is to ____________ and ____________ sound waves. — conduct, amplify

31. The structure that actually contains the auditory receptors is known as the ____________. — cochlea

32. The actual auditory receptors are the ____________ ____________, which are stimulated by deformation of the ____________ ____________. — hair cells, basilar membrane

33. Pitch perception seems to be based on two mechanisms. High frequencies are coded using ____________ of excitation, while lower frequencies are coded by ____________ firing rate. — place, neural

34. ____________ pressure has caused the development of specialized sensory equipment for different species. — Evolutionary

35. The processing of sensory stimuli begins when they impinge on ____________ structures of the body. — accessory

36. For all modalities, stimulus energy must be converted into a form which can be used by the senses. The translation is termed ____________. — transduction

37. Higher neural centers process all sensory input and ____________ this input into various quantitative and qualitative dimensions. — code

38. Any part of a sensory system is in ____________ with the rest of that system. — interaction

VISION

39. Objects can either ____________ or ____________ light. — emit, reflect

40.	Light energy can vary in ____________, thus giving rise to perceived brightness, and in ____________, which determines perceived hue.	intensity wavelength
41.	The visible spectrum extends from roughly ____________ to roughly ____________ nanometers.	400 750
42.	The first place at which light energy from the world interacts with the senses is at the ____________.	retina
43.	The focusing of the eye is affected by ____________ of the lens.	accommodation
44.	____________ are most densely packed in the fovea, while ____________ are most frequent in the periphery.	Cones, rods
45.	The first cells to be stimulated by light are the ____________, which activate the ____________ cells, which in turn stimulate the ____________ cells.	receptors bipolar, ganglion
46.	The axons of the ganglion cells form a bundle, which is known as the ____________ ____________; this exits the eyeball at the ____________ ____________.	optic nerve, blind spot
47.	One person is able to distinguish a one-inch "F" from a one-inch "E" at a distance of 300 feet. Another person is only able to make the same discrimination at 200 feet. These two people have different visual ____________.	acuity
48.	The fact that primarily nocturnal animals have no cones and many rods, while animals that operate in daylight have many cones and few rods, is evidence for a ____________ theory of vision.	duplex
49.	The chemical reaction in which the visual pigment rhodopsin breaks down and then reforms into rhodopsin takes place in the ____________ .	rods
50.	The physical resolution of the eye is not very good. In terms of physics, we shouldn't be able to see as clearly as we do. However, the exaggeration of contrast through ____________ ____________ enhances the visual message.	lateral inhibition
51.	The three attributes used to describe color are ____________, ____________, and ____________.	hue, brightness saturation
52.	____________ colors cannot be distinguished on the basis of hue.	Achromatic
53.	Unique red is that red which appears to have neither any ____________ nor any ____________ in it.	blue yellow
54.	Only ____________ colors can differ in saturation.	chromatic
55.	The ____________ ____________ equates spatial relationships along three dimensions with the three dimensions of color.	color solid
56.	Colored filters placed over two different lights that are focused on the same spot produce an ____________ color mixture.	additive
57.	A ____________ hue is one that, when mixed with another hue in the correct proportion, will produce the color gray.	complementary
58.	A gray color, when surrounded by green, appears reddish. This is known as ____________ ____________ ____________ and is evidence for antagonistic pairing of colors.	simultaneous color contrast

59. ____________ ____________ have the complementary hue and the opposite brightness of the original stimulus.	Negative afterimages
60. Human vision is termed ____________, since there are three cone types.	trichromatic
61. According to the opponent-process theory of color vision, it should never be possible to see a red hue with a trace of ____________ in it.	green
62. Color blindness is most common in ____________ and could entail the ____________ of one of the opponent-process pairs.	males absence
63. ____________ have contributed significantly to the study of form perception by studying the behavior of single nerve cells in the visual system.	Electrophysiologists
64. A nerve cell that selectively responds to some characteristics of a stimulus but not to others is often called a ____________ ____________.	feature detector
65. One of the characteristics that visual nerve cells respond to selectively is ____________.	orientation
66. Studies of ____________ in humans provide some evidence for the importance of feature detectors in visual perception.	adaptation
67. The aftereffect of visual ____________ is a phenomenon that reveals a feature detector.	movement
68. It has been shown that monkeys have feature detectors that are selectively sensitive to very complex stimuli, such as ____________ .	faces or hands

Self Test

1. John Locke, the British empiricist, would most likely agree with which of the following statements?
   a. "All knowledge is determined by innate mechanisms."
   b. "We are born with a fair amount of innate knowledge, with experience playing a small role."
   c. "Knowledge arrives through the senses."
   d. John Locke was not an empiricist and would not have agreed with any of the above statements.
2. The metaphor that best describes the empiricists' view of the human mind at birth is:
   a. a camera
   b. an encyclopedia
   c. a pad and pencil
   d. a blank slate
3. An example of a distal stimulus would be:
   a. the pattern of light energy hitting the retina
   b. a Chevrolet
   c. the sensation produced by a distant mountain
   d. a hallucination
4. An example of a proximal visual stimulus is:
   a. the activity of the retina hit by an array of photons
   b. an object situated very close to the retina
   c. a distant object which appears closer than it really is
   d. all of the above
5. According to the empiricists, linear perspective serves as a depth cue because:
   a. it produces a memory of an associated movement and an experience of depth
   b. it mitigates the effect of convergence
   c. its use by painters has familiarized us with its symbolic representation of depth
   d. we are classically conditioned to accept it as such
6. Immanuel Kant believed:
   a. in innately determined categories of perception
   b. that all knowledge came through the senses
   c. that associations of sensations determined perception
   d. in none of the above

7. Which of the following is an example of transduction?
   a. sound waves in the air being translated into electrical energy by a microphone
   b. electrical waves being translated into sound waves by a loudspeaker
   c. light energy being converted into nerve energy by the retina
   d. all of the above

8. Psychophysics studies the relationship between:
   a. the distal and proximal stimulus
   b. the distal stimulus and sensory experience
   c. nativism and empiricism
   d. the proximal stimulus and sensory experience

9. The absolute threshold depends on:
   a. the magnitude of the difference threshold
   b. the neurophysiological hierarchy of modalities
   c. a critical stimulus energy level required by the sensory system
   d. differences in quality of experience

10. You are shopping for a new car. You have test-driven a number of cars to determine which models have the best performance. You discover that you cannot tell the difference between models A and C. The difference (however measured) between cars A and C is below your:
    a. difference threshold
    b. response bias
    c. criterion
    d. sensitivity

11. Which of the following involves a search for an absolute threshold?
    a. trying to determine whether drink A or drink B has more sugar in it
    b. trying to determine which instrument in an orchestra is playing the loudest
    c. trying to determine whether you were cheated on your Irish coffee (i.e., whether there is really any whiskey in it or not)
    d. trying to determine if you detect any difference in your strength after three months of weight lifting

12. Each of the pairs of numbers below represents a hypothetical difference threshold with its associated stimulus energy value. Which of the Weber fractions that results from these values represents the greatest sensitivity?
    a. 1, 100
    b. 1, 10
    c. 100, 1000
    d. 50, 1000

13. A doctor is scanning a lung X-ray. She sees something which may be either the beginnings of a tumor or harmless scar tissue. It is likely that response bias will come into play when the doctor decides whether to operate or not. Which of the following factors might influence this response bias?
    a. probability that it is a tumor
    b. risks associated with surgery
    c. risks associated with an untreated tumor
    d. all of the above
    e. none of the above; response bias is fixed and cannot be easily changed

14. In the above example, what type of error is worse to make?
    a. false alarm
    b. miss
    c. a and b are equally important
    d. cannot be determined without knowing associated costs and benefits

15. Still considering the example in question 13, imagine that there are five different types of tumors such that each is associated with a different death rate when left untreated. Type I has the highest death rate, and type V has the lowest rate (with the others falling between I and V, in order). Imagine further that these five tumors can be distinguished from each other with X-rays, but none of them can be distinguished from scar tissue (which is harmless). Assuming that everything else is constant from one tumor type to another, under which condition would the doctor be most likely to operate and risk putting the patient under the dangers of surgery?
    a. the patient has either scar tissue or type III tumor
    b. the patient has either scar tissue or type V tumor
    c. the patient has either scar tissue or type I tumor
    d. if the doctor was good, the probability of her operating would be constant, despite the type of tumor

16. Kinesthesis is:
    a. information from the muscles, tendons, and joints
    b. a function of the ossicles in the inner ear
    c. the movement of hair cells in the cochlea
    d. the crystallization of the viscous liquid in the semicircular canals

17. Head rotation is sensed via:
    a. the pressure of crystals on hair cells in the vestibular sacs
    b. the deformation of hair cells in the semicircular canals
    c. dynamic tension of the relevant musculature
    d. the movement of the world relative to ourselves as we walk through it

18. Pressure:
    a. is assessed via the two-point threshold
    b. is one of the four basic skin sensations
    c. depends on the allocation of cortical space
    d. is the sensation elicited by stimulation of capsule receptors
    e. both b and d

19. Rats working in a Skinner box are exposed to air taken from the vicinity of a group of rats that suffered electric shock. What will be the probable result?
    a. the rats will exhibit aggressive behaviors
    b. there is no effect
    c. the rat's bar-pressing performance will be disrupted
    d. the pheromone present in the air will render the rats immobile

20. You are given an acidic solution of lemon and water to drink. After continuously drinking this solution, it appears to be almost tasteless. What phenomenon is being demonstrated?
    a. specificity
    b. adaptation
    c. difference threshold
    d. receptor interaction

21. The sense of taste is enhanced by which of the following senses?
    a. smell
    b. sight
    c. hearing
    d. touch

22. The physical stimulus for hearing is described in terms of amplitude and frequency. The corresponding psychological dimensions are:
    a. loudness and tone
    b. amplitude and pitch
    c. loudness and timbre
    d. loudness and pitch

23. The correct ordering of anatomical structures in the ear (from outside in) is:
    a. eardrum, middle ear, oval window, cochlea
    b. oval window, middle ear, eardrum, cochlea
    c. eardrum, oval window, middle ear, cochlea
    d. none of the above

24. For low frequency tones (below 400 hz), pitch is detected by:
    a. the eardrum
    b. localization on the basilar membrane
    c. firing frequency of the auditory nerve
    d. none of the above

25. For frequencies above 5000, pitch is detected by:
    a. the eardrum
    b. localization on the basilar membrane
    c. firing frequency of the auditory nerve
    d. none of the above

26. A praying mantis needs only one ear because:
    a. it uses its ear to detect only loud sounds
    b. it needs only to detect an ultrasonic sound, not to localize it
    c. it needs to localize an ultrasonic sound, not to detect it
    d. it needs to detect the sound only of another mantis

27. Which of the following are characteristics common to most of the senses?
    a. the presence of anatomical structures
    b. the transduction of the physical stimulus to a neural impulse
    c. the translation of the neural impulse to a dimension of sensation
    d. the interaction of all parts of the sensory system
    e. all of the above

28. One light source appears bluish and another appears greenish. This difference in appearance is due to differences in:
    a. intensity
    b. wavelength
    c. opponent processes
    d. none of the above

29. Intensity is to brightness as wavelength is to:
    a. sensitivity
    b. darkness
    c. wattage
    d. hue

30. Which of the following wavelengths is not considered to be part of the visible spectrum?
    a. 650
    b. 400
    c. 300
    d. 575

31. The structure that bends light rays so that they are projected onto a light-sensitive surface is the:
    a. retina
    b. iris
    c. lens
    d. all of the above

32. During the process of accommodation, a close object will result in ___________ of the lens.
    a. thickening
    b. flattening
    c. no change
    d. increased transparency

33. You arrive late to a movie theater and are forced to sit in the far right-hand seat of the first row. You must then look to your left to see the rectangular screen. What is the image of the screen that is projected onto your retina?

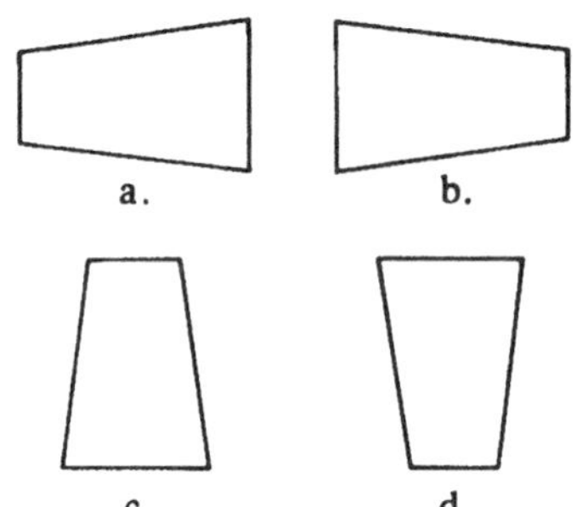

34. The two types of receptors in the human eye are known as ___________ and ___________.
    a. bipolars, horizontals
    b. ganglions, bipolars
    c. rods, cones
    d. bipolars, cones

35. An area near the center of the retina has virtually no rods, consisting entirely of cones. It is approximately two degrees in diameter and is known as the:
    a. periphery
    b. optic nerve
    c. optic chiasm
    d. fovea

36. In order to maximize visual acuity you should:
    a. stare slightly away from the thing that you are trying to see
    b. use only one eye at a time (to reduce interocular rivalry)
    c. reduce the luminance of the area, in order to engage the more sensitive rod system
    d. look directly at the object

37. Which of the following is not in agreement with the duplex theory of vision?
    a. the rods are the receptors for night vision, while cones serve day vision
    b. rods respond to low light levels, cones to high levels
    c. rod vision provides good acuity, cones provide poor acuity
    d. rods result in achromatic vision, cones provide color vision

38. What happens when light hits a visual receptor?
    a. silver bromide molecules combine with light to release silver
    b. light strikes the retina and generates rhodopsin
    c. energy is converted to nervous impulses via a photochemical process which bleaches rhodopsin
    d. the reflected light from the receptor causes a photochemical alteration leading to neural excitation

39. Which of the following is an example of sensory adaptation?
    a. the cold ocean feels warmer after we've been in it for a while
    b. being able to see in a dark room after a period of adjustment
    c. increasing sensitivity to salt with continued exposure
    d. all of the above
    e. a and b

40. The first time you see a friend's new car, it is parked against a black wall. Later you see that same car parked against a white backdrop (at the same time of day) and comment that you remember the car as being much brighter. This is an example of:
    a. brightness contrast
    b. adaptation
    c. temporal interaction
    d. none of the above

41. Which of the following is not used to classify colors?
    a. brightness
    b. hue
    c. amplitude
    d. saturation

42. White and black can be distinguished only on the basis of which dimensions?
    a. brightness
    b. hue
    c. wavelength
    d. saturation

43. Red and green must differ on which dimension (at least)?
    a. brightness
    b. hue
    c. amplitude
    d. saturation

44. White and black cannot possibly differ on which dimension?
    a. hue
    b. saturation
    c. both of the above
    d. none of the above

45. The extent to which a color of some fixed hue is mixed with an achromatic color is represented by a value on the ___________ dimension.
    a. brightness
    b. hue
    c. intensity
    d. saturation

46. Which of the following is true of the color solid?
    a. the central hoop consists of the colors red, green, yellow, blue, orange, purple, in that order
    b. horizontal distance from the central axis represents brightness
    c. the tilt of the central hoop reflects saturation
    d. none of the above

47. An example of a subtractive color mixture is:
    a. two spotlights, each with a different filter, trained on the same location
    b. the use of two filters on one spotlight
    c. the light as it enters the human eye
    d. all of the above

48. All of the following are examples of additive color mixtures except:
    a. color printing
    b. color TV
    c. human color vision
    d. mixing of paints

49. In an additive color mixture, equal amounts of complementary hues mixed together will produce:
    a. a unique hue
    b. a color with a hue intermediate to the two original hues
    c. a color without hue
    d. could be any of the above, depending on the choice of hues

50. All of the following are used as evidence for color antagonism except:
    a. complementary colors
    b. retinal bleaching
    c. simultaneous color contrast
    d. negative afterimages

51. Any wavelength will stimulate:
    a. all three receptor types, but unequally
    b. all three receptor types, and equally
    c. only one or two receptor types
    d. from one to three receptors, depending on the intensity and wavelength

52. In the opponent-process theory, the three pairs of receptors are:
    a. red-blue, green-yellow, black-white
    b. red-yellow, blue-green, black-white
    c. red-green, blue-yellow, black-white
    d. never specified

53. An achromatic color results when which system(s) is(are) in balance?
    a. red-green
    b. blue-yellow
    c. red-green and blue-yellow
    d. black-white

54. A person who is color-blind will probably:
    a. use color names appropriately
    b. be female
    c. be unable to distinguish any hues at all
    d. be unable to imagine how ultraviolet looks to a bee

55. The presence of "bug detectors" in frogs indicates that feature detectors:
    a. can be responsive to quite complex objects
    b. cannot be wired to detect anything but simple attributes of shapes
    c. cannot be shaped by evolutionary pressure
    d. are a minor part of the visual response to objects

56. Adaptation effects in humans can be demonstrated for the perception of:
    a. color
    b. movement
    c. both of the above
    d. none of the above

57. Cases of prosopagnosia and the preference of infants to view faces as opposed to other stimuli suggest that:
    a. there are feature detectors in the human visual system for faces
    b. there is no similarity in how humans and monkeys perceive faces
    c. the perception of faces may be handled by a different part of the visual system than the perception of other objects
    d. none of the above

Answer Key for Self Test

1.	c p. 124	30.	c p. 141
2.	d p. 124	31.	c p. 141
3.	b p. 124	32.	a p. 141
4.	a p. 124	33.	a p. 142
5.	a p. 126	34.	c p. 142
6.	a p. 127	35.	d p. 142
7.	d p. 127	36.	d p. 142
8.	b p. 127	37.	c p. 143
9.	c p. 127	38.	c p. 143
10.	a p. 128	39.	e p. 143
11.	c p. 128	40.	a p. 144
12.	a p. 128	41.	c pp. 145–46
13.	d p. 129	42.	a p. 146
14.	d p. 129	43.	b p. 146
15.	c p. 130	44.	c pp. 145–46
16.	a p. 131	45.	d p. 146
17.	b p. 131	46.	d p. 147
18.	e pp. 131–32	47.	b p. 147
19.	c p. 134	48.	d pp. 148–49
20.	b p. 133	49.	c p. 149
21.	a p. 133	50.	b p. 150
22.	d p. 135	51.	a p. 151
23.	a p. 137	52.	c p. 152
24.	c p. 138	53.	c p. 152
25.	b p. 137	54.	a p. 153
26.	b p. 139	55.	a p. 154
27.	e p. 140	56.	c pp. 154–55
28.	b p. 141	57.	c p. 155
29.	d p. 141		

Investigating Psychological Phenomena

MEASURING BRIGHTNESS CONTRAST

Equipment: Stimuli are included; one sheet of black construction paper needed
Number of subjects: One or more
Time per subject: Ten minutes
Time for experimenter: Twenty minutes

In the "Sensory Processes" chapter, Professor Gleitman describes a phenomenon that clearly illustrates the effect of context on perception. The phenomenon is brightness contrast. Examine Figure 5.12 in the text once again. Note how sharply different in brightness the four central gray squares appear to be; yet they are identical. (You can prove this to yourself by laying a sheet of paper over the figure with holes cut out where the squares are located.) The difference in brightness is apparently a result of interaction between each central square and its surrounding light or dark border. As the text explains, the surrounding border induces a contrast effect such that a patch will appear lighter when surrounded by a dark border, and darker when surrounded by a light border. The greater the difference in lightness between the center and its surroundings, the greater the illusion.

Of course, as you probably suspect, brightness contrast has limits. That is, there is just so much illusion that can be produced by a surrounding context, no matter how great the difference between the center and its surroundings. The present experiment provides an opportunity to examine the extent to which the visual system can be fooled by context. More importantly, however, in this exercise you will have a chance to conduct an actual psychophysical experiment to measure quantitatively the relationship between physical stimuli and psychological experience.

The purpose of the experiment is to measure the magnitude of brightness contrast for a particular test patch of a given, fixed lightness. This test patch will be surrounded by several borders that differ in their lightness, one from another. With this arrangement, we should be able to produce different degrees of brightness contrast. But how do we measure the extent of the effect? One way would be to ask a subject to assign numbers to the test patch corresponding to how bright she thought it was. But we shall use a more accurate technique: each time we present a border around the test patch, we shall ask the subject to match the apparent brightness of the test patch by choosing another patch that seems to match it. The matching patch that is chosen, having been carefully measured for its lightness, will then serve as an index of how light the subject perceived the test patch to be.

First, cut out the matching patches and the borders on the insert for Chapter 5. The matching patches are the ten squares on the left. Note that there is a number on the back of each that corresponds to its lightness. (The units for these numbers have to do with how various lightnesses are actually created by printers, and it is not necessary to know them for this exercise. It is sufficient that the patches are ordered correctly.) Now cut out the six borders on the right side of the insert, and cut out the central square area of each. Note that the borders are also marked with a lightness code on the back. Be very careful with both matching patches and borders to trim away any gray from the adjoining figures so that each cutout is an even gray. On the bottom of the insert is the test patch that has already been placed on a white surrounding region. The test patch has a lightness value of 6. *Do not cut out the test figure!* Leave it on its background and place this in turn on a sheet of black construction paper.

Now you are ready to run the experiment. The procedure is to select one background, place it over the test patch, and ask your subject to select a matching patch from among her ten choices that appears to match the test patch in brightness. (Be sure that she lays down the matching patch on the black area to the right of the background to be certain of her choice.) Be careful to tell the subject not to hesitate to select different matching patches with different backgrounds if she feels this is appropriate. Subjects may think that because the test patch remains the same, they should always select the same matching patch. Do not let the subject see the test patch without a border between trials. as this may also cause a bias toward a particular matching patch.

Place the matching patches at the top of the black construction paper haphazardly. Run the subject through eighteen trials of the experiment, three trials with each background. In order to have the backgrounds presented in a random order in each set of six, here are three random orders that you may use to determine the order in which the backgrounds are presented: 5, 10, 3, 1, 4, 7; 4, 3, 10, 7, 1, 5; 10, 4, 1, 5, 7, 3 (the numbers refer to the lightness codes on the back of each background).

After you have presented a background over the test patch and the subject has chosen her matching patch, place the value of the matching patch in the appropriate space in the table below. After the experiment is complete, add up the values in each column and divide by three to get an average matching patch value for each background.

Now you can plot these data in the graph provided. Along the x-axis are the six values of background that you used. Above each find the average value of matching patch that you calculated from the table, and place a dot at the value (as determined from the y-axis). Now connect the dots and note the shape of the function.

Recall that the test patch has a lightness value of 6. Given this, what shape should the function have? How much of a brightness contrast were you able to obtain? How could you improve the experiment to get an even larger effect?

Reference

Heinemann, E. G. Simultaneous brightness induction as a function of inducing- and test-field luminance. *Journal of Experimental Psychology,* 1955, *50*, 89–96.

Background values:	1	3	4	5	7	10
matching value 1:	______	______	______	______	______	______
matching value 2:	______	______	______	______	______	______
matching value 3:	______	______	______	______	______	______
Total matching value:	______	______	______	______	______	______
Average matching value:	______	______	______	______	______	______

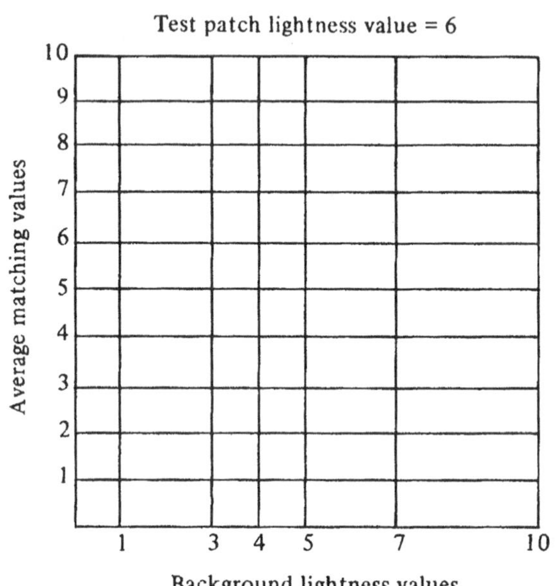

CHAPTER 6

Perception

Learning Objectives

THE PROBLEM OF PERCEPTION

1. Know that the central issue of perception is not why a stimulus is recognized as an object, but why it is even seen as an object.
2. Keep in mind the characteristics of the proximal stimulus in comparison with the distal stimulus.
3. Understand that to organize the sensory world, three questions must be asked of any given stimulus: Where is it? Where is it going? What is it?

THE PERCEPTION OF DEPTH: WHERE IS IT?

Binocular cues

4. Be aware of the significance of binocular disparity in depth perception.

Monocular cues

5. What are the monocular cues to depth perception? How is texture important?

The perception of depth through motion

6. How does motion parallax contribute to our perception of depth?

Innate factors in depth perception

7. What evidence indicates that young infants have at least a rudimentary ability to perceive various aspects of form and space?

THE PERCEPTION OF MOVEMENT: WHAT IS IT DOING?

Illusions of movement

8. Be familiar with the phenomena of stroboscopic and induced movement, and the relevance of these phenomena to the study of real movement.

FORM PERCEPTION: WHAT IS IT?

9. Describe an experiment on young children showing how important form is to object identification.
10. What is transposition and how is it important to the study of form perception?
11. Be aware of the central assumption of Gestalt psychology as it applies to perception.
12. Why does one need to understand both the perception of parts and the relationships among the parts to account for form perception?

The information-processing approach

13. What is the central assumption of the information-processing approach and how is this related to the analogy between mind and computer?

The elements of form

14. Review the evidence for mechanisms in the physiology of the brain that underlie the perception of features.
15. Describe some behavioral evidence for the existence of elementary feature detectors in the visual system.

16. Be aware of the later stage of processing at which features are assumed to be conjoined. How does the study of illusory conjunctions pinpoint the stage of processing that is at work in pattern recognition?

Perceptual segregation

17. What is the role of perceptual segregation in scene perception? Why is it important?
18. Give examples of how perceptual segregation occurs in vision and audition.
19. Be aware of the impact of perceptual segregation on how we think of perception as due to both the stimulus and the perceiver.
20. How is the segregation of figure and ground an example of perceptual segregation?
21. Be familiar with reversible figures and how they contribute to our understanding of perceptual segregation. What proposal has been made about the perception of reversible figures?
22. What are the laws of perceptual grouping and how do they relate to each other?

Pattern recognition

23. What phenomena show that context affects pattern recognition?

Perceptual problem solving

24. What purpose does the perceptual hypothesis serve?
25. The perceptual system follows rules of logic. Explain how and why impossible figures pose a perceptual problem for us.

PERCEPTUAL SELECTION: ATTENTION

26. What is attention?

Selection by physical orientation

27. How can the study of orienting movements tell us about attention?

Central selection

28. Be familiar with the concept of central selection and its manifestations in the auditory and visual modes. What is visual search?
29. What are the conditions that permit parallel visual search, and what are those that require serial search?
30. How does the study of shadowing tell us about attention?
31. What evidence is there about a "filter" theory of attention?

THE PERCEPTION OF REALITY

32. Understand that the goal of all perceptual processes is the perception of reality.
33. The main problem encountered in the perception of reality is interpreting the number of different proximal stimuli produced by one distal stimulus. How is this problem addressed by perceptual constancies?

Empiricism and nativism revisited

34. How do the empiricists explain the discrepancy between the proximal stimulus and the perceived image? What is unconscious inference?
35. What is the nativists' answer?
36. Regarding perceptual organization, understand the difference between the concept of unconscious inference (based on past experience) and the concept of direct response to the complex characteristics and invariant relationships of stimulus patterns.

Size and shape constancy

37. Be familiar with size and shape constancies. What types of cues are necessary for size constancy? How do the empiricists and nativists explain these two phenomena?

THE REPRESENTATION OF REALITY IN ART

Seeing and knowing

38. Explain the odd appearance of figures in Egyptian art. What does this signal about the artist's rendition of reality?

The Renaissance: scenes through a window frame

39. What is the parallel between the struggle of Renaissance painters to represent reality and the psychologist's struggle to understand the perception of reality?

The Impressionists: how a scene is perceived

40. What was the aim of the Impressionists? How is this realized in their paintings?

The Moderns: how a scene is conceived

41. How is the aim of introducing conceptual representations in art achieved by the Moderns?

Programmed Exercises

THE PROBLEM OF PERCEPTION

1. The properties of a three-dimensional distal stimulus are perceived as constant despite continuing variation of the ____________ stimulus. — proximal

2. In order to perceive an object, the observer must ____________ the sensory world into a coherent, meaningful scene. — organize

THE PERCEPTION OF DEPTH: WHERE IS IT?

3. The two eyes look out on the world from slightly different positions and thus obtain a somewhat different view of any solid object on which they converge. This is called ____________ ____________. — binocular disparity

4. Relative size is an example of a ____________ depth cue. — monocular

5. Abrupt change in a ____________ ____________ produces the impression of a sharp drop, a "visual cliff." — texture gradient

6. Far-off objects are blocked from view by other opaque objects that obstruct their optical path to the eye. This is a depth cue called ____________. — interposition

7. As we move our head or body from right to left, the images projected by the objects outside will move across the retina. The direction and speed of this motion is an effective monocular depth cue called ____________ ____________. — motion parallax

8. The reaction of infants to rapidly magnified forms in the visual field is called the ____________ response. — looming

THE PERCEPTION OF MOVEMENT: WHAT IS IT DOING?

9. Suppose we briefly turn on a light in one location in the visual field, then turn it off, and after an appropriate period of time (somewhere between 30 and 200 msec), turn on a second light in a different location. The resulting phenomenon is called ____________ movement. — stroboscopic

10. If the ground is moving and a figure is stationary in the visual field, the figure is seen as moving. This phenomenon of illusory movement is called ____________ movement. — induced

11. The perception of movement in one of two stimuli depends on which is seen as a stationary ____________ of reference. — frame

FORM PERCEPTION: WHAT IS IT?

12. Young children appear to define objects by their ____________. — shape

13. The fact that a triangle appears as such regardless of the elements that make it up is called ____________ of form. — transposition

14. A form is perceived as a ____________, a whole that is different from the sum of its parts. — Gestalt

15. Many investigators believe that form perception is the result of a series of ____________ -____________ steps that transform an input to a perceptual experience.	information-processing
16. A ____________ chart allows one to represent a series of information-processing transformations.	flow
17. A task used frequently to study form perception requires a subject to indicate whether a certain target appears in a briefly presented array. This is called a ____________ ____________ task.	visual search
18. Examples of features that are processed automatically are ____________, ____________, and ____________.	color curvature, orientation
19. An ____________ ____________ occurs when a subject mistakenly ties together two features in an object that did not occur together.	illusory conjunction
20. The process known as ____________ ____________ enables us to separate figure from ground.	visual segregation
21. ____________ figures are ones in which either of two figure-ground organizations is possible.	Reversible (ambiguous)
22. Proximity, similarity, and closure, are examples of the laws of ____________ ____________.	perceptual grouping
23. Contours that continue smoothly along their original course follow the law of ____________ ____________.	good continuation
24. Computer models are examples of ____________ -____________ processing, an approach to pattern recognition that begins with component features and builds up to larger units.	bottom-up
25. The ____________ -____________ process of pattern recognition begins with higher units, because it is often affected by higher-level knowledge and expectations.	top-down
26. ____________ effects demonstrate that there is some top-down processing in the perceptual process.	Context
27. A ____________ ____________ is constantly compared to new stimuli in order to test its validity.	perceptual hypothesis
28. An ____________ figure poses a perceptual contradiction for a subject. It poses a perceptual problem that cannot be solved.	impossible

PERCEPTUAL SELECTION: ATTENTION

29. The ways by which we perceive selectively are grouped under the label "____________."	attention
30. On the average, our eyes move three or four times per second to fixate objects. These fixations are ____________, not random.	purposeful
31. If a stimulus is defined by a ____________ of features in a visual search task, the search for it must be serial.	conjunction

32. When stimuli are presented over earphones so that each ear receives a different message, this is called a ____________ presentation. — dichotic

33. When a subject is asked to ____________ a message, he is repeating it aloud, word for word, as it comes over one of his earphones. — shadow

34. The attentional ____________ attenuates irrelevant messages as a whole, but may pass items from them that are important or familiar. — filter

THE PERCEPTION OF REALITY

35. The perceptual system responds to real objects outside regardless of variations in their proximal images. This is best illustrated by the perceptual ____________: lightness, size, and shape. — constancies

36. According to the empiricists, prior learning of the rules relating retinal image and depth cues leads to the ____________ inference of true size. — unconscious

37. Nativists stress the importance of ____________ relationships within a stimulus pattern in explaining perceptual organization. — invariant (higher-order)

38. A Boeing 747 at a distance of 1,000 feet will look larger than a single-engine two-seater at a distance of 50 feet despite the fact that the retinal image of the latter will be greater than that of the former. This is called ____________ ____________. An analogous phenomenon occurs in the perception of ____________. — size constancy; shape

THE REPRESENTATION OF REALITY IN ART

39. Artists came to appreciate the use of pictorial cues to depth during the ____________. — Renaissance

40. The ____________ tried not to depict reality in their art, but to create certain perceptual experiences in the observer, experiences that would be evoked by a scene on canvas. — Impressionists

41. ____________ try to add conceptual representations such as ambiguity or tension in their art. — Modernists

Self Test

1. Which of the following is *not* true of the proximal stimulus?
   a. it is two-dimensional in vision
   b. it can vary in size and shape
   c. it alone enables us to perceive the constant properties of objects
   d. it is the retinal image of the distal stimulus in vision

2. Binocular disparity is caused by:
   a. a slight difference in the size of the two eyes
   b. small imperfections in the lens and/or cornea
   c. the slightly different position of each eye
   d. the favoring of one eye over the other

3. Binocular disparity:
   a. is an effective cue to depth for long distances
   b. is due to the fact that our eyes receive virtually the same image
   c. is not by itself a sufficient cue to depth
   d. can be simulated by viewing specially designed two-dimensional drawings
   e. is only effective for familiar objects

4. The figure below illustrates all of the following monocular cues to depth except
   a. linear perspective
   b. relative size
   c. binocular disparity
   d. texture gradients
   e. interposition

5. The impression of a "visual cliff" is accounted for by which depth cue?
   a. linear perspective
   b. relative size
   c. texture gradients
   d. interposition

6. Which of the following is *not* true of motion parallax?
   a. Nearby objects move in a direction opposite our own as we move through space.
   b. Objects farther away move in a direction similar to our own as we move through space.
   c. Objects farther away move at a lesser velocity.
   d. Objects closer to us move at a greater velocity.

7. One of the most effective monocular depth cues is ____________, which is absent in pictorial representations but present in real life.
   a. linear perspective
   b. relative size
   c. interposition
   d. motion parallax

8. The results of Gibson and Walk's visual cliff experiment (illustrated above) suggests that:
   a. infants cannot use motion parallax as a cue to depth
   b. infants' eye fixations tend to be directed to edges and vertices
   c. depth perception is largely innately given
   d. texture gradients are not useful cues to distance
   e. none of the above

9. Stroboscopic movement refers to:
   a. the perception of movement when two stimuli are presented in alternation at the proper temporal and spatial intervals
   b. the perception of movement of a target when in fact it is stationary but the background is moving
   c. the perception of self-movement when you are stationary but the scene that you are watching is moving
   d. none of the above

10. Induced movement differs from stroboscopic movement in that:
    a. in the former case it is the figure that moves, while in the latter case it is the ground that moves
    b. the former is a physical phenomenon, while the latter is a retinal phenomenon

c. induced movement is based on relative displacement, while stroboscopic movement is based on absolute displacement
d. none of the above

11. Which two of the following are examples of induced movement?
a. the moon moving through the clouds
b. perceiving movement of a stationary spot of light in darkness
c. perceiving movement of a stationary spot of light when the rectangular frame around it moves
d. perceiving that the moon moves when you move with respect to it
e. perceiving movement in the successive frames in a movie

12. Experiments with young children show that their identification of objects is governed largely by:
a. the color of objects
b. the size of objects
c. the texture of objects
d. the shape of objects

13. One of the most interesting features of form recognition is that forms are recognized in spite of:
a. transpositions of pattern
b. the fact that their apparent lightnesses change with changes in illumination
c. the change in perceived shape that occurs when the angle of regard of an object is changed
d. none of the above

14. According to the Gestalt point of view, the perception of an object depends on
a. the perception of the relations among parts of the object
b. the perception of the elementary features of the object
c. the perception of the object's geons
d. the flow of information as an object is transformed with successive process steps

15. The information-processing view of object recognition draws on an analogy between
a. the brain and a telephone switchboard
b. steps in mental processing of an object and the workings of the brain during processing
c. input and retrieval processes
d. a flow chart of mental processes and a computer program

16. Object recognition begins with
a. recognition of Gestalt properties
b. visual search
c. selective attention
d. conjunction of features
e. feature detection

17. If a target in a visual search task differs from the background items on a feature such as color or curvature, subjects will
a. struggle to detect the target
b. engage in a conjunctive search for the target
c. perceive the target quickly with little search required
d. none of the above

18. If a subject were presented with a display of letters printed in colored inks that included a blue G, a red M, and a yellow B, and if this display were presented briefly, she might see
a. a blue D
b. a red T
c. a yellow R
d. a blue M

19. Which of the following statements about perceptual parsing is *not* true?
a. It is also called visual segregation.
b. It is contributed by the individual and is not a part of the stimulus.
c. It is the first stage of perceptual organization and separates the stimuli into various subcomponents.
d. It occurs only in the realm of visual perception.

20. Segregating figure from ground (as in a reversible figure):
a. is a high-level perceptual process that requires a good deal of preliminary analysis
b. can only be done with reversible figures
c. is accomplished by perceiving the contour separating two regions as belonging to the ground
d. is too elementary a perceptual process to be used effectively by artists
e. none of the above

Reversible figure that can be perceived either as two faces in profile or as a white vase.

21. For reversible figures such as the one above, which of the following is false?
    a. the figure is generally seen in front of the ground
    b. a reversible figure-ground display is characterized by two adjoining regions alternately acting as figures
    c. a contour can be seen as simultaneously belonging to figure and ground
    d. none of the above

22. All of the following are "laws of perceptual organization" *except*:
    a. proximity
    b. similarity
    c. good continuation
    d. simplicity
    e. closure

23. The law of proximity states that:
    a. the closer an object is to an observer, the easier it is to identify it
    b. the closer two objects are to each other, the greater the chance that they will be grouped together perceptually
    c. given any two objects, one is always nearer (perceptually) to an arbitrary third object than the other
    d. none of the above

24. Closure is a special case of:
    a. proximity
    b. similarity
    c. good continuation
    d. perspective

25. Pattern recognition is a:
    a. top-down process
    b. horizontal process
    c. bottom-up process
    d. a and c
    e. a and b

26. A professor is giving a lecture on the state of the U.S. economy. His lecture is suddenly broken up by several coughs, which interrupt but do not stop his speech stream. Although there are physical gaps in the utterance, the students hear and understand the presentation. This is an example of:
    a. feature analysis
    b. context effect
    c. bottom-up processing
    d. attention

27. When a person makes sense of a previously unknown and meaningless stimulus:
    a. he has trouble perceiving it in its original unorganized form
    b. he must constantly reinforce the new pattern in order to retain it in visual memory
    c. he has formed a perceptual hypothesis
    d. a and c

28. A perceptual hypothesis:
    a. once formed, provides fundamental and unchanging laws of perceptual organization
    b. represents the bottom-up aspect of perceptual processing
    c. is formed for every new stimulus encountered
    d. serves as the top-down aspect of visual processing that is compared to the stimulus

29. The problem in perceiving impossible figures is that
    a. the individual features of the figures cannot be accurately detected
    b. the parts of the object individually don't make any sense
    c. top-down processing plays too little a role in their perception
    d. the parts cannot be reconciled together into a whole figure

30. Orienting movements, like turning of the head, are external manifestations of:
    a. differentiation
    b. attention
    c. recalibration
    d. adaptation

31. In a visual search task, if the target is a blue T that is embedded among green R's, blue G's, and red T's, subjects would have to engage in
    a. a serial search for the target
    b. a parallel search for the target
    c. either a serial or a parallel search for the target, depending on their choice
    d. none of the above
32. Which of the following is *not* true of the effects of selective attention?
    a. some information from an unattended channel can trigger attention while the rest is lost
    b. information blocked by an attenuation mechanism nonetheless can affect the connotative meaning of what we attend
    c. response bias effects may account for some selective attention phenomena
    d. response bias may account for the effect of better tachistoscopic recognition of frequent as opposed to infrequent words
    e. none of the above
33. Unconscious inference in depth perception:
    a. is a nativist argument
    b. operates independently of depth cues
    c. operates independently of the retinal image
    d. depends on prior learning of a general rule
34. It is likely that infants exhibit some measure of:
    a. angle constancy
    b. depth constancy
    c. lightness constancy
    d. size constancy
35. The representation of reality in art, especially three-dimensional reality, became a feature in which of the following schools?
    a. early Egyptian art
    b. the Renaissance
    c. Modernism
    d. Impressionism

Answer Key for Self Test

1.	c p. 159	19.	d pp. 168–69
2.	c p. 160	20.	e p. 170
3.	d p. 161	21.	c p. 171
4.	c p. 161	22.	d pp. 171–73
5.	c p. 162	23.	b p. 171
6.	b p. 163	24.	c p. 173
7.	d p. 163	25.	d p. 174
8.	c p. 162	26.	b p. 175
9.	a p. 164	27.	d p. 176
10.	c p. 164	28.	d p. 176
11.	a, c p. 164	29.	d p. 177
12.	d p. 165	30.	b p. 178
13.	a p. 166	31.	a p. 179
14.	a p. 166	32.	d pp. 179–80
15.	d p. 167	33.	d p. 181
16.	e p. 167	34.	d p. 183
17.	c p. 168	35.	b pp. 184–85
18.	d p. 168		

Investigating Psychological Phenomena

THE EFFECT OF MENTAL SET

Equipment: Stimuli are included
Number of subjects: One
Time per subject: Twenty minutes
Time for experimenter: Twenty minutes

The issue of how past experience influences perception (an example of top-down processing) is an important one in psychology and has generated quite a bit of research. This is a difficult issue to resolve because there are many ways in which past experience might influence perceptual processes. In this problem you are asked to consider a series of hypothetical experiments (modeled after a study by Epstein and Rock, 1960) and to provide alternative interpretations of the hypothetical results. As you move through the experiments, try to develop one hypothesis that will account for all of the results described. The stimuli for all the experiments are the ambiguous and unambiguous versions of Leeper's old woman-young woman figure shown below.

Notice that the first picture (A) can be seen either as a young woman or as an old woman—that is, it is ambiguous. The second picture (Y) is quite similar to the first (A) except that some detail has been changed so that it has become a fairly unambiguous picture of a young woman. Likewise, the third picture (O) is a fairly unambiguous version of an old woman. The purpose of all the experiments is to determine how prior exposure to the unambiguous versions of the figure influences whether subjects call the ambiguous version an old woman or a young woman. Imagine that twenty subjects are run in each hypothetical experiment.

EXPERIMENT 1

Each subject is shown the following series of slides (at a rate of one slide every eight seconds) and asked to name each picture as "young" or "old" as it is presented: YYOOOOOOOOA (Y refers to a presentation of the unambiguous young woman, O refers to a presentation of the unambiguous old woman, and A refers to the presentation of the ambiguous image.) All subjects name the Y and O versions of the figure correctly. On the critical trial, the ambiguous picture A, the results are as follows: Twenty subjects call it "old," no subjects call it "young." One interpretation of this result is that the more frequently presented unambiguous version determined the perception of the ambiguous picture. This is listed as hypothesis 1 on the answer sheet. What alternative explanations can you propose to explain the responses of subjects in this hypothetical experiment? Write them on the answer sheet. There are at least three other plausible possibilities.

Before you go on to experiments 2 through 4, check to see whether the hypotheses you have developed coincide with those given in the answers to the problem. If not, use the given hypotheses as the basis for your answers to the questions posed in experiments 2 through 4.

EXPERIMENT 2

A new set of twenty subjects receives the series: YYYYYOOOOOA. Again the responses to all the Y and O stimuli are correct, and the responses to the A stimulus are as follows: Twenty subjects respond "old woman," none respond "young woman." Consider each of the four hypotheses raised to account for the results of experiment 1 and evaluate how each fares with the results of the experiment. Record your responses under experiment 2 on the answer sheet.

EXPERIMENT 3

Twenty subjects each receive the series: OOOOOOOYYYA. All respond correctly to the Y and O stimuli; the responses to A are: Twenty subjects call it "young woman," none call it "old woman." Again evaluate the success of each of the four hypotheses at accounting for these results.*

EXPERIMENT 4

Twenty new subjects are shown the series: YYOYYOYYOA. All O's and Y's are identified correctly; the data on the A presentations are: Eighteen subjects respond "old woman," two subjects respond "young woman." (A reliable difference.) Which of the four hypotheses can explain these results? Is one of the four hypotheses confirmed by the results of all four experiments?

*We continue to consider hypothesis 1 even though experiment 2 cannot be explained by it; scientists do not typically discard an hypothesis because of a single contradictory finding.

A

Y

O

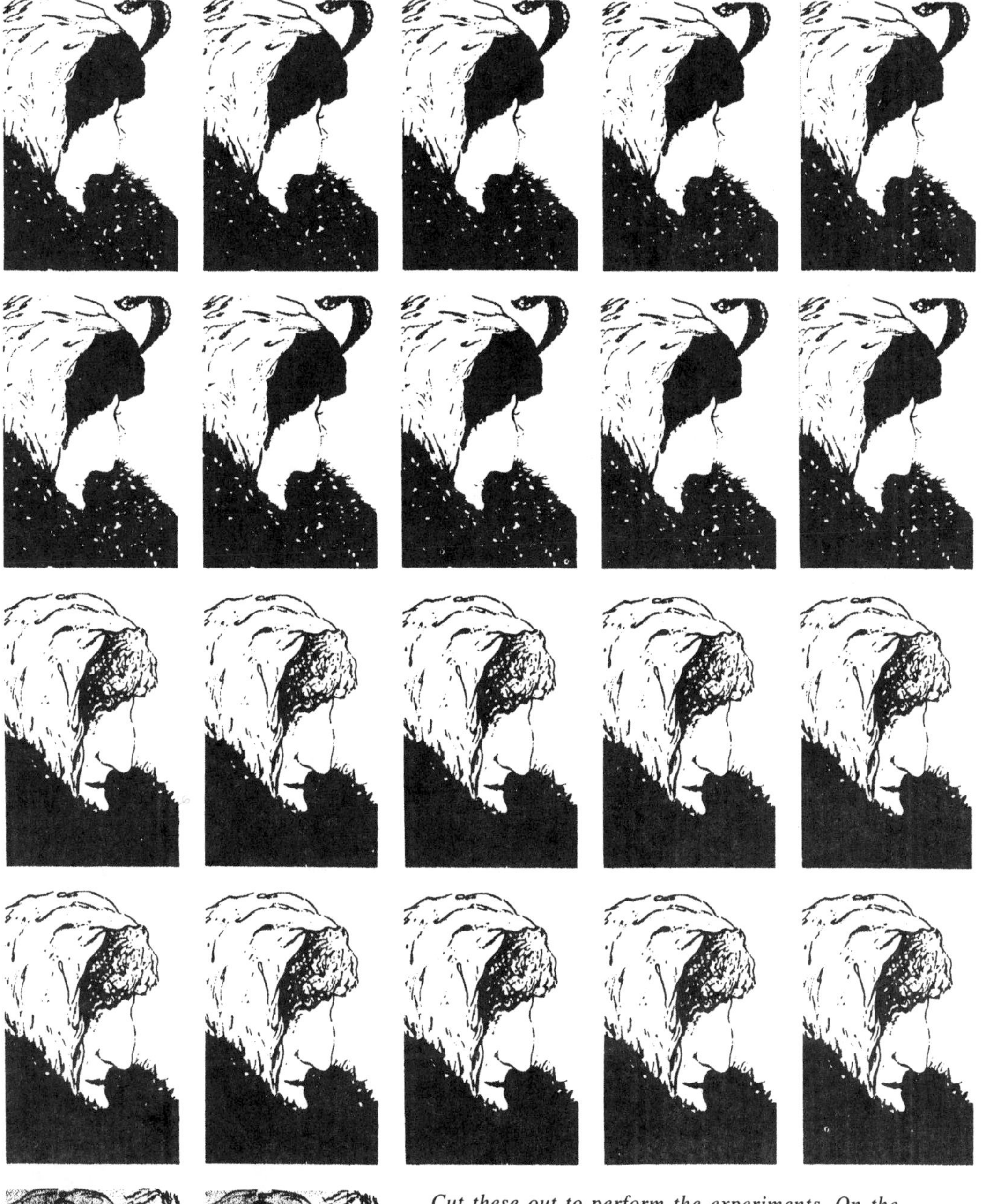

Cut these out to perform the experiments. On the back of each figure are the letters Y (young woman), O (old woman), or A (ambiguous).

Y Y Y Y Y

Y Y Y Y Y

O O O O O

O O O O O

A A

Answers to Problem

EXPERIMENT 1:

Hypothesis 2: It is possible that the interpretation of the ambiguous picture was entirely influenced by the perception of the immediately preceding picture of the old woman. If so, this would be called a "recency effect," because the most recently presented picture would have had the strongest influence on perception of the ambiguous picture.

Hypothesis 3: An alternative possibility has to do with what the subject might be expecting to be presented on the last trial. He has just seen eight consecutive pictures of the old woman and so he might reasonably expect that the next picture will also be that of an old woman. Thus, if this were the case, the subject's cognitive expectations would be guiding his perceptions.

Hypothesis 4: A final possibility is that subjects in general have a bias to respond with the name "old woman." One might suppose that such a bias exists (for some reason) even independently of what the subject actually sees. That is, subjects are biased to call the ambiguous version an "old woman" regardless of what precedes it.

EXPERIMENT 2:

This experiment rules out hypothesis 1, the frequency hypothesis. Both unambiguous versions were presented equally frequently before the ambiguous version was presented. Thus, a subject's perception of the ambiguous version could not have been influenced by the more frequently presented unambiguous version. None of the alternative hypotheses is ruled out by these results: (a) The response to the ambiguous version was the same as that to the most recently presented unambiguous version. Thus, recency is a viable interpretation of these results. (b) Because the responses to the sixth through tenth stimuli were "old woman," the subjects may have built up an expectation that the eleventh stimulus would be an old woman as well. So cognitive expectations may well have guided their response to the ambiguous item. (c) The fact that most subjects identified the ambiguous picture as an old woman is consistent with the possibility that they have a bias to call it that regardless of their immediately prior perceptual experience.

EXPERIMENT 3:

Once again this experiment disconfirms the frequency hypothesis. This time subjects responded to the test picture with the name of the *least* frequently presented unambiguous picture. Also, the experiment rules out hypothesis 4, which states that subjects have a predisposing bias to call the ambiguous version an old woman. Both the recency and the cognitive expectation hypotheses can account for the results.

EXPERIMENT 4:

The cognitive expectation hypothesis probably is ruled out. In responding to the unambiguous versions, subjects were following a regular pattern of two "young woman" responses followed by one "old woman" response. The last unambiguous picture was that of the old woman; thus subjects should have been expecting a young woman next. Instead most responded "old woman," a result that can only be explained by noting that the most recently presented unambiguous picture was that of the old woman. Thus, the recency explanation is compatible with these results. Once again the frequency hypothesis is disconfirmed because the most frequently presented unambiguous picture was the young woman. The response bias explanation might be brought up to explain the results of this experiment except that it was ruled out by experiment 3. Thus, the only explanation which satisfactorily can explain the results of all four experiments is hypothesis 2, which claims that the picture which a subject sees most recently will affect his current perception.

This exercise demonstrates how it is sometimes possible to start with several potential explanations of a phenomenon and successfully rule out the incorrect ones with further experimentation. Initially there were four plausible interpretations of the results of hypothetical experiment 1. The results of hypothetical experiments 2 through 4, however, rule out all but one of the alternatives.

Even though the experiments described above are only hypothetical, they illustrate this process of narrowing down alternative interpretations. You may want to try out any of these experiments to determine the actual results. On page 79 you will find sets of pictures of both the unambiguous versions and the ambiguous version of the figure. Cut them out and return to the previous pages of this section. Perform the experiments as described there and record the results. Do your results correspond to the hypothetical data? Do the same hypotheses apply?

Reference

Epstein, W., and Rock, I. Perceptual set as an artifact of recency. *American Journal of Psychology,* 1960, *73,* 214–228.

ANSWER SHEET

Experiment 1

Hypothesis 1 Frequency of presentation determines the response to the ambiguous figure

Hypothesis 2 ______________________________

____

Hypothesis 3 ______________________________

____

Hypothesis 4 ______________________________

____

Experiment 2

Hypothesis 1 ______________________________

____

Hypothesis 2 ______________________________

____

Hypothesis 3 ______________________________

____

Hypothesis 4 ______________________________

____

Experiment 3

Hypothesis 1 ______________________________

____

Hypothesis 2 ______________________________

____

Hypothesis 3 ______________________________

____

Hypothesis 4 ______________________________

____

Experiment 4

Which of the four hypotheses can account for these results? ______________

____

____

Which hypotheses can account for the results of all four experiments? ______________

____

____

CHAPTER 7

Memory

Learning Objectives

1. Understand what it means for perception to be concerned with organization in space, and memory to be concerned with organization in time.

STUDYING MEMORY

Some preliminary distinctions

2. Be aware of the distinctions between short-term and long-term memory and between explicit and implicit memory.

Encoding, storage, retrieval

3. What is meant by the terms encoding, storage, and retrieval? How do these processes differ from one another?
4. Be familiar with the fact that both recall and recognition are used to measure retrieval. How do these two methods differ from one another?
5. What are the causes of failures to retrieve?

ENCODING

The stage theory of memory

6. What motivates a stage theory of memory, both historically and introspectively?
7. What is the relationship between consciousness and short-term memory?
8. What is the capacity of short-term memory? How is it measured?
9. There are two mechanisms that account for forgetting from short-term memory. What are they, and how do they work?
10. Rehearsal is a process important to short-term memory. Describe its function in relation to both short- and long-term memory.
11. One of the most robust phenomena in the study of memory is the appearance of primacy and recency effects in free recall. Describe these, and indicate what causes them. Be sure you can cite evidence that supports the presumed causes.
12. What is a chunk, and how does this concept apply to the capacity of short-term memory? How do chunks get created?

A changed emphasis: active memory and organization

13. How do findings about rehearsal challenge the stage theory of memory?
14. What is maintenance rehearsal? Does the amount of maintenance rehearsal affect the probability of information's entering long-term memory? Cite the relevant evidence.
15. What is the concept of "working memory," and how does it differ from the concept of "short-term memory"?
16. Mnemonics are tools to increase the capacity of memory. Describe some mnemonics, and understand how they work to affect memory capacity.

RETRIEVAL

17. Understand the role of retrieval cues in increasing the accessibility of memory traces.

The relation between original encoding and retrieval

18. What is the concept of encoding specificity, and how does it influence successful retrieval? Understand the range of contexts in which this principle operates.

Memory search

19. How is memory searched? What does the tip-of-the-tongue phenomenon tell us about memory search?

Implicit retrieval

20. Be aware of the difference between implicit and explicit memory retrieval. What is the essence of an implicit measure, and what are some examples?
21. Describe how repetition priming and word completion given fragments show implicit retrieval effects.
22. What is source memory, and how is it related to implicit retrieval? Be sure you understand the importance of the "overnight fame" experiment and its relation to the concept of source memory.

WHEN MEMORY FAILS

Forgetting

23. What is the shape of the forgetting curve, and how can you plot one?
24. Recount the evidence both for and against a decay theory of forgetting.
25. What is an interference theory of forgetting, and how does it differ from a decay theory?
26. Know the experimental techniques that are used to study proactive and retroactive inhibition.
27. How might a theory based on changing retrieval cues explain everyday forgetting? Explain how such a theory could be applied to the forgetting of childhood memories.
28. Some memories seem to last quite a long time. Give examples.
29. How are flashbulb memories claimed to be different from other memories? Are these memories really treated differently by the memory system? Discuss the evidence.

Conceptual frameworks and remembering

30. How does past knowledge help us remember current material? How is this like the use of top-down processing in perception?
31. Describe some effects that schemas have on memory. What is a "script" and how might it affect memory for some event?
32. Memory is an important issue in the courtroom. What does research tell us about the fallibility of eyewitness testimony? Describe how eyewitness memory may be a reconstruction of earlier events, and explain how evidence might support this view.
33. Describe evidence that might bear on the concept of "accommodative distortions."
34. Is hypnosis a reliable way of helping a witness remember an event? What is the evidence on whether hypnosis improves retrieval?
35. What is the verdict on the tape-recorder theory of memory?
36. Why is there reason to be cautious about the concept of "repressed memories"? What issues should one be concerned about in examining cases of this alleged phenomenon?
37. Discuss the limits to which our memories are distorted.

Disordered memories

38. What are the symptoms of anterograde amnesia, and what are some of its causes?
39. How does retrograde amnesia differ from anterograde amnesia? What mechanism has been proposed to account for retrograde amnesia?

Explicit and implicit retrieval revisited

40. How have the concepts of procedural and declarative knowledge been used to account for the memory deficits of amnesics?
41. Describe how the distinction between explicit and implicit retrieval may be valuable in understanding the performance of amnesics.

TAKING STOCK

42. Discuss the similarity among perception, memory, and thinking.

Programmed Exercises

STUDYING MEMORY

1.	____________-____________ memory holds information for a brief interval. ____________-____________ memory stores information for longer periods of time.	Short-term Long-term
2.	Instances in which we tap our memory quite consciously to retrieve something are called ____________ memory. By contrast, when our memory is used in an indirect way in the service of some other task, this is termed ____________ memory.	explicit implicit
3.	The first stage of memory is ____________, in which information is acquired and brought into the system.	encoding
4.	The records of experience made on the nervous system are called memory ____________.	traces

ENCODING

5.	The second stage of memory is ____________, during which information is filed away. The final stage is ____________, the point at which one tries to remember.	storage retrieval
6.	A ____________ test is a test of retrieval in which a subject is asked to produce an item from memory.	recall
7.	A ____________ test is a test of retrieval in which several items are presented and the subject must decide which ones were presented earlier as part of a studied list.	recognition
8.	The theory of memory that argues for separate memory systems working together is called the ____________ theory.	stage
9.	The ____________ capacity of short-term memory has been estimated as about 7 items.	storage
10.	The ____________ ____________ is the number of items an individual can recall after just one presentation. This quantity, 7 plus or minus 2, is sometimes called the ____________ ____________.	memory span magic number
11.	If it was found that items faded from short-term memory even though no new information entered, this would support a ____________ theory of forgetting.	decay
12.	If one found that forgetting in short-term memory occurred only when new material came into the system, one would have evidence for a ____________ theory of forgetting.	displacement
13.	____________ is one way of either keeping an item in short-term memory or allowing it to pass into long-term memory.	Rehearsal
14.	The method of ____________ ____________ allows a subject who is presented with a list of unrelated items to report them in any order desired.	free recall
15.	Of a long list of presented items, a subject is most apt to remember the first few (known as the ____________ effect) and the last few (known as the ____________ effect).	primacy recency
16.	The process that allows the contents of short-term memory to expand is called ____________. Using this process results in the creation of ____________ of information.	organization, chunks

17. ____________ rehearsal consists of repeating items over and over to keep them in memory for a short time, as in repeating a telephone number. — Maintenance

18. ____________ memory refers to a short-term memory that is involved in processing the information that is held. — Working

19. The various devices designed to improve memory are collectively called ____________. — mnemonics

20. The method of ____________ requires the learner to visualize each of the items he wants to remember in a different spatial location. — loci

21. The most effective kind of image for remembering is one in which the elements of the image are ____________. — interacting

RETRIEVAL

22. When you know a piece of information (i.e., you have stored it), but you cannot retrieve it at the moment, the trace is said to be ____________. — inaccessible

23. A stimulus that provides a trigger to get an item out of memory is called a(n) ____________ ____________. — retrieval cue

24. The principle of ____________ ____________ states that retrieval success is most likely if the context at the time of retrieval approximates that during original encoding. — encoding specificity

25. Many investigators believe that retrieval is generally preceded by an internal process called ____________ ____________. — memory search

26. The ____________-____________-____________ -____________ phenomenon is an example of unsuccessful retrieval in which the subject comes close to the searched-for item in his memory but cannot quite find the right memory location. — tip-of-the-tongue

27. Recall and recognition are both ____________ measures of memory, while word fragment completion is an ____________ measure. — explicit, implicit

28. ____________ priming is a technique used to study implicit memory; words that appear on a study list are identified more readily than words that do not. — Repetition

29. ____________ memory refers to the recollection of the context in which a piece of information was learned. — Source

30. Subjective ____________ can be influenced merely by presenting some material during a study phase so that it is retrieved at the time of judgment, but so that the source of familiarity is forgotten. — fame

WHEN MEMORY FAILS

31. The ____________ curve was first plotted by Ebbinghaus who tested himself on the relearning of lists of nonsense syllables. — forgetting

32. The fact that animals forget when their internal temperatures are higher is evidence for a ____________ theory of forgetting. — decay

33. One cause of forgetting is ____________, in which some items in memory cause the forgetting of others. — interference

34. One example of an interference effect is ____________ inhibition, in which new learning hampers recall of old material. Another example is ____________ inhibition, in which interference is from old material on the recall of newly learned items. — retroactive, proactive

35. One possible reason that we can't recall childhood memories is the drastic change in ____________ cues between childhood and adulthood. This phenomenon is called childhood ____________. — retrieval; amnesia

36. When one learns a language in school, at least some of this material seems to enter a ____________, lasting many years after the learning has ceased. — permastore

37. Brown and Kulik claim that certain salient and emotional events produce what are called ____________ memories, which are quite vivid. — flashbulb

38. As Bartlett demonstrated with subjects' recall of stories, retrieval is often a ____________ event, since partial knowledge of an event is pieced together in recall. — reconstructive

39. The conceptual framework that a person builds on the basis of his knowledge of the world is called a ____________. A special case of this is a ____________, which describes a scenario for a familiar event. — schema; script

40. Eyewitnesses to crimes seem to ____________ the past from their partial knowledge of it in the process of trying to remember it. — reconstruct

41. Retrospective alterations of memory on the basis of some later interpretation are called ____________ distortions. — accommodative

42. The effect of ____________ seems to be to make people overly willing to cooperate with their questioner, not to substantially improve retrieval of information from memory. — hypnosis

43. The ____________-____________ theory of memory asserts that all we have heard or seen is stored in memory. — tape-recorder

44. ____________ memories are alleged to occur when an emotionally traumatic event occurs in early childhood and can't be easily retrieved. — Repressed

45. Lesions in the temporal cortex result in ____________ amnesia, in which the patient has difficulty learning new material. — anterograde

46. A patient has suffered an accident involving trauma to the head. Following this, his ability to learn things is unimpaired, but he seems to have forgotten some things that happened prior to the accident. This is an example of ____________ ____________. — retrograde; amnesia

47. One theory to account for the loss of prior memories after a trauma to the brain is based on the notion of ____________ ____________, according to which newly acquired memories undergo gradual change until they become more firmly established. — trace consolidation

48. An amnesic's memory is relatively unaffected when the memory task involves ____________ knowledge, but her memory is drastically impaired when it involves ____________ knowledge. — procedural; declarative

49. ____________ tests of memory show great performance declines in amnesics, while ____________ tests show little difference from the performance of normals. — Explicit; implicit

Self Test

1. In order for us to remember something, we must first engage in the process of:
   a. storage
   b. rehearsal
   c. encoding
   d. recall

2. An enduring physical record of a memory is called:
   a. a memory trace
   b. a chunk
   c. short-term memory
   d. none of the above

3. Suppose you are given a choice between a multiple-choice test and a short-answer test for the final exam in this course. You want to maximize the chance of doing well. Based on what you know about recall and recognition, all other things being equal, which test should you choose?
   a. short answer
   b. multiple choice
   c. either, there is no difference
   d. it depends on the difficulty of the material

4. Complete the following analogy: Multiple-choice questions are to fill-in-the-blank questions as:
   a. recognition is to recall
   b. recall is to retention
   c. recognition is to retention
   d. learning is to memory

5. In principle, the stages of memory processes must be arranged in which of the following orders?
   a. memory trace—encoding—storage—retrieval
   b. encoding—memory trace—storage—retrieval
   c. encoding—storage—memory trace—retrieval
   d. encoding—memory trace—retrieval—storage

6. The following are all characteristics of short-term memory except:
   a. limited capacity
   b. contents lost without rehearsal
   c. displacement causes forgetting
   d. none of the above

7. It has been found that people can hold about seven items in short-term memory. When more items are presented, complete recall is generally not possible. This demonstrates the ________ of short-term memory.
   a. retention interval
   b. memory trace
   c. displacement
   d. memory span

8. What is true about forgetting from short-term memory?
   a. It can be caused by erosion of the memory trace with time.
   b. The memory trace can be knocked out of short-term memory by another trace.
   c. It can be inhibited by rehearsal of the material stored there.
   d. all of the above

9. Suppose you are given driving directions by a gas station attendant and you repeat them over and over to yourself, "First left, second right, left at the first light, third right." Now suppose that your repetition of the directions is interrupted by an emergency driving maneuver. This would likely cause you to forget the directions, thereby demonstrating the importance of __________ in preserving short-term memory.
   a. storage capacity
   b. retrieval
   c. accessibility
   d. rehearsal

10. Suppose cryogenics (freezing patients and awakening them at some future time) were possible. If you were to discover that, after being awakened, the patients had retained very accurate memories of what they had experienced immediately before freezing, this would be evidence for which hypothesis of forgetting in short-term memory?
    a. interference
    b. decay
    c. neither displacement nor decay
    d. either displacement or decay

11. At a party you are taken around the room by the host and are introduced to the other guests. Some time after the introductions are finished,

one of these people comes up to talk to you. All other things being equal, you have the best chance of remembering her name if she was one of the ___________ people you met. This phenomenon is called ___________.

a. first, primacy
b. middle, inhibition
c. last, recency
d. first or last, the opposition effect

12. Now imagine the same situation (as in No. 11) except that the person comes up to you immediately after you have been very quickly introduced to everyone. Again, other things being equal, you would have the worst chance of remembering her name if she was one of the _________ people you met and the best chance if she was one of the _________.
a. first, last
b. middle, last
c. first, middle
d. last, first

13. Suppose a subject is asked to memorize the following list of words: *apple, horse, desk, carpet, mug, milk, parrot, disk, street, tree.* Which of the following will occur?
a. The word *street* will be rehearsed more than the word *horse*, causing *tree* to be stored in long-term memory.
b. The word *parrot* will be rehearsed more than the word *mug*, causing *parrot* to be stored in short-term memory.
c. The word *apple* will be rehearsed more than the word *carpet*, causing *apple* to be stored in long-term memory.
d. The word *desk* will be rehearsed more than the word *parrot*, causing desk to be stored in short-term memory.

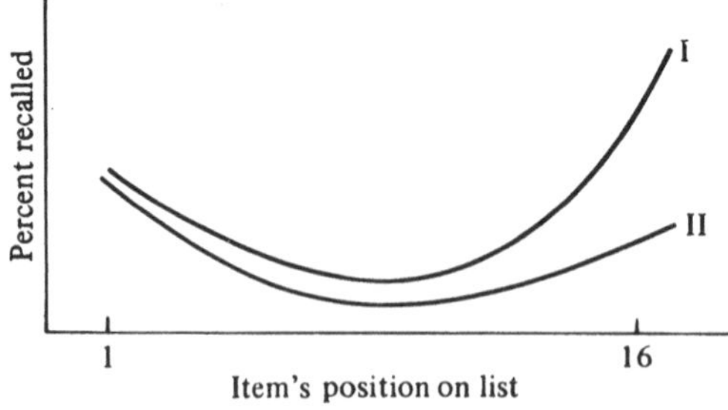

14. The figure above depicts recall curves for a list of 16 items. Two conditions were employed, I and II. What was the difference between the conditions?
a. The interval between each item was longer for II than I.
b. The interval between each item was longer for I than II.
c. The interval between the last item and the recall test was longer for I than II.
d. The interval between the last item and the recall test was longer for II than I.

15. Increasing the capacity of short-term memory is a misnomer because:
a. all one does is to rehearse the material already there, keeping it fresh while new material is added
b. the number of items stored is the same, about 7, just the content of each item has changed
c. it is the number of chunks that has changed, not the capacity of short-term memory
d. it is not possible to increase the capacity of short-term memory

16. Suppose you run an experiment in which you present one word, say *rabbit*, and the subject has to repeat it. Then you present another word, say *pear*, and the subject has to repeat *rabbit, pear*. Then you present a third word, and the subject has to repeat all three, etc. At the end of your list, you test the subject's memory for all words on the list. Based on what you know about the effect of maintenance rehearsal on long-term memory, you predict that:
a. *rabbit* should be entered into long-term memory with higher probability than the last word on the list
b. *rabbit* should be entered into long-term memory with lower probability than the last word on the list
c. *rabbit* should be entered into long-term memory with the same probability as the last word on the list
d. none of the above

17. Working memory is to short-term memory as
a. storage is to processing
b. processing is to storage
c. recall is to recognition
d. recognition is to recall

18. Which of the following processes will *not* result in the effective storage of memory traces in long-term memory?
a. maintenance rehearsal

b. clustering
c. mnemonic devices
d. organization by phrases

19. Mnemonic devices (memorizing aids) use the principle of:
a. consolidation of retrieval
b. recoding
c. retrieval of consolidation
d. all of the above

20. Which of the following images would produce the greatest increase in recall performance for the pair of items *horse-rock*?
a. a horse standing next to a rock
b. a horse dragging a rock
c. a horse and rock pictured separately
d. all of the above would be equivalent

21. You have been trying to remember the name of a street that a friend lives on. Despite all of your efforts you are unable to recall it. While in the kitchen looking for a snack (to console yourself) you reach for a can of nuts, and suddenly the street name comes to you—Walnut. This is an example of the role of ____________ ____________.
a. anterograde amnesia
b. retrograde amnesia
c. mnemonics
d. retrieval cues

22. Retrieval cues are most effective if they:
a. coincide with the way in which a trace was originally encoded
b. are presented at the time of recall, not at encoding
c. are quite concrete
d. elicit visual images

23. The tip-of-the-tongue phenomenon provides us with evidence concerning:
a. the hierarchical organization of long-term memory
b. accessibility in short-term memory
c. the search process in long-term memory
d. the use of retrieval cues in short-term memory

24. Having something "on the tip of the tongue" indicates a problem:
a. in the way the item was chunked
b. with reconstruction
c. with proactive inhibition
d. with retrieval

25. What is the relationship between implicit and explicit memory tests?
a. They must be correlated because they both measure memory.
b. They can be uncorrelated as shown by demonstrations of implicit memory without explicit memory.
c. They must be correlated because the tests measure different aspects of memory.
d. Available evidence does not permit an answer.

26. Each of the following is a test of explicit retrieval except:
a. fragment completion
b. repetition priming
c. free recall
d. memory span
e. more than one of the above

27. It is believed that retrieval is generally preceded by:
a. chunking
b. memory activation
c. memory search
d. recognition

28. If you read the Memory chapter in Professor Gleitman's test, which of the following people should you now think of as more famous than you would have if you had not read the text, assuming that you didn't remember having encountered these names in the text itself?
a. Esther Williams
b. Ted Williams
c. Johnny Carson
d. Sebastian Weisdorf

29. When Ebbinghaus tested himself on memory for nonsense syllables, he found that
a. relearning took just as long as original learning
b. savings was greatest when the retention interval was shortest
c. his implicit memory was better than his explicit memory
d. none of the above

30. According to a decay theory of forgetting, if a subject learning a list of words was then subjected to one of the following procedures, he would forget the greatest number of words if:
a. he slept for four versus two hours
b. he learned other lists for four versus two hours

c. he performed arithmetic problems for four versus two hours
d. all of the above would be comparable

31. Consider the following experimental design:

control group:
learn A → rest → test A
experimental group:
learn A → learn B → test A

This design would be used to test forgetting due to which factor?
a. proactive inhibition
b. retroactive inhibition
c. decay
d. generalization

32. A college sophomore participates in a nonsense syllable learning experiment. The first list takes him only four trials to learn. The second list takes five trials, and the third list takes eight trials. These results can be taken as a demonstration of:
a. memory activation
b. retroactive inhibition
c. proactive inhibition
d. retrograde forgetting

33. One hypothesis about forgetting is that it is due to a change in retrieval cues. Which of the following would be counterevidence for this hypothesis?
a. demonstration of proactive inhibition
b. demonstration of retroactive inhibition
c. demonstration that decay caused forgetting
d. none of the above

34. One of the potential causes of childhood amnesia is that the retrieval cues change massively between childhood and adulthood. Another plausible cause might be:
a. the poor quality of the initial encoding of memory traces
b. retroactive inhibition
c. decay
d. all of the above

35. The concept of a permastore arises from the fact that:
a. some memories are not subject to any forgetting
b. some memories, while they decline initially after learning, remain relatively intact thereafter
c. some memories have a flashbulb character to them
d. all of the above

36. The compelling nature of flashbulb memories has caused some to argue that they are caused by a special memory mechanism. Contrary to this hypothesis, though,
a. the accuracy of these memories may not be all that impressive
b. some of the good memory may come from conversations about the event after it has occurred
c. both of the above
d. none of the above

37. Distortions of memory seem to be accentuated as a function of time between original acquisition of the information and testing. Such distortions could be due to effects of:
a. encoding
b. storage
c. retrieval
d. b and c, but not a

38. Bartlett's experiments and evidence about the fallibility of eyewitness testimony highlight the importance of which of the following factors about recall?
a. reconstruction
b. proactive inhibition
c. retrieval cues
d. retroactive inhibition

39. One could have a script for:
a. mowing the lawn
b. visiting the eye doctor
c. going to a fast food restaurant
d. all of the above

40. Suppose two groups of subjects watched a videotape of a minor theft, in which someone in a room full of people reached into a drawer and took a $20 bill. After the videotape, group 1 was asked "Did you see the custodian reach into the drawer?" while group 2 was asked "Did you see a custodian reach into the drawer?" (Actually, there was no custodian in the room.) Which group is more likely to accuse the custodian of the theft?
a. group 1
b. group 2
c. group 1 and group 2 will be equally likely to accuse the custodian
d. can't tell from the available detail

41. Suppose an eyewitness to a crime was hypnotized and asked to recall as much as she could of the events of the crime. She would most likely:

a. recall more of what she had seen
b. recall less of what she had seen
c. recall about the same as if she had not been hypnotized, but report more
d. resist recalling more about the crime because of its emotional impact

42. These are reasons to believe that some of the recent reports of repressed memories of childhood sexual abuse are not correct. Among the factors that may be exaggerating the number of such reports are:
a. the fact that some of the therapists involved in eliciting them are using hypnosis, which is known to cause the patient to report more things that may be confabulations in the hopes of pleasing the therapist
b. the fact that some of the therapists who work on this problem have a bias to find childhood causes of adult problems even when there may be no such causes
c. the fact that highly charged memories such as those of childhood abuse are not likely to be repressed for such a long time without having come out before
d. all of the above

43. Retrograde amnesia may be caused by:
a. a disruption in the mechanism that causes new material to be placed into long-term memory, thus preventing any new learning
b. a disruption of trace consolidation at the time of the trauma
c. a difficulty in retrieving events that occurred just prior to the trauma
d. more than one of the above

44. One experiment has shown that while amnesics get better at reading mirror-reversed text, they cannot recognize the words they have read later on, while normals can. This indicates that:
a. amnesics lose the ability to learn new information
b. amnesics lose the ability to learn declarative information, but not procedural information
c. amnesics can learn procedural skills, but only if the very same stimuli are repeated over and over
d. anterograde amnesics are different from retrograde amnesics

45. Three major symptoms characterize anterograde amnesia. They are:
a. accurate memory for pretrauma events, normal short-term memory, inaccurate memory for most posttrauma events
b. inaccurate memory for pretrauma events, normal short-term memory, inaccurate memory for most posttrauma events
c. accurate memory for pretrauma events, abnormal short-term memory, accurate memory for most posttrauma events
d. inaccurate memory for pretrauma events, normal short-term memory, accurate memory for most posttrauma events

46. Milner's subject H.M. (an anterograde amnesic) was tested for his memory span for unrelated nouns. What is your best guess about his span?
a. 0
b. 4
c. 7
d. 10

47. A theory of memory which says that memory needs time to be fixed into a permanent form is called:
a. rehearsal
b. spreading activation
c. trace consolidation
d. memory priming

48. You witness an automobile accident in which one of the drivers hits his head on the windshield. He appears uninjured, but when a policeman asks him what happened just prior to the accident, the man seems confused and is unable to answer. The policeman is about to haul the man off to jail (assuming that he must be drunk) when you step forward and (having studied your psychology text) say, "This man is suffering from ____________ ____________!"
a. trace consolidation
b. anterograde amnesia
c. retrograde amnesia
d. Korsakoff syndrome

49. The problem with anterograde amnesics may be:
a. impaired explicit memory but normal implicit memory
b. impaired declarative learning but normal procedural learning
c. impaired long-term memory processes but normal short-term memory processes
d. all of the above
d. none of the above

Answer Key for Self Test

1. c p. 192
2. a p. 192
3. b p. 192
4. a p. 192
5. b p. 194
6. c p. 194
7. d p. 194
8. d pp. 194–95
9. d p. 195
10. d p. 194
11. a p. 195
12. b p. 195
13. c p. 195
14. d p. 196
15. b p. 196
16. c pp. 197–98
17. b p. 199
18. a p. 198
19. b p. 200
20. b p. 200
21. d p. 201
22. a p. 201
23. c p. 203
24. d p. 203
25. b pp. 203–4
26. e p. 204
27. c p. 202
28. d p. 204
29. b p. 206
30. d p. 206
31. b p. 206
32. c p. 206
33. d pp. 206–7
34. d pp. 207–8
35. b p. 208
36. c pp. 209–10
37. d p. 210
38. a pp. 210–11
39. d p. 211
40. a pp. 212–13
41. c pp. 213–14
42. d pp. 214–15
43. d p. 218
44. b p. 219
45. a pp. 216–17
46. c p. 217
47. c p. 218
48. c p. 218
49. d pp. 218–19

Investigating Psychological Phenomena

THE EFFECT OF IMAGERY INSTRUCTIONS ON MEMORY

Equipment: None
Number of subjects: One
Time per subject: Fifteen minutes
Time for experimenter: Twenty minutes

As Professor Gleitman discusses, there are several mnemonic techniques that will improve memory performance. One of these is the use of images. By now there is a good deal of research that demonstrates the memorial effectiveness of asking subjects to create images of the objects or events that they are trying to commit to memory. In the present experiment you will have an opportunity to demonstrate the effectiveness of imagery instructions for yourself in an experiment that involves learning paired-associate lists.

The procedure is quite simple. Below you will find two lists of twenty noun pairs each that you can use as stimuli for the experiment. You will need just one subject to participate in the experiment. The procedure is as follows.

First, read the following instructions to the subject:

> This is a memory experiment in which you will be required to memorize and recall two lists of words, each of which is composed of twenty pairs of fairly common nouns. First I will read aloud the twenty noun pairs from list 1 at the rate of one pair every seven seconds or so. While I am reading the pairs, just sit quietly and listen to them, trying as best you can to memorize the words in each pair. After I have presented all the pairs, I shall go through the list again, this time reading only the first noun in each pair. As I read each of these nouns, I would like you to recall the appropriate second noun that was paired with it when I originally presented the list. You will have seven seconds or so to recall the second noun for each pair and to write it in the space provided on your answer sheet. Do you have any questions?

After you have read these instructions to the subject, give him or her the report sheet for this chapter in Appendix B. Then follow the testing procedure outlined in the instructions. After you have completed the procedure for list 1, read the following instructions to the subject:

> Now I shall present you with another list of twenty noun pairs that I would like you to memorize. The procedure for this list will be identical to that for the first list except for one change: This time, when you are presented with each pair, try to form a mental image of the words in which there is some sort of interaction. For example, if you were presented with the pair "horse-rock," you might form an image of a horse that is harnessed to a large boulder, dragging the boulder along the ground. Such images should help you memorize the words. Do you have any questions?

Now present list 2 exactly as list 1 was presented after you have given the subject another answer sheet for list 2.

To score the subject's performance, simply count up the number of items that were answered correctly on each list. If all went well, the subject should have scored better on list 2 (unless the subject was already forming mental images for the nouns in list 1).

Now at this point you may raise a question. Was the subject's performance on list 2 better because of the influence of the imagery instructions, or could it have been better for some other reason? For example, it may have already occurred to you that performance on list 2 may have been better than list 1 because list 2 was presented *after* list 1, and therefore the subject may simply have been better practiced at memorizing words. Before reading on, try to think of a way that you might have run this experiment that would have avoided this problem.

One way to have avoided a practice effect would have been to use two different subjects. This first subject would have received only list 1 with its instructions while the second would have received only list 2 with its imagery instructions. If performance on list 2 was still better than on list 1, you might feel more confident in attributing this difference to the effect of the instructions (assuming that your two subjects were fairly comparable in their overall memory ability). At least practice could not account for the difference.

But, you might object, there might *still* be an explanation for the difference between lists that has nothing to do with the effect of imagery instructions. Suppose, for instance, list 2 was composed of words that were more common or concrete than the words on list 1 (e.g., horse versus liberty). This alone might make list 2 more memorable. There are two ways that one might control for this possibility. The first is to choose words for the two lists that are equated for frequency of usage and concreteness (and, for that matter, whatever else you might think of that would affect the memorability of words). The second method is to balance experimentally which word lists are paired with which instructions. The following table shows one arrangement that should work in which you would have to run at least 4 subjects:

	neutral instructions	imagery instructions
word list 1	subject 1	subject 2
word list 2	subject 3	subject 4

If you were to run this experiment, then you could tell whether the word lists differ from one another in memorability and/or whether there is an effect of instructions. If word list 2 is more memorable than word list 1, then subjects 3 and 4 should perform better than 1 and 2. If imagery instructions produce better performance than neutral instructions, then subjects 2 and 4 should perform better than 1 and 3. If list 2 is more memorable than list 1 *and* imagery instructions produce better performance than neutral instructions, then subject 4 should perform best of all.

If you want to check on the possible influence of practice in the experiment that you ran, and if you want to be sure that the word lists are comparable (they have actually been balanced for meaningfulness and commonness of the words), then you should try this last experiment. Whether you do try it or not, however, you should realize that one of the points of this exercise was to show that even a fairly simple experiment such as the one that you ran with the word lists is sometimes open to several interpretations. To find the right one requires careful experimentation.

Noun pairs for list 1	Noun pairs for list 2
1. building-letter	1. sail-bowl
2. grass-meat	2. coffee-lake
3. animal-village	3. girl-flood
4. house-lip	4. corn-river
5. sky-seat	5. stone-bottle
6. dress-apple	6. paper-shore
7. fur-mountain	7. dust-army
8. flag-coast	8. ocean-fire
9. sugar-ship	9. clothing-board
10. mother-city	10. door-king
11. market-church	11. butler-tree
12. plant-baby	12. gold-chair
13. sea-iron	13. flower-car
14. woods-engine	14. bird-skin
15. arm-boulder	15. hall-child
16. woman-forest	16. garden-book
17. table-wood	17. money-shoes
18. queen-college	18. cat-camp
19. bar-diamond	19. wife-storm
20. cotton-street	20. dollar-machine

CHAPTER 8

Thought and Knowledge

Learning Objectives

1. What is directed thinking, and how does it differ from other senses of the word "thinking"?

ANALOGICAL REPRESENTATIONS

2. Be able to define a mental representation and to distinguish it from an external representation.
3. Understand the difference between analogical and symbolic representations. Be able to give examples of each.

Mental images

4. While there are individual differences in imagery, understand that these differences are not clearly related to performance on tasks requiring imagery.
5. Be familiar with the term "eidetic imagery" and what the characteristics of this imagery are.
6. Understand how our visual imagery has some of the qualities of a pictorial representation. Be familiar with the phenomenon of mental scanning. But also understand the evidence showing that images are not truly internal pictures.

Spatial thinking

7. Be familiar with the evidence showing that some spatial knowledge is symbolic and conceptual.

SYMBOLIC REPRESENTATIONS

8. Be able to describe the definition of a concept and to give examples.
9. Be familiar with the term "proposition" and with its elements, the "subject" and the "predicate."

Knowledge and memory

10. Describe the differences between episodic and generic memory. What is semantic memory, and how is it related to episodic and generic memory?
11. What is meant by the claim that semantic memory is organized hierarchically? Explain how judgments of typicality contradict this claim.

THE PROCESS OF THINKING: SOLVING PROBLEMS

Organization in problem solving

12. How is thinking goal directed? Describe how Duncker's ray problem illustrates the goal-directedness of problem solving.
13. How is thinking hierarchical? How are the concepts of chunking and subroutine related to the hierarchical nature of thought?
14. What is the shape of the learning curve in the development of a skill, and what does this shape tell us about the course of learning?
15. Be able to describe how chunking ability differentiates novices from experts. What is the role of automatization in skill development?
16. Describe the Stroop effect and discuss its relevance to automaticity.
17. What are the major differences between masters and beginners in problem solving? What skills do masters have that novices don't?

Obstacles to problem solving

18. Be aware of the effects of set and motivation on problem solving. How does set influence solution

strategies? What is functional fixedness and how does it hinder problem solving?

Overcoming obstacles to solution

19. How do novices and masters use the strategy of working backwards? How can this strategy help a novice in problem solving?
20. What does it mean to change the way a problem is represented in order to facilitate solving that problem? How do changes in representation help in problem solution?

Restructuring

21. What is restructuring? How is it related to creative thinking?
22. How is incubation related to the effects of set? Understand how it is related to creative thinking.

Artificial intelligence: problem solving by computer

23. Why are computers valuable analogs to humans as problem solvers? How is the analogy weak?
24. Understand the goal of the field of artificial intelligence.
25. Define the terms "algorithm" and "heuristic." Describe some useful heuristics in problem solving.
26. What is MYCIN and what can it do?
27. Why are different strategies required for well-defined versus ill-defined problems? What is the difference between these two kinds of problems, and how is this difference relevant to the comparison of humans and computers?
28. How is the concept of "common sense" important in understanding the limitations in the ability of computers to solve problems?

THE PROCESS OF THINKING: REASONING AND DECISION MAKING

29. Are the laws of logic the laws of thought?

Deductive reasoning

30. What is a syllogism? What reasons cause many subjects to do poorly in solving syllogisms?
31. What sort of heuristics do people use to solve syllogisms?

Inductive reasoning

32. Be able to explain the difference between deductive and inductive reasoning and give examples of each.
33. What is the confirmation bias? Why are disconfirmations more helpful in testing hypotheses than confirmations? Can you give an example of the confirmation bias?

Decision making

34. People are poor at estimating probabilities, but they can use shortcuts to get at these estimates. What are some of these shortcuts?
35. What is the representativeness heuristic? How does it affect people's use of base-rate information?
36. Why can the availability heuristic sometimes lead to grave errors in estimating likelihoods? Be able to state examples in which the availability heuristic may affect estimations.

COGNITION AND CONSCIOUSNESS

37. What are the essential questions in the study of consciousness?

Mental processes that go on below the surface

38. Be able to distinguish between unconscious and nonconscious.
39. Be familiar with the phenomenon of blindsight and what its implications are for consciousness in perception.
40. What does it mean to use memory unconsciously? Give examples of the use of memory in comprehension that show its influence even when we're not conscious of it.
41. Describe how actions may be taken without conscious awareness.
42. Understand what it means to be aware of the products of processing without being aware of the processing itself.

What's consciousness good for?

43. How might consciousness be useful in situations requiring choice and reciprocity?

TAKING STOCK

44. How do the broad domains of cognition (perception, memory, and thinking) overlap? Give examples.

Programmed Exercises

1. The word "____________" may be used as a synonym for remembering, attention, or belief.	thinking
2. If one is talking about ____________ thinking, one is referring to reasoning or reflecting on some problem, with some goal in mind.	directed

ANALOGICAL REPRESENTATIONS

3. Mental ____________ refer to internal codes that stand for external ____________.	representations, representations
4. An ____________ representation is one that captures some of the characteristics of what it represents; a ____________ representation stands for what it represents, but does not resemble it in any simple way.	analogical symbolic
5. If you use a symbolic representation that encodes information in an all-or-none way, you can call that a ____________ representation.	digital
6. ____________ imagery is sometimes called photographic memory, referring to a literal representation of some external visual event.	Eidetic
7. You can show that people can ____________ images by showing that the time it takes them to traverse from one part of an image to another is linearly related to the distance that must be traversed, as if they were looking over an actual map of the space.	scan
8. ____________ thinking is sometimes picture-like and sometimes requires conceptual representations. This is illustrated by examining several phenomena of mental maps.	Spatial

SYMBOLIC REPRESENTATIONS

9. A ____________ is an internal representation of a class or category for which some instances can be enumerated.	concept
10. A ____________ asserts a relationship between concepts such that it relates a ____________ and a ____________, the former of which is what the ____________ is about and the latter of which is what is asserted.	proposition subject, predicate proposition
11. A mental average might constitute some concept, in which case it is called a ____________.	prototype
12. It is generally believed that there are two kinds of memory representations, ones that tag an event with its time or place of occurrence (called ____________ memory), and ones that constitute memory for items of knowledge (called ____________ memory).	episodic generic
13. One type of generic memory is ____________ memory, which concerns the meanings of concepts.	semantic
14. One popular type of model for semantic memory involves a representation called a ____________, in which various ____________ are linked together by lines and arrows in a complex system of relationships to show how they are interrelated.	network, nodes
15. A network in which one concept was stored under others that subsumed it throughout would be called ____________.	hierarchical

THE PROCESS OF THINKING: SOLVING PROBLEMS

16. In an analogy to computer programming, psychologists often call mental operations that are run off under the control of higher-level mental operations ____________.	subroutines

17. The use of master plans to organize subsidiary actions suggests that thought is organized into ___________.	hierarchies
18. The ability to organize many details into larger ___________ is one of the crucial features of directed activity, including thinking.	chunks
19. Much of the difference between a master and an apprentice is in the degree to which subcomponents of an activity have been chunked hierarchically; to the master, the substeps have become ___________.	automatic
20. The ___________ and subsequent rise found in many learning curves for motor skills suggest that the learner gradually transforms this task.	plateau
21. The ___________ effect is an example of how reading letter strings has become an automatized activity for adults. Reading incompatible color names interferes with naming colors in which the color words are printed.	Stroop
22. As Adrian de Groot demonstrated with chess, master problem solvers use ___________ that contain more information than do those of beginners.	chunks
23. When a person becomes ___________ on one approach to a task, it is hard for him to approach it any other way.	fixated
24. A person who attempts to solve a problem by thinking along a line of thought created by previous thinking is operating under a ___________ ___________.	mental set
25. The Luchins water jug problem, an example of mental set, is one of the classic demonstrations of ___________ in problem solving.	mechanization
26. In general, the greater the ___________ toward reaching a solution, the greater the ___________ with which the problem is approached.	motivation set
27. Thinking of objects in terms of their normal function is termed ___________ ___________ and can hinder problem solving.	functional fixedness
28. ___________ ___________ is a problem-solving strategy frequently used by novices but not characteristic of experts.	Working backwards
29. Sometimes it is necessary to change the way a problem is ___________ to achieve a solution.	represented
30. Solutions of difficult problems often involve a perceptual ___________ of the problem in order to break a false perceptual set.	restructuring
31. The phenomenon whereby one arrives at an insightful solution to a problem after intense preparation followed by rest is called ___________.	incubation
32. One way in which humans and computers are similar is that both are ___________ -___________ systems.	information- processing
33. The field of ___________ ___________ is concerned with programming computers to solve various intellectual problems.	artificial intelligence
34. A procedure in which all of the operations required to achieve the solution are specified step by step is called an ___________.	algorithm
35. A ___________ differs from an algorithm in that it is a rule of thumb rather than a fixed sequence of steps.	heuristic
36. ___________ ___________ are problem-solving programs that deal with problems in a limited domain of knowledge.	Expert systems
37. ___________ is an example of a problem-solving program that helps doctors in the treatment of infectious diseases.	MYCIN

38. A newspaper proofreader is asked to check a piece of text for spelling errors. This is an example of a(n) ___________ -___________ problem. — well-defined

39. A student is asked to write a "good" paper. This is an example of a(n) ___________ -___________ problem. — ill-defined

40. Some computer scientists feel that the crucial difference between human and artificial intelligence is that computer programs lack ___________ ___________. — common sense

THE PROCESS OF THINKING: REASONING AND DECISION MAKING

41. A ___________ contains two premises and a conclusion. — syllogism

42. The statement "All A are B and therefore all B are A" is a(n) ___________ inference. — invalid

43. In ___________ reasoning we apply a general rule to a particular case. — deductive

44. In ___________ reasoning we consider different cases and try to find the rule that covers them all. — inductive

45. The fact that people primarily seek evidence that will confirm their hypotheses suggests that there is a strong ___________ ___________. — confirmation bias

46. One ___________ shows that a hypothesis is false, but countless ___________ cannot prove that it is true. — disconfirmation, confirmations

47. The ___________ heuristic involves judging the probability that an object belongs to a category by judging the similarity of that object to the category. — representativeness

48. When we estimate the frequency of certain events by considering how many such events readily come to mind, we are using the ___________ ___________. — availability heuristic

49. There is a good deal of evidence that throws a poor light on human ___________; we make all sorts of reasoning errors. — rationality

COGNITION AND CONSCIOUSNESS

50. Major advances in the study of consciousness have come about through the study of when it is ___________. — absent

51. Freud's conception of the ___________ included the notion that memories were actively kept out of our awareness. — unconscious

52. There are patients with damage to the occipital lobe of the brain who experience ___________, the ability to make judgments about visual objects with no conscious experience of those objects. — blindsight

53. By and large, we seem to be unaware of mental ___________; but, by contrast, we are sometimes aware of the ___________ of mental operations. — processes, products

54. In relying on automatic routines, we give up ___________. — flexibility

TAKING STOCK

55. There are no clear boundaries among the domains of ___________, ___________, and ___________. — perception, memory, thinking

Self Test

1. All of the following are examples of directed thinking *except*:
   a. discovery of a geometric proof
   b. deciding on the next move in a chess game
   c. daydreaming about last night's meal
   d. trying to figure out why a car will not start
2. A hand drawing of a tractor is what kind of representation, as compared to an actual tractor?
   a. analogical
   b. symbolic
   c. both of the above
   d. neither of the above
3. The relationship between the quality of mental images and the ability to perform tasks that require imagery is:
   a. positive
   b. negative
   c. sometimes positive, sometimes negative
   d. unstudied
4. Eidetic imagery is more prominent in:
   a. young children
   b. older adults
   c. middle aged adults
   d. no one; it is not a reliable phenomenon
5. It appears that the relationship between scanning mental images and scanning actual pictures is:
   a. symbolic
   b. representational
   c. haphazard
   d. analog
6. Studies of mental images for ambiguous figures show that:
   a. subjects can "see" either form of the figure
   b. subjects cannot reverse the figure in their mind's eye
   c. subjects can see both versions of the figure simultaneously, in contrast to what they see when they are viewing such a figure
   d. none of the above
7. A concept:
   a. may designate a quality
   b. must have a finite number of instances
   c. must not refer to a relationship
   d. all of the above
8. A proposition:
   a. can be simply a mental image
   b. can be simply a sentence
   c. has a truth value
   d. none of the above
9. A proposition must have:
   a. a subject and a predicate
   b. a product and a process
   c. a node and a relation
   d. none of the above
10. Remembering what you did on your last birthday is an example of
    a. semantic memory
    b. generic memory
    c. hierarchical memory
    d. episodic memory
11. Semantic memory is to generic memory as:
    a. processes are to products
    b. episodic memory is to generic memory
    c. concepts are to knowledge
    d. all of the above
12. A hierarchical network theory of semantic memory won't work because:
    a. *apple* and *olive* are not coequal members of the category *fruit*
    b. *red* is a more typical color than *mauve*
    c. people rate *chairs* as being more representative of the category *furniture* than *ottomans*
    d. all of the above
13. Organization in problem solving is often:
    a. lacking
    b. ill-defined
    c. determined working backward
    d. goal-determined
14. Learning curves involving such tasks as receiving Morse code have a characteristic plateau preceded and followed by rises. This is because:
    a. people tend to get bored with tasks like this, and so their performance falls off
    b. people begin to use mental imagery after a little practice
    c. with practice people can make more efficient use of chunks
    d. none of the above

15. Which of the following is *not* a characteristic of learning for a new motor skill?
    a. periods in which there is no apparent change in the learning curve
    b. periods of relatively sharp increases in skill
    c. a steady increase in skill from the beginning of learning to the end
    d. a scalloped shape to the learning curve

16. The Stroop effect clearly shows that:
    a. certain mental activities become automatized
    b. colors are named faster than words
    c. words are named faster than colors
    d. none of the above

17. Research has shown that master chess players are better than novices in:
    a. solving algorithms
    b. chunking chess moves
    c. memorizing in general
    d. memorizing random patterns of chess pieces

18. A person is asked to solve a series of math problems. The first five problems can be solved only one way, each the same. The sixth problem can also be solved using this method, but there is also a much simpler solution. The subject solves this problem in the way he solved the first five. This person's problem-solving ability has been hampered by:
    a. functional fixedness
    b. a lack of motivation
    c. mental set
    d. an improper heuristic

19. Several subjects are told that they will receive ten dollars if they are able to solve a problem in fifteen minutes. A second group is given no such promise. These groups demonstrate the inverse relationship between ____________ and ____________.
    a. motivation, set
    b. effort, success
    c. attitude, money
    d. none of the above

20. An inability to think of objects except in terms of their normal function can be a hindrance in problem solving and is known as:
    a. perceptual set
    b. restructuring
    c. functional fixedness
    d. none of the above

21. Some problems require a change in representation in order for the problem solver to work toward a solution. This phenomenon is quite different from:
    a. restructuring
    b. incubation
    c. functional fixedness
    d. analogy

22. All of the following problems discussed in the text require perceptual restructuring for a solution *except*:
    a. the nine-dot problem
    b. the match puzzle
    c. the horse-and-rider problem
    d. unscrambling words (anagrams)

23. All of the following often contribute to insights *except*:
    a. a period of intense preparation
    b. a period of retreat
    c. a different environment
    d. functional fixedness

24. One likely reason that incubation helps in reaching a problem solution is that:
    a. it allows for perceptual restructuring
    b. it helps break mental set
    c. it gives time to set up subgoals
    d. none of the above

25. The concept of an incubation period (in the explanation of insight) is unsatisfactory because:
    a. it tells us nothing of the underlying processes
    b. the term "unconscious thought" is too vague
    c. it has been demonstrated to be false
    d. a and b, but not c

26. The use of the computer as an analog to the human problem solver depends on:
    a. the sequential nature of computer programs
    b. the fact that computers use algorithms to solve their problems
    c. the fact that computers are limited to solving well-defined problems
    d. the irrelevance of the underlying hardware in humans and computers

27. Humans and computers are similar in that:
    a. both are information-processing systems
    b. both can use heuristics
    c. both can use algorithms
    d. all of the above

28. A food recipe specifies what ingredients are to be added together, in what amounts, and in what order. Such a recipe would be:
   a. a heuristic
   b. an algorithm
   c. a subgoal
   d. a scheme

29. Which of the following would make most efficient use of heuristics?
   i. an initial diagnosis made by a physician
   ii. an architect designing a hotel
   iii. a search for a particular word in the dictionary
   iv. deciding where to hang a new picture

   a. i, ii, iii
   b. ii, iii, iv
   c. iii, iv
   d. i, ii, iv

30. Examples of the appropriate use of subgoals and heuristics might be:
   a. trying for a position in the center of a board in a game of chess
   b. going for a checkmate
   c. finding the general area of an automotive problem (i.e., electrical vs. mechanical)
   d. all of the above

31. Ill-defined problems differ from well-defined problems in that:
   a. ill-defined problems have more difficult and complex solutions
   b. well-defined problems always have solutions, while ill-defined problems are unsolvable
   c. it is hard to define what changes are needed to reach the goal stated in ill-defined problems
   d. all of the above

32. The analogy between computers and the human mind is weak because:
   a. computers are made of transistors
   b. the mind uses nerve signals, not electrical impulses
   c. humans can solve well-defined problems
   d. none of the above

33. Expert systems are limited in their similarity to human problem solving in that:
   a. they are too rigid in their approaches to problems
   b. they are restricted to a narrow area of competence
   c. they are confined to working on well-defined problems
   d. all of the above

34. One of the limitations of artificial intelligence is its lack of common sense. This could be addressed by:
   a. giving the computer a better set of algorithms to map out all possibilities that might occur in any given situation
   b. providing the computer with better background knowledge so that it can anticipate what might occur
   c. making ill-defined problems well-defined
   d. having the computer stick strictly to relevant information, ignoring any information about a problem that is not directly relevant to its algorithm for the solution

35. All A are B
   Some B are C
   Therefore, some A are C. This is a(n):
   a. invalid syllogism
   b. valid syllogism
   c. invalid algorithm
   d. valid algorithm

36. Which of the following statements is true?
   a. People often set out to see whether their hypotheses are false.
   b. People rarely set out to see whether their hypotheses are false.
   c. People do not seek evidence that will confirm their hypotheses.
   d. none of the above

37. In making predictions about the outcome of situations, people seem to make too little use of:
   a. salient information that is presented in the form of a memorable scenario
   b. base-rate information that tells one the past history of a situation
   c. deductive reasoning
   d. none of the above; people appropriately balance these sources of information

38. When a decision is affected by events that come readily to mind, this is a manifestation of:
   a. inductive reasoning
   b. deductive reasoning
   c. the representativeness heuristic
   d. the availability heuristic

39. All of the following are shortcomings of human rationality *except*:
    a. people cannot perform the operations of addition, subtraction, multiplication, and division adequately
    b. people make errors in deductive reasoning
    c. people make errors in inductive reasoning
    d. people are not concerned with demonstrating that their hypotheses are wrong

40. The study of consciousness has been aided by the study of:
    a. blindsight
    b. incubation
    c. functional fixedness
    d. mental set

41. Which of the following phenomena has been instrumental in the study of consciousness?
    a. perception without awareness
    b. memory without awareness
    c. action without awareness
    d. all of the above

42. It has been suggested that consciousness is needed for:
    a. flexibility in processing
    b. automaticity in processing
    c. avoiding the deleterious effects of mental set
    d. promoting the use of analogy in reasoning

Answer Key for Self Test

1. c p. 223
2. c p. 224
3. c p. 225
4. a p. 226
5. d p. 226
6. b p. 227
7. a p. 229
8. c p. 230
9. a p. 230
10. d p. 230
11. c p. 230
12. d p. 231
13. d p. 232
14. c p. 234
15. c p. 234
16. a p. 236
17. b p. 235
18. c p. 236
19. d p. 238
20. c p. 238
21. c pp. 239–40
22. d pp. 232, 237, 241
23. d pp. 239–40
24. b p. 240
25. d p. 240
26. d p. 241
27. d p. 241
28. b p. 241
29. d pp. 241–42
30. d p. 242
31. c pp. 242–43
32. d p. 243
33. d p. 243
34. b p. 243
35. a p. 244
36. b p. 246
37. b p. 248
38. d p. 248
39. a p. 249
40. a p. 251
41. d pp. 251–52
42. a p. 253

Investigating Psychological Phenomena

THE STROOP EFFECT

Equipment: Included (see insert)
Number of subjects: One
Time per subject: Thirty minutes
Time for experimenter: Forty minutes

It is frequently observed that as people are given more experience at the task of reading, the skill becomes more and more automatic in character. One symptom of this increasing automatization is that it is difficult to prevent a skilled reader from reading material that he is exposed to. This appears to be a general characteristic of skills that become automated. Given the proper conditions for the occurrence of such a skill, it is difficult to inhibit it.

Since automatization is a prominent characteristic of skilled activities ranging from reading to motor behavior to problem-solving routines, it is useful to investigate it to determine its characteristics. One task that has been studied extensively in this regard is the Stroop task (turn to p. 235 in the text for a full description of the task). The following three experiments are designed to demonstrate the basic Stroop effect and to extend it somewhat so that you can develop some intuitions about why it occurs.

EXPERIMENT 1

First, before performing Stroop's actual demonstration you should conduct a simple version of it that will provide some baseline data on the effectiveness of our ability to ignore irrelevant information (see Chapter 6, "Perception," for a full discussion of this ability). In this experiment subjects are required to name colors. In the control condition of the experiment the colors are simply displayed in patches. In the experimental condition the colors are presented by having randomly ordered letter strings, each string of a different color. The question is whether having the letters present interferes with a subject's ability to name the colors. In principle, if the subject is capable of selectively attending to color, having the letters present should not interfere with his color-naming performance. Thus, naming the colors of the letter strings should be as easy as naming the colors of the color patches. On the other hand, the extent to which the subject cannot ignore the letter information is the extent to which his performance in color naming will decline.

Your measure of ease of color naming will be the amount of time it takes a subject to name a string of fifteen colors. To obtain reliable data you should have the subject name the colors in five lists of color patches and in five lists of letter strings, alternating between the two kinds of lists (see the number below each list).* The procedure is as follows: Cut out the ten lists of stimuli for experiment 1. On each trial have the appropriate list in front of the subject turned over so that he cannot see the stimuli (see book insert for these lists). Then read the following instructions:

> When I say "go," turn over the list in front of you and name the colors in the list from top to bottom. there will be fifteen colors total. Name these colors as fast but as accurately as possible. After you have named the last color, say "stop!" We will do this with ten different lists. Five have the colors printed in patches of ink the other five have the colors printed in strings of randomly arranged letters. You should *ignore* how the colors are presented and simply name them. Any questions?

You should keep time from when you say "go" until when the subject says "stop." Make sure to present the ten lists in the order indicated by the number under the list. Record the time elapsed for each list and the number of errors for each list in the spaces provided on the report sheet.

Average the times for each type of list and total the errors. Does it appear that there is a difference between the average naming time or the total number of errors comparing the two types of lists? How would you interpret the data?

EXPERIMENT 2

In this experiment you are going to duplicate Stroop's demonstration. In the previous experiment you probably found either no effect or a very small effect of list type. The question we now ask is: Are there any conditions under which the subject cannot selectively attend well? In this experiment we have constructed such a condition by having the letters in the experimental condition spell color words themselves. Subjects are still required to name the color of the word, not what it spells, but now the name of what it spells is itself going to be a color name. If selective attention is not very effective, these names should interfere with the subject's response and slow him down relative to a control condition that has neutral (noncolor) words printed in color.

Following the same procedure as before, but read the following set of instructions:

> In this experiment you are going to perform the same task as in the previous experiment. This time, however, the ink colors will be printed in the form of words. For half the lists, the words will be randomly chosen. For the other half, they will be color words. In both lists, however, you are to ignore the meaning of the words themselves and simply name the colors in which they are printed from the top to the bottom of each list. Remember that you should be as fast and as accurate as possible. Don't turn over each list until I say "go," and when you have finished be sure to say "stop!"

When you record the data, keep track of both the time to read the list and the number of errors made. Average the time and errors for each type of list. Is the difference in average time and total errors between list types greater than the difference found in experiment 1? How would you interpret this?

EXPERIMENT 3

Now we will try a somewhat more subtle version of the Stroop experiment to get a better idea of the extent to which the subject can selectively attend. In the experimental condition, the words printed in color represent nouns whose referents themselves have a characteristic color (this color is never the same as the color in which the word is written). If the word suggests the characteristic color of its referent to the subject, this color might interfere with naming the color in which the word is printed (Majeres, 1974).

Follow the same procedure as in experiments 1 and 2, but read the following instructions to the subject:

> In this experiment you are going to perform the same task as in the previous experiment; that is, you will be naming colors. This time the ink colors will be printed in the form of words that themselves are not colors. For example, one of the lists might contain the word "stove" printed in green ink. Disregard the word that is present and simply name the ink color of each word in the list. Remember that you should not turn over

* Notice that the two types of lists are matched for the length of the stimulus,. That is, the color patches of lists 1, 3, 5, 7, and 9 are matched in length to the letter strings of length 2, 4, 6, 8, and 10. Why is this an important control? How have the lists of experiments 2 and 3 been matched? Why?

the list until I say "go," you should name the colors as quickly as possible, and you should say "stop" when you are done.

Conduct this experiment as you did the others. Is there a difference in performance between the lists? It it larger or smaller than in experiment 2? What does this suggest about selective attention? What does it suggest about the automaticity of the reading process? *(If your instructor collects the data, fill out the report sheet in Appendix B.)*

References

Stroop, J. R. Studies of interference in serial verbal reactions. *Journal of Experimental Psychology,* 1935, *18,* 643–62.

Majeres, R. L. The combined effects of stimulus and response conditions on the delay in identifying the print color of words. *Journal of Experimental Psychology,* 1974, *102,* 868–74.

Report Sheet

Experiment 1

Color patch list

List 1 __________ sec. ___________ errors

List 3 __________ sec. ___________ errors

List 5 __________ sec. ___________ errors

List 7 __________ sec. ___________ errors

List 9 __________ sec. ___________ errors

Average = ___________ sec.

Total errors = ___________

Letter string list

List 2 __________ sec. ___________ errors

List 4 __________ sec. ___________ errors

List 6 __________ sec. ___________ errors

List 8 __________ sec. ___________ errors

List 10 _________ sec. ___________ errors

Average = ___________ sec.

Total errors = ___________

Experiment 2

Neutral words

List 1 __________ sec. ___________ errors

List 3 __________ sec. ___________ errors

List 5 __________ sec. ___________ errors

List 7 __________ sec. ___________ errors

List 9 __________ sec. ___________ errors

Average = ___________ sec.

Total errors = ___________

Color words

List 2 __________ sec. ___________ errors

List 4 __________ sec. ___________ errors

List 6 __________ sec. ___________ errors

List 8 __________ sec. ___________ errors

List 10 _________ sec. ___________ errors

Average = ___________ sec.

Total errors = ___________

Experiment 3

Neutral words

List 1 __________ sec. ___________ errors

List 3 __________ sec. ___________ errors

List 5 __________ sec. ___________ errors

List 7 __________ sec. ___________ errors

List 9 __________ sec. ___________ errors

Average = ___________ sec.

Total errors = ___________

Color referent words

List 2 __________ sec. ___________ errors

List 4 __________ sec. ___________ errors

List 6 __________ sec. ___________ errors

List 8 __________ sec. ___________ errors

List 10 _________ sec. ___________ errors

Average = ___________ sec.

Total errors = ___________

CHAPTER 9

Language

Learning Objectives

MAJOR PROPERTIES OF HUMAN LANGUAGE

Language is creative

1. Describe some phenomena that undermine the view that language is a habit.

Language is structured

2. What are the descriptive rules of language? Explain the difference between descriptive rules and prescriptive rules.

Language is meaningful

3. How do the words and grammar of a language contribute to meaning?

Language is referential

4. What does it mean for language to be referential?

Language is interpersonal

5. Give examples of how an unspoken principle of conversation makes communication successful in different social situations.

THE STRUCTURE OF LANGUAGE

6. What are the major hierarchical levels of linguistic structure?

Phonemes

7. What is a phoneme? Give examples.
8. Given what you now know about phonemes, and about human perception (Chapter 6), state why it is difficult for humans to understand unfamiliar speech.

Morphemes and words

9. What is a morpheme? Give examples.
10. How are morphemes combined?

Phrases and sentences

11. What is syntax?
12. How is the organization of words into phrases related to meaning?

THE LINGUISTIC HIERARCHY AND MEANING

13. How is the human ability to deal with the infinite number of items in any language explained?

The meaning of words

14. What is semantics?
15. Be prepared to argue why meaning is not the same as reference.
16. According to the definitional theory, how are word meanings stored in memory?
17. What convincing evidence exists for the prototype theory? How does this theory differ from the definitional theory?
18. What is a family resemblance structure?
19. How can one reconcile definitional and prototype theories?

Organizing words into meaningful sentences

20. Describe the subject-predicate structure of sentences and how this conveys meaning.

LANGUAGE DEVELOPMENT

Is language learning the acquisition of a skill?

21. Why is imitation insufficient to account for either sentence or word acquisition?

22. Characterize the kinds of speech corrections that children often receive and what these imply about language learning.

The social origins of speech production

23. Characterize the verbal behavior of the prelinguistic child.

Discovering the forms of language

24. Initially, infants are capable of responding to all sound distinctions made in any language. What change occurs in the later stages of language learning? Describe how the habituation paradigm is used to reveal this developmental change.

The one-word speaker

25. What kinds of words do children learn first? What kinds of words do children rarely learn first? Why?
26. Why is it difficult to study the acquisition of word meaning by children?
27. What are two common problems for the language learner who is trying to comprehend the meaning of a word?
28. Describe the selective looking experiment and its use in answering this question: Can propositions be conveyed by the child's single words?

The two-word (telegraphic) speaker

29. What changes in language take place around two years of age?
30. How are words ordered in two-word speech?

Later stages of language learning: syntax

31. What are typical language errors made by a two-and-a-half year old? What do these errors indicate about the structure of language?

Further stages of language learning: word meaning

32. Explain the categorization bias held by most language learners. What evidence helps psychologists to observe this bias?
33. Describe how children use their growing knowledge of word classes and semantics to interpret a word meaning.

LANGUAGE LEARNING IN CHANGED ENVIRONMENTS

34. What characteristics about the course of language acquisition suggest that it is a biological process?

Wild children

35. What does the study of wild children tell us about the nature-nurture controversy?

Isolated children

36. What does the study of isolated children tell us about language acquisition?

Language without sound

37. Describe the characteristics of American Sign Language (ASL). Why is this an important example of language from a theoretical point of view?

Language without a model

38. Describe the language-learner studies with deaf children of hearing parents. What do the results imply?

Children deprived of access to some of the meanings

39. Theoretically, blind children should learn sentence meanings more slowly than sighted children because blind children are cut off from opportunities to observe word referents. Nevertheless, evidence shows that the rate of language acquisition is not significantly different. Explain this finding, and relate it to what you have learned about categorization.

The case of Helen Keller

40. If isolated from language forms, a human infant begins to invent her own language. Describe how Helen Keller and Anne Sullivan invented language. Which characteristics of communication were carefully developed by Sullivan?

LANGUAGE LEARNING WITH CHANGED ENDOWMENTS

The critical period hypothesis

41. Summarize the evidence that points out the importance of critical periods in language learning.
42. Describe the initial difference between young learners of a second language and old learners. How does this difference change over time?
43. How does age relate to achieving native-level fluency?
44. Can you teach an old dog new tricks when it comes to language? Describe the evidence.

Language in nonhumans

45. Compare vocabulary learning in chimpanzees and humans. Which method works best to teach chimpanzees vocabulary?

46. Describe the evidence that suggests the use of primitive propositions by chimpanzees.
47. What evidence has suggested early syntax acquisition in chimpanzees? Be able to evaluate the quality of this evidence.
48. If we say that trained chimpanzees use language, what does our definition of language exclude?

LANGUAGE AND ITS LEARNING

49. Evidence suggests that language acquisition is a complex interaction of the child's innate capabilities, and the social, cognitive, and linguistic supports in the child's environment. Give examples of how each factor plays a role in learning language.

Programmed Exercises

MAJOR PROPERTIES OF HUMAN LANGUAGE

1. There are about ____________ human languages now in use on earth. — 4,000
2. Although animal and human languages are similar in that both have sounds and words (or something like words), animal languages do not have ____________. — sentences
3. We are able to make up novel sentences at will. This tells us that language is ____________. — creative
4. An estimate of the number of English sentences that are twenty words or fewer is ____________. — 10^{30}
5. A rule such as "it is not correct to say ain't" is a ____________ rule. — prescriptive
6. Each ____________ in a language expresses a meaningful idea or concept. — word
7. We are able to understand which words refer to which things, scenes, and events in the world. This tells us that language is ____________. — referential
8. A communicating pair takes the utterance and its context as the basis for making a series of complicated inferences about the meaning of a conversation. This tells us that language is ____________. — interpersonal

THE STRUCTURE OF LANGUAGE

9. We can think of language as existing at a number of levels, from sounds to ideas. The structure of language, then, is ____________. — hierarchical
10. The spoken words *bed* and *dead* differ only in the "b" and "d" sounds at the beginning. This is a difference in one ____________. — phoneme
11. English uses about ____________ speech sounds. — forty
12. Morphemes are the smallest language units that carry ____________. — meaning
13. "Strange," "er," and "s" are all ____________. — morphemes
14. The system by which we combine words into meaningful sentences is known as ____________. — syntax
15. An organized grouping of words is known as a ____________, the unit from which sentences are composed. — phrase

THE LINGUISTIC HIERARCHY AND MEANING

16. The fact that ____________ of units exists at each level of the hierarchy enables us to generalize what we know about constructing sentences. — organization

17. An old (and insufficient) view of word and phrase meaning is that meaning is whatever a word or phrase points to in the real world. This view equates meaning and ____________. — reference

18. Another view states that meaning is a kind of internal picture of whatever it refers to. This theory says that meanings are ____________ ____________. — mental images

19. Another theory says that the meaning of a word is synonymous with a list of characteristics, or ____________. This theory of meaning is called the ____________ theory. — features, definitional

20. The ____________ theory of meaning is similar to the feature theory, except that no one feature is necessary or sufficient. Instead, a whole group of features may be present. This theory accounts nicely for the fact that certain words are better examples of their respective categories than other words. — prototype

21. Words are related through groups of features shared unequally among word meanings. This concept is termed the ____________ ____________ structure. — family resemblance

22. When we say, "The girl climbed the tree," "climbed the tree" is the ____________ of the sentence, and "the girl" is the ____________. — predicate, subject

LANGUAGE DEVELOPMENT

23. Language learning by ____________ is not a sufficient explanation, since children often speak novel sentences. — imitation

24. ____________ cannot account for language learning, since it is impossible for the child to know what parts of a sentence are being praised. — Reinforcement

25. ____________ cannot account for language learning, since grammatical errors are seldom successfully changed by parents. — Correction

26. Childish sounds that make no real sense, but often sound like real words, are called ____________ . — babbles

27. Speech production is preceded by ____________ interactions such as looks, gestures, and caresses. — social (interpersonal)

28. Although infants can respond to all sound distinctions made in any language, they learn to ____________ the distinctions that don't matter in their language. — ignore

29. Two-word speech is known as ____________ speech. — telegraphic

30. Even though children utter only two-word sequences at one stage in their acquisition of language, there is reason to believe that they have ____________ parts to their propositional ideas. — three

31. After a child learns that the past tense of the verbs *play* and *walk* are *played* and *walked*, *runned* may be given as the past tense of *run* although *ran* was previously used. This phenomenon is known as ____________ . — overgeneralization

32. By two years old, the child is seeking ____________ ____________ that operate over the whole vocabulary or set of sentence structures. — general rules

LANGUAGE LEARNING IN CHANGED ENVIRONMENTS

33. Cases of wild children raised by animals were initially regarded as crucial cases for the ____________-____________ controversy about language development. — nature-nurture

34. Evidence that language can develop without sound comes from studies of ____________ children. — deaf

35. A widely used manual communication system among deaf people is ____________ ____________ ____________. — American Sign Language (ASL)

36. A biological ____________ enables children to learn language basics, whether they invent the basics themselves (if there is no language model) or follow the model that they are exposed to. — predisposition

LANGUAGE LEARNING WITH CHANGED ENDOWMENTS

37. When language capacities are lost or diminished because of damage to a cerebral hemisphere (usually the left), this state is termed ____________. — aphasia

38. One hypothesis of language learning postulates an ideal time to learn languages, after which the learning process is significantly more difficult. This time is known as the ____________ ____________. — critical period

39. In comparing adults with children, it is clear that ____________ pick up a second language more quickly than ____________ do. — children; adults

40. After having been taught ASL for four years, Washoe had learned __________ signs. Some of these were acquired by ____________, others by having her hands physically molded into a desired position. — 130; imitation

41. Premack's studies of the concept of ____________ in chimpanzees showed that they were quite successful in performing a task in which they were required to identify an object that could produce a change of state in another object. — causation

42. Even if chimpanzees were shown to have some sense of ____________, this would not be sufficient to claim that they have knowledge of syntax. — sequence

43. Studies with chimpanzees show that a precursor to language may be primitive ____________ thought. — propositional

LANGUAGE AND ITS LEARNING

44. Language acquisition is a task combining the child's innate capacities as well as the ____________, ____________, and ____________ environment of the child. — social, cognitive, linguistic

Self Test

1. A new group of people is discovered possessing a language that has never been studied before. After a good deal of work, linguists are able to translate anything said in this language into English. This is further evidence that all language:
   a. is unrelated
   b. is similar in the ideas that can be expressed
   c. uses the same sounds
   d. uses the same words

2. All of the following describe language use *except*:
   a. it is creative
   b. it has a rule-governed structure
   c. it is imitative
   d. it is interpersonal

3. The fact that there is an infinite number of sentences that can be uttered upon seeing a rabbit is an argument against the behaviorist position and demonstrates the ________ of language.
   a. uncertainty
   b. variability
   c. creativity
   d. rigidity

4. The fact that the words *boys*, and *kiss*, and *girls*, can be arranged in different orders to give different meanings (i.e., "Boys kiss girls," "Girls kiss boys") demonstrates another universal characteristic of language. Language is:
   a. rule-governed
   b. unpredictable
   c. implicit
   d. prototypical

5. The rules of grammar that structure a language are called:
   a. features
   b. morphemes
   c. semantics
   d. descriptive rules

6. The belief that knowledge of word meanings sets humans above animals is:
   a. a new belief
   b. a belief dating back to antiquity
   c. widely held by psychologists today
   d. both b and c

7. The problem of reference is complex because:
   a. speech is not an automatic response of the nervous system
   b. language is referential
   c. language is meaningful as well as referential
   d. all of the above

8. The actual speech acts that pass between people are merely hints about the thoughts being conveyed. Hidden from the observer are the unspoken, yet guiding:
   a. descriptions of conversation
   b. principles of conversation
   c. dialects
   d. utterances

9. When we say that language is hierarchical, we mean that:
   a. different language uses demonstrate social class differences
   b. language structure exists at many levels
   c. language has developed from other cognitive functions
   d. modern languages are descended from other languages

10. Which of the following represents the actual hierarchy of language structures?
    a. phrase, word, phoneme, morpheme
    b. word, morpheme, phrase, phoneme
    c. phoneme, morpheme, word, phrase
    d. morpheme, phoneme, word, phrase

11. The perceptual units of speech are:
    a. phonemes
    b. morphemes
    c. syllables
    d. words

12. One reason that foreign languages sound strange is that:
    a. the same phonemes are pronounced differently
    b. other languages are spoken more rapidly
    c. there are fewer "gaps" in foreign languages than in English
    d. some of the phonemes are different from those of English

13. A morpheme is a:
    a. word
    b. single sound
    c. perceptual unit
    d. unit of meaning

14. A phrase is:
    a. several sentences put together
    b. unrelated to the meaning of the sentence
    c. an organized group of words
    d. always delineated by grammatical markings

15. What makes possible the understanding of infinite numbers of sentences in a language?
    a. human memory alone
    b. the organization of units and patterns
    c. psychologists and neurolinguists cannot agree on what makes it possible
    d. humans cannot understand infinite numbers of sentences

16. The area of knowledge dealing solely with meaning is called:
    a. linguistics
    b. semantics
    c. phonetics
    d. none of the above

17. The study of semantics proceeds by:
    a. inventing new meanings for words
    b. updating standard dictionaries
    c. eliminating what is false about word meaning
    d. voting on the meaning of words

18. A view of meaning as simply referring to objects in the world is not sufficient since:
    a. the same object can be referred to in more than one way
    b. it's difficult to describe the reference of words like *truth*
    c. both of the above
    d. none of the above

19. The definitional theory attempts to define the ____________ attributes that define a given concept.
    a. necessary
    b. sufficient
    c. both of the above
    d. none of the above

20. One problem with the definitional theory is that:
    a. some attributes are used to describe more than one concept
    b. some concepts involve more than one attribute
    c. some concepts have no attributes
    d. some members of a category seem to be better examples of that category than other members

21. The major characteristics of a prototype theory of meaning is that:
    a. no feature is individually necessary
    b. no feature is individually sufficient
    c. a whole set of features describes word meaning
    d. all of the above

22. A robin will be judged to be an exemplary member of the bird family because:
    a. it has wings
    b. it has feathers
    c. the robin is close to the presumed prototype of a bird
    d. a robin is more like a bird than an ostrich

23. A family resemblance structure is an analogy to support which theory?
    a. prototype
    b. definitional
    c. interpersonal
    d. language attribution

24. Sentence meanings are often called:
    a. propositions
    b. predicates
    c. paraphrases
    d. phonemes

25. Which of the following can be used to explain first-language learning?
    a. imitation
    b. reinforcement
    c. correction
    d. none of the above

26. A major difference between deaf and hearing infants is that:
    a. while both babble, deaf children eventually stop vocalizing
    b. deaf children babble for a longer period of time than do hearing children

c. deaf children only babble in the presence of an adult
d. deaf children do not babble

27. All of the following are forms of preverbal communication *except*:
a. crawling
b. babbling
c. gesturing
d. touching

28. Which of the following statements is true about sound discrimination in early language learning?
a. Initially infants respond only to the sounds of their own language.
b. Initially infants respond to all sounds in all languages.
c. Initially infants cannot respond to sound distinctions at all.
d. Initially infants respond only to the most common sound distinctions of their own language.

29. Which of the following words is most likely to be among a child's first words?
a. push
b. wall
c. the
d. pain

30. Two-word speech is known as ________ speech.
a. functor
b. telegraphic
c. syntactic
d. propositional

31. By two-and-a-half years of age knowledge of ____________ begins to develop.
a. phonemes
b. propositions
c. syntax
d. synapses

32. The use of a word form like "sitted" by a child is known as:
a. telegraphic
b. undergeneralization
c. overgeneralization
d. syntactics

33. Which of the following is a "basic level" word?
a. beagle
b. animal
c. poodle
d. dog

34. Children are disposed to organize the world into broad ____________.
a. categories
b. syntax
c. phrases
d. ideas

35. Which statement(s) describe(s) how children learn language?
a. They use the forms of new words as clues to their meanings.
b. They use their knowledge of words to predict their forms.
c. They use their knowledge of sentence structure to plug in new words.
d. all of the above

36. Evidence from wild children who have been found reveals that:
a. some can be rehabilitated to use language without problems
b. some can learn to speak a few words
c. all can learn to speak a few words
d. none of the above

37. Language development does not depend on hearing language, as evidenced by:
a. wild children
b. ASL
c. isolated children
d. retarded children

38. Deaf children whose parents did not teach them sign language demonstrated language development similar to that of hearing children in that:
a. the children went through one-word speech, two-word speech, etc.
b. they began by pointing to "action objects," and only later "talking" about things like "walls"
c. they eventually put signs together to form sentences
d. all of the above

39. The following individuals were deprived of exposure to language since birth. Which one has the best chance of learning to speak?
    a. an eight-year-old girl
    b. a fourteen-year-old boy
    c. a twenty-year-old man
    d. a thirty-year-old woman

40. Helen Keller's experience is an example of how when human infants are isolated from language forms, they will:
    a. become incommunicative until adolescence
    b. need to be taught how to think
    c. begin to invent their own language
    d. become permanently incommunicative

41. The loss of language function is known as:
    a. aphasia
    b. anorexia
    c. asphyxia
    d. aphaeresis

42. The speech disorder characterized by loss of content in words is:
    a. Broca's aphasia
    b. expressive aphasia
    c. Wernicke's aphasia
    d. none of the above

43. First-language learning, second-language learning, and recovery from aphasia may depend on:
    a. intelligence
    b. the particular language involved
    c. generalization
    d. the critical period

44. When Washoe teaches some of her human signs to an adopted chimpanzee baby, it is an example of:
    a. cultural transmission
    b. language acquisition among chimpanzees
    c. syntax
    d. both a and b

45. Language in chimpanzees:
    a. seems to involve propositions
    b. uses a hierarchical structure
    c. approaches the complexity of human language
    d. progresses at about the same rate as for children

46. Some linguists argue that chimpanzees are held back by their basic ____________.
    a. syntax
    b. vocabulary
    c. intonation
    d. words

47. The nature of human language can be described by which of the following statement(s)?
    a. Fundamentally, languages are the same all over the world.
    b. All languages consist of a hierarchy of sentences.
    c. Language can flourish in virtually any exposure condition.
    d. all of the above

Answer Key for Self Test

1. b p. 257	25. d p. 270
2. c p. 258	26. a p. 271
3. c p. 259	27. a p. 271
4. a p. 259	28. b p. 271
5. d p. 259	29. a p. 272
6. d p. 260	30. b p. 275
7. d p. 260	31. c p. 276
8. b pp. 260–61	32. c p. 276
9. b p. 261	33. d p. 277
10. c pp. 262–63	34. a p. 277
11. a p. 262	35. d p. 277
12. d p. 262	36. b p. 278
13. d p. 262	37. b p. 280
14. c p. 263	38. d p. 281
15. b p. 264	39. a p. 286
16. b p. 264	40. c pp. 283–84
17. c p. 264	41. a p. 285
18. c pp. 264–64	42. c p. 285
19. c p. 265	43. d pp. 285–87
20. d p. 266	44. a p. 288
21. d p. 266	45. a p. 288
22. c p. 266	46. a p. 288
23. a p. 266	47. d pp. 289–90
24. a p. 267	

Investigating Psychological Phenomena

IMPLICIT LEARNING

Equipment: A stopwatch or a watch that indicates seconds, index cards
Number of subjects: One
Time per subject: Thirty minutes
Time for experimenter: Forty minutes

One of the most impressive aspects of language is its acquisition: Children learn an enormous amount about their language without ever being explicitly taught. Consider syntax, for instance. Not until children have already learned a substantial number of syntactic rules do parents correct syntactic constructions that their children use. Somehow the growing child manages to induce the syntactic rules of language from the variety of utterances that he or she happens to encounter. This ability to induce complex rules from examples is an ability that we use all the time, but its use without intention, or even awareness, and with complex linguistic construction is what makes it impressive as a characteristic of language acquisition. Having just learned about language acquisition, you can now begin to appreciate how complex the language-learning process must be, especially since it is largely mediated by implicit induction.

You can demonstrate this implicit induction process using the following experiment modeled after one by Arthur Reber (1967). There are two phases to the experiment. In the first place, your subject will memorize a series of strings letters after being told only that she is a subject in a memory experiment. In the second phase, the subject will be told that the letter strings from the first phase were constructed using a rule. Then the subject will be shown twenty-four new strings that she has never seen before and asked to judge which twelve of these were constructed from the same rule used in phase 1. If the subject correctly categorized more of these twenty-four strings than we would expect by chance alone (twelve by chance, since there are only two responses the subject can make), then we can conclude that the subject has learned something about the rule even though she wasn't trying to in phase 1.

PHASE 1

Instruct your subject as follows:

"This experiment concerns memory for unmeaningful material. You will be presented with twenty strings of letters that you must memorize and recall. These strings of letters will be presented in groups of four which you can study for fifteen seconds. Then the groups will be taken away and you will be required to recall all four strings (in any order). Following this you will be presented with the same strings again for another fifteen-second study period. This will be followed by another recall attempt. In all, the five groups of strings will be presented five times each for study and recall."

The stimulus materials for this first phase are at the end of this section. Write each of the five lists of strings on index cards and present them to the subject individually. Provide the subject with twenty slips of paper on each of which she can recall one quadruplet of strings. Be sure to remove each recall attempt before showing the next repetition of a set of strings or before going on to a new set of strings.

PHASE 2

Instructions:

"The strings of letters were constructed according to a rule. The rule dictated the order in which letters were allowed to follow one another. In the second phase you will be shown twenty-four new strings of letters, and you must decide for each one whether it was or was not constructed according to the same rule for the letter strings in phase 1. When you decide, you should place your answer in the appropriate place on the answer sheet."

Score the subject's answers after she has completed phase 2, using the answer key provided. Did she do better than chance? Ask her whether she has any guesses about what the rule is. You will probably be surprised to discover how little the subject appears to be aware of the rule even though she can use it (in some sense) to make judgments about individual instances.

A diagrammatic representation of the rule is shown below. It works as follows: If you begin at "start" and trace through the diagram along any path in the direction of the arrows, you can get to "end." By noting the order of the letters that you pass along the way, you can construct a string. Notice that because of loops, some strings may be quite long but still permissible according to the rule.

Think about some of the following issues: In what way does this experiment mimic language learning? In what way is language learning different? As a model of language learning, why was it important not to tell subjects about the rule until the end of phase 1? What do the results suggest about language learning?

Reference

Reber, A. S., Implicit learning of artificial grammars, *Journal of Verbal Learning and Verbal Behavior*, 1967, *6*, 855–63.

PHASE 1: STIMULUS LISTS

(Write these letter strings on index cards or pieces of paper for presentation to the subject.)

List 1	List 2	List 3	List 4	List 5
VVTRXRR	VVRXRR	VTRRR	VVTRXR	XMVTRX
XMVTTRX	XXRR	XMVRXRR	VTRR	XMTRRRR
XMVRXR	VVRMVRX	VVTTRMT	VVRMTRR	XMVRX
VVTRX	XMVRMT	VVRMTR	XMVTRMT	XXRRR

PHASE 2: LIST OF ALTERNATIVES FOR RECOGNITION TEST

(Write these letter strings on index cards as well.)

1.	RXTTVMXR	13.	VVTTRX
2.	XMTR	14.	VVRX
3.	MXXR	15.	VVRRRTX
4.	XMVRXRRR	16.	MT
5.	VVRXR	17.	VVTRMVRX
6.	VTTX	18.	VM
7.	MVTTXVR	19.	XXR
8.	XX	20.	XMT
9.	VRT	21.	RXTMV
10.	VVTTTRX	22.	XXM
11.	TTV	23.	TTRXXM
12.	VT	24.	VTR

RECOGNITION TEST REPORT SHEET

(You can find this report sheet in Appendix B; cut it out and give it to the subject.)

ANSWERS

1.	no	13.	yes
2.	yes	14.	yes
3.	no	15.	no
4.	yes	16.	no
5.	yes	17.	yes
6.	no	18.	no
7.	no	19.	yes
8.	yes	20.	yes
9.	no	21.	no
10.	yes	22.	no
11.	no	23.	no
12.	yes	24.	yes

RULE FOR LETTER-STRING CONSTRUCTION

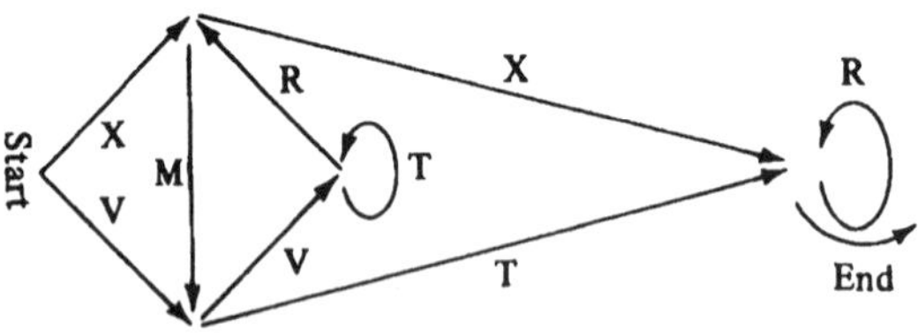

CHAPTER 10

The Biological Basis of Social Behavior

Learning Objectives

THE SOCIAL NATURE OF HUMANS AND ANIMALS

1. Explain Hobbes's conception of human nature.

Natural selection and survival

2. Outline the basic principles of Darwin's theory of evolution.
3. Distinguish personal from genetic survival, and indicate the role of sexual competition in the latter.
4. Does natural selection operate on behavior as well as on physical traits?
5. Are humans an inherently social species? Does Darwin's theory of evolution answer this question?

Built-in social behaviors

6. Describe the basic principles of ethology, including the concepts of display, fixed-action patterns, and releasers.
7. What is sociobiology?

BIOLOGICAL SOURCES OF AGGRESSION

Conflict between species: predation and defense

8. Is aggression a component of predatory attack?
9. Is it fair to describe much of aggressive behavior between different species as defensive? Explain.

Conflict between like and like

10. Discuss the relation between testosterone and aggression.
11. Discuss the nature and function of territories.
12. Explain mechanisms for limiting aggression in humans and in animals.
13. What are dominance hierarchies, and what are their functions?
14. Are humans territorial? Explain.

THE BIOLOGICAL BASIS OF LOVE: THE MALE-FEMALE BOND

15. What is bonding, and what is the role of grooming in primates in cementing relationships?

Sexual behavior

16. What is the selective advantage of sexual reproduction?

Sexual choice

17. Describe the nature and function of courtship rituals.
18. Discuss the evolutionary origin of displays, and indicate how the comparative method helps to discover this.
19. Explain why the female is more selective in mate selection than the male.

Reproduction and timing

20. Explain the role of sex-hormones in sexual behavior in animals and humans. Why is it said that the human female is emancipated from hormonal control?

Evolution and mating systems

21. Define polygyny, polyandry, and monogamy. Explain why most bird species are monogamous, while most mammals species are polygamous.
22. What is the relation between polygyny and sexual dimorphism?
23. What are differences in important characteristics sought in mates by human males versus females? What is the sociobiological account of these differences?
24. What is the sociobiological explanation of the predominance of polygyny in human cultures,

and the widespread tendency of men to be more interested in multiple sexual partners than women? What is the culturally oriented rejoinder to the sociobiological explanation?

THE BIOLOGICAL BASIS OF LOVE: THE PARENT-CHILD BOND

The infant's attachment to the mother

25. To what extent is the child's love for the mother explained by the fact that the mother fulfills the child's basic biological needs?

The mother's attachment to the infant

26. What is the function of maternal attachment?
27. What characteristics of the infant are important is establishing maternal attachment?

COMMUNICATING MOTIVES

Expressive movements: animal display

28. Describe the role of displays in communication. Why are displays sometimes called expressive movements?

The expression of emotions in humans

29. Review the evidence for human facial expressions as products of both biology and culture.

SOCIAL COGNITION IN PRIMATES

30. Describe evidence indicating that some primates identify individuals in their troop, and are aware of some of the relationships between individuals.

SELF-SACRIFICE AND ALTRUISM

Altruism in animals

31. Explain how self-sacrifice ("altruism") is consistent with evolutionary theory.
32. Distinguish among enlightened self-interest, kin selection, and reciprocal altruism as accounts for altruistic behavior.

Altruism in humans

33. Discuss sociobiological accounts of altruism in humans, and the criticism of this approach.
34. What, if any, are the ethical implications of something being a "part of human nature"?

ETHOLOGY AND HUMAN NATURE

35. Indicate the extent to which human social behavior can be explained in biological terms.

Programmed Exercises

THE SOCIAL NATURE OF HUMANS AND ANIMALS

1. The view that man is an inherently solitary creature, who invents society as a means of taming his brutish nature, is associated with the British philosopher ____________.	(Thomas) Hobbes
2. According to Darwin, evolution proceeds because variants of a species with superior characteristics are more likely to survive. This process is called ____________ ____________.	natural selection
3. Essentially, natural selection is not about literal survival, or ____________ survival, but about reproductive success, which amounts to ____________ survival. The latter leads to selection of traits that produce an advantage in ____________ competition.	personal genetic sexual
4. Those characteristics that confer survival and reproductive advantage are considered to have high ____________ ____________.	adaptive value
5. The branch of biology that studies animal behavior, particularly under natural conditions and within an evolutionary framework, is called ____________. It focuses on ____________-specific behavior.	ethology species

6. Stereotyped, species-specific movements are called ___________-__________ ___________. — fixed-action patterns

7. When a female stickleback enters a nest, the male prods her rhythmically at the base of her tail. This action causes the female to deposit her eggs, a species-specific response. We can term such prodding a __________ ___________. — releasing stimulus

8. Since this prodding stimulus is a product of the male's behavior, it can also be called a ___________. — display

9. ___________ is a branch of biology that emphasizes the evolutionary basis of social behavior. — Sociobiology

BIOLOGICAL SOURCES OF AGGRESSION

10. An attack by a lion on a zebra seems qualitatively different from a fight or threat sequence between two members of the same species. We call the former ___________ and the latter ___________. — predation, aggression

11. The generally higher level of aggression seen in males of most species has been attributed to higher levels of the male hormone ___________. — testosterone

12. Animals often defend a particular area against other members of their species. This area probably serves to guarantee them essential ___________ and is called a ___________. — resources, territory

13. Animals limit aggression by making ritualized communications, called ___________ ___________. — threat displays

14. One mechanism for limiting aggression involves a display that essentially indicates "surrender." Such a display is called an __________ ___________. — appeasment signal

15. In a ___________ ___________, a group of animals of the same species develops a stable social order based on the establishment of rank as a result of mutual aggressive encounters. — dominance hierarchy

16. A person walks up to a stranger, approaching her until their bodies are just inches apart. This can be considered a violation of ___________ ___________. — personal space

THE BIOLOGICAL BASIS OF LOVE: THE MALE-FEMALE BOND

17. The tendency to affiliate with others of one's own kind is called __________. — bonding

18. This is accomplished in some animals, such as monkeys, by activities including caring for the fur of another member of the species. This activity is called ___________. — grooming

19. In sexual reproduction, the ___________ and ___________ unite to produce the fertilized egg, or ___________. — sperm, ovum, zygote

20. The rooster's comb, the stag's antlers, and possibly the enlarged breast of the human female are all instances of structural ___________. — displays

21. The relatively complex behavior patterns that constitute sexual displays in many animals are called ___________ ___________. — courtship rituals

22. Courtship rituals indicate both the animal's ___________ and ___________. — intentions, species

23. In most species the ____________ (male or female) has the major role in "deciding" whether or not to mate. — female

24. Except for primates, mammals mate only when the female is in "heat" or ____________. — estrus

25. Implantations of male hormones, that is, ____________, into the part of the brain called the ____________, can cause a castrated male animal to show male sexual behavior. — androgens; hypothalamus

26. While the biological aspects of the human female reproductive cycle are controlled by hormones, in the human female, ____________ ____________ is relatively independent of hormones. — sexual activity (sexual behavior)

27. In general, in terms of mating systems, bird species are ____________, whereas mammal species are ____________. — monogamous; polygynous

28. There is usually more ____________ ____________, that is, structural differences between the sexes, in species that are ____________. — sexual dimorphism; polygynous

29. In human mate selection, males are more inclined to emphasize ____________ ____________, while females are more inclined to emphasize ____________ ____________ ____________. — physical attractiveness (youth); good financial (social) prospects

30. The sociobiological view predicts that, because of the lower investment that male mammals have in any reproductive act, the mating system of ____________ will be more common than its opposite, ____________, and that males will seek more ____________ in sexual partners than will females. — polygyny; polyandry; variety

THE BIOLOGICAL BASIS OF LOVE: THE PARENT-CHILD BOND

31. The human infant's cry or the chirp of a newly hatched bird are examples of ____________ calls. — distress

32. The ____________ is the human infant's built-in means of communicating with adults and maintaining their attention while indicating a generally positive state. — smile

COMMUNICATING MOTIVES

33. The message of a display can be inferred by noting the ____________ between the occurrence of the display and the animal's behavior just before and after the occurrence. — correlation (relation)

34. Some prefer to describe displays as indications of an animal's emotional state. In this respect, displays are referred to as ____________ ____________. — expressive movements

35. Human ____________ ____________ are displays that probably indicate emotional states. — facial expressions

36. Although there are some variations across cultures, there seem to be a number of ____________ human facial expressions. — universal

SOCIAL COGNITION IN PRIMATES

37. There is evidence that at least some free-living primates, such as vervet monkeys, are aware of the ____________ between other pairs of monkeys in their troop. — relationship

SELF-SACRIFICE AND ALTRUISM

38. "Self-sacrifice" by a parent animal can be understood within an evolutionary framework, since it may ultimately serve to increase the number of the parent's ___________ in the population.	genes
39. When this (question 38) is accomplished by sparing the lives of relatives, it is called ___________ ___________.	kin selection
40. "Unselfish" acts may also be adaptive because the recipients of these acts may later return the favor. This is called ___________ ___________.	reciprocal altruism
41. Certain "altruistic" behaviors, such as alarm calls, may actually promote personal survival, and hence are examples of ___________ ___________-___________.	enlightened self-interest
42. Edmund Wilson's view that altruism in humans is based in our genes is part of the general position of ___________.	sociobiology
43. The sociobiological view emphasizes genetic relatedness, or ___________, in explaining altruism.	kinship
44. Opponents of sociobiology argue that human altruism derives from __________ as opposed to ___________.	culture biology (genes)

ETHOLOGY AND HUMAN NATURE

45. Contrary to the position taken by Hobbes, it now seems clear that the human organism is, in its biological nature, a ___________ creature.	social

Self Test

1. Hobbes and Darwin agree that:
   a. natural selection is the key to understanding human nature.
   b. humans are basically solitary creatures
   c. humans are basically destructive
   d. humans enter a "social contract" to protect themselves from their brutish nature
   e. none of the above

2. Animal A lives 10 years and has 6 offspring. Animal B lives 8 years and has 10 offspring. Therefore:
   a. A has greater personal, B has greater genetic survival
   b. B has greater personal, A has greater genetic survival
   c. B is more successful in sexual competition
   d. A is more successful in sexual competition
   e. a and c

3. The Darwinian principle of natural selection implies that:
   a. social behavior cannot be subject to evolution because it is not inherited
   b. in the struggle to survive and reproduce, human beings are self-centered and solitary creatures restrained only by the constraints imposed by society
   c. social or altruistic behavior may evolve only if it serves to increase the frequencies of the genes of the animal showing this behavior
   d. coupled with the principles of ethology and genetics, social and altruistic behavior will evolve as long as there is appropriate display or communication
   e. a and b

4. Ethologists are particularly concerned with the study of:
   a. species-specific behavior
   b. behavior in natural settings
   c. social behavior
   d. all of the above
   e. none of the above

5. Releasing stimulus is to fixed-action pattern as:
   a. species-specific is to general
   b. cause is to effect
   c. learned is to innate
   d. predation is to aggression
   e. house is to door

6. Sociobiology:
   a. is concerned with evolutionary explanations of behavior
   b. claims a biological, evolutionary origin for some human social behavior
   c. holds, along with ethology, that many behaviors have a genetic basis
   d. all of the above
   e. none of the above

7. An observer notes that animal A, a male of a particular species, is, at a particular time, more aggressive than animal B. In an effort to increase the aggressiveness of animal B, the observer could:
   a. introduce a dominant animal of the same species into B's environment
   b. inject B with any sex hormone in an appropriate dose
   c. place B in its own territory and arrange for another male to approach the territory border
   d. place B in the territory of another male
   e. limit B's resources and deprive B of the releasers it would normally encounter

8. Aggressive encounters between members of the same species are often concerned with the establishment of:
   a. mobbing
   b. predation
   c. appropriate defense mechanisms
   d. territories
   e. displays

9. The adaptive value of territories is that they:
   a. increase the aggressiveness of the territory holder
   b. provide resources for the territory holder
   c. prevent threat displays
   d. decrease personal space and allow for greater reproduction
   e. c and d

10. The damage caused by aggressive encounters within a species is controlled by all but one of the following. Which of the alternatives is *not* a means of controlling aggression?
    a. appeasement signals
    b. assessing the strength of the enemy
    c. displays
    d. establishment of territories
    e. imprinting

11. Dominance hierarchies
    a. exist only in males
    b. are the basis of personal space
    c. confer reproductive advantages on those at the top
    d. guarantee equal distribution of resources
    e. increase aggressive encounters

12. This picture illustrates one stage of:

    a. predation
    b. defense
    c. feeding
    d. courtship
    e. contact comfort

13. Courtship rituals serve all but one of the following purposes. Which of the items below is *not* a function of courtship rituals?
    a. to synchronize the sexual activities of male and female
    b. to attract members of the opposite sex
    c. to increase the size of a territory
    d. to identify the sex and sexual readiness of the partners
    e. all of the above are functions of courtship rituals

14. To the extent that the male of a species spends time and energy in the care of the young, we would expect that:
    a. he would be more selective about mating partners

b. he would have higher levels of testosterone than expected
c. he would show more structural sexual displays
d. he would be less likely to have a territory
e. he would show more appeasement signals

15. During estrus, the female (nonprimate) mammal is:
a. secreting testosterone
b. most receptive to sexual approach of males
c. fertile
d. all of the above
e. b and c

16. In some species where the female has a clearly defined estrus cycle, the male is always ready for sexual activity. This would make sense if it were the case that in these species:
a. all females come into estrus at the same time
b. estrus is dependent on the season
c. estrus occurs throughout the year and females are not synchronized in their cycles
d. hormonal factors are especially important in determining the receptivity of the female
e. a and b

17. Which of the following features of human sexual behavior is shared most completely with other mammals?
a the hormone independence of female receptivity
b. the existence of sexual displays
c. the importance of learning in the sexual response
d. the persistence of sexual behavior following castration
e. b and d

18. Sociobiologists' predictions about male-female differences in mammalian mating systems and variety-seeking in sexual partners are based on the fact that female mammals have a greater investment in reproduction because they:
a. carry the offspring during pregnancy
b. take the greater responsibility for the early care of infants
c. account for a greater part of the genetic material of their offspring
d. all of the above
e. a and b

19. If you knew that in a particular species, the males sought more variety in sexual partners than did the females, you would guess that this species had a ____________ mating system.
a. monogamous
b. polyandrous
c. polygynous
d. dimorphic
e. b or c

20. According to the sociobiological account, a human female is inclined to emphasize financial/social security in selecting a mate because:
a. this improves the prospects for a successful upbringing of her children
b. males with higher status are more likely to be fertile
c. she is likely to give birth to more children
d. males with higher status are less likely to prefer polygyny
e. b and c

21. There is a tendency for human males to seek more variety in mates ("male promiscuity") than females. Which of the following is *not* evidence that this difference has a biological basis?
a. males have higher economic and social status in almost all cultures
b. male promiscuity appears cross-culturally
c. male promiscuity occurs in most mammalian species
d. male mammals have a lower investment than females in any particular offspring
e. female mammals carry and nurse their young

22. Features of the human infant, such as the upturned nose and chubby cheeks, are:
a. the stimuli through which we learn to recognize specific children
b. the vehicles for the establishment of basic trust
c. releasers of parental behavior
d. instances of distress displays
e. more common in monogamous cultures

23. Expressive movements by animal A may inform other members of its species about:
a. its current motivation
b. a motivational conflict that it is experiencing
c. how likely it is that it will behave in one way or another
d. a and b
e. all of the above

24. Some claim that at least some human facial displays are innately linked to certain emotional states. Which of the following *invalidate* such a view?

a. Across many cultures, people seem to associate the same facial expressions with the same situations (emotions).
b. Blind children show some of the basic facial expressions in appropriate situations.
c. Deaf children show some of the appropriate facial expressions in some situations.
d. On some occasions, some people can mask the facial expression they would normally make under the circumstances.
e. none of the above

25. Which of the following is (are) evidence for social cognition in nonhuman primates?
a. insight learning
b. awareness of kinship relationships between other members of the troop
c. awareness of dominance relations between other members of the troop
d. all of the above
e. b and c

26. Consider a case in which an animal risks death from a predator by distracting it from the children of the animal's sister. Which of the possibilities listed below is the most likely account of this "altruistic" behavior?
a. kin selection
b. reciprocal altruism
c. emancipation from hormonal control
d. all of the above
e. none of the above

27. Consider a different case, one in which animal A risks death from a predator by distracting the predator from another adult, B, of its species. And suppose that B is not related to A, and furthermore, that B is not a member of A's group, and is only transiently in A's presence. This apparently altruistic act would be easily accounted for as:
a. kin selection
b. reciprocal altruism
c. emancipation from hormonal control
d. a and b
e. none of the above

28. On a sociobiological (evolutionary and genetic) account, which of the following "altruistic" human acts would be most difficult to explain?
a. a man sacrificing his life to save four of his sister's children
b. a woman sacrificing her life to save four of her sister's children
c. a grandmother sacrificing her life to save one grandchild
d. a grandchild sacrificing his life to save one grandparent
e. a and c

29. Which of the following support(s) the cultural critique of sociobiology?
a. parents leave more money in their wills to their biological as opposed to their adopted children
b. some people list their best friend as the person to be called in an emergency
c. male homosexuals are more promiscuous than female homosexuals
d. in some societies, some close relatives (e.g., the maternal side) are ignored
e. b and d

30. Hobbes and the sociobiologists would agree that:
a. there is something that might be called basic (biological) human nature
b. humans are inherently social
c. any apparently selfish act of humans is a result of culture and works against basic human nature
d. humans are basically aggressive
e. none of the above

Answer Key for Self Test

1. e p. 296
2. e p. 297
3. c p. 297
4. d p. 298
5. b p. 298
6. d p. 299
7. c p. 301
8. d p. 301
9. b p. 301
10. e pp. 302–3
11. c p. 303
12. d p. 307
13. c pp. 307–8
14. a p. 308
15. e p. 309
16. c p. 309
17. b pp. 309–10
18. e pp. 311–12
19. c p. 310
20. a p. 311
21. a p. 312
22. c p. 315
23. e p. 316
24. e p. 316
25. e p. 319
26. a p. 321
27. e pp. 321–22
28. d p. 322
29. e pp. 322–23
30. a p. 323

Investigating Psychological Phenomena

PERSONAL SPACE: BEHAVIOR IN ELEVATORS

Equipment: A bank of at least two public elevators
Number of subjects: None
Time pre subject: None
Time for experimenter: Thirty minutes to one hour

Whatever one's view of the precise way in which the basic phenomena of territoriality in animals are experienced in humans, it is clear that humans prefer to avoid close contact with strangers. Strangers interact at respectable distances, and one typically feels uncomfortable when a stranger approaches to within much less than a meter. Observations of this sort lead to the notion of personal space, a "territory" around the body. The distance spacing of students seated at libraries or riders on public transportation speaks to the same issue.

In this study we will attempt to gather direct evidence for the idea of personal space. To do so, we must find a common situation in which strangers find themselves in close confinement. Elevators seem particularly suited for this study.

Our study will be based on observations of where people stand in elevators. Given that an elevator already requires that all riders stand in close proximity, a personal space approach would certainly predict that *strangers* would maximize the distance between them. In order to test this idea, we will have to make some decisions about where, when, and how to make observations. (Although it would seem easy to just go and observe people in elevators, to do so without some thought, planning, and preliminary casual observation, would almost surely result in unreliable and not very meaningful data.)

What are the predictions? We must realize that elevators are typically asymmetrical: there is a door on one wall, and there is usually a button panel on one or both sides of the door. When people enter, they normally go to the panel to see if their floor has been pressed. Since it is likely that each person who gets on will go to the panel, it would be natural to maximize the distance from the panel in anticipation of the arrival of the next person. A personal space approach would also predict that strangers would not look at each other, but rather would tend to look straight ahead (toward the door) or up or down. On the basis of personal space, we would make the following predictions with respect to the positions in the schematic elevator diagrammed below.

1. In elevators with only one rider, the rider would usually stand along the back wall. In anticipation of a second rider, the first rider would be expected to stand in one back corner, thus leaving the other back corner for the second rider (and keeping both away from the button panels, which an additional rider would approach on entering). In terms of the schematic elevator layouts on the next page, a single person should be located either in square 7 or square 9.
2. The second rider would be inclined to maximize distance from both the first rider and a potential third rider, who would be expected to approach the button panel(s) on entering the elevator. Therefore, in the schematic elevator layout below, two people should occupy squares 7 and 9. (Note: squares 7 and 6, 4 and 9, and 4 and 6 would also constitute reasonable distributions, but would not be as optimal as 7 and 9.)

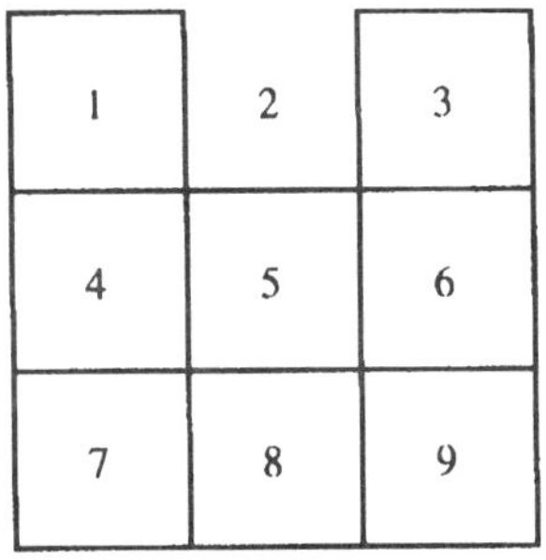

1	2	3
4	5	6
7	8	9

Schematic elevator, divided into a 3×3 unit array. The door is at 2.

Conditions of Observation: The observer cannot be on the elevator, as he would then be influencing the results. Therefore, observations must be made when an elevator arrives or departs and the door is open. Since people are likely to be leaving or entering, quick observations will be necessary at a stable moment: just as the doors open or just as they close. (If you are lucky enough to be near an office or other building with video security monitors for the elevators in the lobby, you can use the monitors to record the positions of people between floors.)

Personal space rules would not necessarily hold among friends, and certainly not between lovers.

Therefore, a fair test of personal space should eliminate any data including people who know each other well. To do this as best as possible, we will adopt two policies:

1. We will eliminate any observation (that is, the data collected from any particular elevator at a particular time) if any two people in the elevator are talking to one another or showing personal involvement in any way (e.g., holding hands).
2. We will try to make observations at places and at times when the number of people knowing each other well would be minimal. Ideal locations would be elevators in department stores or office buildings. Time would also be an important factor. We should avoid taking observations around the noon hour. (Why? Because it is very common to go out to lunch with friends, so the level of friend pairs or groups in elevators might be particularly high. This holds as well for people returning from lunch.)

Finally, precise conditions of measurement must be determined. Only record stable patterns: No one should be moving. Your critical time for observation is the moment before the doors close (it is harder to use the moment they open, because it is likely that a passenger intending to exit has moved toward the door as the elevator comes to his or her floor). If, at the time of departure, the elevator contains one or two people who have settled into position and if they do not appear to be friends (by the criteria above) then record their location on the data sheet. Assign each person to whichever of the nine squares best locates him or her.

To minimize data collection time, try to find a bank of elevators (at least two), and try to go at a time of moderate use, so you won't have to deal with infrequent or empty elevators. But don't use the lunch period, as discussed above. Normally the first floor is the natural place to make observations. But if you have a great deal of trouble with subjects moving in the elevator, you could go to another floor and push the call button, so that the elevator will stop on your floor. (The second floor would be best for these purposes. Why?)

Make sufficient observations so that you can get fifteen cases of elevators with one rider and fifteen of elevators with two riders. Indicate on the two data sheets the plan of the elevator, its location, and the time of day. Record one-person elevators on one data sheet and two-person elevators on the other.

When you have fifteen observations of each type, enter your data in the boxes in the table below. Do your data support the personal space theory? In order to help you make this evaluation, we have given you an indication of what would be statistically significant findings.

For the one-person elevator, there are nine possible positions. The theory predicts that one of two positions (7 or 9) will be occupied. If people positioned themselves randomly in the elevator, we would expect them to be at 7 or 9 2/9 of the time, or for fifteen cases, $2/9 \times 15 = 3.3$ times (see table). By statistical calculations, we have determined that if there was actually an equal chance of someone's standing in any square, the chances of finding nine or more subjects out of fifteen in squares 7 or 9 is less than one in 100. This seems highly unlikely, so we would reject the idea that people stand randomly in the elevator and claim that the results supported the personal space hypothesis. These calculations are worked out in the table.

For the case of two people in the elevator, we have made similar calculations. It turns out that there are thirty-six different pairs of spaces that could be occupied in our 9-square elevator. The 7-9 combination is just one of them, and hence, if people were standing in random positions, there would only be one case in thirty-six where the 7-9 position was occupied. Therefore, the expected number of 7-9 locations in fifteen trials would be $15 \times 1/36 = 0.4$. A value of three or more people in this pair of locations would come about by chance less than one time in 100.

We can use one other measure with the two-person elevators. Personal space theory predicts, in general, that these people will stand far apart. We can translate this into the prediction that two people will not stand in boxes that are touching (even on the diagonal). Pairs 7-9, 4-6, 1-9 and others would meet this criterion. Although, of the thirty-six pairs of locations, twenty are touching (contiguous). Thus, we would expect that (since there are sixteen nontouching pairs), in 16/36 × 15 cases, we would expect people in nontouching pairs, assuming that people distributed themselves randomly. A score of twelve or more pairs in nontouching squares would come about less than one time in 100 by chance and would be evidence for the personal space hypothesis. (See calculations in table below.)

For comparison purposes, we have made measurements like those we asked you to make in this study. We took advantage of a special situation that allows unusually easy data collection. The data we present comes from elevators in an office building in New York City. In this building, there is a video security camera in the ceiling of each elevator. Therefore, we could watch the bank of video monitors, and record the location of people. Furthermore, we could make the measurements between floors, so that there was no movement to or from the door. *(If your instructor collects the data, fill out the report sheet in Appendix B.)*

Analysis of Results

Elevator type	Location prediction	# in predicted place/Total	Expected random #	# significant*
1 person	7 or 9	□/15	3.3	9
2 person	7 and 9	□/15	0.4	3
New York data				
1 person	7 or 9	28/57	12.7	20
2 person	7 and 9	15/32	0.9	5

		# in noncontiguous squares/Total	Expected random #	# significant*
2 person	16 noncontiguous pairs out of 36 total pairs	□/15	6.7	12
New York data				
2 person	16 noncontiguous pairs out of 36 total pairs	31/32	14.2	21

* # significant means that one would expect this or a larger number of cases by chance no more than one time in one hundred.

Indicate panel location and other unusual features on diagram below.

Name ____________________ Location ____________

1 Person in Elevator

Time ____________

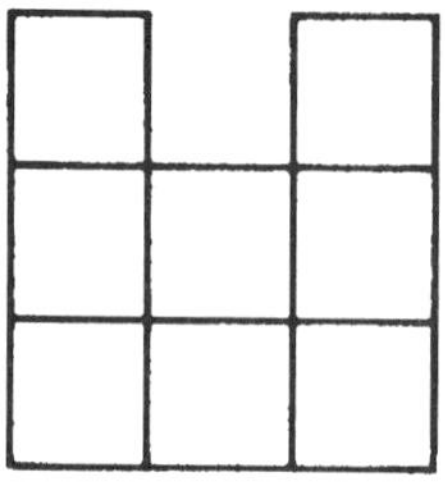

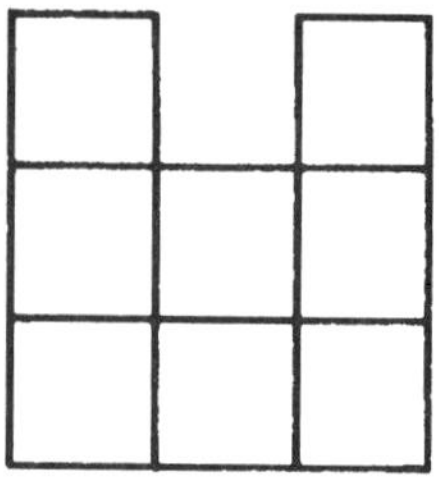

1

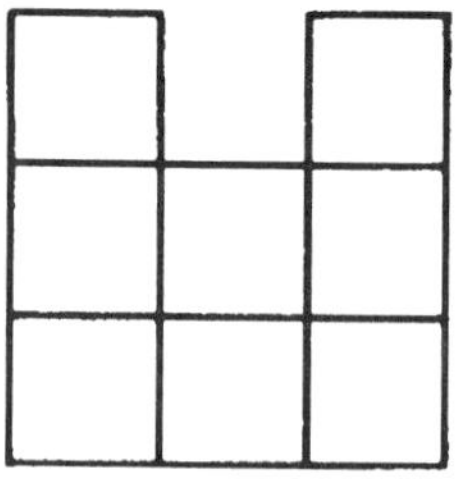

2

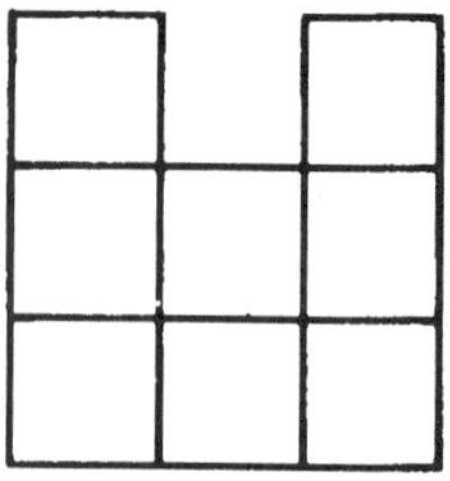

3

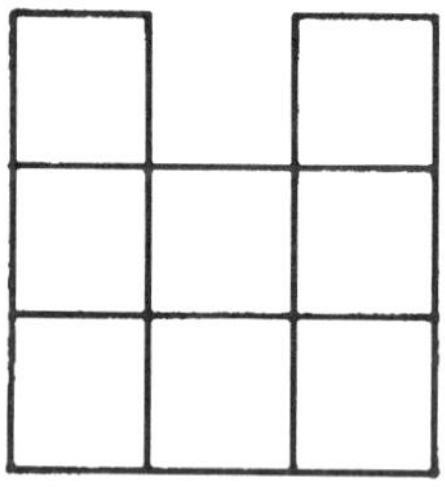

4

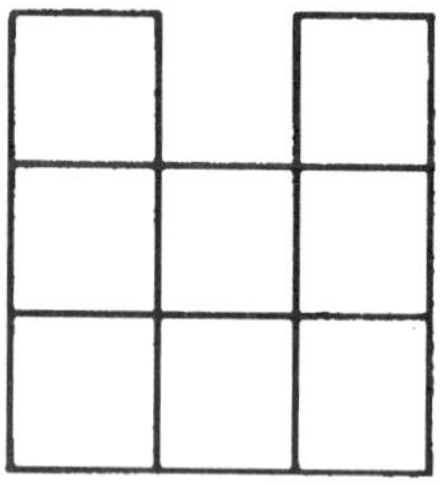

5

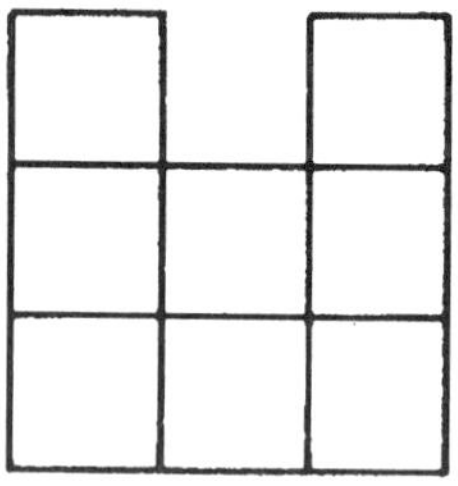

6

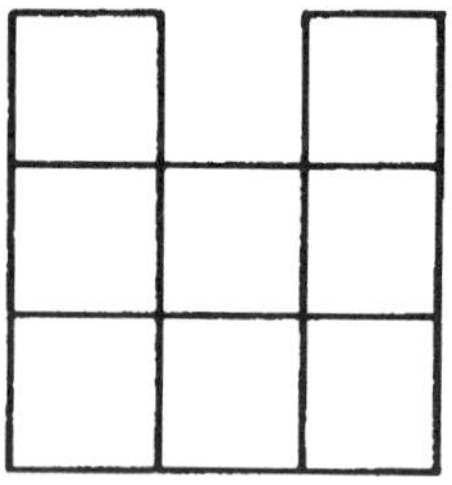

7

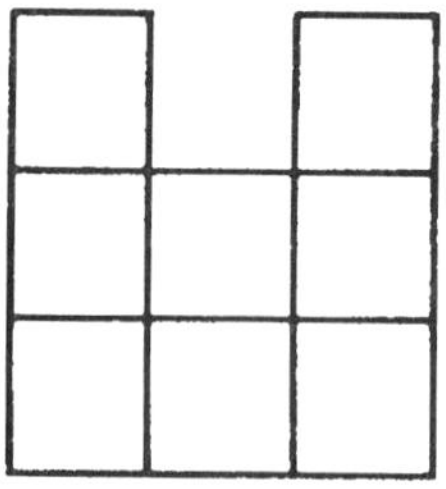

8

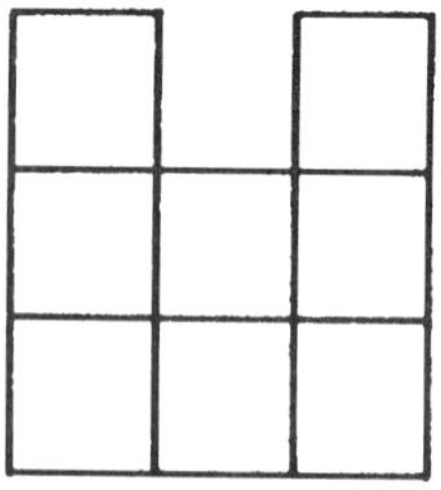

9

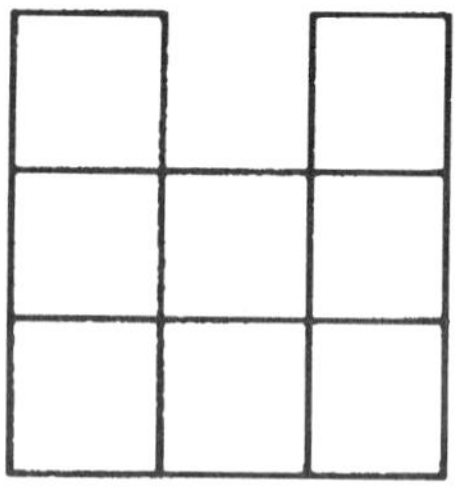

10

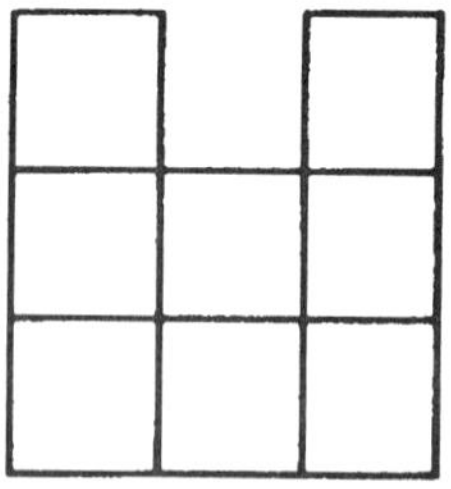

11

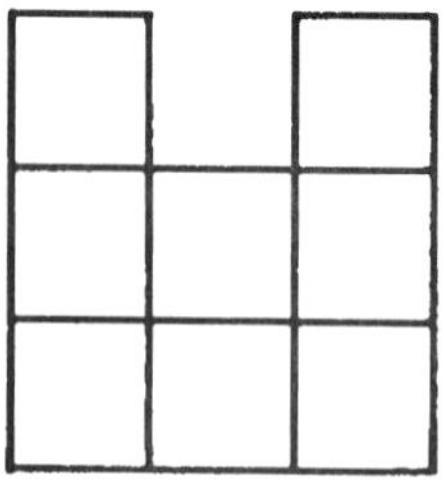

12

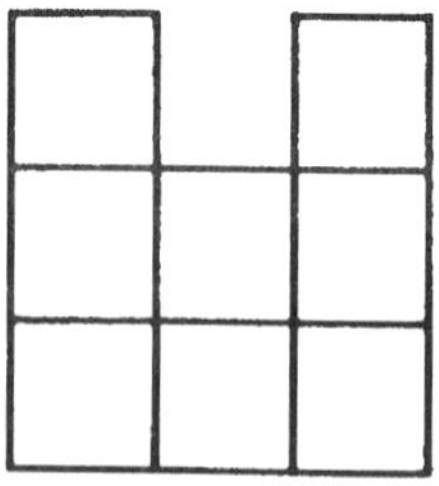

13

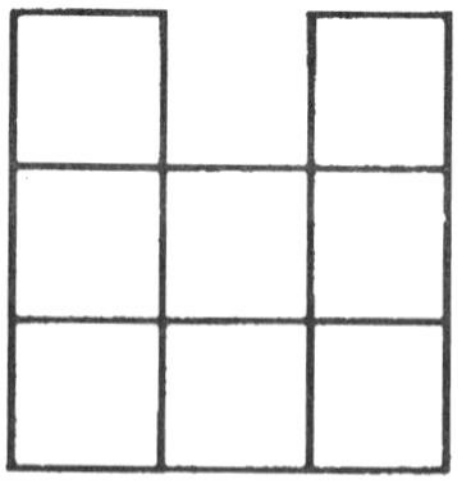

14

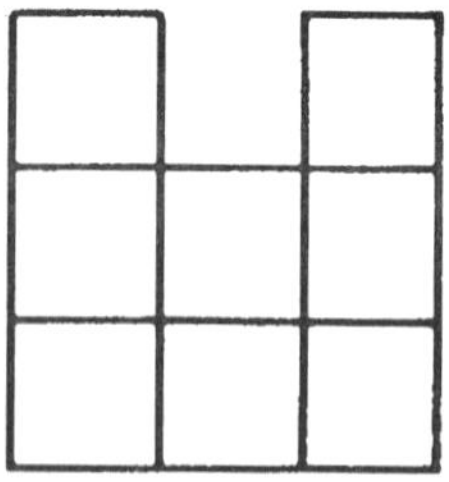

15

Indicate panel location and other unusual features on diagram below.

Name ______________________ Location ____________

2 Persons in Elevator Time ______________

1

2

3

4

5

6

7

8

9

10

11

12

13

14

15

FURTHER STUDIES

1. You can extend these observations. In elevators with a button panel on one side of the door, you can make the further predictions that: 1. the first person will stand in the back corner opposite to the panel; 2. in three-person elevators, the third person should stand in the front corner that does not have the button panel.
2. You can extend this study to elevators with three persons. In elevators with two-button panels, it is hard to make precise predictions about where people will stand (see item 1 above, for predictions in single-panel elevators). However, personal space theory would predict that people would stand as far apart as possible, so that they should not stand in contiguous squares. There are eighty-four possible arrangements of three people, assigned to three of the nine squares. Only nine of these eighty-four arrangements involve no person in a square contiguous to another (e.g., 1, 3, 9; 6, 1, 7; 1, 3, 8). Run another fifteen elevators, this time with three persons. How many have no one in a square contiguous with any other? We would predict, based on random location of people, 9/8 4 × 15 = 1.6 cases of people in noncontiguous squares. A significant result (less than one time in 100, by chance) would be six or more cases out of fifteen with no one in contiguous squares.
3. You can make observations like the elevator observations in any place where strangers are in an enclosed area. Library tables or seats on vehicles of public transportation are natural places to see if distance between strangers are maximized.
4. What do you think would happen if the rules of personal space were purposely violated? How would the desire for privacy and isolation from strangers affect the behavior of the person violated? Also, do you think that the sex of the subjects, in cases when there are two or more persons per elevator, would be influential in any way?

CHAPTER 11

Social Cognition and Emotion

Learning Objectives

1. Distinguish human from animal social behavior in terms of complexity, culture, and social cognition.

SOCIAL COGNITION AND SOCIAL REALITY

The interpersonal nature of belief

2. What is social cognition?
3. Describe Asch's experiment on the social basis of physical "reality," and indicate why subjects become upset in this study.

Social comparison

4. What is social comparison, and how does it function in ambiguous situations?

Cognitive processes and belief

5. What is meant by cognitive consistency?
6. Explain cognitive dissonance and give an example.

ATTITUDES

7. Define attitudes and distinguish between attitudes and beliefs.

Attitudes and behavior

8. How good is the relation between attitudes and behavior? Indicate some factors that could explain discrepancies between attitudes and behavior.

Attitude change

9. What accounts for the effectiveness of persuasive communications? Review the role of the message source and the message.
10. Describe the central and peripheral routes to persuasion, and indicate the role of heuristics.
11. Explain how aspects of cognitive dissonance, particularly bringing one's own behavior into line with one's attitudes, causes attitude change. Include justification of effort and forced compliance in the discussion.
12. Describe how protecting the self-picture can account for many instances of attitude change, and distinguish this motivation from cognitive consistency.

PERCEIVING OTHERS

Forming impressions

13. How is visual perception analogous to social perception?

Impressions of others as patterns

14. Describe Asch's experiments on impression formation.

Impressions of others as cognitive constructions

15. What are the parallels between cognitive constructions of the physical and social worlds?
16. Indicate the roles of schemas and implicit theories of personality in social cognition and impression formation.
17. What are stereotypes, and what is the role of illusory correlation in maintaining inaccurate stereotypes?

ATTRIBUTION

Attribution as a rational process

18. Indicate the parallels between scientific thinking and the attribution process.

19. What are situational dispositional factors in the attribution process?

Errors in the attribution process

20. Evaluate the roles of situational and dispositional factors in judgments about other people. What is the fundamental attribution error?
21. What is the actor-observer difference?
22. Why are people more inclined to make situational attributions about their own behavior, as opposed to the behavior of others (the actor-observer difference)? Indicate the role of different information and different perspectives.
23. What is the self-serving attributional bias?

PERCEIVING ONESELF

The self-concept

24. Describe the factors that contribute to the developing perception of the self.

Self-perception and attribution

25. What is self-perception theory? What is the evidence for the influence of one's own behavior on one's attitudes?

EMOTION: PERCEIVING ONE'S OWN INNER STATES

The James-Lange theory

26. Describe the James-Lange theory of emotion and the major objections to it.

The attribution-of-arousal theory of emotion

27. Describe the attribution-of-arousal theory of emotion put forth by Schachter and Singer. Contrast this theory with the James-Lange theory. What is the role of physiological state in each theory?
28. Discuss the misattribution of emotion in light of the attribution-of-arousal theory.

Beyond attribution-of-arousal theory

29. What is the relation between facial expressions and emotion? What is the evidence for a group of fundamental emotions?
30. How can a small number of fundamental emotions produce a much larger number of experienced emotions?

TAKING STOCK

31. Evaluate the contribution of motivational (passion) and cognitive (reason) factors in social cognition and emotion.

Programmed Exercises

1. Human social behavior is more ____________ than animal social behavior, and includes a major influence from ____________.	complex (flexible) culture

SOCIAL COGNITION AND SOCIAL REALITY

2. The way we try to interpret and understand social events, that is, ____________ ____________, is like the way we comprehend nonsocial events.	social cognition
3. In Asch's experiment on judging line length, subjects become disturbed because the behavior of the confederates challenges their shared sense of ____________ ____________.	physical reality
4. When people have to make difficult judgments, they often seek the opinion of others, demonstrating the need for ____________ ____________.	social comparison
5. ____________ ____________ refers to people's tendency to resolve contradictions between their attitudes and beliefs.	Cognitive consistency

6. The perception by a person of inconsistency in beliefs, feelings, or behavior sets up an unpleasant internal state called____________ ____________. — cognitive dissonance

ATTITUDES

7. An ____________ is a rather stable, evaluative mental position held toward some idea or object or person. — attitude
8. Unlike beliefs, attitudes are ____________. — evaluative (or emotionally tinged)
9. ____________ as opposed to ____________ attitudes are better predictors of behavior. — Specific, general
10. Messages that openly try to convince us of something, called ____________ communications, are more effective if they come from a ____________ and ____________ source. — persuasive, credible, trustworthy
11. There may be two routes to persuasion. One, the ____________ route to persuasion, involves careful consideration of arguments. The other, the ____________ route to persuasion, demands less attention and makes use of shortcuts, or ____________. — central, peripheral, heuristics
12. According to dissonance theory, a goal will be valued all the higher, the ____________ it was to reach. — harder
13. Attitudes toward a goal often become more positive after a person makes sacrifices to attain the goal. This is called retrospective ____________ of ____________. — justification, effort
14. If people behave inconsistently with their beliefs under ____________ ____________, they are unlikely to change their beliefs or attitudes. — forced compliance
15. An alternative to cognitive consistency as an explanation of attitude change involves more emotional or evaluative factors, and is described as protecting the ____________ - ____________. — self-picture

PERCEIVING OTHERS

16. In both object and person perception, the observer extracts certain ____________ from the flow of events. — consistencies (invariances)
17. According to Asch, both form perception and person perception result from combinations of attributes into ____________ wholes. — organized
18. Impressions of others can be seen as patterns, based on the relations among elements. One basis for this process is a set of organized expectations about the way in which different behaviors of people hang together, called a ____________ or an ____________ ____________ of personality. — schema, implicit theory
19. Simplified schemas applied to whole groups are called ____________. Some inaccurate stereotypes are maintained by a tendency for people to see expected relations, even if these relations do not actually exist. This process is called ____________ ____________. — stereotypes, illusory correlation

ATTRIBUTION

20. ___________ is a process through which people infer the causes of other people's behavior.	Attribution
21. Studies of attribution show that in judging others people tend to rely too much on internal causation, or ___________ factors, as opposed to ___________ factors in explaining behavior. This is called the ___________ ___________ ___________.	dispositional, situational fundamental attribution error
22. People are more likely to attribute their own (as opposed to others') behavior to situational factors. This is called the ___________-___________ ___________.	actor-observer difference
23. The tendency to make dispositional attributions for one's own success, and situational attributions for one's own failures, is called the ___________-___________ bias.	self-serving

PERCEIVING ONESELF

24. Bem and some other cognitive social psychologists believe that conceptions of the self are built up from attribution processes of the same type used in forming conceptions of other people. This position is called __________-___________ ___________.	self-perception theory
25. According to this theory, ___________ determines attitudes, rather than the other way around.	behavior
26. The " ___________-__________-__________-___________" technique is an example of how behavior can lead to attitude change.	foot-in-the-door

EMOTION: PERCEIVING ONE'S OWN INNER STATES

27. According to the ___________-___________ theory, the subjective experience of emotion results from our awareness of bodily changes in the presence of certain stimuli.	James-Lange
28. According to Schachter and Singer's ___________-___________-___________ theory of emotion, emotion depends on the interpretation of autonomic ___________ by a subject, in light of the total situation.	attribution-of-arousal arousal
29. Studies of facial response patterns in different emotional situations suggest that there are about six to ten ___________ emotions.	fundamental
30. According to the ___________-___________ view, facial expressions are primarily representations of internal emotional states.	read-out
31. Some suggest that facial expressions can be suppressed or enhanced by learned, culture-based ___________ ___________.	display rules

Self Test

1. Primate and human social behavior have in common:
   a. displays
   b. a role for social cognition
   c. some type of territorial defense
   d. all of the above
   e. a and c

2. In Asch's experiment on the effect of social pressure on judgments of noticeably different line lengths, he found that:
   a. many subjects yielded to social pressure, but their perception of line length did not necessarily change
   b. the actual perceptions of line length were changed in the subject
   c. the perceptions of line length were changed in the confederates
   d. the shared sense of physical reality can affect perception
   e. a and b

3. Indicate which of the following statements about social comparison is *false*:
   a. Social comparison is more likely to occur when someone is faced with a difficult decision.
   b. Social comparison is more likely to occur in a situation in which there is some ambiguity.
   c. Social comparison is more likely to occur when people feel they need more information.
   d. Social comparison is more likely to occur when the decision involves social issues.
   e. none of the above are false

4. Fred supports the cause of the A's, in their war against the B's. He then sees on television that the A's are killing innocent children. He decides that the A's must have been forced to do this by the B's and that the A's have no choice. This type of thinking in Fred is an example of:
   a. social comparison
   b. stimulus-response association
   c. resolution of cognitive dissonance
   d. reference to comparison groups to change attitudes
   e. all of the above

5. Sandy holds that French food is good and Canadian food is bad. These views represent:
   a. attitudes
   b. beliefs
   c. cognitive consistency
   d. cognitive dissonance
   e. actions

6. Attitudes are usually measured by:
   a. questionnaire
   b. observation of behavior
   c. experimental studies
   d. physiological measures
   e. a and c

7. Attitudes do not always predict behavior. This could be because:
   a. attitudes, as measured, are often very general, and behavior deals with specific situations
   b. attitudes are evaluative and behavior is not
   c. behavior is hard to measure accurately
   d. behavior is not affected by cognitive consistency or cognitive dissonance
   e. a and c

8. Someone using the peripheral route to persuasion is likely to:
   a. have cognitive dissonance
   b. use heuristics
   c. show more cognitive consistency
   d. have fewer attitudes
   e. pay special attention to events in the periphery

9. According to cognitive dissonance theory, which of the following would be the best way to cause people to change attitudes?
   a. pay them a lot to make them believe they hold the new attitude
   b. force them to behave as if they support the new attitude for at least a few weeks

c. tell them that they will be considered prejudiced if they continue with their current attitude
d. show them that their current attitude is inconsistent with their actual behavior
e. urge them to consult with an appropriate social comparison group

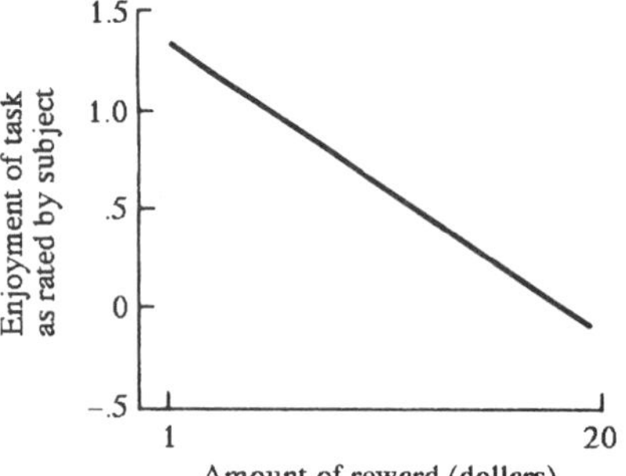

10. The graph above illustrates the relation between:
    a. attitudes and beliefs
    b. cognitive dissonance and forced compliance
    c. cognitive dissonance and cognitive consistency
    d. social comparison and ambiguity
    e. cognitive dissonance and beliefs

11. After working as a volunteer for a political candidate for a month, Jonathan finds that his support for the candidate has increased, even though he has never met her. This is an instance of:
    a. forced compliance
    b. justification of effort
    c. persuasive communications
    d. a and b
    e. all of the above

12. Which of the following techniques is *not* considered an effective way to produce a positive change in attitude toward a message?
    a. use of a credible and trustworthy source
    b. use of a message that is regarded favorably by a social comparison group
    c. openly forcing a person to behave in a way that supports the message
    d. linking the message to past behavior by the person that supports the message
    e. c and d

13. An alternative to the view that attitude change results from attempts to create logical consistency invokes emotional factors that motivate creation of:
    a. cognitive consistency
    b. a favorable self-picture
    c. retrospective reevaluation
    d. justification of effort
    e. post-decision dissonance

14. Perception of objects and people have in common the fact that:
    a. both rely almost exclusively on vision
    b. both involve the construction of stable or invariant characteristics
    c. both are fixed in their nature by first impressions
    d. both involve the resolution of cognitive dissonance between the object (or person) and its perception
    e. none of the above

15. Stereotypes:
    a. are always inaccurate
    b. may be distorted because of illusory correlation
    c. are not like heuristics, because they lead to incorrect conclusions
    d. may be accurate
    e. b and d

16. There are parallels between nonsocial and social cognitions. Which of the following processes does *not* appear in both types of situations?
    a. illusory correlation
    b. use of heuristics
    c. use of schemas
    d. attempts to simplify complex situations
    e. all of the above appear in both types of situations

17. The decision by a person that another person's behavior was internally caused, e.g., as a result of his aggressive nature, is an example of:
    a. cognitive consistency
    b. illusory correlation
    c. stereotypes
    d. attribution
    e. situational factors

18. People have a tendency to believe that actors in the theater are really like the roles that they play. This is an example of:

a. the resolution of cognitive dissonance
b. the dominance of dispositional over situational factors in attribution
c. impression formation
d. the distinction between the bodily self and the social self
e. the interaction of social and biological factors in the determination of behavior

19. The actor-observer difference describes the fact that people are *less* likely to make __________ attributions about themselves than others.
a. dispositional
b. correct
c. cognitively consistent
d. situational
e. c and d

20. Explanations of the actor-observer difference include the fact that:
a. people know themselves better than they know others
b. people cannot literally see themselves in social situations
c. attribution theory only applies to judging other people
d. a and b
e. all of the above

21. The self-serving bias is designed to explain:
a. the fundamental attribution error
b. the actor-observer difference
c. the greater inclination to make dispositional attributions about the self in cases of success
d. a and b
e. all of the above

22. According to self-perception theory:
a. one's own behavior can influence one's attitudes
b. cognitive dissonance is a self-fulfilling prophecy
c. social roles determine behavior
d. social factors are not involved in the concept of the self
e. attitudes are formed more or less independent of behavior

23. Which of the following illustrates how one's feelings or beliefs may be the result of one's actions?
a. the "foot-in-the-door" technique
b. impression formation
c. the social nature of the self
d. the need for comparison groups
e. none of the above

24. Bert, after a great deal of effort, convinces Sarah to go to a movie with him. Although Sarah finds Bert's company to be exactly what she expected, she ends up liking him more than she had anticipated. This could be explained in terms of:
a. the James-Lange theory of emotion
b. the principle of displacement
c. either self-perception theory or cognitive dissonance
d. the notion of emotion as an attribution process
e. Bert's captivating, but subtle, personality

25. Both self-perception theory and the James-Lange theory of emotion make the similar claim that:
a. emotion depends on appraisal
b. behavioral or bodily events cause mental changes
c. subjective phenomena cannot be studied
d. attribution plays no role in emotion
e. impression formation is of central importance

26. After running for a quarter mile, a person shows increased heart rate and various other signs of arousal but may not feel any strong emotion. This fact is particularly damaging to which of the following theories?
a. the attribution-of-arousal theory
b. the James-Lange theory
c. Cannon's idea that subjective emotion leads to physiological responses
d. a and b
e. all of the above

27. An experiment has shown that subjects alter their ratings of the attractiveness of nude photos in response to feedback about the increase or decrease of their heart rate. This result can be taken to support:
a. the attribution-of-arousal theory of emotion
b. the James-Lange theory
c. Cannon's theory (subjective emotion leads to the physiological responses, but the latter do not cause the former)
d. a and b
e. all of the above

28. The existence of display rules presents serious problems for:
    a. the read-out view of facial expressions
    b. the idea of fundamental emotions
    c. the attribution-of-arousal theory
    d. all of the above
    e. none of the above

29. Forced compliance, interpretation of emotions, and the self-serving bias all share:
    a. cognitive interpretations
    b. motivational interpretations
    c. an involvement with attitude change
    d. a and b
    e. a and c

Answer Key for Self Test

1.	d p. 327	16.	e pp. 337–39
2.	a p. 329	17.	d p. 340
3.	e p. 330	18.	b p. 340
4.	c p. 331	19.	a p. 340
5.	a p. 332	20.	d pp. 341–42
6.	a p. 332	21.	c p. 342
7.	a p. 333	22.	a p. 344
8.	b p. 334	23.	a p. 344
9.	d p. 335	24.	c pp. 343–44
10.	b p. 335	25.	b pp. 343–45
11.	b pp. 334–35	26.	b p. 346
12.	c pp. 333–34	27.	d pp. 345–46
13.	b p. 336	28.	e pp. 348–49
14.	b p. 337	29.	d p. 350
15.	e pp. 338–39		

Investigating Psychological Phenomena

PERSON PERCEPTION: THE EFFECT OF CONTEXT OR SET ON FIRST IMPRESSIONS

Equipment: Paper and pencil, a stopwatch or a watch that indicates seconds
Number of subjects: At least eight
Time per subject: Five minutes
Time for experimenter: Forty minutes

Social perception bears many analogies to more traditional areas of perception (see pp. 336–39 in the text). In both cases, information is taken in selectively and put together into some organized percept. This aspect of person perception was illustrated in the text with special reference to the classic studies of Solomon Asch. Asch's work argued for an organizational basis for impression formation. This approach is in keeping with the position of Gestalt psychology. In Asch's view, impressions were not formed by "summing" different items of information about a particular person. One particular aspect of the active process of impression formation is the effect of set. One is constantly forming impressions of people. New information on any person is integrated with an already existing impression: the new information will be interpreted to be as consistent as possible with the existing impression. Under the circumstances, one would expect that the first information one gets about a person would be especially important, since it might color what comes in later. Therefore, an organizational view would predict that the *order* of items of information about a person would affect the resulting impression, whereas a simple *summation* hypothesis would not matter.

Asch tested his hypothesis in a very simple manner: He gave college students a list of six adjectives that ostensibly described someone and recorded the impressions that they subsequently formed of this imaginary person. By manipulating the types of adjectives used and the order of their presentation, Asch attempted to produce systematic changes in the elicited impression formations. We will repeat his experiment on word order in precisely the same way that it was performed by Asch.

Try to get at least eight (student) subjects. It might be useful for you to team up with a few friends from the course and run up to twenty subjects, so that your results might be more meaningful. Subjects must be divided into two groups. You can run as many subjects as you want at the same time, so long as they are all from the same group. Since this experiment will compare the results of subjects from one group with the results from another group, it is important that the two groups be similar in general characteristics. For example, keep the percentage of females the same in both groups, and try not to run a group of friends together, since they may share many similar characteristics. If you run one subject at a time, simply assign the first subject to group A, the second to group B, and so on. This should give you a random and "unbiased" sample.

The list for group A	The list for group B
intelligent	envious
industrious	stubborn
impulsive	critical
critical	impulsive
stubborn	industrious
envious	intelligent

Note that the adjectives in group B are in the reverse order of group A. This arrangement is designed to enhance any effect of order, by putting adjectives that would lead to quite different impressions on opposite ends of the adjective list.

Subjects should be seated comfortably, and should have in front of them a blank piece of paper and a pencil. Make sure to put the group letter (A or B) on the paper and on the checklist. The experimenter reads the following instructions:

> I shall read you a number of characteristics that belong to a particular person. Please listen to them carefully and try to form an impression of the kind of person described. You will later be asked to give a brief characterization of the person in just a few sentences. I will read the list slowly and will repeat it once.

Read the list of six adjectives out loud in a steady voice, with an interval of five seconds between terms. Then say:

> I will now read the list again.

(Repeat the reading of the list)

> Now please write a brief characterization of this person.

(Subject writes)

Finally, tell the subjects while handing them the checklist (see pages 143 and 145):

> Here is a list of pairs of adjectives. For each pair, please circle the adjectives that better characterize the person we have been describing.

After the subject has completed this task, he or she is finished.

NOTES ON PROCEDURE

In setting up any experiment, many decisions must be made. Here, these include selecting the adjectives for the list, and for the checklist, deciding on the number of adjectives in the list, and so on. In most cases there are specific reasons for making these decisions. In this experiment, for example, ask yourself:

1. Why does the experimenter read the list instead of allowing the subject to read the list?
2. Why is the subject asked to write an impression before seeing the checklist rather than after filling out the checklist?

RESULTS

You should end up with eight or more written sketches and eight or more marked checklists. About half should be in each group. There is no simple way to score the written impressions. Read them over and try to summarize the impressions written by the two groups (the procedure used by Asch). You could also give the written impressions to another person and ask that person to sort them into piles, about equal in size. One pile would be for the more desirable impressions (persons) and the other for the less desirable ones. See if the impressions based on the adjective list with more desirable traits first are usually classified as more desirable. (It would be a good idea to fold back the part of the impressions paper with the group letter on it before reading and analyzing the character summaries.)

It is easier to analyze the data from the checklists. Simply record the percent of subjects who selected the more favorable adjective of each pair for each group. This is the procedure used by Asch. His results, based on twenty-four student subjects in group A and thirty-four in group B, are presented in the table on the next page. Record your data in the columns next to his data. Compare your results with his. If we take a difference of 20 percentage points as worthy of note, he reported big differences, in favor of group A, on happy, humorous, sociable, popular, good-looking, and restrained.

(You can increase the significance of your data by combining it with data from a few friends in the class, so that you would have 20 or more subjects in each group.)

Based on your results, what is the conclusion about the validity of the organization (set, Gestalt) versus simple summation explanations of impression formation?

Try to explain why some particular adjectives show clear effects and others do not. Obviously, in real life people form impressions from interactions with other people or by hearing about them from other people. To what extent do you think that Asch's procedure gives an indication of how people actually form impressions? The hallmark of a good experiment is that it simplifies a situation but still preserves its essential features. Is that true of this experiment?

FURTHER STUDY

You can use Asch's technique to address other questions. You can change specific adjectives on the list. You can use brief statements about a person's *behavior* (e.g., John consistently drives over the speed limit; John is always on time, etc.), rather than general characteristics. You can see which types of adjectives cause a subject to guess that a person is male or female. There are many possibilities, should this problem interest you. Some of the possibilities that you will come up with may never have been investigated.

Reference

Asch, S. E. Forming impressions of personality. *Journal of Abnormal and Social Psychology*, 1946, *41*, 258–90.

Percent of subjects checking favorable adjective at left

	Asch's Data		Your Data	
Adjective Pair	group A (24 students)	group B (34 students)	group A (__ students)	group B (__ students)
generous	24	10		
wise	18	17		
happy	32	5		
good-natured	18	0		
humorous	52	21		
sociable	56	27		
popular	35	14		
reliable	84	91		
good-looking	74	35		
serious	97	100		
restrained	64	9		
honest	80	79		

CHECKLISTS

There are eight checklists on the next two pages. Cut one out for each subject. (Asch used eighteen adjective pairs. We use twelve of these pairs.)

Circle the most relevant adjective:

generous–ungenerous
shrewd–wise
unhappy–happy
irritable–good-natured
humorous–humorless
sociable–unsociable
popular–unpopular
unreliable–reliable
good-looking–unattractive
frivolous–serious
restrained–talkative
dishonest–honest
Group ____________________

Circle the most relevant adjective:

generous–ungenerous
shrewd–wise
unhappy–happy
irritable–good-natured
humorous–humorless
sociable–unsociable
popular–unpopular
unreliable–reliable
good-looking–unattractive
frivolous–serious
restrained–talkative
dishonest–honest
Group ____________________

-- *Cut here* --

Circle the most relevant adjective:

generous–ungenerous
shrewd–wise
unhappy–happy
irritable–good-natured
humorous–humorless
sociable–unsociable
popular–unpopular
unreliable–reliable
good-looking–unattractive
frivolous–serious
restrained–talkative
dishonest–honest
Group ____________________

Circle the most relevant adjective:

generous–ungenerous
shrewd–wise
unhappy–happy
irritable–good-natured
humorous–humorless
sociable–unsociable
popular–unpopular
unreliable–reliable
good-looking–unattractive
frivolous–serious
restrained–talkative
dishonest–honest
Group ____________________

Circle the most relevant adjective:

generous–ungenerous
shrewd–wise
unhappy–happy
irritable–good-natured
humorous–humorless
sociable–unsociable
popular–unpopular
unreliable–reliable
good-looking–unattractive
frivolous–serious
restrained–talkative
dishonest–honest
Group ____________________

Circle the most relevant adjective:

generous–ungenerous
shrewd–wise
unhappy–happy
irritable–good-natured
humorous–humorless
sociable–unsociable
popular–unpopular
unreliable–reliable
good-looking–unattractive
frivolous–serious
restrained–talkative
dishonest–honest
Group ____________________

Cut here

Circle the most relevant adjective:

generous–ungenerous
shrewd–wise
unhappy–happy
irritable–good-natured
humorous–humorless
sociable–unsociable
popular–unpopular
unreliable–reliable
good-looking–unattractive
frivolous–serious
restrained–talkative
dishonest–honest
Group ____________________

Circle the most relevant adjective:

generous–ungenerous
shrewd–wise
unhappy–happy
irritable–good-natured
humorous–humorless
sociable–unsociable
popular–unpopular
unreliable–reliable
good-looking–unattractive
frivolous–serious
restrained–talkative
dishonest–honest
Group ____________________

CHAPTER 12

Social Interaction

Learning Objectives

RELATING TO OTHERS: ONE-ON-ONE INTERACTIONS

Social exchange and reciprocity

1. What is social exchange?
2. Explain the reciprocity principle, and give examples of it from different cultures.
3. How is the reciprocity principle used in bargaining and persuasion? What are reciprocal concessions and what is the door-in-the-face technique?
4. Discuss self-disclosure in the context of reciprocity, and gender differences in self-disclosure.

Altruism

5. Under what circumstances do people fail to help others in distress? Consider the role of ambiguity, pluralistic ignorance, and diffusion of responsibility.
6. What is the bystander effect?
7. Indicate the possible costs that someone who offers aid might incur.
8. In there any genuine altruism?

Attraction

9. Why is proximity a major determinant of attraction?
10. Review the evidence for similarity and physical attractiveness in attraction.
11. What is the evidence for the importance of physical attractiveness in attraction?
12. Describe the matching hypothesis.
13. Evaluate the roles of biological and cultural factors as determinants of sexual attractiveness.

Love

14. Describe the phenomenon of romantic love. What is the role of culture in defining it and establishing its importance?
15. What factors affect the intensity of romantic love? Include a discussion of the Romeo-and-Juliet effect.
16. Distinguish romantic from companionate love.

SOCIAL INFLUENCE: MANY-ON-ONE INTERACTIONS

17. What is social influence?

Social facilitation: social influence by the presence of others

18. Define social facilitation. Indicate the conditions under which it occurs, and in particular, the role of arousal and facilitation of dominant responses.

Conformity

19. What is conformity? What is the role of cognitive and motivational factors in causing conformity?
20. What is the ally effect?

Blind obedience

21. What characterizes the authoritarian personality? How does the trait relate to prejudice against minorities?
22. Describe Milgram's basic study on obedience.
23. Discuss the importance of seeing oneself as another's agent.
24. Discuss how dehumanization, psychological distance, and gradual escalation (slippery slope) influence blind obedience. Illustrate these influences with the example of the Milgram experiments.
25. Contrast personality factors with situational factors as causes of blind obedience.

LEADERSHIP: ONE-ON-MANY INTERACTIONS

Great person or social forces

26. Evaluate the relative roles of situational and dispositional factors in determining leadership.

Leadership in the laboratory

27. Illustrate how leadership has been studied in the laboratory. What personality and situational factors promote leadership?

CROWD BEHAVIOR: MANY-ON-MANY INTERACTIONS

The emphasis on the irrational: deindividuation

28. What is deindividuation? What is the evidence linking it to crowds? What is the role of group size and anonymity?

Cognitive factors and the panicky crowd

29. Evaluate the statement that "people become 'primitive' or irrational in crowds."
30. Describe the circumstances under which panic is likely to spread in a crowd.
31. What is the prisoner's dilemma? Provide examples of payoff matrices as illustrations.
32. Show how the prisoner's dilemma analysis can account for panic in crowds. How does it relate to the rationality-irrationality issue?
33. Discuss the prisoner's dilemma analysis of social dilemmas, such as air pollution, and indicate strategies that might produce more cooperation.

THE GENERALITY OF SOCIAL PSYCHOLOGY

34. Evaluate the extent to which principles of social psychology discussed in this and the preceding chapter are general features of human nature, as opposed to principles specific to United States culture in the late twentieth century.

Programmed Exercises

RELATING TO OTHERS: ONE-ON-ONE INTERACTIONS

1. According to the principle of ____________ ____________, each partner in a relationship gives something to the other, and expects to receive something in return.	social exchange
2. The notion that favors and gifts must be repaid is embodied in the ____________ principle.	reciprocity
3. An application of this principle is the ____________-____________-____________-____________ technique, in which, after a major request is refused, a smaller request from the same source is more likely to be granted. This is based on the principle of ____________ ____________.	door-in-the-face reciprocal concession
4. In the non-material domain, ____________-____________ is an example of reciprocity. At least in the United States, it is more common in ____________.	self-disclosure women (females)
5. Three factors that account for people's failure to help someone in distress are ____________, ____________ ____________, and ____________ ____________ ____________.	ambiguity, pluralistic ignorance, diffusion of responsibility
6. The larger the size of the group a person is in the less likely he is to come to a victim's assistance. This is called the ____________ ____________.	bystander effect
7. The costs of helping include loss of ____________ and possible ____________ ____________.	time physical danger

8. Two people who have spent a fair amount of time in physical ____________ to one another are more likely than not to become friends. — proximity

9. In addition to proximity, two major factors that cause one to like another are ____________ and ____________ ____________. — similarity, physical attractiveness

10. The strong tendency for people to marry other people very similar to themselves is called ____________. — homogamy

11. The personal characteristic that most influences initial liking for a person in American culture is ____________ ____________. — physical attractiveness

12. The view that people select mates who are similar to them on many characteristics (such as physical attractiveness) is called the ____________ ____________. — matching hypothesis

13. Although there may be some universal characteristics that lead to sexual attraction, to a large extent the criteria of sexual attractiveness vary in different ____________. — cultures

14. Two contrasting types of love are a passionate type, or ____________ love, and another type that emphasizes mutual trust, care, and sharing, called ____________ love. — romantic; companionate

15. Parental opposition tends to intensify romantic love. This is called the ____________-____________-____________ effect. — Romeo-and-Juliet

SOCIAL INFLUENCE: MANY-ON-ONE INTERACTIONS

16. The study of the way an individual is affected by different social forces acting simultaneously, is the study of ____________ ____________. — social influence

17. The improvement in performance in the presence of other members of one's species is called ____________ ____________. — social facilitation

18. According to Zajonc, social facilitation operates by producing ____________, which strengthens the tendency to perform the ____________ response. — arousal; dominant

19. Going along with what other people think or do is called ____________. — conformity

20. Conformity is more likely if the other persons involved are ____________ in the position they take. A single other dissenter may reduce conformity considerably. This is called the ____________ ____________. — unanimous; ally effect

21. People who emphasize the importance of power, dominance, and obedience have been described as having an ____________ personality. — authoritarian

22. In Milgram's first experiment on obedience, approximately ____________ percent of subjects shocked the learner up to the maximum amount. — 65 (50–75 percent would be acceptable)

23. Milgram's experiments suggest that it is not necessary to have an ____________ personality to exhibit blind obedience. — authoritarian

24. An important factor that causes people to perform acts that they might otherwise consider abhorrent is the feeling that they are another person's ____________. — agent

25. Blind obedience is more likely when ____________ ____________ between the "subject" and the "victim" is increased. — psychological distance

26. The obedient person who causes pain to another person may treat that person as an object. This is called ____________. — dehumanization

27. The cognitive reorientation required in producing obedience is best accomplished by a ____________ ____________ in obedience requirements. This is called the ____________ ____________. — gradual increase; slippery slope

LEADERSHIP: ONE-ON-MANY INTERACTIONS

28. The most important one-on-many interaction is ____________. — leadership

29. Leadership is associated with dispositional characteristics, such as ____________ and ____________. — (2 of) dominance, intelligence, sociability (extraversion, "outgoingness")

30. Situational factors that encourage leadership include ____________ and ____________. — (2 of) authority, clear-cut task, good interpersonal relations

31. Evidence suggests that part of leadership depends on dispositional characteristics, so that there is an effect for ____________ ____________ as well as social factors. — great persons

CROWD BEHAVIOR: MANY-ON-MANY INTERACTIONS

32. ____________, a weakened sense of personal identity, disinhibits impulsive actions that are normally under restraint. It occurs more often in ____________. — Deindividuation; crowds

33. ____________ and ____________ ____________ ____________ promote deindividuation. — Anonymity, large group size

34. The prisoner's dilemma presents an individual with a choice in a situation with mixed risks and benefits, described in a ____________ ____________. — payoff matrix

35. The prisoner's dilemma analysis is an attempt to explain the apparently ____________ behavior of a crowd in terms of the ____________ behavior of individuals. — irrational, rational

36. The prisoner's dilemma can be applied to problems of society, such as industrial pollution and other ____________ dilemmas. — social

THE GENERALITY OF SOCIAL PSYCHOLOGY

37. Some principles of social psychology described in this and the preceding chapter may be universal aspects of ____________ ____________, or they may be much more specific to this ____________ and this ____________. — human nature; culture, time

Self Test

1. The idea of social exchange is:
   a. tit-for-tat (exchange of favors)
   b. the money economy
   c. the slavery system
   d. forced compliance
   e. altruism

2. The relation between the foot-in-the-door and the door-in-the-face techniques is the same as the relation between:
   a. social exchange and the reciprocity principle
   b. altruism and sharing
   c. perception and memory
   d. gradual commitment and downside bargaining
   e. display and communication

3. Both gift-giving and self-disclosure:
   a. are altruistic
   b. encourage reciprocity
   c. encourage ambiguity
   d. are examples of the door-in-the-face technique
   e. a and d

4. The bystander effect is accounted for by:
   a. ambiguity
   b. diffusion of responsibility
   c. pluralistic ignorance
   d. a and c
   e. all of the above

5. Diffusion of responsibility is:
   a. an example of social exchange
   b. an example of cost of intervention
   c. less if there are fewer observers
   d. b and c
   e. a and c

6. Which of the following is a possible basis for true altruism?
   a. the bystander effect
   b. hopes for reciprocal altruism
   c. empathy: sharing another's feelings
   d. social exchange
   e. proximity

7. Proximity is an important factor in attraction. There is evidence that this relation results from the fact that:
   a. one must ordinarily meet someone in order to be attracted to him/her
   b. familiarity promotes attraction, and familiarity is increased by proximity
   c. proximity explains the matching hypothesis
   d. a and b
   e. all of the above

8. Mildred and Herb have been dating for years. Both are physically unattractive, and one acquaintance wonders what they see in each other. Which of the following factors could contribute to their mutual attractiveness?
   a. proximity
   b. similarity
   c. matching
   d. a and c
   e. all of the above

9. In a particular culture, relatively thin males tend to marry relatively plump females. According to the matching hypothesis, this implies that:
   a. relative thinness in males is as desired (attractive) as relative plumpness in females
   b. physical attractiveness is not important in this culture
   c. body shape is not important in this culture.
   d. the plumpness and thinness of relatives is important in this culture
   e. c and d

10. Romantic love has been described as having three components: intimacy, passion, and commitment. In comparison, companionate love would differ most from romantic love in that it would have less of:
    a. intimacy
    b. passion
    c. commitment
    d. b and c
    e. a and c

11. Baseball player A is a better hitter in batting practice than in actual games, while player B shows the opposite pattern. We can say that:
    a. A shows social facilitation and B does not
    b. B shows social facilitation and A does not
    c. hitting optimally is more likely to be a dominant response for player A
    d. hitting optimally is more likely to be a dominant response for player B
    e. b and d

12. The situations that lead to conformity are similar to those that lead to failure to help a person in distress. Both conformity and failure to help others in distress are increased by all of the following *except*:
    a. ambiguity in the situation
    b. a need for additional information
    c. presence of a large number of other people
    d. a desire to be liked by others
    e. a feeling of a lack of competence for the problem at hand

13. A single dissenter in a conformity experiment is likely to have more of an effect on an otherwise lone nonconforming subject if:
    a. she is in agreement with the nonconforming subject
    b. her dissent is clear, but not in agreement with the nonconforming subject
    c. the problem in question is a matter of minimal importance
    d. a and c
    e. all of the above

14. An explanation of blind obedience that emphasizes the authoritarian personality of the person in question relies on:
    a. situational factors
    b. dispositional factors
    c. cognitive dissonance
    d. cognitive consistency
    e. attribution of emotional experience

15. Both Milgram's obedience experiment and Asch's line judgment studies show the importance of ____________ in determining behavior.
    a. attribution
    b. cognitive dissonance
    c. compliance
    d. dispositional factors
    e. none of the above

16. Which of the following would tend to *prevent* obedience in a situation of the type that Milgram studied?
    a. making a person feel like the agent of another
    b. dehumanizing the person being punished
    c. describing the experiment as a scientific enterprise
    d. decreasing the psychological distance between the subject and the person being punished
    e. none of the above

17. It is probably easier for a bombardier to drop bombs on an inhabited building than for the same person to kill someone standing in front of him. This presumed fact can be accounted for in terms of:
    a. anonymity
    b. psychological distance
    c. dehumanization
    d. all of the above
    e. none of the above

18. The fact that people underestimate the percent of people who comply in the Milgram obedience study can be accounted for in terms of:
    a. the fundamental attribution error
    b. social exchange theory
    c. social facilitation
    d. conformity
    e. b and c

19. The tendency to account for leadership almost entirely in terms of "great persons" can be explained by:
    a. leadership theory
    b. conformity
    c. the fundamental attribution error
    d. the above-average effect
    e. statistics

20. Which of the following makes it *less* likely that Cynthia will emerge as a leader:
    a. she is in a position of authority
    b. the goal (situation) is ambiguous
    c. she is sociable
    d. she is dominant
    e. there are good relationships among members of the group

21. Anonymity promotes:
    a. social exchange
    b. the fundamental attribution error
    c. the actor-observer difference
    d. social facilitation
    e. deindividuation

22. Brown suggests that panic is more likely in situations where:
    a. a serious danger is perceived
    b. the escape routes appear to be inadequate
    c. the people involved have well-defined roles
    d. a and b
    e. all of the above

23. The prisoner's dilemma analysis explains:
    a. the use of payoff matrices
    b. how obedience is based on a past history of stern parental treatment
    c. how maladaptive crowd behavior can result from rational behavior of individuals
    d. the importance of roles in controlling the crowd panic reaction
    e. b and c

24. The cultural critique holds that much of modern social psychology is a description only of 20th-century people in Western-developed countries. Which of the following argues *against* the cultural critique?
    a. absence of a bias to dispositional attributions in Hindu Indians
    b. absence of a word for embarrassment in some cultures
    c. suppression of self for communal concerns in some cultures
    d. our ability to understand narratives from different cultures and times
    e. all of the above argue against the cultural critique

Answer Key for Self Test

1. a p. 353
2. d pp. 354–55
3. b p. 355
4. e pp. 356–58
5. c p. 358
6. c p. 359
7. d p. 360
8. e pp. 360–62
9. a pp. 361–62
10. b p. 364
11. e p. 365
12. d pp. 365–66, 356–57
13. a p. 367
14. b p. 368
15. c pp. 368–69
16. d p. 370
17. d p. 370
18. a p. 371
19. c p. 373
20. b p. 374
21. e p. 375
22. d p. 376
23. c p. 377
24. d p. 379

Investigating Psychological Phenomena

MATCHING FOR INTELLIGENCE AND ATTRACTION

Equipment: None
Number of subjects: One, yourself
Time per subject: Twenty minutes
Time for experimenter: Twenty minutes

As described in the text, one of the major features of romantic couples is that they are similar along a wide variety of dimensions. Much of this similarity seems to be a reason for the formation of the relationship, rather than a consequence of it. Although certain characteristics may become more similar the longer a couple is together, this cannot be so for the many characteristics unlikely to change in adulthood, such as height. Furthermore, individuals are likely to seek a partner with a high rating on characteristics for which there can be a clear positive or negative evaluation (such as intelligence or attractiveness), with competitive selection and fear of rejection tending to sort people out with others at their own level of achievement, ability, beauty, and so forth. Thus, one would expect similar ratings on almost all traits.

This study will demonstrate the principles of homogamy and matching by examining the similarity of couples on two characteristics: physical attractiveness and intelligence. You will be the one subject in this study. First, select ten heterosexual couples that you know fairly well. The couples should be selected according to the following criteria:

1. All should be romantically involved: married or together for at least one year.

2. The couples should be about the same age in two senses: The members of the couple should be no more than ten years apart in age and the oldest person should be no more than twenty years older than the youngest person of the same sex on the list. (If you cannot generate the ten couples that this study calls for, you can ask a friend to generate the data for you.)

DO NOT INCLUDE YOURSELF IN ANY OF THESE COUPLES.

List the couples (by first name of each partner) in the tables on the next page. Now rank the ten women and the ten men separately for both physical attractiveness and intelligence. Thus, for physical attractiveness, rank the most attractive man number one, the next most attractive number two, and so on until all ten numbers have been assigned. Rank the women in the same fashion.

Now calculate a rank-order correlation, a statistic that represents the correlation between the ranking for men and women in each couple. (See the Statistical Appendix in the text, but use the formula on page 156 to calculate the correlation.) If the members of a couple match perfectly on a characteristic (that is, if the man ranked number one for attractiveness is involved with the woman ranked number one on this same trait, and so on), the correlation coefficient would equal 1.00—the highest possible value for correlation. If the members of a couple are inversely matched (that is, if the man ranked number one for attractiveness is involved with the woman ranked number ten on that trait), then the correlation coefficient would equal –1.00 (the lowest possible value). If there is no relation between the ranking of the man and woman in a couple on the trait in question, then the correlation coefficient would be 0. (For a sample calculation and table, see page 156.)

Attractiveness

	Couple (man's/woman's name)	Man's Rank	Woman's Rank	Difference	Difference^2
1					
2					
3					
4					
5					
6					
7					
8					
9					
10					

Correlation for attractiveness = ____________________

Intelligence

	Couple (man's/woman's name)	Man's Rank	Woman's Rank	Difference	Difference^2
1					
2					
3					
4					
5					
6					
7					
8					
9					
10					

Correlation for intelligence = ____________________

Use the formula below to calculate the correlation, *r*.

$$r = 1 - \frac{6(\text{Sum of the difference in ranking between couple members}^2)}{\text{number of couples (number of couples}^2 - 1)}$$

Sample data on intelligence:

Couple (man's/woman's name)	Man's Rank	Woman's Rank	Intelligence Difference	Difference^2
1 A/B	1	2	–1	1
2 C/D	5	3	2	1
3 E/F	3	1	2	4
4 G/H	9	6	3	9
5 I/J	2	7	–5	25
6 K/L	7	5	2	4
7 M/N	4	4	0	0
8 O/P	8	9	–1	1
9 Q/R	10	8	2	4
10 S/T	6	10	–4	16

Sum of Difference^2 = 65

Correlation for intelligence = .61

For the sample table, the equation would read:

$$r = 1 - \frac{6(65)}{10(100 - 1)} = -.61$$

Compare your results to those in the list below generated by other students in introductory psychology. These correlation coefficients were calculated by eleven students for intelligence and thirteen students for attractiveness and have been arranged in order of increasing correlation. How do your values compare to theirs?

Correlations

Attractiveness	Intelligence
–.16	–.01
–.01	.18
.02	.26
.07	.35
.36	.39
.45	.42
.46	.56
.50	.63
.55	.68
.60	.75
.60	.76
.76	
.76	

Finally, try to think of the characteristic that would be most likely to show similarity in mates, as well as the characteristic that might, perhaps because of its lack of importance, not show matching in mates. Calculate the correlation coefficient for each of these characteristics, using the same ten couples you have already used. You might also consider doing a similarity/matching score for ten same-sex couples or non-romantic friends. Would you expect them to show similarity/matching effects as well? Would you expect this on the same characteristics as with heterosexual romantic partners?

CHAPTER 13

Physical and Cognitive Development

Learning Objectives

WHAT IS DEVELOPMENT?

Development as differentiation

1. What is differentiation, and how does it account for similarities in the embryos of different species?

Development as growth

2. Review the major events in physical growth of humans from conception to adulthood.
3. How does humans' physical growth (especially of the nervous system) compare with that of other animals? What is the effect of the difference?
4. Review the basic sensory and response capacities of the human infant.

Development as orderly progression

5. Describe the sequence of early development in humans, and indicate how the order of many accomplishments is fixed.

PIAGET'S THEORY OF COGNITIVE DEVELOPMENT

6. What are the major philosophical positions on development? How does Piaget's theory relate to these? What are the four developmental stages, according to Piaget?

Sensory-motor intelligence

7. Describe the hallmarks of this stage. How does the child see himself and objects around him? What distinctions develop during this period?
8. Why is object permanence seen as an end to this stage of development?
9. What do the terms *assimilation* and *accommodation* mean according to Piaget? What is a schema?
10. What does Piaget mean by the term *representation*? What are some examples of representations?

The preoperational period

11. How is the name of this period derived?
12. Be familiar with various tests of conservation. How does the child's conservation ability develop during this period? Why do children fail to conserve at the beginning of this period? What operations are crucial for conservation?
13. Describe a test that demonstrates egocentrism.

Concrete and formal operations

14. What is the difference between these stages? How does Piaget study formal operations? Give examples of thinking patterns that would qualify for this stage.

What is the cognitive starting point?

15. How is Piaget compared to empiricists?

Space and objects in infancy

16. What is occlusion? How does it affect adult object perception?
17. What is the habituation procedure, and how has it been used to study infant perception?
18. What evidence suggests that infants have some notions of the principles that govern objects in space?

Social cognition in infancy: the existence of other minds

19. Describe the evidence that very young infants are capable of discriminating a face from other stimuli, a skill that is fundamental to early social interaction.
20. A next important step in social interaction is sharing attention with another person. Be familiar

with the data showing that this skill develops early as well.

COGNITIVE DEVELOPMENT IN PRESCHOOLERS

The meaning of mental stage

21. What are the characteristics of a developmental "stage" as Piaget uses the term? How is this contradicted by modern evidence?

Numerical skills in preschoolers

22. Even though preschoolers may use idiosyncratic counting terms, how does evidence show that they may nonetheless have a rudimentary understanding of counting principles?
23. Studies of numerical quantity show that young children have an appreciation of number. Describe the evidence for this claim.
24. How do modern studies of number cast doubt on the Piagetian concept of a stage?

Social cognition in preschoolers: developing a theory of mind

25. What are some basic assumptions of a theory of mind?
26. How has it been shown that young children have the rudiments of an understanding of some of these assumptions?
27. Describe the evidence that even two-year-olds have a primitive conception of the principles of perception.
28. Some subtle evidence, that you should be able to describe, shows that the notion of a belief may be primitively represented in children as young as three.

Sequence or stages?

29. Understand the argument that Piaget's fundamental conception of stages still has plausibility even in spite of modern evidence about his tasks.

THE CAUSES OF COGNITIVE GROWTH

The nativist approach: maturation

30. Be aware of the role of cross-cultural data in evaluating the maturational hypothesis.

The empiricist approach: specific learning

31. Be able to discuss the basic issue distinguishing the positions of learning and maturation. What is Piaget's position? What is the relevant evidence?
32. How does a learning position explain the fairly fixed orders of development that characterize various stages? What are the results of studies to train young children on conservation?

Piaget's approach: assimilation and accommodation

33. Describe how Piaget sees assimilation and accommodation as explanations of cognitive growth.

The information-processing approach: chunking and strategies

34. What are the memory limitations of young children? How do neo-Piagetians account for these?
35. Describe some strategies for remembering that adults and children use. How do young children approach a memory task, and how does their approach change as they mature?
36. What is meant by the term *metacognition*? How is metacognition manifested in memory, perception, language, thinking, and problem solving? At what approximate age does metacognition manifest itself?

COGNITIVE DEVELOPMENT FROM A CROSS-CULTURAL PERSPECTIVE

37. How is the poor performance of non-Western people on standard cognitive tests explained? Are they capable of abstract thought without formal schooling? Give examples.
38. Explain how the concept of transfer of skills may account for cross-cultural differences.

TAKING STOCK

39. What is the proper balance between maturational and environmental factors in development? Discuss.

Programmed Exercises

WHAT IS DEVELOPMENT?

1. The process of ____________ involves a progressive change from the more general to the more particular, from the simple to the more complex.	differentiation
2. Differentiation predicts and accounts for the fact that development occurs in an ____________ progression.	orderly
3. Physical growth continues until approximately the end of the ____________ decade of life.	second
4. The part of the human body that grows at a disproportionately high rate before birth is the ____________.	head (brain)
5. Because of extensive growth of the brain after birth, humans have a longer period of ____________ than most other species.	dependency
6. The ____________ reflex is elicited in an infant by a touch to the cheek, which makes the infant turn his head toward the stimulating object.	rooting
7. In general, the infant's sensory capacities are ____________ advanced at birth than his ____________ capacities.	more response (motor)
8. The human baby begins to walk alone at an age of about ____________ months.	15 (12 to 18)
9. The first words typically occur at about ____________ months.	10 (8 to 12)
10. Although some children develop faster than others, the major motor and language accomplishments occur in a ____________ sequence.	fixed (orderly)

PIAGET'S THEORY OF COGNITIVE DEVELOPMENT

11. Jean Piaget and other developmental psychologists usually look for ____________ differences between children and adults; they do not see children as adults in miniature.	qualitative
12. Piaget regards cognitive development as a dynamic process in which the child progresses through several ____________.	stages
13. A child has begun to learn that he lives in a stable world which can be distinguished from his sensory impressions. This child is most likely in the ____________-____________ stage.	sensory-motor
14. Children develop the notion of ____________ ____________ near the end of the sensory-motor stage as they become aware that objects exist independently of their sensory experience and motor manipulations.	object permanence

15. Perhaps the most significant accomplishment of children in the last phase of the sensory-motor stage is their ability to ____________ objects or events in their absence, rather than merely reacting to their presence. — represent

16. Recurrent action patterns (such as sucking, swallowing, and head and eye movement) are the first mental elements, or ____________. It is in terms of these that the infant organizes the world. — schemas

17. Representations may be internalized actions, images, or words; in all cases they function as ____________, which stand for whatever they may signify. — symbols

18. ____________ imitation is a case in which a child imitates an action that occurred in the past, such as a playmate's temper tantrum observed a day before. — Deferred

19. According to Piaget, a conceptual system of thought can only be constructed by means of higher-order schemas. These ____________ allow the internal manipulation of ideas according to a stable set of rules and emerge at age seven or so; the period from two to seven is therefore termed ____________. — operations; preoperational

20. Piaget states that the ability to form ____________ precedes linguistic expression and is a prerequisite for it. — representations

21. A characteristic of children in the preoperational stage is their inability to ____________ quantity, as shown by their lack of knowledge about relative quantities of liquids in two glasses. — conserve

22. One of the crucial concepts which children must grasp if they are to conserve is that manipulations upon objects are ____________. — reversible

23. A preoperational child is incapable of attending to all of the relevant ____________ of an object simultaneously. — dimensions

24. Piaget believes that a child can learn to chunk dimensions together when he learns to focus upon the ____________ from one experience to another rather than upon the individual experiences themselves. — transformations

25. A preoperational child believes his point of view is the only one. Such a belief is known as ____________. — egocentrism

26. A child can determine whether a given number is odd or even and can also add one to any number. The child finds that 3 + 1 is even, and 5 + 1 is even, but doesn't understand that any odd number added to one results in an even number. This child would be categorized as being in the ____________ ____________ stage. — concrete operations

27. A child in the concrete operations stage has operations which are applicable to ____________ events but which do not work too well when applied to ____________ concepts. — concrete; abstract

28. The ability to entertain hypothetical possibilities and deal with potential relationships is characteristic only of the stage of ____________ ____________. — formal operations

WHAT IS THE COGNITIVE STARTING POINT?

29. The fact that an infant can perceive an object that is partially blocked by another object gives evidence that infants are capable of reacting appropriately to the perceptual effect of ____________. — occlusion

30. The procedure in which a perceptual display is kept in view until an infant becomes bored is called ____________. — habituation

31. It appears that young infants have some knowledge of the fact that two objects cannot occupy the same ____________ at the same time. — space (place)

32. Studies of the knowledge of number in infants have relied on the ____________ method, which depends on showing a stimulus repeatedly and then testing with it and a novel stimulus. — habituation

33. Studies of numerical reasoning show that infants as young as five months had a primitive understanding of ____________ operations: They could distinguish when a stimulus had been added to an array. — arithmetical

34. Investigations of infants minutes after birth have demonstrated that they have a preference for looking at normal rather than scrambled ____________. — faces

35. Infants will turn their ____________ in the direction in which the mother is looking. — attention

COGNITIVE DEVELOPMENT IN PRESCHOOLERS

36. According to Piaget, cognitive development is characterized by a series of ____________, each qualitatively different from the others. — stages

37. Even though children may use idiosyncratic symbols to denote given numbers of objects, they may still have the basic principle of ____________. — counting

38. Piaget had demonstrated failure of young children to ____________ number, in that if a number of items was stretched out, the children thought there were more items present. — conserve

39. Recent studies of cognitive development suggest that stages are not ____________ -____________- ____________ in nature. The demarcations between stages are not sharp. — all-or-none

40. The fact that young children will turn a photograph in the proper orientation when showing it to another person suggests that they have a rudimentary theory of ____________. — mind

41. There are two crucial components to the notion of a ____________. One is that they can be true or false; the other is that different people can have different ones. — belief

42. The ____________ ____________ test asks a child to predict what another being will know in a certain situation. This test compares the child's own knowledge with what the child knows about another's knowledge. — false belief

43. One critical difference between preschoolers and school age children is that the latter can apply their knowledge to a wider range of ____________. — problems

44. Most developmental psychologists would say that Piaget's cognitive milestones are not a succession of mental stages, similar to those found in embryological development, but rather a ____________ of mental steps. — sequence

THE CAUSES OF COGNITIVE GROWTH

45. Nativists would state that mental development depends on ____________, a preprogrammed growth process based on changes in underlying neural structures. — maturation

46. While children of different cultures may reach each Piagetian stage at different ____________, they pass through these stages in the same ____________. — ages, order

47. The alternative to the maturation-centered approach is one that emphasizes the acquisition of specific ____________ through exposure to the environment. — patterns (learning)

48. Piaget believes that at the same time that the environment is ____________ to the child's schemas, the schemas ____________ to the environment. — assimilated accommodate

49. A more current approach to cognitive development asserts that it results from a change in ____________ ____________. — information processing

50. According to this approach, mental growth is partly based on the acquisition of better and larger ____________ of information and of various ____________ for thinking and remembering. — chunks, strategies

51. As children get older, ____________ repetition, also called ____________, is used as a strategy for remembering. — rote, rehearsal

52. The fact that adults can reflect on the cognitive operations whereby they gain knowledge shows that they are capable of ____________. — metacognition

COGNITION DEVELOPMENT FROM A CROSS-CULTURAL PERSPECTIVE

53. One reason for cross-cultural differences in cognitive performance is the lack of formal ____________ in some cultures (for example, Australian aborigines, New Guinea tribesmen, and Kpelle farmers in Liberia). — schooling

54. Another reason for cross-cultural differences in performance may be that some _____-__________ cultures simply do not understand the nature of the answer expected by the Western experimenter. — non-Western

TAKING STOCK

55. Development is best characterized as a function of both ____________ and ____________. — maturation environment

Self Test

1. The fact that, at early stages, embryos of many very different species look very much alike, and have a much simpler structure than adults, can be taken as evidence for:
   a. physical development
   b. differentiation
   c. the inheritance of behavior
   d. all of the above
   e. b and c

2. The figure below corresponds to a human being of about what age (beginning with conception as zero)?

   a. one month
   b. four months
   c. eight months
   d. birth (nine months)
   e. one year (postconception)

3. All but one of the following are distinctive features of human development, in comparison with most other mammals. Which is *not* a distinctly human feature?
   a. long period of dependency on the parent
   b. being born at a very immature stage
   c. presence of reflex at birth
   d. continuation of growth until about twenty years of age
   e. b and c

4. Major features of motor, language, and other types of development often occur in a fixed order in children who develop at different rates. A major reason for this is that:
   a. development must occur in stages
   b. some capacities depend on the existence of other capacities
   c. sense organs mature before response capacities
   d. language depends on locomotion ability
   e. the infant begins with reflexes like grasping before it can learn

5. A nativist:
   a. thinks of the child's mind as similar to an adult's, only with fewer associations
   b. thinks of a child's mind as qualitatively different from an adult's
   c. conceptualizes the growth of a child's mind as progression through a series of natural stages
   d. views basic cognitive categories as given *a priori* at birth

6. A child has learned that whether a toy box is open or closed, there are toys inside. It could be said that the child has attained the concept of:
   a. object permanence
   b. representations
   c. directed action
   d. solipsism

7. When a child just becomes aware that objects exist independent of his own sensory experience, he would most likely have completed which Piagetian stage?
   a. sensory-motor
   b. preoperational
   c. concrete operations
   d. formal operations

8. Recurring action patterns, such as sucking and swallowing, are:
   a. simple reflexes that have little developmental interest
   b. the first mental elements with which the infant organizes the world
   c. examples of intentional acts
   d. none of the above

9. The two processes that Piaget sees as being responsible for cognitive development are:
   a. deferred imitation and assimilation
   b. schemas and representations
   c. assimilation and accommodation
   d. none of the above

10. A toy is hidden under a box in the presence of a child. The child is prevented from reaching the box for a few seconds. When he is released he immediately lifts the box off the toy. The earliest stage that this child could be in is __________.
    a. sensory-motor
    b. preoperational
    c. concrete operations
    d. formal operations

11. Demonstrations of the child's understanding that symbols (i.e., internalized actions, images, or words) may stand for objects but are not equivalent to them include all of the following *except*:
    a. object permanence
    b. deferred imitation
    c. make-believe play
    d. metacognitions

12. The concept unknown to a child who doesn't conserve quantity is:
    a. reversibility
    b. accuracy
    c. size
    d. weight

13. Children who don't conserve are:
    a. unable to attend to all of the relevant dimensions of a stimulus
    b. usually in the concrete operations stage
    c. usually in the formal operations stage
    d. none of the above

14. The social counterpart of an inability to attend to more than one dimension in a conservation task is:
    a. aggressive behavior
    b. having only one friend during a particular time interval
    c. egocentrism
    d. none of the above

15. The major difference between a child in the concrete operations stage and one in the formal operations stage is:
    a. The former is incapable of following the rules.
    b. The former cannot deal with numbers.
    c. The former cannot deal with abstract concepts.
    d. all of the above

16. The idea behind using habituation to study knowledge of occlusion is:
    a. to have an infant habituate to an occluded stimulus and then see whether it sees the whole unoccluded stimulus as novel
    b. to have an infant habituate to an unoccluded stimulus and then see whether it sees the whole occluded stimulus as novel
    c. to have an infant see a stimulus and then see whether it habituates to that stimulus faster when it is occluded
    d. none of the above

17. The experiment showing that infants have knowledge about objects and about the fact that two objects cannot occupy the same place at the same time made use of a procedure in which a screen moved over an object and either stopped when it reached the object or seemed to pass through it. This procedure indicated that the infants had a sense of objects because:
    a. they habituated to the moving screen
    b. they spent more time looking at the screen when it stopped at the object behind it
    c. they moved their hands and arms more while the screen was moving, indicating that they anticipated its stopping when it hit the object
    d. they spent less time looking at the screen when it stopped at the object behind it

18. A rudimentary theory of mind has been demonstrated in young children by the result that:
    a. they will appropriately orient a picture they are showing to an adult so that it faces the adult
    b. they will be egocentric in trying to take the perspective of another person in how that person views a scene
    c. they can recognize faces only minutes after birth
    d. none of the above

19. What are two characteristics of a developmental stage as Piaget uses the term?
    a. consistent, continuous
    b. continuous, discrete
    c. consistent, concrete
    d. consistent, discrete

20. One way of reconciling modern evidence with Piaget's view of stages of development is to say that:
    a. young children begin with very few cognitive capacities and need to learn them all
    b. young children have some cognitive skills but cannot apply them to very many situations
    c. Piaget was essentially correct in all of his assertions about stages, but he was wrong in when the stages begin
    d. none of the above

21. According to the theory of maturation:
    a. behavior change is associated with neurological changes
    b. environmental changes have great impact on the development of the child
    c. learning takes place independently of age
    d. all of the above

22. According to the theory of specific learning:
    a. learning is the acquisition of specific patterns
    b. most things could be learned at any time
    c. the speed with which a child learns depends on his age
    d. a and b but not c

23. Which of the following statements about Piaget is true?
    a. he asserts that development involves a constant interchange between the child and the environment
    b. he asserts that specific learning causes the progression from one stage to another
    c. he asserts that the age at which each stage begins is consistent across cultures
    d. he says that the child's schemas assimilate to the environment, as well as the environment being accommodated to the schema

24. An approach to cognitive development asserts that mental growth is based partly on the acquisition of better and larger chunks of information. This approach explains cognitive development as a change in:
    a. maturation
    b. information processing
    c. specific learning
    d. assimilation

25. Which of the following is *not* an example of metacognition?
    a. being realistic about how many numbers you can recall at one time
    b. recognizing the difference between reality and illusion
    c. using strategies for reaching solutions
    d. reading and following directions for a recipe

26. Which of the following is true?
    a. Unschooled people are incapable of abstract thought.
    b. Schooled and unschooled people think alike.
    c. Schooled people cannot apply their knowledge to a variety of contexts or situations.
    d. none of the above

Answer Key for Self Test

1.	b	p. 386	14.	c	p. 396
2.	b	p. 386	15.	c	p. 396
3.	c	p. 387	16.	a	p. 398
4.	b	p. 389	17.	d	p. 399
5.	d	p. 391	18.	a	p. 403
6.	a	p. 392	19.	d	p. 401
7.	a	p. 392	20.	b	pp. 404–5
8.	b	p. 393	21.	a	p. 406
9.	c	p. 393	22.	d	p. 407
10.	b	p. 393	23.	a	p. 407
11.	d	pp. 392–393	24.	b	p. 408
12.	a	p. 394	25.	d	pp. 410–11
13.	a	p. 394	26.	d	pp. 411–13

Investigating Psychological Phenomena

CONSERVATION OF NUMBER

Equipment: Thirty-three red poker chips and thirty-four blue ones
Number of subjects: One, age four or five (preoperational stage, according to Piaget)
Time per subject: Fifteen minutes
Time for experimenter: Thirty minutes

In Chapter 13, Professor Gleitman discusses the development of conservation ability as children move into what Piaget calls the stage of concrete operations. The characteristic of this ability is that children come to use a set of mental rules, or operations, to govern their thought about objects in the world. For example, they learn that a certain volume of water is unchanged by the characteristics of the container that happens to contain it. Thus, pouring a certain amount of water from a low and wide container into one that is tall and thin does not change its volume even though the water achieves a greater height in the tall container.

There is also research suggesting that Piaget may have underestimated the ability of children to conserve. Apparently, when faced with somewhat less demanding tasks, which nevertheless are formal tests of conservation ability, young children who should be in a preoperational stage show some signs of conservation. This has been shown most impressively with the conservation of number. The problem that preoperational children face in conserving number is that they confuse numerosity with the physical length of the series which contains the items whose number must be judged. For example, they frequently judge that a row of items contains more items if it is simply longer than another row of items.

The present exercise allows you to take an empirical look at this issue. One of the variables that may influence whether children show evidence of conservation or not is the number of items that are included in a test. Common sense suggests that the more objects in a set whose number must be judged, the more difficult will be the judgment. We shall test this hypothesis in the context of a number conservation test in which the number of objects whose number must be judged will vary. In both conditions of the experiment, your subjects will be asked to judge which of two rows contains more objects. In one condition, the number of objects in each row will be less than in the other condition.

In order to conduct this experiment most efficiently, and with the greatest chance of keeping the attention of your subject, prearrange the stimulus arrays before you begin. The figure on the next page shows you the five stimulus arrangements for each of the two numerosity conditions. Each letter in the figure represents a chip of the appropriate color (B = blue, R = red). On the left are the arrangements for the lower numerosity condition. The first arrangement is the control condition in which each row contains the same number of chips, and in which the two rows are of equal length. In the second figure, the two rows contain the same number, but the lengths of the rows differ. In the third figure, the lengths are equal, but one row contains more chips than the other. The fourth arrangement pits the two variables against one another: the row that is longest also contains fewer chips than the shorter row. On the right are comparable arrangements for the condition in which more chips are used. The four arrangements are in the same order as the ones on the left of the figure.

Make each of the eight arrangements on a separate piece of cardboard, and place them out of sight. Then seat your subject comfortably and explain to him/her that you are going to play a game in which the child has to say which row of chips has more chips. Take out arrangement 1 first and ask the child, "Which row has more, the one with red or the one with blue, or are they the same?" If the child answers that they are not the same, then lengthen or shorten one of the rows so that the child agrees that they are equal. Be sure that the red and blue chips are equal. Be sure that the red and blue chips line up above one another, so there is a one-to-one correspondence.

Now move on to arrangement 2. Continue with the same line of questioning, asking which row contains more, the red one or the blue one. After getting an answer, which you should record on the given protocol form, ask your subject to explain his/her response. That is, ask why he/she judged one of the rows as having more (or less, or equal, depending upon his/her answer) chips, and record the substance of this answer on the protocol form. Continue with arrangements three and four, after which you should move on to arrangements five through eight. In each case, record the data in the spaces provided on the answer sheet. For each arrangement decide whether your subject was paying attention to the number or the length of the series in making his/her judgment. Which condition shows better number conservation overall?

The critical comparison that is of interest in this experiment is whether your subject shows evidence of competence in number conservation with fewer chips, but falters with a greater number of chips. If this is so, how does it fit in with the discussion in the text about the development of conservation? What does it imply about a stage theory of development?

Some other questions that might be raised by this exercise are the following: Would your results have been any different if the two conditions had been run in the opposite order, from the more to the less difficult? Is there something inherent in the questioning of the subject that may bias him/her to attend to length rather than number? Why might number conservation be better with fewer chips in the stimuli? What kinds of operations did your subject seem to be using as the basis for his/her judgment? What kinds of tests could be constructed to discover whether other conservation skills might also develop earlier than previously thought?

STIMULI FOR NUMBER CONSERVATION EXPERIMENT

Small Numbers

1. B B B
R R R

2.   B B B
R   R   R

3. B   B
R R R

4. B   B
 R R R

Large Numbers

5. B B B B B B
R R R R R R

6.   B B B B B B
R R R R R R

7. B B B B B
R R R R R R

8. B B B B   B
 R R R R R R

ANSWER SHEET FOR NUMBER CONSERVATION EXPERIMENT

1. More blue ______________________
More red ______________________
Both equal ______________________

Explanation:

2. More blue ______________________
More red ______________________
Both equal ______________________

Explanation:

3. More blue ______________________
More red ______________________
Both equal ______________________

Explanation:

4. More blue ______________________
More red ______________________
Both equal ______________________

Explanation:

5. More blue ______________________
More red ______________________
Both equal ______________________

Explanation:

6. More blue ______________________
More red ______________________
Both equal ______________________

Explanation:

7. More blue ______________________
More red ______________________
Both equal ______________________

Explanation:

8. More blue ______________________
More red ______________________
Both equal ______________________

Explanation:

CHAPTER 14

Social Development

Learning Objectives

1. What are the major ways in which the individual's social world expands as the individual develops? What principles of development did Freud suggest?

ATTACHMENT

The roots of attachment

2. Describe the view (the "cupboard" theory) that attributes the infant's love for the mother to the fact that she fulfills basic biological needs.
3. How do Harlow's experiments on monkeys cast doubt on the "cupboard" view?
4. Explain Bowlby's theory of attachment, including both positive and negative aspects of attachment seeking. Contrast Bowlby's theory with Freud's "cupboard" theory.
5. Describe the process of imprinting in animals.

Patterns of attachment

6. Describe Ainsworth's procedure for measuring attachment. What characterizes the securely attached child?
7. What is the evidence that the early parent-child relationship, as assessed in the Strange Situation, is a major determinant of later social and emotional adjustment?
8. What is the evidence of attachment to the father? What is the difference between paternal and maternal attachment?

The effect of early maternal separation

9. What are the effects of maternal separation and the effects of career mothers and day care on later social adjustment?

Are the effects of early social deprivation reversible?

10. Summarize the effects of maternal deprivation on humans. Are the effects of early social deprivation reversible?
11. Describe circumstances under which it is possible to reverse effects of early maternal deprivation in humans.
12. Evaluate the Freudian claims that early experience is a critical factor in social development, and that its effects are irreversible. Describe the general process of social development.

CHILDHOOD SOCIALIZATION

Mechanisms of socialization

13. Describe observational learning and modeling. Indicate the way in which this process differs from instrumental learning.
14. Outline cognitive developmental theory. Indicate how it views imitation.
15. Summarize the basic differences among the Freudian-reinforcement, social learning, and cognitive developmental approaches to socialization.

The first agents of socialization: the parents

16. Describe the autocratic, permissive, and authoritative-reciprocal patterns of child rearing. What are the characteristic behaviors of children raised under each of these approaches?

The child's effect on the parents

17. Explain the interaction between the child's temperament and the parent's pattern of child rearing, and indicate how this interaction complicates the task of relating patterns of child rearing to the child's personality.

THE DEVELOPMENT OF MORALITY

Not doing wrong

18. What does it mean to internalize moral values? What is the role of punishment in internalization?

Doing good

19. What is empathy, and how does it function in supporting altruistic behavior?

Moral reasoning

20. Describe Kohlberg's stages of moral reasoning.
21. According to Gilligan, what is the fundamental sex difference in moral attitudes or reasoning? What is the evidence on this potential sex difference?
22. Discuss cultural differences in moral reasoning and moral behavior.

THE DEVELOPMENT OF SEX AND GENDER

23. Distinguish among gender roles, sexual orientation, and gender identity.

Gender roles

24. What is gender typing and what are gender role stereotypes?

Constitutional factors and sex differences

25. Evaluate the role of nature (biological-genetic) factors in establishing gender roles, with respect to gender differences in aggression and pattern of intellectual abilities.

Social factors and sex differences

26. Discuss how small constitutional differences can be amplified by social forces.

Theories of gender typing

27. Compare and contrast three theories of gender typing: psychoanalytic, social learning, and cognitive developmental. What is the critical mechanism of gender typing for each theory?

Sexual orientation

28. Discuss the incidence of homosexuality at different historical times and in different cultures.
29. What is the evidence on age of onset of homosexuality and the effects of early experience?
30. Discuss some possible biological causes of homosexuality, or, more generally, sexual orientation. Include consideration of genetic effects and brain differences.
31. What possible adaptive value could there be to homosexuality?

DEVELOPMENT AFTER CHILDHOOD

32. Describe Erik Erikson's conception of human growth. What are his "eight ages of man"? To what extent do they hold across cultures?

Adolescence

33. Discuss the particular problems of adolescence as a transition to adulthood in the United States and in other cultures. Is adolescence always turbulent?

Adulthood

34. Indicate how changes in American society have markedly changed the experience of old age.

Programmed Exercises

ATTACHMENT

1. According to Freud, love for the mother derives from the fact that she is associated with the ____________ of hunger, thirst, and pain.	alleviation (reduction, decrease)
2. Harlow's experiments with terry-cloth mothers suggest that, in monkeys, the nutrient provided by the mother is less important for attachment than the ____________ ____________ that she provides.	contact comfort
3. According to Bowlby's theory of attachment, fear of the ____________ forms one basis of attachment. Another basis is a tendency to engage in ____________ ____________.	unknown (unfamiliar) social interaction
4. The built-in fear referred to above is initially unspecific, and corresponds to what psychiatrists call ____________-____________ anxiety.	free-floating

5. The formation of strong attachments by the young of a species to objects (typically the parent) encountered early in life is called ___________. — imprinting

6. This type of attachment (imprinting) tends to occur during a special time, early in life, called the ___________ ___________. — critical period

7. According to Bowlby, proximity to an attachment figure provides ___________ and ___________, and separation from it leads to ___________. — comfort security, distress

8. Fear of strangers and specific recognition of the mother occur at about the same time, cross-culturally. This time is from ___________ to ___________ months of age. — six, eight

9. In Ainsworth's "Strange Situation" measurements, a child who explores freely when the mother is present, shows some distress at her leaving, and greets her return with enthusiasm is called ___________ ___________. — securely attached

10. In Ainsworth's "Strange Situation" measurements, a child who doesn't explore even in the mother's presence, becomes intensely upset when she leaves, and shows ambivalence during reunion is called ___________. — resistant

11. In Ainsworth's "Strange Situation" measurements, a child who is distant and aloof toward its mother, shows little distress when she leaves, and ignores her when she returns is called ___________. — avoidant

12. In the "Strange Situation," disappearance of the father produces some ___________, but ___________ than that shown when the mother disappears. — distress, less

13. While mothers are preferred sources of care and comfort for most children, fathers are often the preferred ___________. — playmate

14. Evidence indicates that the effects of maternal separation in humans are ___________, and that maternal ___________, with consequent day care, may not compromise social adjustment. — reversible, employment (careers)

15. Humans reared in some ___________ show marked deficits in social performance. — institutions

16. Maternal deprivation has severe long-term effects in humans, but not if it occurs for no more than a few ___________. — months

17. Freud claimed that early experience (in the first six years or so of life) was ___________ for appropriate adult social adjustments, and that the effects of normal early experience were ___________. — critical irreversible

18. Studies on children put in nurturant environments after being in institutions indicate that many of the effects of maternal deprivation are ___________. — reversible

CHILDHOOD SOCIALIZATION

19. ___________ is the process by which the child acquires the patterns of thought and behavior that are characteristic of the society in which she is born. — Socialization

20. Both Freudian and reinforcement theories explain socialization in terms of the opposite influences of ___________ and ___________. — pain (punishment), pleasure (reward)

21. Researchers who believe that the basic Pavlovian and instrumental learning process must be supplemented to explain socialization are called ____________ ____________ theorists. — social learning

22. Such theorists (see previous question) add to the basic learning processes the mechanism of ____________ ____________. — observational learning (modeling)

23. In order to preform an observed act, there must be something to ____________, which is called the ____________. — imitate model

24. The ____________ approach to socialization emphasizes the role of understanding or competence in the socialization process. — cognitive (cognitive developmental)

25. The child-rearing style in which the parent controls the child strictly, and does not explain the justification for the governing rules to the child, is called the ____________ pattern. The opposite extreme is called the ____________ pattern. An intermediate approach, in which the parent exercises power, but also recognizes the child's point of view, is called the ____________-____________ pattern. — autocratic, permissive authoritative-reciprocal

26. Of these patterns (see question 25), the one that leads to the best-adjusted children is the ____________ ____________ pattern. — authoritative-reciprocal

27. Some differences in the pattern of child rearing may result from differences in ____________ in children, some of which are present at birth. — temperament

THE DEVELOPMENT OF MORALITY

28. We say a moral value is ____________ when an individual avoids transgressions because he feels that they are wrong, and not because he is afraid of being punished. — internalized

29. The ____________-____________ child-rearing style is most likely to lead to successful internalization. — authoritative-reciprocal

30. A direct emotional response to another person's emotions is called __________. — empathy

31. Kohlberg has interviewed both adults and children in an attempt to describe the development of ____________ ____________. — moral reasoning

32. Kohlberg describes this development in a series of successive ____________. — stages

33. According to Kohlberg, moral reasoning develops along a course in which right and wrong are defined by, first: ____________ _______ ____________; second: _____________; and third: _____________ _____________ _____________. — 1. fear of punishment and/or gain; 2. convention; 3. internalized (or abstract) moral principles

34. According to Gilligan, in making moral decisions, men tend to emphasize ____________, while women tend to be more influenced by ___________. — justice, compassion (caring)

THE DEVELOPMENT OF SEX AND GENDER

35. A definition of maleness or femaleness would have to consider three different "domains" or aspects. One is our inner sense of being male or female, called ____________ ____________. — gender identity

36. A second aspect (see above) is a group of behavior patterns that our culture deems appropriate for each sex, called ____________ ____________. gender roles

37. A third aspect (see above) is our choice of sexual partner, called ____________ ____________. sexual orientation

38. The expectation that someone "labeled" as male will be more aggressive and more interested in things than people is an example of ____________ ____________. gender typing

39.

This figure illustrates the phenomenon of gender role ____________. stereotypes

40. Characteristics of the female gender role stereotype in American society include (list 3) ____________, ____________, and ____________. submissiveness, interest in people, emotionality, fear of success, talkativeness, gentleness

41. There seems to be a constitutional basis for some sex differences: for example, in the area of motivation, males tend to be more ____________ than females. aggressive

42. There may also be a constitutional basis for male superiority in ____________ ability. spatial (spatial-mathematical)

43. In many cases, culture or social factors act to ____________ existing small constitutional sex differences. exaggerate (or amplify or increase)

44. A female who sees herself as female and is sexually attracted to males but is aggressive and athletic could be said to have some characteristics of the male ____________ ____________. gender role

45.	According to Freud, the basic mechanism of gender typing is ___________.	identification
46.	According to the social learning view, little girls show typical female interests because they are ___________ for doing so.	rewarded (reinforced)
47.	Cognitive developmental theories point out that a three-year-old who believes that a girl can become a boy if given a haircut fails to show ___________ ___________.	gender constancy
48.	According to cognitive developmental theory, and in contrast to social learning theory, identification with a same-sex model ___________ (precedes or follows) the acquisition of gender identity.	follows
49.	According to social learning theories, the first aspect of sex differences that is established is ___________ ___________.	gender role
50.	The majority of men and women are ___________ in that they seek sexual partners of the opposite sex. The minority who seek partners of the same sex are called ___________.	heterosexual homosexuals
51.	The incidence of exclusive male homosexuality in the United States is about ___________ percent of all adult males (as of 1948).	4
52.	Research indicates no major differences between homosexuals and heterosexuals in ___________ experience. Overall, it seems homosexuals experience an attraction to the same sex ___________ (before/after) having sexual experiences.	early before
53.	___________ studies suggest a genetic influence on homosexuality.	Twin
54.	There is evidence for a difference in ___________ structure between male heterosexuals and homosexuals.	brain (hypothalamus)

DEVELOPMENT AFTER CHILDHOOD

55.	Erikson's "Eight Ages of Man" spans the entire life cycle, each stage accompanied by a critical ___________.	conflict (or crisis)
56.	The stage of transition from childhood to adulthood is called ___________. At this stage, the major conflict is described as an ___________ ___________.	adolescence identity crisis
57.	In some cultures, the transition to adulthood is marked clearly, with a ceremony or more extended set of activities called ___________ ___________.	initiation rites
58.	In Erikson's scheme, although there are some important biological markers in growth past childhood, such as ___________, the quality and duration of each stage is substantially influenced by ___________.	puberty (or menopause) culture

Self Test

1. Harlow's results, showing a preference by infant monkeys for a "terry-cloth mother" over a wire mother that provides food, argue:
   a. in favor of Freud's view of attachment
   b. in favor of Bowlby's view of attachment
   c. that nutrition has no effect in producing attachment between infant and mother
   d. a and b
   e. all of the above

2. Bowlby's theory of attachment:
   a. may include imprinting to a familiar object
   b. assumes that infants fear unfamiliar objects
   c. assumes infants have a tendency to be attached to objects with certain characteristics
   d. all of the above
   e. none of the above

3. Which of the following statements about imprinting is *false*?
   a. Imprinting depends on the fact that the parents will be the most salient objects around the offspring in the first part of life.
   b. Imprinting is based on experience.
   c. Animals may lose the capacity to imprint after a certain age.
   d. One would not expect to find imprinting in a "parasitic" species that is typically raised by adults of another species.
   e. none of the above

4. Proximity is to comfort as separation is to
   a. imprinting
   b. critical periods
   c. providing nutrients
   d. distress
   e. satisfaction

5. Infants show less distress at their fathers' than their mothers' departure, in Ainsworth's Strange Situation. Which of the following would be most likely to increase the infants' distress response to the fathers' disappearance?
   a. dress the father as a woman
   b. dress the father as a strange man
   c. find a father who had much more contact with his child
   d. find a child who had been severely punished by his mother
   e. give the child a free-floating anxiety toy

6. A conclusion that can be drawn from human maternal deprivation studies is that:
   a. adequate nutrition is not sufficient to produce normal social behavior
   b. behavior to peers is unaffected by maternal deprivation
   c. imprinting does not have anything to do with later sexual or maternal behavior
   d. maternal deprivation effects are especially severe if the deprivation occurs in the first few months of life
   e. all of the above

7. Institutionalized human children show social abnormalities characterized by:
   a. a "critical period" beginning at the time of birth and ending at about three months
   b. social withdrawal
   c. long-term effects that are irreversible
   d. a and b
   e. all of the above

8. Freud claimed that early experience had (1) a critical and (2) an irreversible effect on social development. Results from research up to this time suggest that:
   a. these two principles are basically correct
   b. early experiences have important effects, but many are reversible
   c. these two principles are totally incorrect
   d. early experiences have some significant effects, and these effects are irreversible
   e. none of the above

9. Both the Freudian approach and social learning or reinforcement theory agree that __________ is a major factor in socialization.
   a. imitation
   b. modeling
   c. the child's understanding of the importance of older people
   d. gender identity
   e. none of the above

10. According to social learning theory, a critical aspect of socialization is:
    a. observational learning from models
    b. making models
    c. Pavlovian conditioning
    d. imprinting
    e. none of the above

11. Wendy sees her big sister smoking a cigarette. A few hours later she sneaks over to a pack of cigarettes, takes one out, holds it with two fingers, and puts it into her mouth, looking as debonair as possible. Then she lights it up, and inhales

her first breath, coughing and gagging. But she continues to smoke the whole cigarette. This performance presents problems for a simple reinforcement view of socialization because:
   a. there is observational learning without immediate performance
   b. there seems to be negative reinforcement (gagging) for smoking
   c. there seems to be no basic biological reinforcement for her smoking
   d. it is not clear why she would want to imitate her sister
   e. all of the above

12. Ironically, children raised in the opposite autocratic and permissive styles share some common behavioral characteristics. Both types of children tend to:
   a. be socially responsible
   b. be more attached to their father
   c. lack independence
   d. be high in originality
   e. a and c

13. Imagine that a study reports that most cranky five-year-olds had parents who closed the door to their infants' bedrooms at night, so the baby wouldn't wake them. What might be possible explanations of this result?
   a. Isolating infants causes them to be cranky later in life.
   b. Cranky infants are more likely to be isolated by their parents.
   c. Parents who isolate their children in this way also do other things in child rearing that cause crankiness.
   d. Crankiness is inherited; cranky parents are more likely to be irritated by a crying child, and so are more likely to isolate it.
   e. all of the above

14. Authoritative-reciprocal rearing style is to optimal adjustment as mild social pressure is to ____________.
   a. doing good
   b. not doing wrong
   c. maximum internalization
   d. permissive rearing style
   e. autocratic rearing style

15. Forced compliance is an ineffective way of producing attitude change. This finding is in accord with:
   a. the permissive rearing style
   b. the principle of minimal sufficiency
   c. the principle of imitation
   d. attachment theory
   e. none of the above

16. The occurrence of unselfish helping behavior by A suggests that A:
   a. experiences empathic distress
   b. is at a high stage of moral reasoning
   c. knows how to be helpful in the particular situation
   d. a and b
   e. a and c

17. Consider the following three objections to making three reservations on different airlines at the same time for one person: A. It is against the unwritten rules of the airlines. B. It interferes with the access of others with no tangible gain to the party in question. C. It can be detected, and penalties can be assessed. According to Kohlberg, how would these three reasons be arranged in terms of the development of moral reasoning; indicate the earliest stage first.
   a. A, B, C
   b. B, C, A
   c. C, B, A
   d. B, A, C
   e. C, A, B

18. A person says that one shouldn't double park because it is against the law. This explanation is an example of:
   a. preconventional morality
   b. conventional morality
   c. postconventional morality
   d. empathy
   e. none of the above

19. According to Gilligan, moral reasoning in men is relatively more influenced by justice, while in women it is relatively more influenced by compassion. But men and women don't differ on scores on Kohlberg's tests of moral reasoning. Why?
   a. Kohlberg's tests value compassion as much as abstract principles.
   b. Compassion is more abstract than justice.
   c. The male-female difference has more to do with emphases than abilities.
   d. a and b
   e. a and c

20. Which of the following is illustrative of gender role?
   a. thinking of oneself as a female
   b. attraction to the opposite sex

c. submissiveness and emotionality in a female
d. homosexual tendencies
e. none of the above

21. The finding that, in American culture, females express emotion more readily than do males, should be interpreted to mean:
a. that females are constitutionally more inclined to express emotions
b. that our society teaches females to be more expressive
c. that the average female is more emotionally expressive than the average male, but that there is a great deal of overlap
d. gender typing is not a sufficient explanation of sex difference, and one must also consider gender identity
e. a and d

22. The idea that there is a constitutional factor contributing to sex differences in aggression or spatial orientation is (or would be) supported by all of the following *except*:
a. in early humans, the stronger male was responsible for almost all hunting and fighting
b. these differences are seen in many cultures
c. some of these differences are also seen in animals
d. male hormone increases aggression
e. all of the above

23. According to the psychoanalytic view, the basic mechanism of gender typing is:
a. imitation
b. conditioning
c. repression
d. identification
e. imprinting

24. Kohlberg's cognitive developmental view criticizes both the Freudian concept of identification and the social learning notion of imitation in the first few years of life on all *except*:
a. Little children don't show gender constancy.
b. Little children don't have a basis for recognizing which of their parents is of their sex.
c. Gender role precedes gender identity.
d. Young children may not understand that males have a penis and females don't.
e. b and c

25. The psychoanalytic notion that the young boy identifies with his father in order to avoid punishment for his erotic feelings toward his mother assumes:
a. a necessary linkage among gender role and identity and sexual orientation
b. that the boy understands his fundamental sexual similarity to his father
c. that erotic factors form the basis for gender typing
d. all of the above
e. none of the above

26. According to Kohlberg's cognitive view of gender typing, gender identity depends critically on:
a. identification
b. constitutional factors
c. achievement of gender constancy
d. hormones
e. imprinting

27. Male homosexuality:
a. is not stigmatized in all cultures
b. was quite acceptable in ancient Greece
c. seems to be more common than female homosexuality
d. is almost always associated with male gender identity
e. all of the above

28. The psychoanalytic view suggests that male homosexuality may result when the child resolves fears aroused during the Oedipal conflict by identifying with the mother instead of the father. This theory would have difficulty explaining:
a. the absence of evidence for differences in the early experience of homosexuals and heterosexuals
b. the occurrence of a normal homosexual phase in adolescents in some cultures
c. the fact that, typically, male homosexuals have traditional male gender identity and roles
d. all of the above
e. a and b

29. An argument can be made for the adaptiveness of homosexuality in terms of inclusive fitness. This might be analogous to:
a. the existence of sterile female worker bees
b. the adaptive value of grandparents
c. gender identity crises

d. all of the above
e. a and b

30. The transition from childhood to adolescence:
a. occurs at the same age in all cultures
b. is always a turbulent period
c. usually occurs at the onset of sexual maturity
d. all of the above
e. none of the above

31. Initiation rites, retirement parties, and weddings have in common that they:
a. explicitly mark important life transitions
b. occur in virtually all cultures
c. are explicitly predicted by Erikson's scheme
d. match Freud's views of major life events
e. make for gradual transitions from one stage to another

32. In some societies, children gradually assume adult responsibilities, and in some societies, old family members live in the home, taking care of grandchildren (or great-grandchildren) and giving advice. These traditions:
a. emphasize transitions from one stage of life to another
b. ease transition from one stage of life to another
c. emphasize the importance of biological factors in life history
d. prove the correctness of Erikson's stages
e. none of the above

Answer Key for Self Test

1.	b	p. 419
2.	d	pp. 419–20
3.	e	pp. 420–21
4.	d	p. 421
5.	c	p. 422
6.	a	p. 424
7.	b	p. 424
8.	b	p. 425
9.	e	pp. 426–27
10.	a	p. 426
11.	e	p. 426
12.	c	p. 429
13.	e	pp. 428–29
14.	c	p. 429
15.	b	p. 431
'6.	e	pp. 431–32
17.	e	p. 433
18.	b	p. 433
19.	c	p. 433
20.	c	p. 435
21.	c	p. 436
22.	e	pp. 437–38
23.	d	p. 439
24.	c	p. 440
25.	d	pp. 439–40
26.	c	p. 440
27.	e	pp. 441–42
28.	d	pp. 441–42
29.	e	p. 444
30.	c	p. 446
31.	a	p. 447
32.	b	p. 450

Investigating Psychological Phenomena

SEX DIFFERENCES

Equipment: None
Number of subjects: Twelve
Time per subject: Five minutes
Time for experimenter: Sixty minutes

Sex differences can be analyzed into three different categories:
1. Gender identity—thinking of oneself as male or female.
2. Sexual orientation—sex of desired sexual partners, leading to the heterosexual-homosexual distinction.
3. Gender role—behavior patterns or attitudes associated with one or the other sex.

The relative role of experience (nurture) and genes (nature) has been debated for each of these aspects of sex. But before such studies can be done definitively, we must be clear on the nature of the differences to be explained. This is more or less clear for gender identity and sexual orientation. But the major behavioral and attitudinal differences between the sexes are not obvious and surely differ across cultures.

This study is an attempt to define some reliable sex differences among American college students. We have developed seventeen questions that promise to reveal sex differences (we will use as a criterion of a question that discriminates between the sexes a response pattern in which there is at least a 25 percentage point difference between males and females).

First: Answer the questionnaire. *Do not read on until you finish it.*

Questionnaire on Sex Differences

Sex: Male Female (Circle one)

1. Would you be willing to kill a cockroach by slapping it with your hands?
a) yes b) no
2. What is Queen Anne's lace?
a) flower d) doily
b) embroidery e) spice
c) perfume

3. How many times in the last twenty-four hours have you used the word "shit"?
   a) less than 5 times b) 5 or more times
4. Can you sew well enough to make clothes?
   a) yes b) no
5. Do you believe in sexual intercourse only after a spiritual love exists between you and your partner?
   a) yes b) no
6. Do you walk around freely in the nude in a locker room?
   a) yes b) no
7. How often do you cry?
   a) very often d) very infrequently
   b) often e) never
   c) only with good reason
8. At times I feel like smashing things.
   a) true b) false
9. Do you know your chest measurement?
   a) yes b) no
10. Can you change a tire easily?
   a) yes b) no
11. I spend no more than one hour during an average school day playing the radio or listening to records.
   a) true b) false
12. Would you prefer to be the dominant one in a relationship?
   a) yes b) no
13. Do you think that you are overweight?
   a) yes b) no
14. When you get depressed, does washing your hair make you feel better?
   a) yes b) no
15. Do you sleep in the nude?
   a) yes b) no
16. Which parent are you closest to?
   a) mother b) father
17. I try to keep my room as neat as possible.
   a) true b) false

These questions have been made up by faculty and students in introductory psychology courses. Each question has been "tested" with at least 100 undergraduate students in psychology courses. Therefore, we know how well these questions discriminate between college-age males and females (at least in 1971–1973, when the questions were tested). Of the seventeen questions, we know from past testing that five do not discriminate males from females. Try and guess, in advance, which questions would not discriminate. Then, check your guesses against the data presented on the final page of this study. *Guess before you read on.*

List questions that would not discriminate.

Note the type of successful questions in this questionnaire. Some relate to traditional male-female differences. Thus, males are more aggressive (item 12 on dominance, but note no difference on item 8—smashing things). Similarly males are less squeamish (item 1, cockroach) and more restrained emotionally (item 7, crying).

Other questions refer to knowledge or abilities that tend to go with gender in our society. This would include information about flowers (item 2, Queen Anne's lace), sewing ability (item 4), ability to change a tire (item 10), and knowledge of body measurements (item 9).

There are in addition some "miscellaneous" questions that tap into reliable differences (item 5, attitudes to intercourse; item 6, attitude to walking around nude in a locker room; item 13, perception of fatness in self; item 14, washing of hair as a response to depression; and item 17, neatness).

Second, collaborate with at least one or two other students in the class, so that you can collect enough data. Give the twelve copies of this questionnaire, located on pp. 181–186, to twelve undergraduates, six males and six females. (Try to get them to fill out the questionnaire when you give it to them; otherwise, you will find that you don't get a very high return rate.) Aim for a minimum of five completed questionnaires for each sex. Combine your results with the results of as many classmates as you can: It would be desirable to end up with at least fifteen students of each sex.

Third, tabulate your results (see p. 179) in the following way. For the "yes" or "no" questions (e.g., item 1), add up the number of subjects who answered "yes." Then calculate what percentage answered "yes." For the "true" or "false" questions (e.g., item 8), record those who answer "true." For other items (e.g., item 2), add up the number of subjects whose answers are the same as those indicated in parentheses under "Item" (e.g., item 1–flower).

Fourth, we have devised a "femaleness" score, by indicating the more common female response to each of the questions that discriminates sex. Compute such a score for each of your subjects by counting one point for each of the following answers:

1.	no	9.	yes
2.	flower	10.	no
4.	yes	12.	no
5.	yes	13.	yes
6.	no	14.	yes
7.	very often, often, or with good reason	17.	yes

Indicate here the total number of subjects of each sex from whom you have collected data:

Male ______________ Female ______________

Item	Your data (combined with classmate's data)				U. of Pa. Students**	
	Male		Female		Male	Female
	#	%	#	%	%	%
1. Killing cockroach	____	____	____	____	37	7*
2. Queen Anne's lace (correct answer: flower)	____	____	____	____	50	82*
3. Using word "shit" (less than 5 times)	____	____	____	____	49	50
4. Sew clothes	____	____	____	____	4	59*
5. Intercourse only after spiritual love	____	____	____	____	30	75*
6. Nude in locker room	____	____	____	____	72	31*
7. Crying frequently (very often, often, or only with good reason)	____	____	____	____	22	78*
8. Feel like smashing things	____	____	____	____	75	70
9. Chest measurement	____	____	____	____	28	78*
10. Change tire	____	____	____	____	76	13*
11. Playing radio	____	____	____	____	41	42
12. Prefer dominance in relationship	____	____	____	____	72	10*
13. Overweight	____	____	____	____	17	60*
14. Washing hair when depressed	____	____	____	____	19	53*
15. Sleep in nude	____	____	____	____	39	44
16. Closest parent (mother)	____	____	____	____	61	72
17. Keep room neat	____	____	____	____	51	77*

* A male-female difference of a least 25 percentage points.

** Responses to items in the sex difference questionnaire by undergraduate introductory psychology students at the University of Pennsylvania (1971–1973). Responses are based on from 70 to 270 males and from 88 to 292 females, depending on the item.

SCORES OF MALES AND FEMALES ON "FEMALENESS" SCORE

Plot the number of males and females with each score. Use solid lines for the males and broken lines for the females. The graph at the left contains data gathered from fifteen undergraduate males and seventeen undergraduate females in 1980. Plot your data on the blank graph on the right. How well does this score separate biological females from biological males? What percent of females score less than the highest male? How would you go about making a better behavioral discriminator of the sexes? (Note: We have avoided asking questions that might trivially distinguish males from females, such as: Do you wash the hair on your chest? or Do you ever wear dresses?)

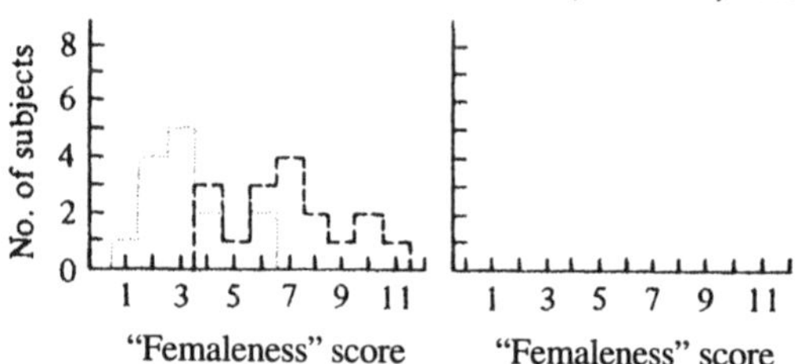

You may note some major differences between your data and the data we reported in 1971–1973. In fact, we tried the questionnaire on fifteen male and seventeen female undergraduate students in 1980 (the subjects used in the femaleness ratings), and found some differences from our 1971–1973 study. The biggest effects were that male-female differences disappeared for Queen Anne's lace (question 2), overweight (question 13: Over half of the men as well as women thought they were overweight), and washing hair when depressed (question 14: Practically no one in our recent sample answered yes to that).

There are basically three ways to explain discrepancies (our recent data or your data) from the original large sample of 1971–1973.

1. A general change in society over the last decade. It would seem fair to say that female gender roles have become more like male gender roles in this period. Does your data show this trend for any items? (Note that this would mean that female scores could move closer to male scores, and *not* that male scores would move closer to female scores. Of course, it is also possible to argue that the roles are becoming less distinct, but not necessarily moving toward the traditional male role.)

2. A difference in the populations sampled. Students from different parts of the country or from institutions with different styles or emphases might differ markedly in gender roles. Do you think your student sample would be likely to be very different from University of Pennsylvania students? In what ways? Is this reflected in differences on any scores? (Note, the differences might not just appear as male-female differences, but as generally higher or lower levels of response. For example, one might expect a generally higher positive response on sewing or changing a tire in people from rural backgrounds.)

3. Sampling error. Some observed differences may simply result from the fact that all samples from the same population don't have precisely the same scores (see Statistical Appendix to the textbook). With a small sample such as you have collected (as opposed to the large sample that we originally used), a wider variation from sample to sample would be expected. We would ordinarily use statistical methods to indicate how confident we would be that a difference between samples was not due to chance.

FURTHER ACTIVITIES

You might wish to try out some other questions that would relate gender identity to gender role. You could get a suggestion as to whether your questions were good discriminators with samples as low as twenty.

You can also try to use behavior rather than verbal responses to questionnaires. Can you think of obvious differences in such activities as: manner of walking or eating, facial expressions, behavior in front of mirrors, motorcycle riding, etc. Test your hypothesis by direct observation.

(If your instructor collects the data, fill out the report sheet in Appendix B.)

Questionnaire on Sex Differences

Sex: Male Female
(Circle one)

1. Would you be willing to kill a cockroach by slapping it with your hands?
   a) yes b) no
2. What is Queen Anne's lace?
   a) flower d) doily
   b) embroidery e) spice
   c) perfume
3. How many times in the last twenty-four hours have you used the word "shit"?
   a) less than 5 times b) 5 or more times
4. Can you sew well enough to make clothes?
   a) yes b) no
5. Do you believe in sexual intercourse only after a spiritual love exists between you and your partner?
   a) yes b) no
6. Do you walk around freely in the nude in a locker room?
   a) yes b) no
7. How often do you cry?
   a) very often d) very infrequently
   b) often e) never
   c) only with good reason
8. At times I feel like smashing things.
   a) true b) false
9. Do you know your chest measurement?
   a) yes b) no
10. Can you change a tire easily?
    a) yes b) no
11. I spend no more than one hour during an average school day playing the radio or listening to records.
    a) true b) false
12. Would you prefer to be the dominant one in a relationship?
    a) yes b) no
13. Do you think that you are overweight?
    a) yes b) no
14. When you get depressed, does washing your hair make you feel better?
    a) yes b) no
15. Do you sleep in the nude?
    a) yes b) no
16. Which parent are you closest to?
    a) mother b) father
17. I try to keep my room as neat as possible.
    a) true b) false

Questionnaire on Sex Differences

Sex: Male Female
(Circle one)

1. Would you be willing to kill a cockroach by slapping it with your hands?
   a) yes b) no
2. What is Queen Anne's lace?
   a) flower d) doily
   b) embroidery e) spice
   c) perfume
3. How many times in the last twenty-four hours have you used the word "shit"?
   a) less than 5 times b) 5 or more times
4. Can you sew well enough to make clothes?
   a) yes b) no
5. Do you believe in sexual intercourse only after a spiritual love exists between you and your partner?
   a) yes b) no
6. Do you walk around freely in the nude in a locker room?
   a) yes b) no
7. How often do you cry?
   a) very often d) very infrequently
   b) often e) never
   c) only with good reason
8. At times I feel like smashing things.
   a) true b) false
9. Do you know your chest measurement?
   a) yes b) no
10. Can you change a tire easily?
    a) yes b) no
11. I spend no more than one hour during an average school day playing the radio or listening to records.
    a) true b) false
12. Would you prefer to be the dominant one in a relationship?
    a) yes b) no
13. Do you think that you are overweight?
    a) yes b) no
14. When you get depressed, does washing your hair make you feel better?
    a) yes b) no
15. Do you sleep in the nude?
    a) yes b) no
16. Which parent are you closest to?
    a) mother b) father
17. I try to keep my room as neat as possible.
    a) true b) false

Questionnaire on Sex Differences

Sex: Male Female
(Circle one)

1. Would you be willing to kill a cockroach by slapping it with your hands?
   a) yes b) no
2. What is Queen Anne's lace?
   a) flower d) doily
   b) embroidery e) spice
   c) perfume
3. How many times in the last twenty-four hours have you used the word "shit"?
   a) less than 5 times b) 5 or more times
4. Can you sew well enough to make clothes?
   a) yes b) no
5. Do you believe in sexual intercourse only after a spiritual love exists between you and your partner?
   a) yes b) no
6. Do you walk around freely in the nude in a locker room?
   a) yes b) no
7. How often do you cry?
   a) very often d) very infrequently
   b) often e) never
   c) only with good reason
8. At times I feel like smashing things.
   a) true b) false
9. Do you know your chest measurement?
   a) yes b) no
10. Can you change a tire easily?
    a) yes b) no
11. I spend no more than one hour during an average school day playing the radio or listening to records.
    a) true b) false
12. Would you prefer to be the dominant one in a relationship?
    a) yes b) no
13. Do you think that you are overweight?
    a) yes b) no
14. When you get depressed, does washing your hair make you feel better?
    a) yes b) no
15. Do you sleep in the nude?
    a) yes b) no
16. Which parent are you closest to?
    a) mother b) father
17. I try to keep my room as neat as possible.
    a) true b) false

Questionnaire on Sex Differences

Sex: Male Female
(Circle one)

1. Would you be willing to kill a cockroach by slapping it with your hands?
   a) yes b) no
2. What is Queen Anne's lace?
   a) flower d) doily
   b) embroidery e) spice
   c) perfume
3. How many times in the last twenty-four hours have you used the word "shit"?
   a) less than 5 times b) 5 or more times
4. Can you sew well enough to make clothes?
   a) yes b) no
5. Do you believe in sexual intercourse only after a spiritual love exists between you and your partner?
   a) yes b) no
6. Do you walk around freely in the nude in a locker room?
   a) yes b) no
7. How often do you cry?
   a) very often d) very infrequently
   b) often e) never
   c) only with good reason
8. At times I feel like smashing things.
   a) true b) false
9. Do you know your chest measurement?
   a) yes b) no
10. Can you change a tire easily?
    a) yes b) no
11. I spend no more than one hour during an average school day playing the radio or listening to records.
    a) true b) false
12. Would you prefer to be the dominant one in a relationship?
    a) yes b) no
13. Do you think that you are overweight?
    a) yes b) no
14. When you get depressed, does washing your hair make you feel better?
    a) yes b) no
15. Do you sleep in the nude?
    a) yes b) no
16. Which parent are you closest to?
    a) mother b) father
17. I try to keep my room as neat as possible.
    a) true b) false

Questionnaire on Sex Differences

Sex: Male Female
(Circle one)

1. Would you be willing to kill a cockroach by slapping it with your hands?
   a) yes b) no
2. What is Queen Anne's lace?
   a) flower d) doily
   b) embroidery e) spice
   c) perfume
3. How many times in the last twenty-four hours have you used the word "shit"?
   a) less than 5 times b) 5 or more times
4. Can you sew well enough to make clothes?
   a) yes b) no
5. Do you believe in sexual intercourse only after a spiritual love exists between you and your partner?
   a) yes b) no
6. Do you walk around freely in the nude in a locker room?
   a) yes b) no
7. How often do you cry?
   a) very often d) very infrequently
   b) often e) never
   c) only with good reason
8. At times I feel like smashing things.
   a) true b) false
9. Do you know your chest measurement?
   a) yes b) no
10. Can you change a tire easily?
    a) yes b) no
11. I spend no more than one hour during an average school day playing the radio or listening to records.
    a) true b) false
12. Would you prefer to be the dominant one in a relationship?
    a) yes b) no
13. Do you think that you are overweight?
    a) yes b) no
14. When you get depressed, does washing your hair make you feel better?
    a) yes b) no
15. Do you sleep in the nude?
    a) yes b) no
16. Which parent are you closest to?
    a) mother b) father
17. I try to keep my room as neat as possible.
    a) true b) false

Questionnaire on Sex Differences

Sex: Male Female
(Circle one)

1. Would you be willing to kill a cockroach by slapping it with your hands?
   a) yes b) no
2. What is Queen Anne's lace?
   a) flower d) doily
   b) embroidery e) spice
   c) perfume
3. How many times in the last twenty-four hours have you used the word "shit"?
   a) less than 5 times b) 5 or more times
4. Can you sew well enough to make clothes?
   a) yes b) no
5. Do you believe in sexual intercourse only after a spiritual love exists between you and your partner?
   a) yes b) no
6. Do you walk around freely in the nude in a locker room?
   a) yes b) no
7. How often do you cry?
   a) very often d) very infrequently
   b) often e) never
   c) only with good reason
8. At times I feel like smashing things.
   a) true b) false
9. Do you know your chest measurement?
   a) yes b) no
10. Can you change a tire easily?
    a) yes b) no
11. I spend no more than one hour during an average school day playing the radio or listening to records.
    a) true b) false
12. Would you prefer to be the dominant one in a relationship?
    a) yes b) no
13. Do you think that you are overweight?
    a) yes b) no
14. When you get depressed, does washing your hair make you feel better?
    a) yes b) no
15. Do you sleep in the nude?
    a) yes b) no
16. Which parent are you closest to?
    a) mother b) father
17. I try to keep my room as neat as possible.
    a) true b) false

Questionnaire on Sex Differences

Sex: Male Female
(Circle one)

1. Would you be willing to kill a cockroach by slapping it with your hands?
   a) yes b) no
2. What is Queen Anne's lace?
   a) flower d) doily
   b) embroidery e) spice
   c) perfume
3. How many times in the last twenty-four hours have you used the word "shit"?
   a) less than 5 times b) 5 or more times
4. Can you sew well enough to make clothes?
   a) yes b) no
5. Do you believe in sexual intercourse only after a spiritual love exists between you and your partner?
   a) yes b) no
6. Do you walk around freely in the nude in a locker room?
   a) yes b) no
7. How often do you cry?
   a) very often d) very infrequently
   b) often e) never
   c) only with good reason
8. At times I feel like smashing things.
   a) true b) false
9. Do you know your chest measurement?
   a) yes b) no
10. Can you change a tire easily?
    a) yes b) no
11. I spend no more than one hour during an average school day playing the radio or listening to records.
    a) true b) false
12. Would you prefer to be the dominant one in a relationship?
    a) yes b) no
13. Do you think that you are overweight?
    a) yes b) no
14. When you get depressed, does washing your hair make you feel better?
    a) yes b) no
15. Do you sleep in the nude?
    a) yes b) no
16. Which parent are you closest to?
    a) mother b) father
17. I try to keep my room as neat as possible.
    a) true b) false

Questionnaire on Sex Differences

Sex: Male Female
(Circle one)

1. Would you be willing to kill a cockroach by slapping it with your hands?
   a) yes b) no
2. What is Queen Anne's lace?
   a) flower d) doily
   b) embroidery e) spice
   c) perfume
3. How many times in the last twenty-four hours have you used the word "shit"?
   a) less than 5 times b) 5 or more times
4. Can you sew well enough to make clothes?
   a) yes b) no
5. Do you believe in sexual intercourse only after a spiritual love exists between you and your partner?
   a) yes b) no
6. Do you walk around freely in the nude in a locker room?
   a) yes b) no
7. How often do you cry?
   a) very often d) very infrequently
   b) often e) never
   c) only with good reason
8. At times I feel like smashing things.
   a) true b) false
9. Do you know your chest measurement?
   a) yes b) no
10. Can you change a tire easily?
    a) yes b) no
11. I spend no more than one hour during an average school day playing the radio or listening to records.
    a) true b) false
12. Would you prefer to be the dominant one in a relationship?
    a) yes b) no
13. Do you think that you are overweight?
    a) yes b) no
14. When you get depressed, does washing your hair make you feel better?
    a) yes b) no
15. Do you sleep in the nude?
    a) yes b) no
16. Which parent are you closest to?
    a) mother b) father
17. I try to keep my room as neat as possible.
    a) true b) false

Questionnaire on Sex Differences

Sex: Male Female
(Circle one)

1. Would you be willing to kill a cockroach by slapping it with your hands?
   a) yes b) no
2. What is Queen Anne's lace?
   a) flower d) doily
   b) embroidery e) spice
   c) perfume
3. How many times in the last twenty-four hours have you used the word "shit"?
   a) less than 5 times b) 5 or more times
4. Can you sew well enough to make clothes?
   a) yes b) no
5. Do you believe in sexual intercourse only after a spiritual love exists between you and your partner?
   a) yes b) no
6. Do you walk around freely in the nude in a locker room?
   a) yes b) no
7. How often do you cry?
   a) very often d) very infrequently
   b) often e) never
   c) only with good reason
8. At times I feel like smashing things.
   a) true b) false
9. Do you know your chest measurement?
   a) yes b) no
10. Can you change a tire easily?
    a) yes b) no
11. I spend no more than one hour during an average school day playing the radio or listening to records.
    a) true b) false
12. Would you prefer to be the dominant one in a relationship?
    a) yes b) no
13. Do you think that you are overweight?
    a) yes b) no
14. When you get depressed, does washing your hair make you feel better?
    a) yes b) no
15. Do you sleep in the nude?
    a) yes b) no
16. Which parent are you closest to?
    a) mother b) father
17. I try to keep my room as neat as possible.
    a) true b) false

Questionnaire on Sex Differences

Sex: Male Female
(Circle one)

1. Would you be willing to kill a cockroach by slapping it with your hands?
   a) yes b) no
2. What is Queen Anne's lace?
   a) flower d) doily
   b) embroidery e) spice
   c) perfume
3. How many times in the last twenty-four hours have you used the word "shit"?
   a) less than 5 times b) 5 or more times
4. Can you sew well enough to make clothes?
   a) yes b) no
5. Do you believe in sexual intercourse only after a spiritual love exists between you and your partner?
   a) yes b) no
6. Do you walk around freely in the nude in a locker room?
   a) yes b) no
7. How often do you cry?
   a) very often d) very infrequently
   b) often e) never
   c) only with good reason
8. At times I feel like smashing things.
   a) true b) false
9. Do you know your chest measurement?
   a) yes b) no
10. Can you change a tire easily?
    a) yes b) no
11. I spend no more than one hour during an average school day playing the radio or listening to records.
    a) true b) false
12. Would you prefer to be the dominant one in a relationship?
    a) yes b) no
13. Do you think that you are overweight?
    a) yes b) no
14. When you get depressed, does washing your hair make you feel better?
    a) yes b) no
15. Do you sleep in the nude?
    a) yes b) no
16. Which parent are you closest to?
    a) mother b) father
17. I try to keep my room as neat as possible.
    a) true b) false

Questionnaire on Sex Differences

Sex: Male Female
(Circle one)

1. Would you be willing to kill a cockroach by slapping it with your hands?
   a) yes b) no
2. What is Queen Anne's lace?
   a) flower d) doily
   b) embroidery e) spice
   c) perfume
3. How many times in the last twenty-four hours have you used the word "shit"?
   a) less than 5 times b) 5 or more times
4. Can you sew well enough to make clothes?
   a) yes b) no
5. Do you believe in sexual intercourse only after a spiritual love exists between you and your partner?
   a) yes b) no
6. Do you walk around freely in the nude in a locker room?
   a) yes b) no
7. How often do you cry?
   a) very often d) very infrequently
   b) often e) never
   c) only with good reason
8. At times I feel like smashing things.
   a) true b) false
9. Do you know your chest measurement?
   a) yes b) no
10. Can you change a tire easily?
    a) yes b) no
11. I spend no more than one hour during an average school day playing the radio or listening to records.
    a) true b) false
12. Would you prefer to be the dominant one in a relationship?
    a) yes b) no
13. Do you think that you are overweight?
    a) yes b) no
14. When you get depressed, does washing your hair make you feel better?
    a) yes b) no
15. Do you sleep in the nude?
    a) yes b) no
16. Which parent are you closest to?
    a) mother b) father
17. I try to keep my room as neat as possible.
    a) true b) false

Questionnaire on Sex Differences

Sex: Male Female
(Circle one)

1. Would you be willing to kill a cockroach by slapping it with your hands?
   a) yes b) no
2. What is Queen Anne's lace?
   a) flower d) doily
   b) embroidery e) spice
   c) perfume
3. How many times in the last twenty-four hours have you used the word "shit"?
   a) less than 5 times b) 5 or more times
4. Can you sew well enough to make clothes?
   a) yes b) no
5. Do you believe in sexual intercourse only after a spiritual love exists between you and your partner?
   a) yes b) no
6. Do you walk around freely in the nude in a locker room?
   a) yes b) no
7. How often do you cry?
   a) very often d) very infrequently
   b) often e) never
   c) only with good reason
8. At times I feel like smashing things.
   a) true b) false
9. Do you know your chest measurement?
   a) yes b) no
10. Can you change a tire easily?
    a) yes b) no
11. I spend no more than one hour during an average school day playing the radio or listening to records.
    a) true b) false
12. Would you prefer to be the dominant one in a relationship?
    a) yes b) no
13. Do you think that you are overweight?
    a) yes b) no
14. When you get depressed, does washing your hair make you feel better?
    a) yes b) no
15. Do you sleep in the nude?
    a) yes b) no
16. Which parent are you closest to?
    a) mother b) father
17. I try to keep my room as neat as possible.
    a) true b) false

CHAPTER 15

Intelligence: Its Nature and Measurement

Learning Objectives

1. Explain the relationship between the rise of mental testing and the structure of society.

MENTAL TESTS

2. Distinguish between achievement and aptitude tests.
3. Describe the purpose of intelligence and personality tests.

The study of variation

4. Define frequency distribution, mean, variance, standard deviation, and normal curve.
5. Explain the meaning of correlation.

Evaluating mental tests

6. Explain the concept of reliability and different measures of reliability.
7. Explain predictive and construct validity, and the procedure of standardization.

Using tests for selection

8. Discuss the value of a cutoff score.

INTELLIGENCE TESTING

9. Indicate the difficulties in defining intelligence.

Measuring intelligence

10. Outline the major events in the history of intelligence testing.
11. Define and explain the rationale behind intelligence quotients (as calculated by Binet) and deviation IQs.
12. Describe the different types of intelligence tests. Contrast the Wechsler, Binet, and the Kaufman Assessment Battery for Children.
13. How are intelligence tests modified to deal with culture differences, native language differences, and the exploration of neurological impairment?

An area of application: mental retardation

14. Discuss the definition of mental retardation and the relationship between retardation and productive functioning in society.

Intelligence and age

15. What is the relation between age and intelligence test performance, and what might account for these changes?

WHAT IS INTELLIGENCE? THE PSYCHOMETRIC APPROACH

16. What is the psychometric approach?

The structure of mental abilities

17. Describe the evidence for "g," and differentiate general factor and group factor theories.

WHAT IS INTELLIGENCE? BEYOND IQ

18. What are the limitations of intelligence tests, in terms of the range of mental abilities measured?

Practical intelligence

19. What is tacit knowledge, and how does it contribute to practical intelligence?

The notion of multiple intelligences

20. What are Gardner's multiple intelligences, and what is the evidence for them?

The culttural context of intelligence

21. How might cultural differences produce different performances on questions on intelligence tests?
22. Explain and evaluate the statement: "We may be able to measure intelligence, but we don't really know what it is."

NATURE, NURTURE, AND IQ

Some political issues

23. Review the history of positions on genetic factors in intelligence differences related to racial groups or social class.
24. What are the results on the effect of preschool enrichment programs on intelligence and school performance? How are these interpreted by those inclined to genetic or environmental explanations?

Genetic factors

25. Review basic terms in genetics (gene, chromosome, phenotype, genotype, dominant, recessive) and the relation between genotype and phenotype.
26. Describe the cause and genetic basis of phenylketonuria, and know how it illustrates the fact that inborn characteristics may be changeable.
27. Explain polygenic inheritance.
28. Explain why studies of the similarity in intelligence of members of the same family cannot be used to distinguish between genetic and environmental factors.
29. Explain how twin and adoption studies can be used to make this same distinction. Summarize the results of these studies and indicate problems in interpreting them.

Environmental factors

30. Summarize the evidence for and against genetic and environmental explanations of differences in intelligence (IQ) in American whites, from twin and adoption studies and from situations where major environmental differences were studied.

Group differences in IQ

31. Explain how the degree of genetic determination within groups can differ markedly from the degree of genetic determination of the same trait between groups.
32. Evaluate each of the following explanations of the reported difference between average IQ scores of American whites and blacks:
    1. the difference doesn't exist
    2. unfairness of the tests and test situations for blacks
    3. differences in environments between the groups
    4. genetic differences between the groups
33. What would be the consequences of a clear finding that some of the black-white IQ differences was attributable to genetic factors?

Programmed Exercises

MENTAL TESTS

1.	Tests of ____________ measure what an individual can do now, his present knowledge and competence in a particular area.	achievement
2.	Tests of ____________ predict what an individual will be able to do later.	aptitude
3.	____________ tests measure general aptitude.	Intelligence
4.	____________ tests assess behavioral dispositions.	Personality
5.	The frequency with which individual cases are distributed over different intervals of some measure is called a(n)____________ ____________.	frequency distribution
6.	The most common measure of central tendency is the ____________.	mean
7.	The most common measure of variability is the ____________ ____________. This is the square-root of the____________.	standard deviation variance
8.	Many physical and mental attributes show symmetrical bell-shaped frequency distributions, which are described as ____________ ____________.	normal curves

9. In evolution, ____________ provides the basis on which natural selection works. — variability

10. Each point in the figure here represents the weight and IQ of one person. This display is called a ____________ ____________. — scatter diagram

Weight

IQ

11. The ____________ ____________ is a statistic that describes the relations between two sets of measures. — correlation coefficient

12. If a test shows consistency in repeated measurements in similar circumstances, it is said to be ____________. — reliable

13. This is measured as the ____________ of the scores on two versions of the same test. — correlation

14. The higher the positive correlation between the score on a driving test and the number of years driving without an accident, the greater the ____________ ____________ of this test. The number of years without an accident is called the ____________. — predictive validity; criterion

15. A test based on a theoretical scheme that accounts for the attribute being measured is said to have ____________ ____________. — construct validity

16. If test A is a better measure of C than is test B, we can say that test A has a higher ____________ ____________. — validity coefficient

17. In order to obtain norms against which to evaluate a test score, the test is administered to a large number of people, called the ____________ ____________. — standardization sample

18. In using a test for selection, one often sets a ____________ score; people scoring below this value are rejected. — cutoff

INTELLIGENCE TESTING

19. According to Binet's system, a six-year-old who passed all the items at the nine-year-old level and none at the ten-year-old level would have a ____________ ____________ of nine years. — mental age

20. A person who gets the mean score for people of his age would have a deviation IQ of ____________. — 100

21. A person with an IQ of 100 would have a ____________ ____________ of 50. — percentile rank

22. The Wechsler Adult Intelligence Scale was in part a response to the emphasis on language in the Binet-Simon IQ tests. The Wechsler test has two parts, labeled ____________ and ____________. — performance, verbal

23. The Kaufman Assessment Battery for Children focuses on intelligence as a form of __________ processing. It has nonverbal scales, which make it particularly appropriate for testing of __________ or __________ children. — information; handicapped, minority (non-English-speaking)

24. The majority of people classified as mentally retarded can function __________ in relatively simple life situations. — adequately

25. Measurements of changes in intelligence in later life are ideally done by testing the same person at different ages in what is called a __________ study. — longitudinal

WHAT IS INTELLIGENCE? THE PSYCHOMETRIC APPROACH

26. In the __________ approach, the results of intelligence tests are studied and analyzed in an attempt to discover the structure of intelligence. — psychometric

27. The fact that scores from a variety of different intelligence tests, specific and general, are positively __________, led Spearman to introduce the factor of __________ __________. — correlated; general intelligence (g)

28. The fact that some specific parts of intelligence tests correlate very highly with only some other parts, and that there are clusters of tests which highly correlate with one another, is evidence for the __________ __________ theories. — group factor

WHAT IS INTELLIGENCE? BEYOND IQ

29. __________ __________, derived from experience in specific domains is an important part of practical intelligence. — Tacit knowledge

30. Gardner's theory of __________ __________ holds that there are six different, __________ mental capacities. — multiple intelligences; independent

31. Evidence for these independent capacities is the presence of retarded people who show outstanding performance on a task related to one of these activities. Such people are called __________ __________. — retarded savants

32. People from different __________ may know different things, respond to tests differently, and make different interpretations of the meaning of the same question. — cultures

NATURE, NURTURE, AND IQ

33. The unit of hereditary transmission is the __________. These are located in specific positions on one of the pairs of __________. — gene; chromosomes

34. The observed characteristics of an organism are called its __________. But the underlying genetic blueprint is called the __________. — phenotype; genotype

35. A gene that expresses itself in the phenotype regardless of the other gene member of the pair is called __________. A gene that will express itself in the phenotype only if there is an identical gene in the corresponding locus of the other chromosome is called __________. — dominant; recessive

36. A form of mental retardation that is caused by a single recessive gene is __________. — phenylketonuria (PKU)

37. Traits that are controlled by genes but show many different values are determined by __________ inheritance. — polygenic

38. The fact that members of the same family have positively correlated intelligence and often share special abilities can be used as evidence for both ____________ and ____________ factors. — hereditary (genetic), environmental

39. Two basic methods for estimating the role of inherited factors in intelligence or other traits are ____________ and ____________ studies. — twin, adoption

40. The pattern of a higher correlation of IQ scores in ____________ twin pairs than in ____________ twin pairs, argue for a role for heredity in intelligence. — identical, fraternal

41. The fact that the IQ of early-adopted children correlates more highly with the IQ of the biological as opposed to adoptive mother is evidence for ____________ determinants of intelligence. — genetic (biological, hereditary)

42. The negative effects of poor environments on IQ are illustrated by data showing that the longer a child is in a deprived environment, the lower his IQ. This appears as a ____________ correlation between IQ and age. — negative

43. Some have argued that at least part of the American black-white difference in average IQ scores can be attributed to the fact that the test was designed for the white middle class, that is to say, that the tests are not ____________ fair. — culture

44. One cannot infer that, if a trait has high genetic determination within two populations, then population differences will also be explainable as largely due to ____________. — heredity

45. A number of studies indicate that when differences in the environment of blacks and whites during childhood are markedly reduced or equated, the black-white IQ difference is markedly ____________. — reduced (diminished)

Self Test

1. Mental testing is primarily an American product, dating from the beginning of this century. America was a natural place for mental testing because:
   a. Americans embraced Freudian theory
   b. the American idea that all men are created equal required mental tests to show up their subtle differences
   c. of the high social and occupational mobility in America
   d. reinforcement was a popular concept in America
   e. Binet and Simon were Americans

2. One group of five people gets the following scores on a mathematics test: 85, 85, 90, 95, 95. Another group gets these five scores: 80, 80, 90, 100, 100. Which of the following statements about these groups is true?
   a. Both have the same means and different standard deviations.
   b. Both have the same means and the same standard deviation.
   c. Both have different means and the same standard deviation.
   d. Both have different means and standard deviations.
   e. It is impossible to say which group has a greater standard of deviation.

3. The diagram below represents the hypothetical scores of individual subjects on an IQ test and on a history achievement test. The correlation displayed would be closest to:
   a. +1.00
   b. + .50
   c. +0.00
   d. –.50
   e. –1.00

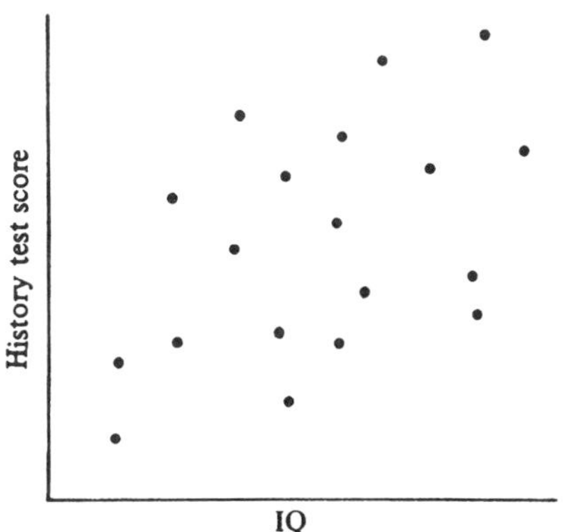

4. For which of the following pairs of variables would one expect to see a negative correlation?
   a. age and vocabulary
   b. height and visual acuity
   c. brain size and intelligence
   d. long-distance running ability and weight (among adults)
   e. social security number and intelligence (among adults)

5. If X is correlated with Y, then:
   a. if we know X, we can guess better than chance at the value of Y
   b. if we know Y, we can guess better than chance at the value of X
   c. there is no variability in X and Y
   d. X causes Y
   e. a and b

6. A hypothetical air force needs a test to help select people for training as pilots. There is no adequate theory of the acquisition of flying skills, but air force investigators discover that the speed with which one can tap with the third finger correlates +.80 with good performance in flying school. On the basis of this observation, one could say that the test had:
   a. high reliability
   b. high predictive validity
   c. high construct validity
   d. good standardization
   e. a standard deviation

7. An appropriate standardization sample for a test of artistic talent in elementary school children would be:
   a. elementary school children
   b. elementary school children fifty years ago
   c. older children who have selected art as a career
   d. elementary school children with artistic talent
   e. representative adults from the same country

8. Intelligence testers face special problems because:
   a. intelligence changes with age
   b. intelligence tests are not reliable
   c. all questions require prior knowledge, so that past experience determines the test score
   d. there is no clear basis for determining construct or predictive validity
   e. it is difficult to calculate percentile ranks for intelligence

9. The deviation IQ is a better measure than the older intelligence quotient (mental age/chronological age), because:
   a. it is newer
   b. the deviation IQ is more reliable and is based on better tests
   c. a person's deviation IQ will stay about the same, from age fifteen to fifty, for example
   d. the deviation IQ increases with age, as does intelligence
   e. it is based on the idea of 100 being average

10. Harry is eighteen and has a deviation IQ of 110. Carol is ten and has the same deviation IQ. In comparing them, we can say that:
   a. both have the same percentile rank in their age group
   b. both have the same mental age
   c. both get the same number of questions correct
   d. a and b
   e. none of the above

11. The SATs are a type of intelligence test. The scores are calculated in the same way as deviation IQs, with 500 as the mean score of those who have taken the test over the past few years. The mean deviation IQ of people with SAT scores of 500 is well over 100. This can be explained as a result of:
   a. different types of questions on the two tests
   b. high reliance on verbal ability in most IQ tests
   c. superior intelligence in the standardization population for the SATs
   d. a higher cutoff score in the SATs, which elevates the scores
   e. a higher intake of meat and other high protein foods in high school seniors

12. A student takes the same test of reaction time at 10:00 A.M. on two consecutive days. She gets very different scores on these two days. If this was true of many other test takers, it would suggest that this test is not:
   a. valid
   b. standardized
   c. reliable
   d. none of the above
   e. all of the above

13. A test administered like the SAT but measuring subjects' abilities to do jigsaw puzzles would be a ____________ test.

a. group performance
b. group verbal
c. unreliable performance
d. standardized performance
e. verbal performance

14. A psychometrician examines a verbal and a spatial intelligence test, and finds that the scores on these two tests correlate +.38. From this he might conclude that:
   a. performance on both tests is partly determined by "g" but mostly by more specific or group factors
   b. these tests measure very different things, and there is no "g" component here
   c. both of these tests are excellent measures of "g"
   d. these results constitute proof of the group factor theories
   e. none of the above

15. One occasionally finds people who are highly intelligent, but terrible at spatial relations. This fact supports:
   a. Gardner's theory of multiple intelligence
   b. group-factor theory
   c. a limit on the importance of "g"
   d. a and c
   e. all of the above

16. The fact that in the period between the two World Wars IQ scores of Eastern European immigrant groups improved, the longer they were in the United States:
   a. justified a policy of excluding Eastern Europeans from immigrating to the United States
   b. raises questions about U.S. immigration policy in the period between the wars
   c. demonstrates that intelligence is primarily under genetic control
   d. demonstrates that intelligence is primarily under environmental control
   e. none of the above

17. Jane and Phyllis have brown eyes. All of Jane's relatives have brown eyes. Phyllis's father has brown eyes, but her mother has blue eyes (brown eye color is dominant). From this information, we can guess that Jane and Phyllis have:
   a. the same genotype and phenotype
   b. the same genotype and different phenotypes
   c. different genotypes and the same phenotype
   d. different genotypes and phenotypes
   e. c or d

18. A genetic female who is exposed to androgens (male hormones) as a fetus and develops male genitals, and a person with phenylketonuria who is treated at birth and develops no symptoms, both illustrate that:
   a. inborn, genetically determined traits can be changed by environmental factors
   b. recessive traits can occur in both sex and intelligence
   c. behavior is inherited
   d. environmental factors, under some circumstances, have no influence on behavior
   e. behavior is related to sex chromosomes

19. The clustering of specific talents (e.g., music in the Bach family) or high intelligence in particular families, *across generations*, argues for:
   a. a significant role for genetics in these abilities
   b. a significant role for environment in these abilities
   c. polygenic inheritance
   d. a and b
   e. a and/or b

20. If, counter to the results actually found, it was reported that fraternal and identical twins had the same high correlation in intelligence and that this was *higher* than the correlation between other siblings (e.g., brothers and sisters of different ages), one would be most justified in concluding that:
   a. the higher correlation in twins was due to environmental factors
   b. the higher correlation in twins was due to genetic factors
   c. fraternal twins are more closely related, genetically, than are other siblings
   d. a and c
   e. b and c

21. Environmentalists explain the significant correlation between the IQ of adopted children and their biological parents in terms of *selective placement* of these children in adopted homes. (Children with higher IQ biological parents are placed with higher IQ adoptive parents.) This argument, however, is strongly weakened by:

a. the studies on identical twins
b. the fact that the IQ of adopted children correlates more highly with biological than adoptive parents
c. the fact that there is a positive correlation between the IQ of adopted children and their adoptive parents
d. b and c
e. none of the above

22. All but one of these findings supports or is consistent with the idea of a hereditary component in intelligence differences. Which finding does *not* support such a view?
a. higher IQ correlation in identical than fraternal twins
b. higher IQ correlation between adoptive children and their biological parents than between these same children and their adoptive parents
c. higher IQ correlation between siblings than between half siblings (sharing only one parent)
d. higher correlations in IQ between fraternal twins than between other siblings
e. the stability of IQ over decades

23. On the whole, the IQs of biological parents giving children up for adoption are below those of adopting parents (since the latter are screened by agencies). The observation that, whatever the correlation between IQ of adopted child and biological parent, the actual IQ of such adopted children tends to be considerably higher than that of the biological parents, is evidence for:
a. hereditary effects
b. environmental effects
c. a and b
d. multiple intelligences
e. polygenic inheritance

24. Many have argued that IQ tests and the circumstances under which they are given favor whites over blacks. All but one of the following reported findings argue against this view: that is, all but one indicate that the tests are reasonably culture fair. Select the one reported finding that does *not* argue in favor of the culture fairness of tests or test situations:
a. the black-white IQ difference remains about the same when the black version of the test is translated into black English
b. the black-white difference is about the same for verbal tests and for the abstract Raven's progressive matrices
c. the black-white difference remains about the same whether the tester is black or white
d. the black-white difference remains about the same for tests of verbal and tests of spatial intelligence
e. the black-white difference decreases in the children in families that have children of both races through adoption

25. Assume two breeds of cattle: In both, size differences within the breed are completely determined by genes. Assume further that one breed is found in New Zealand and the other in central Africa and that the New Zealand breed averages about 10 percent bigger than the African breed. What inferences can be made about the origin of this difference between breeds?
a. it is certainly due to heredity
b. it is certainly due to environment
c. it must be due to both heredity and environment
d. there must be some (although it may be small) genetic determination
e. no certain inference can be drawn about breed differences from this information

26. A fair summary of studies on environmental matching or change, as applied to the black-white IQ difference, would be:
a. there is generally a decreased black-white IQ difference when attempts are made to equalize environments in the comparison groups, and an improvement in black IQs when the environment is improved
b. appropriate manipulation of environments, to provide blacks with the full advantages of the white environment, leads to elimination of the black-white IQ difference
c. there is very little effect of environmental change or equalization on black IQ or black-white differences
d. a and b
e. none of the above

27. What would be educationally and scientifically *appropriate* sociopolitical responses to a *hypothetical* proof that a fair proportion of the difference in IQ scores between American blacks and whites could be assigned to hereditary factors?
a. curtailment of early enrichment programs
b. establishment of racial quotas

c. inclusion of race as an important factor in determining the ability of applicants for jobs involving intelligence
d. cessation of affirmative action programs
e. none of the above

Answer Key for Self Test

1. c p. 457
2. a p. 459
3. b pp. 460–61
4. d p. 460
5. e p. 460
6. b p. 462
7. a p. 463
8. d p. 465
9. c p. 466
10. a p. 467
11. c pp. 463, 468
12. c p. 462
13. a p. 468
14. a p. 473
15. e p. 473
16. b p. 478
17. c pp. 479–80
18. a p. 480
19. e pp. 481–85
20. a p. 484
21. b p. 484
22. d p. 482
23. b p. 484
24. e pp. 486–89
25. e pp. 486–89
26. a p. 488
27. e pp. 488–89

Investigating Psychological Phenomena

"INTELLIGENCE TESTS"

Equipment: None
Number of subjects: One (yourself)
Time per subject: (Thirty minutes)
Time for experimenter: Thirty minutes

This is an experiment that will help you to understand the construction of intelligence tests. The procedure that you will go through will be like the procedure that might be used in the development of an intelligence test. The main concern is that you understand how a distribution of test scores is generated, and how an individual score is interpreted with respect to that distribution.

For this purpose, rather than making up a so-called intelligence test, we have chosen to try out a measure of a characteristic that is rarely tested: One's knowledge of foods and cooking. In this case, one begins with some idea of the ability or knowledge base that one is trying to assess. Questions or tasks are constructed that seem to measure these. Then, pilot tests, like those we will give you, are distributed to a representative sample of the population for which the tests are intended. In your case, your class might serve as a sample of college undergraduates. Of course, students differ in schools and in different regions, so this would not be anything like the random sample we would actually need were this a real test.

The results of the test are examined. Typically, most of the questions which all subjects get right or all get wrong are discarded, because such questions do not help to measure *differences* among people in the abilities under study. Then, some sort of retest studies are done, to make sure the test is reliable, and a validity study is done, to assure that the test measures what it is supposed to measure.

We will only deal with one phase of test construction here. We have made up a test that has never been used by psychologists before. (It is certainly not clear why a food knowledge test would be of interest to anyone in the real world.) We ask each of you to take the test. It is brief. The food knowledge test is in the format of a written test, with unlimited time. It is, of course, "closed book." Fill it out in a quiet place. Then score your answers, using the list of correct answers at the end of this section.

FOOD KNOWLEDGE TEST

Sex ______________

Listed below are five countries

Italy (southern Italy)
China
India
Mexico
Germany

Each of the following food items (1–14) is particularly characteristic of the cuisines of one of the five countries listed above. Write the name of the appropriate cuisine (country) beside the food item.

1. potatoes ______________
2. corn ______________
3. sesame oil ______________
4. olive oil ______________
5. soy sauce ______________
6. cumin (two possible answers) ______________
7. oregano ______________
8. curry ______________
9. chili pepper (two possible answers) ______________
10. liverwurst ______________
11. turmeric ______________
12. yogurt ______________
13. bean curd ______________
14. ghee ______________

Write in the name of the country associated with each of the following items:

15. sushi ______________
16. lasagna ______________
17. taco ______________
18. paella ______________
19. moussaka ______________
20. goulash ______________
21. sukiyaki ______________
22. mousse ______________
23. sate (pron: sā′ • tāy) ______________
24. biryani ______________
25. mole (pron: mǒ′ • lāy) ______________
26. trifle ______________
27. kim chee ______________
28. champagne ______________
29. What is the primary ingredient used in raising (leavening) bread? ______________
30. What is yogurt made from? ______________
31. What are raisins made from? ______________
32. What is meringue made of? ______________
33. What animal does bacon come from? ______________
34. What are prunes made from? ______________
35. What type of fish is lox made from? ______________
36. What vegetable are pickles usually made from? ______________
37. What fruit is wine usually made from? ______________
38. What is sauerkraut made from? ______________
39. What are chitterlings made from? ______________
40. What does caviar come from? ______________
41. What is marzipan made from? ______________
42. What is the primary ingredient in guacamole? ______________

Indicated below are five common cooking methods:

baking
sautéing or pan frying
braising
boiling
broiling

For each dish or food below, indicate by writing in the correct term from those listed above the primary cooking method used.

43. chicken soup ____________
44. bread ____________
45. scrambled eggs ____________
46. pot roast ____________
47. shish-kebab ____________
48. spaghetti ____________
49. soufflé ____________
50. hash-brown potatoes ____________
51. collard greens ____________

TEST RESULTS AND "IQ" CALCULATIONS

The food knowledge test was taken by 153 University of Pennsylvania undergraduates in the introductory psychology course and twenty-one students in a University of Michigan class in learning and memory. The results were:

Mean score: 35.9 for 174 subjects
Standard deviation: 5.03
Range of scores: 22 (lowest) to 47 (highest)

Females do slightly better than males on this test (mean female score: 36.8: mean male score: 35.1).

CALCULATION OF A "CULINARY IQ"

As we will discuss below, much more work would have to be done with this test before it could actually be used in a meaningful way. For the sake of illustrating the scaling of psychological tests, we will use the data generated by undergraduates taking this test to develop a "deviation" scale like that used in IQ tests. You can then calculate your "culinary IQ."

The basic principle behind scaling of tests is the deviation score. Like a percentile score, it expresses where a particular score stands with respect to all of the other scores. The distribution of scores for tests usually falls into what is called a normal distribution. An ideal normal distribution is drawn in the next column. Normal distributions are typically described by their mean value and their standard deviation, a measure of the spread or variability of the curve (see the statistical appendix to the text). In a normal distribution, 68 percent of all observations fall within one standard deviation of the mean, and 96 percent of all observations fall within two standard deviations of the mean (see figure in the next column). Test scores are measured in units of deviation from the mean. For all IQ type tests, 100 is set as the mean value and 15 point as the standard deviation. Thus, an IQ of 115 corresponds to the score one standard deviation above the mean (85 to one standard deviation below); 130 corresponds to a score of two standard deviations above the mean (70 to two below), and so on. (An IQ of 105 would then be one-third of a standard deviation above the mean.) In percentile terms, an IQ of 130 would be at the 98th percentile, and an IQ of 85 would be at the 16th percentile (see figure).

Normal distribution

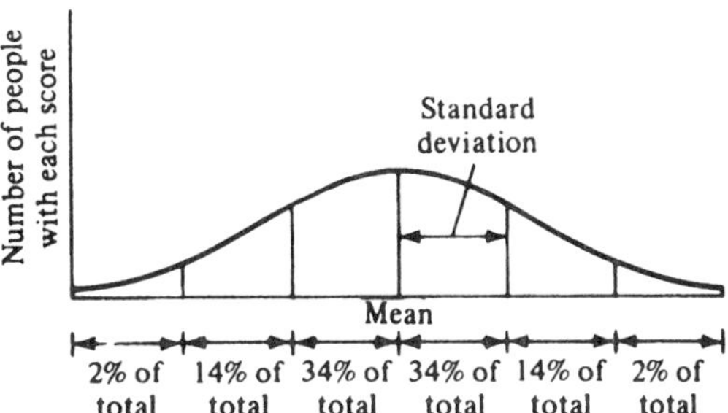

Applying these ideas to our test, the mean score (35.9) on the food test would be assigned a scaled score of 100. Subtracting one standard deviation (5.03) from this score, we get approximately 31, a score that would be assigned a scaled score of 85 (one standard deviation below the mean corresponds to 15 scaled points). We have performed the appropriate arithmetic for the food test, and provided the raw score (your actual score) and scaled score (converted to deviation units) equivalents in the table on the next page. Because the standard deviation for the food knowledge scores is almost exactly 5, each additional point on the test is worth one-fifth of a standard deviation, or 3 "IQ" points.

FOOD TEST

Raw score (your actual score)	Scaled score ("IQ")
18	46
19	49
20	52
21	55
22	58
23	61
24	64
25	67
26	70
27	73
28	76
29	79
30	82
31	85
32	88
33	91
34	94
35	97
36	100
37	103
38	106
39	109
40	112
41	115
42	118
43	121
44	124
45	127
46	130
47	133
48	136
49	139
50	142
51	145

The next step in developing a test would be to improve the first version. For example, in the food knowledge test, there are a number of useless items: These are items that do not contribute to the measurement of differences in people. For three items (number 16—lasagna, 37—wine, and 44—bread), all 174 subjects got the right answer. Because of this, these items would normally be discarded. Three additional items were missed by less than 2% of the subjects and might also be discarded. There were no questions that were missed by all subjects. The "hardest" question was about the country of origin of sate (number 23—Indonesia), and 8.6% of subjects were correct on this item.

We would also eliminate any questions that turned out to be ambiguous. In this test, for example, some of the "What is X made from?" questions need clarification. Thus, for number 39—chitterlings (chitlings), some people answered "pig," and others said "intestine." We scored both as correct, but should have been more specific in the question. Similarly, for number 30—what is yogurt made from?—we intended that milk be the correct answer. But bacteria cultures are also components of yogurt. We should have asked, "What is the primary ingredient in yogurt?" See if you can find some other ambiguous questions. Finally, we would examine the correlation of correctness on each question with the total score on the test. Are there any items which don't seem to be measuring the same sort of thing as the rest of the test? (See the experiment on personality testing in the next chapter.) Such items might or might not be included but would at least be reexamined. Along these same lines, one might look at any questions which the top performers on the test all missed. Often such items are badly worded, or perhaps even in error. For the food test, there was no single item missed by all of the six top scorers.

Having streamlined the test, we would then use some type of test-retest procedure to determine reliability. (Will the same person score about the same on two different occasions?) The reliability measures would be complicated, since one would expect improvement on the second time through.

We would then perform some sort of validity test. Is the test measuring what it is supposed to measure? If the food knowledge test is supposed to predict likely candidates for success in a cooking school, does it actually do so?

Finally, having satisfied ourselves that we had a reliable and valid test, we would then administer the test to a large sample of people (hundreds to thousands of people) randomly selected from the population of people for whom the test was designed (e.g., high school seniors, all adults, etc.).

Ask yourself whether you believe the food test is meaningful. How would you validate it? What might it be used for? What would it correlate with?

FURTHER ACTIVITIES

Sketch out what you think would be an appropriate test for use in predicting success in a particular profession: e.g., fighter pilot, baseball player, or architect. Then ask yourself how you would validate the test.

Answer Sheet

Score one point for each correct answer
(Listed next to each answer are the percentages correct out of 174 students.)

1. potatoes–Germany (83.9%)
2. corn–Mexico (78.7%)
3. sesame oil–China (28.2%)
4. olive oil–Italy (93.7%)
5. soy sauce–China (97.7%)
6. cumin–India or Mexico (78.2%)
7. oregano–Italy (90.2%)
8. curry–India (73.0%)
9. chili–India or Mexico (90.2%)
10. liverwurst–Germany (97.7%)
11. turmeric–India (48.3%)
12. yogurt–India (44.8%)
13. bean curd–China (44.8%)
14. ghee–India (60.3%)
15. sushi–Japan (55.7%)
16. lasagna–Italy (100%)
17. taco–Mexico (98.8%)
18. paella–Spain (40.2%)
19. moussaka–Greece (43.7%)
20. goulash–Hungary (73.6%)
21. sukiyaki–Japan (76.4%)
22. mousse–France (74.7%)
23. sate–Indonesia (8.6%)
24. biryani–India (37.4%)
25. mole–Mexico (14.9%)
26. trifle–England (47.7%)
27. kim chee–Korea (13.2%)
28. champagne–France (80.4%)
29. bread–yeast (97.1%)
30. yogurt–milk (88.5%)
31. raisins–grapes (96.0%)
32. meringue–egg white (74.1%)
33. bacon–pig (99.9%)
34. prunes–plums (77.0%)
35. lox–salmon (66.7%)
36. pickle–cucumber (97.7%)
37. wine–gapes (100%)
38. sauerkraut–cabbage (89.1%)
39. chitterlings–pig or intestine (29.3%)
40. caviar–fish eggs (91.4%)
41. marzipan–almond or sugar (31.0%)
42. guacamole–avocado (48.3%)
43. chicken soup–boiling (96%)
44. bread–baking (100%)
45. scrambled eggs–pan frying (98.3%)
46. pot roast–braising (46.6%)
47. shish kebab–broiling (57.5%)
48. spaghetti–boiling (97.7%)
49. soufflé–baking (83.3%)
50. hash-brown potatoes–pan fry-sautéing (96.6%)
51. collard greens–boiling (55.7%)

CHAPTER 16

Personality I: Assessment, Trait Theory, and the Behavioral-Cognitive Approach

Learning Objectives

1. What are the four orientations from which the subject of personality is approached, and what are their historical origins?

METHODS OF ASSESSMENT

Structured personality tests

2. Understand the construction and the use of the Minnesota Multiphasic Personality Inventory (MMPI). What is the importance of score profiles and validity scales?
3. Why isn't the MMPI a commonly used test for normal people? What is one of the tests that is used instead?
4. Be familiar with test validity and how personality tests measure up.

Unstructured personality tests

5. What is the rationale for projective techniques? Describe some of these procedures.
6. What scoring categories are used in the interpretation of Rorschach inkblots, and what general rules are employed?
7. Be familiar with the difference in interpretation between the Rorschach and the Thematic Apperception Test (TAT) in regard to perceived content.
8. Why is TAT interpretation impressionistic and global?
9. Summarize the issues and arguments in assessing the validity of the TAT and the Rorschach.
10. Of what value are projective tests in a clinical setting? Do they have incremental validity?

THE TRAIT APPROACH

The search for the right taxonomy

11. What is the trait approach to personality?
12. What was Cattell's approach to developing a taxonomy of personality traits? What modifications of Cattell's analysis have been suggested and why?
13. Discuss Eysenck's taxonomy of neuroticism and extroversion-introversion.

The trait-situation controversy

14. What is the importance of cross-situational consistency, or inconsistency, in the argument against trait theory? How does this affect the validity of personality tests?
15. What is situationism, and how is it related to personality?
16. How do situationists explain how we see our friends' personalities as consistent?
17. Review the evidence on consistency of behavior across time and situations. Describe how superficially different expressions of a personality trait contribute to apparent behavioral inconsistency. What are the implications for trait theory?
18. What is an interaction effect? Understand the importance of the interaction between a personality and situation in personality assessment. What is the drawback to this approach?

19. Realize that consistency may be a personality trait. How does Snyder's self-monitoring scale measure behavioral consistency in different situations?
20. How is the study of cross-situational consistency similar to the study of attribution in social psychology?
21. In the light of available evidence, evaluate the concept of person constancy.

Traits and biology

22. What is the definition of the word *temperament*, and what effect does it have on a person's personality?
23. How stable is an individual's temperament, as demonstrated by Buss and Plomin's temperament scale?
24. Discuss the evidence that personality traits may have a genetic component.
25. Describe how Eysenck compares introverts and extroverts in terms of their arousal systems. What research on sensation-seeking has Zuckerman done that correlates with Eysenck's findings?

THE BEHAVIORAL-COGNITIVE APPROACH

26. What is the central assumption of the behavioral-cognitive approach to personality?
27. How have the principles of behavior theory applied to the explanation of personality differences?

Social learning theory

28. Describe some of the cognitive dimensions on which some social learning theorists think that people differ.
29. What is the evidence that control over a situation is a cognitive dimension that people seek?
30. How does attributional style have an effect on such conditions as depression?
31. Describe how self-control is seen as an important personality characteristic. Discuss evidence that children can be influenced in their self-control depending on physical and cognitive factors.
32. How is the early ability to delay gratification related to late coping ability?
33. How are social learning theorists still similar to behaviorists in orientation?

Programmed Exercises

1.	The way that people differ in their desires, feelings, and in the expression of these feelings reflects their ____________ ____________.	personality differences
2.	In the comic dramas that they performed, the Greeks and Romans thought of the different characters and their respective personalities as ____________. The same characterizations were used in literature.	types
3.	Some felt that these stock characters were two-dimensional, and that more ____________ characterizations were needed.	rounded
4.	Others were concerned over the ____________ versus ____________ forces that caused a character to act as he did.	internal, external
5.	These arguments between the different schools of drama and literature are analogous to debates between different psychological theories of personality. The ____________ theory holds that personality is best understood by the description and analysis of underlying personality dispositions.	trait
6.	Achieving selfhood and actualizing one's own potential would be consistent with the ____________ approach to personality.	humanistic
7.	The behavioral-cognitive approach insists that an individual's actions and thoughts are produced by the ____________ that he is in at any given time.	situation
8.	According to ____________ theory, the important aspects of personality originate from buried unconscious conflicts and desires.	psychodynamic

METHODS OF ASSESSMENT

9. Implicit in the use of personality tests is the assumption that personality patterns are essentially ____________ over time.	consistent
10. ____________ tests were developed to enable us to predict people's future behavior.	Personality
11. The first personality test was administered to army recruits and was meant to identify ____________ ____________ soldiers.	emotionally disturbed
12. The MMPI is termed ____________ because it assesses a number of personality ____________ simultaneously.	multiphasic traits
13. The authors of the MMPI emphasize the ____________ power of a question in distinguishing between the criterion group and normal subjects.	discriminatory
14. In interpreting scores on the MMPI, it is necessary to examine score ____________, which present the scores on all the scales in graphic form.	profiles
15. In order to detect whether or not subjects are lying on test items or are trying to fake mental illness, the MMPI uses two ____________ ____________ made up of items no one can honestly deny and of items so bizarre that few would endorse them.	validity scales
16. It is difficult to interpret MMPI scores for ____________ subjects since the criterion groups used to define the scales were composed of ____________ patients.	normal psychiatric
17. One test that was developed using normal subjects as the criterion group is the ____________ ____________ ____________.	California Psycho-logical Inventory
18. The degree to which a test can predict real-world events is called its ____________ ____________.	predictive validity
19. The use of ____________ techniques was, in part, a protest against the highly ____________ nature of paper-and-pencil techniques.	projective structured
20. One of the concerns of the originators of projective techniques was that a subject could ____________ to ____________ when taking a test like the MMPI.	lie, himself
21. The idea behind projective techniques is that in structuring unstructured materials, a subject will reveal deeper facets of his ____________.	personality
22. Three categories used in scoring Rorschach inkblots are the portion of the blot used, the attributes of the stimulus that the subject responds to, and the ____________ of what the subject sees.	content
23. In interpretations of Rorschach inkblots, use of the entire blot is said to reflect ____________ thinking, while attention to details suggests ____________.	integrative (or concep-tual), compulsiveness (or rigidity)
24. Rorschach responses dominated by color suggest ____________ and ____________.	emotionality impulsivity
25. The ____________ ____________ ____________, in which subjects tell stories about pictures, places a major emphasis on content.	Thematic Apper-ception Test (TAT)

26. In addition to predictive validity, it is desirable for a test to have ____________ validity, so that the test provides knowledge not found by other means. — incremental

THE TRAIT APPROACH

27. The major task in determining the proper traits with which to classify personality is the development of a(n) ____________ of personality difference. — taxonomy

28. Cattell's taxonomy of personality is based on ____________, using factor analysis to discover how ____________ words are interrelated. — language, trait

29. According to Eysenck, both ____________ and ____________ are unsociable and withdrawn, but the former's unsociability is not tainted by fear of social activities. — introverts, neurotics

30. Some psychologists have argued that the reason that many tests are not good predictors of future behavior is that most people exhibit a lack of ____________-____________ consistency. — cross-situational

31. ____________ maintains that human behavior is largely determined by the situation a person is in, rather than by the actual, internal traits of the person. — Situationism

32. Contrary to situationistic claims, some ____________ studies have shown a fair amount of consistency of personality. — longitudinal

33. Another argument against situationism is that perceived behavior inconsistency may be more ____________ than ____________ since the expression of a constant trait may vary over time. — apparent, real

34. When a person's reactions cannot be predicted adequately solely by situation or by ____________ ____________, the critical factor may be the ____________ of these two. — individual differences, interaction

35. Since cross-situational consistency varies from person to person, it may be regarded as a ____________ that only some individuals possess. — trait

36. One can assess how much a person adjusts his behavior to fit a situation by having him complete the ____________-____________ scale developed by Mark Snyder. — self-monitoring

37. The intuitive belief that most people remain unchanged over time is known as ____________ ____________ and is similar to size and shape constancy in perception. — person constancy

38. It is believed that a person's ____________ ultimately originates from her biological makeup. — temperament

39. Identical twins show more similarity of personality than do fraternal twins, indicating some ____________ of personality traits. — heritability

40. According to Eysenck, introversion corresponds to a high level of ____________; thus, persons of this type are actually more awake than others. — arousal

41. Zuckerman's research on ____________ ____________ indicates that those people with a higher arousal system (introverts) have higher levels of the neurotransmitter ____________ in their brains. Those with lower levels of this neurotransmitter are underaroused, and as a result are likely to seek thrills and take risks. — sensation seeking, norepinephrine

THE BEHAVIORAL-COGNITIVE APPROACH

42. The behavioral-cognitive approach, in contrast to ____________ theory, emphasizes the importance of external forces in the determination of behavior. — trait

43. This view is a direct descendent of ____________, an important movement early in this century that emphasized the role of learning, and de-emphasized the role of cognition. — behaviorism

44. A modification of behaviorism that recognizes the importance of internal cognitive states, such as expectations and beliefs, is ____________ ____________ theory. — social learning

45. According to Mischel, some of the cognitive qualities on which people may differ are their ____________, their ____________ strategies, their subjective ____________, and their ____________-____________ systems. — competencies, encoding, values, self-regulatory

46. Patients who are allowed the opportunity to ____________ their environments are more active and feel better than patients who are not. — control

47. A person's ____________ style indicates the extent to which he designates the causes of events as internal versus external. — attributional

48. Measures of ____________ of gratification in young children show that this characteristic predicts behavior in adolescence. — delay

49. Social learning theorists can still be regarded as behaviorists in that they continue to stress the importance of the ____________ in determining behavior, and they insist on the importance of ____________ in acquiring various personality characteristics. — situation, learning

Self Test

1. Personality differences include:
   a. intelligence, ability, and insight
   b. desires, feelings, and modes of expressing these needs and feelings
   c. none of the above
   d. both a and b

2. The four orientations to personality are:
   a. Trait Theory, Psychoanalytic Theory, Attribution Theory, Behavioral-Cognitive Theory
   b. Trait Theory, Humanistic Theory, Psychogenic Theory, Behavioral-Cognitive Theory
   c. Psychodynamic Theory, Humanistic Theory, Behavioral-Cognitive Theory, Projective Theory
   d. Trait Theory, Humanistic Theory, Psycho-dynamic Theory, Behavioral-Cognitive Theory

3. The first personality and intelligence tests were similar in that both were ____________ but differed in that the former was ____________ and the latter was ____________.
   a. diagnostic, unstructured, structured
   b. unstructured, descriptive, normative
   c. diagnostic, poorly validated, well-validated
   d. structured, descriptive, diagnostic

4. An appropriate criterion group for a diagnostic test of paranoid schizophrenics would be:
   a. normal individuals
   b. paranoid schizophrenics
   c. a mixture of a and b
   d. no criterion group is needed when the test is used as a diagnostic tool

5. The California Psychological Inventory (CPI) uses ____________ criterion groups.
   a. no
   b. pathological
   c. normal
   d. random

6. When a test can foretell some real-world event, it is said to have:
   a. score profiles
   b. incremental validity
   c. predictive validity
   d. unproven validity

7. Projective techniques differ from tests such as the MMPI and CPI in that the former are more:
   a. structured
   b. quantitative
   c. variable
   d. all of the above
   e. none of the above

8. In structuring unstructured materials, it is expected that a subject:
   a. will reveal his capacity for conceptual organization
   b. will be relieved of objective test anxiety and will thus perform most effectively and honestly
   c. will project his deepest feelings and conflicts upon the ambiguous stimulus
   d. will be distracted from the psychologist's analysis of the subject's voice tone, body language, and gestures in responding.

9. Two examples of projective tests are:
   a. the MMPI and the Thematic Apperception Test (TAT)
   b. the Rorschach and the TAT
   c. the Rorschach and the CPI
   d. all of the above

10. Three categories used in interpreting the Rorschach are:
    a. location, negativism, color
    b. content, attributes, and location
    c. content, impulsiveness, use of white space
    d. impulsiveness, happiness, truth value

11. While the TAT has not fared well as a diagnostic tool, it has shown some promise as an indicator of:
    a. intelligence
    b. motives
    c. hidden fears
    d. imagination

12. A taxonomy is a:
    a. classification system
    b. rating scale used in psychiatric diagnosis
    c. type of mental disorder
    d. class of stable personality traits

13. Eysenck has formed a hypothesis that all personalities can be classified on the basis of a rating on two independent scales. They are ____________ and ____________.
    a. paranoid, schizophrenic
    b. shy-outgoing, anxiety
    c. neuroticism, extroversion-introversion
    d. psychopathic deviance, extroversion-introversion

14. Introverts differ from extroverts in all of the following ways *except*:
    a. they are solitary
    b. they are cautious
    c. they are slow to change
    d. they have a lower pain threshold
    e. none of the above

15. Walter Mischel found that children are ____________ in their behavior in different circumstances. He saw this as evidence ____________ the validity of personality traits.
    a. consistent, for
    b. inconsistent, for
    c. consistent, against
    d. inconsistent, against

16. The concept of situationism is most opposite to the assumptions underlying:
    a. the MMPI and CPI
    b. the Rorschach and TAT
    c. both of the above
    d. none of the above

17. Situationists:
    a. deny the existence of individual differences
    b. believe that social roles play a large part in the situations people get into
    c. claim that situations themselves are the best predictors of people's reactions
    d. believe that past situational experiences determine personality traits

18. In ____________ with Mischel, some authors have claimed that there is a higher level of consistency in people's behavior than previously believed. They hypothesize that reactions that appear ____________ in gross analysis are really different manifestations of ____________ underlying sources.
    a. agreement, dissimilar, different
    b. agreement, dissimilar, the same
    c. disagreement, similar, different
    d. disagreement, dissimilar, the same

19. In defense of trait theory, one could cite evidence that behavior is:
    a. consistent over time
    b. consistent across situations
    c. both of the above
    d. none of the above

20. Studies by Endler and Hunt have looked at person-situation interactions. Their results suggest that the practicality of assigning traits like fear to people:
    a. is useless
    b. has been experimentally validated
    c. should be qualified to be more specific to individual circumstances
    d. is minimal since internal fluctuations in trait strength cause behavior to vary from situation to situation

21. High self-monitors are:
    a. not adaptable
    b. inconsistent
    c. consistent
    d. rigid

22. Person constancy involves the notion that:
    a. all people behave in essentially the same way for a particular situation
    b. people are not consistent, and we perceive them as being that way
    c. we tend to see a person in only one situation, so we think of her only in that situation
    d. all of the above
    e. none of the above

23. Which of the following is true of sensation seekers?
    a. They have underactive norepinephrine systems in their brain.
    b. They are overaroused in certain systems of their brain.
    c. They have a low pain tolerance.
    d. They react more to external stimuli than those who are not sensation seekers.

24. The behavioral-cognitive approach to personality does *not* attribute differences in personality to:
    a. enduring traits in personality that may be a function of hereditary influences
    b. differences in how a person will behave in different situations
    c. learning that occurs during the life of an individual that may cause certain behaviors to appear in certain situations
    d. classical and operant conditioning

25. Social learning theory is a modification of behaviorism in that it admits to the influence of:
    a. an individual's competencies
    b. an individual's encoding strategies
    c. an individual's subjective values
    d. all of the above

26. The Attributional Style Questionnaire is an important instrument to measure control because:
    a. it assesses the extent to which an individual thinks the causes of events are internal to her or due to external forces
    b. it has value in predicting clinical depression
    c. it is related to the idea of learned helplessness in animals that may be related to depression
    d. all of the above

27. The extent to which a child is willing to delay gratification is related to:
    a. later academic performance
    b. later social competence
    c. later coping skills in adolescence
    d. all of the above

28. Social learning theory has strayed away from its behaviorist origins, but it still shares similarities with that school because:
    a. it stresses the importance of learning
    b. it stresses the role of traits in determining behavior
    c. it emphasizes the value of situational differences in exerting an influence on behavior
    d. a and b
    e. a and c

Answer Key for Self Test

1.	b	p. 493	15.	d	p. 507
2.	d	pp. 494–95	16.	c	p. 507
3.	c	p. 496	17.	c	p. 507
4.	b	p. 496	18.	d	p. 508
5.	c	p. 498	19.	c	pp. 508–9
6.	c	p. 498	20.	c	p. 510
7.	e	p. 499	21.	b	p. 511
8.	c	p. 499	22.	e	p. 512
9.	b	p. 499	23.	a	pp. 514–15
10.	b	p. 500	24.	a	p. 515
11.	b	p. 502	25.	d	p. 516
12.	a	p. 504	26.	d	pp. 517–18
13.	c	p. 505	27.	d	p. 519
14.	e	pp. 505, 514	28.	e	p. 520

Investigating Psychological Phenomena

CONSTRUCTING A PERSONALITY INVENTORY

Equipment: None
Number of subjects: One (yourself)
Time per subject: Forty-five minutes
Time for experimenter: Forty-five minutes

Constructing a test to assess a personality trait is an involved process. It requires the creation of test items and the validation of these items through administration of the test to large groups of subjects. While it would be impossible to illustrate all the steps in this process through a short exercise such as this, it is possible to provide an idea about some of the issues that are involved. That is the purpose of this demonstration.

A first draft of a test for a particular personality trait has been created.* Before reading on, you should take this test. Listed on the opposite page are twenty-one questions for you to answer. Try to put yourself in each of the following situations and on the answer sheet mark the choice that would best describe your reactions. Limit your replies to the choices given and answer every question.

* We thank Lisa Lange, John Prevost, Barb Merriam, Laurie Tunstall, and Julie Nuse for their permission to use the shyness inventory that was prepared as part of a course project supervised by Dr. Charles Morris. We also thank Dr. Morris for kindly supplying the correlational data.

Draft Personality Inventory

	strongly disagree	slightly disagree	slightly agree	strongly agree
1. I am in a crowded bar sitting with some friends. A good-looking individual comes up to me and asks me to dance. I like to dance but I notice that the dance floor is empty and answer no.	1	2	3	4
2. I get an important exam back and I disagree with the grading on one of the problems. But I accept my grade, avoiding a confrontation with the professor.	1	2	3	4
3. I enjoy attending seminars and discussion groups as opposed to large lectures.	1	2	3	4
4. I'm in a restaurant and receive some bad food. Instead of saying something, I stay quiet but leave a small tip.	1	2	3	4
5. My family is moving to another state and I will be attending a new school. I look forward to meeting new people and making new friends.	1	2	3	4
6. I find it easy to liven up a dull occasion.	1	2	3	4
7. I am required to form groups in a class and interact on a subject. The groups are formed but I tend to listen more than offer information.	1	2	3	4
8. If I were in the waiting room of a doctor's office and a stranger sat down next to me, introduced himself, and started asking me questions, I would feel nervous and uncomfortable.	1	2	3	4
9. I can usually enjoy myself at a party even if I know almost no one there.	1	2	3	4
10. A teacher asks questions to which I know the answers, but I never raise my hand for fear that the answers might not be what the teacher is looking for.	1	2	3	4
11. I become uncomfortable and at a loss for words, usually blushing, when I am given a compliment.	1	2	3	4
12. I often find myself taking charge in group situations.	1	2	3	4
13. I prefer being with people and going to parties rather than spending my spare time alone pursuing personal interests or hobbies.	1	2	3	4
14. If someone was smoking a cigarette in a nonsmoking section and the smoke was bothering me, I wouldn't hesitate to ask the person to put out the cigarette.	1	2	3	4
15. I often look back at a situation and think of things I should have done or said.	1	2	3	4
16. I feel proud to be called on to give a toast at a social gathering.	1	2	3	4
17. I would go out of my way to make a stranger feel comfortable in a group in which the people are unfamiliar to him.	1	2	3	4
18. When I've been waiting in line for service for a long time and someone cuts in front of me, I feel angry but don't say anything about it.	1	2	3	4
19. I prefer not to answer the door when I know it's a salesman because I have a hard time getting him to leave once he's inside the door.	1	2	3	4
20. When I've struck up a conversation with the person sitting next to me, a long plane flight seems more enjoyable.	1	2	3	4
21. I consider myself to be a shy person.	1	2	3	4

Now that you have answered the questionnaire, you are probably aware that it is intended to assess shyness. The questions themselves were constructed as candidates that might have something to do with predicting how shy people are. How can one tell if the questionnaire accomplishes its purpose or which questions are the best predictors of shyness?

One possibility is to examine the face validity of each of the questions. Since you have just completed the questions yourself and since you are now aware that its purpose is to test for shyness, you can do this yourself. Examine each question and decide for yourself whether you think that it would be a good predictor of shyness. That is, does the question ask subjects about a reaction that should depend on how shy the subjects are? Try to pick out the four questions that you think would best predict shyness and the four that would be least relevant. Note, by the way, that the questions are constructed so that for some (items 1, 2, 4, 7, 8, 10, 11, 15, 18, 19, and 21) a high score (e.g., 4) would indicate more shyness, while for the rest, a low score (e.g., 1) would indicate more shyness. This is only done to provide variety; your assessment of each question should be independent of this point.

Questions that would best predict shyness	Questions that would least predict shyness
1. ______	1. ______
2. ______	2. ______
3. ______	3. ______
4. ______	4. ______

Your judgment of the quality of a question is a measure of face validity (that is, the extent to which a question, on the face of it, is a good predictor of shyness), but this is not the only possible measure of validity. Another criterion is to have some independent measure of a subject's shyness and correlate responses to each question with the measure (predictive validity). Presumably, if a question were a good predictor of shyness, it would correlate highly with this measure.

One such measure is a subject's response to question 21. This question directly asks subjects for their own assessment of whether they consider themselves to be shy. In order to determine how well each test question correlates with this self-assessment of shyness, sixty-nine subjects were given this questionnaire and correlations of each question with question 21 were calculated. They are presented in Table 1 below.

TABLE 1

Correlations of each question in the questionnaire with question 21. A low correlation (a positive or negative value close to 0) indicates that there is little relationship between the answer to that question and the answer to question 21; a high correlation (a value closer to –1 or +1) indicates a relationship between responses to that question and responses to question 21. For example, item 10 has a correlation of .42 with item 21. This means that subjects who tend to agree with the statement in question 10 tend to agree also with the statement in question 21. Likewise, subjects who tend to disagree with the statement in question 10, also tend to disagree with the statement in question 21. A negative correlation, such as in question 6, indicates that subjects who tend to agree with the statement in 6 tend to disagree with the statement in 21. Likewise, those who tend to disagree with the statement in 6 tend to agree with the one in 21 (note that even though a correlation is negative, it still means that there is a relationship between the two items in question, but a reverse relationship).

Question:	1	2	3	4	5	6	7	8	9	10
Correlation:	.23	.08	–.15	–.08	–.20	–.28	.38	–.24	–.24	.42
Question:	11	12	13	14	15	16	17	18	19	20
Correlation:	.29	–.22	–.20	–.27	.32	–.37	–.16	.17	.09	–.07

Compare your judgments of question quality against these correlations to see whether the ones you judged as good have either high positive or high negative values; also, check whether the questions you judged as poor have correlations near 0.

Another validity criterion that may be reasonable is the total score on the test. The logic of using this criterion is that individual questions may vary in how well they indicate shyness, but the test *as a whole* may be a much better indicator. If this were so, then it would be sensible to correlate scores on individual questions with those on the whole test to see which questions best predict the total test score. This was done for the same sixty-nine subjects as above; the correlations are presented in Table 2 below.

TABLE 2

Correlations of each question with the total test score. As in Table 1, a low value means little relationship of that question with the total test score, while a higher value (either positive or negative) means that there is some relationship. For example, the correlation of .55 for question 10 indicates that subjects who tend to agree with the statement in item 10 tend to have a high total score on the questionnaire, while subjects who tend to disagree with the statement in 10 tend to score low on the whole questionnaire. Another illustration is the correlation of –.49 for question 5. This means that subjects who tend to disagree with the statement in 5 tend to get a high total score, while subjects who tend to agree with the statement in 5 tend to have a low score.

Question:	1	2	3	4	5	6	7	8	9	10
Correlation:	.45	.41	–.54	.13	–.49	–.44	.46	.42	–.53	.55
Question:	11	12	13	14	15	16	17	18	19	20
Correlation:	.37	–.42	–.35	–.44	.40	–.46	–.27	.35	.25	–.01

Again, see how well your judgments of question quality are related to these correlations. Note also an interesting pattern in the two sets of correlations presented in Tables 1 and 2. Item 10 has both the highest absolute correlation with question 21 and the highest correlation with the total test score. Also, item 7 has very high correlations with both criterion measures. This consistency suggests that these two items may well be good, valid indices of shyness. How did you rate these items? Examine the items themselves to see if you can explain why they might be better than others.

Note also that two items, 4 and 20, have very low correlations with both criterion measures. How did you judge these items? Why to you think they have such low correlations?

If we were to continue to develop a "shyness inventory," we might well try to use other validity criteria as well as the three described above. For example, we might try to use the inventory to predict some behavior that is characteristic of shy people. This would allow us to assess the predictive validity of the test. Whatever the criteria, though, the objective of test construction is to find questions that best predict that which you are trying to assess. This exercise should have given you some insight into the process by which this objective is reached.

CHAPTER 17

Personality II: Psychodynamic, Humanistic, and Sociocultural Approaches

Learning Objectives

THE PSYCHODYNAMIC APPROACH: FREUD AND PSYCHOANALYSIS

The origins of psychoanalytic thought

1. How did Freud view the process of taming the savage, selfish human nature?
2. Compare Freud's and Hobbes's views of human nature and its taming.
3. Describe the symptoms of hysteria. Why is this illness termed a psychogenic disorder?
4. What is catharsis?
5. What are repression and resistance, and how do they relate to catharsis?
6. What did Freud mean by the unconscious?
7. How did Freud propose to study the unconscious?
8. What is psychoanalysis, and how does it relate to the understanding of psychopathology and the normal personality?

Unconscious conflict

9. Understand the nature of unconscious conflict and its effect on behavior.
10. What are the three divisions of personality according to Freud? How do these develop, and how do they interact to give rise to conflict and resolution?
11. Be cognizant of the major role of anxiety as a motivating force in keeping unacceptable urges repressed.
12. How does repression affect the realm of thought in addition to that of behavior?
13. What are defense mechanisms?
14. Describe the specific defense mechanisms (repression, displacement, reaction formation, rationalization, projection, and isolation).

The origins of unconscious conflict

15. What are Freud's stages of psychosexual development, and what is the relation of these stages to sexuality and pleasure?
16. What are oral and anal characters?
17. In Freud's view, the Oedipus complex is the most important aspect of psychosexual development. Discuss this theory with respect to both sexes.

Windows into the unconscious

18. What is the psychopathology of everyday life, and how does it reflect underlying motives and conflicts?
19. Explain Freud's theory of dreams. Understand the motive of wish fulfillment and its symbolic expression, and the difference between the latent and the manifest dream.

A critical look at Freudian theory

20. Recount some of the methodological and conceptual difficulties with Freud's theories.
21. What are different conceptions of the role of biological factors, especially sexuality, versus social factors in personality development? What is the position of the neo-Freudians on this point?
22. Review the evidence on the validity of the existence of anal and oral characters, and their

link to childhood toilet training and feeding experiences.

23. How universal is the Oedipus complex? Summarize evidence from the Trobriand Islanders.
24. What evidence militates against Freud's emphasis on wish fulfillment in the interpretation of dreams?
25. Freud believed that the manifest dream was a disguised and censored version of the latent dream that deals with unacceptable urges. What is the evidence for this? What is an alternative view?
26. Summarize the issues and arguments against and in favor of Freud's reliance on repression in dealing with unconscious conflicts. What is the evidence for repression, as opposed to a less "motivation-oriented" view of retrieval blocking?
27. What are the basic ideas of psychoanalysis?
28. What are Freud's major contributions to our understanding of human nature and to the field of psychology? What are the shortcomings of his approach and theory?

THE PSYCHODYNAMIC APPROACH: PERSONALITY DIFFERENCES

29. What are dominant patterns of defense, and what, according to the neo-Freudians, is their role in accounts of personality differences?

Patterns of neurotic conflict

30. Describe Karen Horney's views about patterns of neurotic conflict, including mention of basic anxiety and vicious circles.

Coping patterns and mental health

31. Distinguish between the Freudian position, Karen Horney's position, and the view of the ego psychologists.
32. What are coping mechanisms and how do they relate to Freudian defense mechanisms?
33. What do longitudinal studies tell us about the importance and consistency of coping patterns?

THE HUMANISTIC APPROACH

The major features of the humanistic movement

34. Describe the basic differences between the humanistic approach and all of the other approaches to personality that have been discussed.
35. Explain the hierarchy of needs, including definitions of deficiency needs and self-actualization.

Evaluating the humanistic approach

36. What are the empirical and conceptual problems of the humanistic approach?
37. Indicate the sense in which humanistic psychology is a protest movement. Relate it to other movements of a similar character in history, especially the Romantic movement.

THE SOCIOCULTURAL PERSPECTIVE

38. What are the basic sociocultural criticisms of the four personality theories already discussed?

Human diversity

39. Indicate important cultural variations in basic personality features and gender roles.

Human sameness

40. Describe the cross-cultural method. What does it indicate about common themes in personality across cultures?
41. What are personality correlates of socioeconomic level?

Collectivism and individualism

42. Describe collectivism and individualism. What are the different features of each? Indicate countries or areas of the world in which one or the other is dominant.

Cultural differences in the concept of the self

43. Review evidence indicating a different concept of self in some Asian cultures.
44. What are the consequences for current personality theory if the sociocultural critique is basically correct?

TAKING STOCK

45. Summarize the five basic views of personality presented in this chapter. Evaluate their contribution to a total theory of personality, and describe the analog, in drama, for most of these approaches.

Programmed Exercises

THE PSYCHODYNAMIC APPROACH: FREUD AND PSYCHOANALYSIS

Exercise	Answer
1. According to the psychodynamic approach, understanding of human personality requires understanding of ___________ psychological forces.	hidden (deep, unconscious)
2. The psychodynamic approach derives from ___________, founded by ___________.	psychoanalysis Freud
3. Freud has been compared to Hobbes, since both men believed that humans are basically ___________. But Freud differs from Hobbes in that Freud believed that the taming force of society is ___________ in each of us.	savage (or selfish) internalized
4. A patient exhibiting partial blindness, glove anesthesia, or memory gaps would likely be diagnosed as suffering from ___________.	hysteria
5. If organic damage is ruled out in the above case (number 4), then the origin of the symptoms must be ___________.	psychogenic
6. Freud and Breuer came to the conclusion that the symptoms of hysteria could not be just suggested away; the underlying ___________ that such symptoms block must be recovered. The resulting ___________ will then have therapeutic effects.	memories catharsis
7. Although Freud began by using hypnosis, he later abandoned this approach, since not all of his patients were hypnotizable and since the same crucial memories could be obtained in the waking state through the method of ___________ ___________.	free association
8. A patient is told to say anything that enters his mind, yet struggles at times to change the subject or forgets what he was going to say. This subject is demonstrating ___________ to the recovery of ___________ memories.	resistance, repressed
9. According to Freud's view, forbidden impulses are never completely controlled, despite repressive measures by the individual. This division of the individual (one part fighting another) gives rise to ___________ conflicts.	unconscious
10. According to Freud, repression is a ___________ against the intolerable pain that would be caused by becoming aware of unacceptable thoughts and wishes.	defense
11. Repressed wishes are usually related to ___________ ___________, the direct expression of which is forbidden by society.	biological urges
12. Freud investigated unconscious conflicts: their origin, effects, and removal. He termed his exploration and interpretation of these phenomena ___________.	psychoanalysis
13. The three distinct systems of the human personality, according to Freud, are the ___________, the ___________, and the ___________.	id, ego, superego
14. The most primitive portion of personality is the ___________. It operates according to the ___________ principle, with the single goal being immediate satisfaction.	id pleasure
15. As the id-dominated infant encounters the frustration of the real world, he develops a(n) ___________, which attempts to satisfy the urges of the id according to a ___________ principle.	ego reality

16. The young child refrains from doing wrong only through fear of being caught. As the rules and admonitions of the parents are ___________, however, the ___________ develops and suppresses forbidden behavior even in the absence of negative consequences.	internalized superego
17. ___________ is the crucial factor in the mechanism underlying repression. Internal thoughts and feelings that evoke this state must be escaped and are thus suppressed.	Anxiety
18. Repression can be regarded as the primary, initial ___________ ___________ ___________.	mechanism of defense
19. When fear of retaliation blocks the expression of anger, a person may vent his feelings on another recipient, resulting in ___________ ___________.	displaced aggression
20. When a repressed thought or wish manifests itself as a diametrically opposite wish or thought, it is a result of ___________ ___________.	reaction formation
21. ___________ is another defense mechanism in which a repressed thought is reinterpreted in more acceptable terms.	Rationalization
22. Cognitive reorganization also plays a role in ___________, in which forbidden urges are attributed to others rather than to the self.	projection
23. ___________ is another defense mechanism in which memories are allowed back into consciousness, but the emotions that accompany them are not.	Isolation
24. Freud's theory of ___________ development postulates biologically determined stages of emotional and sexual development.	psychosexual
25. Freud maintained that the young child seeks pleasure. This pleasure is often obtained by touching body parts which are particularly sensitive, such as the mouth, anus, and genitals. These parts are known as ___________ ___________.	erogenous zones
26. Seeking pleasure through the mouth is characteristic of the ___________ stage, which yields to the ___________ stage as toilet training begins. The ___________ stage focuses on the stimulation of the genitals, while interest in the satisfaction of others as well as one's own satisfaction characterizes the ___________ stage.	oral anal phallic genital
27. The ___________ character recapitulates the pleasure and passive dependency of nursing at her mother's breast.	oral
28. The ___________ character is typically excessively clean, obstinate, and stingy.	anal
29. The family drama from which grows the child's internalized morality and identification with the same-sex parent is called the ___________ ___________.	Oedipus complex
30. According to the theory of the Oedipus complex the ___________ urges of the boy at ages three and four are directed toward the ___________ as the source of previous gratification during the oral stage.	phallic (sexual) mother
31. The young boy's ___________ of the father leads to ___________ and a fear of retaliation by the father, which is termed ___________ ___________.	jealousy, hostility castration anxiety

32. As the young boy's anxiety about retaliation increases, the boy ____________ with the father in the hope that this will eventually secure him an erotic partnership like the father's. identifies

33. The renunciation of genital pleasures endures from about five to twelve years of age and is termed the ____________ ____________. latency period

34. Through his study of dreams, Freud came to the conclusion that dreams are an attempt at ____________ ____________. Desires suppressed by considerations of reality and by the superego emerge and are gratified in dreams. wish fulfillment

35. The ____________ dream is the disguised expression of the ____________ dream, which represents hidden and forbidden wishes. manifest, latent

36. The manifest dream employs ____________ in representing the hidden wishes and concerns of the dreamer. symbolism

37. The fact that psychotherapists cannot be totally objective about a patient's behavior patterns and problems is one of the difficulties of ____________ theory. psychoanalytic

38. Freud believed that the progression of emotional development is rooted in ____________, and is thus universal. biology

39. Some psychoanalytic practitioners acknowledge the importance of social factors in development. These psychologists are termed ____________. neo-Freudians

40. Freud maintained that neurotic conflict centers on the repression of ____________ impulses. Others, such as Erich Fromm, emphasize the area of ____________ relationships. erotic interpersonal

41. Evidence from ____________ anthropology supports the importance of social as opposed to biological factors in personality development. cultural

42. Evidence suggests that while some of the supposed features of the ____________ character cluster together and run in families, there is no relation between this "character" and ____________ ____________ in childhood. anal toilet training

43. Studies of Trobriand Islanders have suggested that the hostility of the young boy toward the father in our culture may be a product, not of sexual ____________, but rather of the father's role as a ____________. jealousy, disciplinarian

44. Freud's belief that dreams reflect current emotional preoccupations is supported by the dreams of ____________ patients. preoperative

45. The same urge may sometimes be disguised and sometimes be expressed openly in a dream. Freud's assertion that the manifest dream represents a ____________ disguise cannot handle this facet, but C. S. Hall's proposal that the dream functions to ____________ an underlying idea can. defensive express

46. Some laboratory research suggests that memory findings indicating "repression" may not involve motivated forgetting but rather be a particular case of ____________ failure. retrieval

47. Despite the criticisms of Freud's theoretical proposals, his conception of ____________ conflict and the sheer scope of his ideas rank him as one of the giants of psychology. internal (or unconscious)

THE PSYCHODYNAMIC APPROACH: PERSONALITY DIFFERENCES

48. The ___________-___________ differ from Freud in that they emphasize inner conflicts based on interpersonal as opposed to biological sources. — neo-Freudians

49. The neo-Freudians describe personality differences in terms of ___________ ___________ of defense. — dominant patterns

50. According to Horney, neurotic conflicts are caused by ___________ ___________, an all-pervading feeling of being alone and helpless in a hostile world. These conflicts may harden into personality characteristics, because the conflicts create a self-perpetuating ___________ ___________. — basic anxiety; vicious circle

51. In ___________ ___________, there is an emphasis on cultural and interpersonal factors, as well as stress, on the healthy modes of ___________ with the world. — ego psychology; coping

52. ___________ ___________ by Vaillant indicate consistency in coping patterns, with more ___________ coping patterns in older and better-adjusted people. — Longitudinal studies; mature

THE HUMANISTIC APPROACH

53. In contrast to the behavioristic and psychoanalytic approaches to personality, humanistic psychologists describe themselves as having a ___________ view of human motivation. — positive

54. Maslow describes the behaviorists and psychoanalysts as focusing on physiological needs such as hunger, thirst, and escape from pain, which Maslow calls ___________ ___________. — deficiency needs

55. Maslow places the needs referred to above at the bottom of the ___________ ___________ ___________. At the top is the desire to realize oneself to the fullest, called ___________-___________. — hierarchy of needs; self-actualization

56. According to Maslow, satisfaction of lower-level needs and a reasonable sense of self-worth allow for the expression of the desire for ___________-___________. — self-actualization

57. Self-actualized persons are more likely to report profound and deeply felt moments in their lives, called ___________ ___________. — peak experiences

58. One problem with the humanistic approach is that there is little ___________ to support the assertions made about human nature. — evidence

59. Another problem is that, in an important sense, people like Adolf Hitler fit the description of being ___________-___________. — self-actualized

60. In parallel with the Romantic movement, humanistic psychology can be seen as a ___________ movement. — protest

THE SOCIOCULTURAL PERSPECTIVE

61. Evidence from ___________ ___________ suggests wide difference across cultures in ___________ and gender ___________. — cultural anthropology; personality, roles

62. The ___________-___________ method compares different cultures, with the aim of extracting common themes. — cross-cultural

63. Evidence indicates that the same ____________ of personality exist cross-culturally. — dimensions

64. There is evidence from studies both within and across cultures that higher socioeconomic status is associated with more ____________-____________. — self-control

65. Cultures in which there is more emphasis on relations with and obligations to the family and community are called____________, as opposed to ____________. — collectivist, individualist

66. Collectivists belong to fewer ____________-____________ than individualists, but show more loyalty to them. — in-groups

67. In contrast, individualists are more influenced by ____________-____________, and restrict much of their loyalty to the ____________ ____________. — out-groups, nuclear family

68. Evidence for different concepts of the self in different cultures comes from the way Asian Indians ____________ other persons, and the nature and use of personal ____________ in Bali. — describe, names

TAKING STOCK

69. The five different approaches to personality represent five different theoretical ____________, each of which may have some validity. — perspectives

70. Some of the different approaches correspond to different approaches to the presentation of character in ____________. — drama

Self Test

1. Behavioral-cognitive approach is to psychodynamic approach as
   a. psychiatry is to psychology
   b. normality is to pathology
   c. surface is to deep
   d. airplane is to surface transportation
   e. pleasure is to pain

2. Which of the following adjectives would *not* be used by Freud to describe basic human nature?
   a. sexually motivated
   b. selfish
   c. pleasure-seeking
   d. conflict-free
   e. b and d

3. At first the child's behavior is based on a fear of direct social consequences. Later he will avoid certain behaviors even when there is no chance of punishment. Freud would say that the control put on the child by society is then ____________.
   a. eliminated
   b. internalized
   c. externalized
   d. repressed
   e. conflicted

4. Freud and Hobbes agree:
   a. about the basic savageness of human nature
   b. that there is a taming of basic human nature
   c. about the way that human nature is tamed
   d. about the importance of unconscious conflict
   e. a and b

5. Freud made a major contribution to the understanding of human nature when he suggested that the apparent irrationality of much human behavior was a symptom of ____________ ____________.
   a. basic insanity
   b. severe hysteria
   c. unconscious conflicts
   d. wish fulfillment
   e. internalized standards

6. Which of the following are symptoms of hysteria?
   i. partial or total blindness
   ii. paralysis
   iii. feelings of helplessness
   iv. anesthesia of a body part
   v. uncontrollable urges
   a. i, iii, v
   b. i, ii, iv, v
   c. ii, iii, iv
   d. i, ii, iv
   e. all are symptoms of hysteria

7. Charcot and Freud believed that hysteria is ____________.
   a. inherited
   b. psychogenic
   c. the result of physical trauma (injury to the brain)
   d. incurable
   e. unimportant

8. The explosive release of emotions that accompanies the remembrance of certain long-forgotten memories is called ____________.
   a. resistance
   b. memory release
   c. transference
   d. catharsis
   e. unconscious conflict

9. A patient is asked merely to say whatever comes to his mind during a therapy session. The term applied to this psychoanalytic technique is:
   a. transference
   b. free association
   c. resistance formation
   d. wish fulfillment
   e. hypnosis

10. All of the following statements (made by a patient during free association) are examples of resistance *except*:
    a. "I really can't think of anything right now."
    b. "I just forgot what I was about to say."
    c. "I'm thinking of something which has nothing to do with my problem."
    d. "I just remembered a terrible experience from my childhood."
    e. "What I'm thinking about now is too unimportant to tell you."

11. According to Freud, repressed thoughts:
    a. are connected to a wish or thought that a person is unable to face without intense anxiety
    b. are linked to basic biological urges
    c. often date back to early life
    d. all of the above
    e. none of the above

12. Which of Freud's subsystems would be responsible for a desire to eat or drink?
    a. ego
    b. superego
    c. id
    d. a combination of ego and superego
    e. all of the above

13. If a child wants a drink, we often find that he asks for something rather than just taking it. This is evidence for the operation of:
    a. the ego
    b. repression
    c. the id
    d. a and c
    e. b and c

14. The reality principle controls:
    a. the ego
    b. the superego
    c. the id
    d. a and b
    e. all of the subsystems to one degree or another

15. When a child begins to think of himself as if he were the parent, the ____________ has begun to develop.
    a. ego
    b. superego
    c. id
    d. a and b
    e. impossible to tell from this description

16. On what is the mechanism underlying repression based?
    a. irrationality
    b. biological urge reduction
    c. anxiety reduction
    d. fear reduction
    e. ego expansion

17. Why are thoughts and memories repressed as well as actions?
    a. thinking about an act is similar to performing it
    b. young children cannot properly distinguish between thought and action
    c. young children do not realize thoughts are private
    d. a and b
    e. all of the above

18. A child is punished for something he did. He then hits his brother. This is an example of:
    a. repression
    b. transference
    c. hysteria
    d. displaced aggression
    e. anxiety

19. A child has deeply hidden feelings of hostility toward a younger sibling. However, the child treats his sibling with apparent love. This is an example of the defense mechanism known as:
    a. projection
    b. reaction formation
    c. rationalization
    d. displacement
    e. repression

20. A child who displays a behavior diametrically opposed to his frustrated true desires is demonstrating:
    a. reaction formation
    b. displacement
    c. projection
    d. isolation
    e. none of the above

21. After failing to be offered a good job, an applicant decides that he wouldn't have liked the job anyway. This person is displaying a defense mechanism called:
    a. rationalization
    b. projection
    c. reaction formation
    d. isolation
    e. repression

22. When a person attributes his own thoughts and feelings to someone else, we call this:
    a. rationalization
    b. projection
    c. reaction formation
    d. repression
    e. isolation

23. The relation of defense mechanisms to unacceptable unconscious thoughts is about the same as:
    a. rationalization to irrationalization
    b. blocking or rerouting to river
    c. track to trolley
    d. predator to prey
    e. oral to anal

24. Parts of the body which are particularly sensitive to touch are called:
    a. arousal zones
    b. pleasure zones
    c. sensitivity zones
    d. erogenous zones
    e. projection zones

25. Which of the following presents the correct stages of psychosexual development in the right order?
    a. oral, anal, erogenous, phallic, genital
    b. oral, anal, phallic, genital
    c. anal, oral, erogenous, phallic
    d. oral, anal, phallic, erogenous
    e. none are in the correct order

26. An adult who likes eating, kissing, and smoking, would, according to Freud, be described as:
    a. repressed
    b. ego-dominated
    c. an oral character
    d. an anal character
    e. a remnant

27. The anal and oral characters have in common:
    a. unusually strong superegos
    b. strong attachments or conflicts related to a particular stage of development
    c. a concern for orderliness
    d. a lack of normal sexual interests
    e. none of the above

28. All of the following are components of Freud's family triangle *except*:
    a. love
    b. inadequacy
    c. fear
    d. jealousy
    e. b and d

29. The drama of the Oedipus complex unfolds according to the following progression of events:
    a. identification, love, fear, hate, renunciation
    b. love, fear, hate, renunciation, identification
    c. hate, fear, renunciation, identification
    d. love, hate, fear, renunciation, identification
    e. none of the above

30. The motivation for the young boy's identification with his father is:
    a. perception of sexual similarities
    b. castration anxiety
    c. the father's acts of retaliation
    d. vicarious enjoyment of the mother through the father
    e. none of the above

31. The stage following resolution of the Oedipus complex comprises:
    a. the latency period
    b. increased masturbation
    c. puberty
    d. genital stage
    e. all of the above

32. Freud believed that the basis of every dream was:
    a. projection
    b. schizophrenia
    c. wish fulfillment
    d. day residues
    e. castration anxiety

33. Freud distinguished between two parts of the dream, which he termed:
    a. conscious and unconscious
    b. latent and manifest
    c. normal and deviant
    d. wish fulfillment and disguise
    e. normal and abnormal

34. Problems with the psychoanalytic view include:
    a. lack of objectivity of clinical practitioners in reporting patients' statements
    b. so much flexibility that an outcome or its opposite can be predicted
    c. suggestion or influence of patients to report certain kinds of events or feelings
    d. a and c
    e. all of the above

35. Neo-Freudians believe that Freud erred in:
    a. emphasizing unconscious conflict
    b. his views of dreams as wish fulfillments
    c. his perception of oral and anal characteristics
    d. his assertion that the key to emotional development is in biology
    e. being concerned about anxiety

36. For which claims of psychoanalytic theory is there specific positive evidence?
    a. universality of the Oedipus complex
    b. link between hostility to the father and his sexual link to the mother
    c. existence of a cluster of traits predicted by the anal character
    d. a link between toilet training and the anal character
    e. no evidence for any of the above

37. In a recent study, a test was made of Freud's view of the dream as an attempt at gratification. Most very thirsty subjects reported:
    a. dreams in which they drank
    b. dreams in which they did not drink
    c. no dreams whatsoever
    d. dreams in which the act of drinking was represented symbolically
    e. dreams about eating

38. Which of the following statements is *not* in accordance with C. S. Hall's view about dreams?
    a. the dream symbol expresses, rather than disguises, an underlying idea
    b. the dream is a concrete form of mental shorthand that embodies a feeling or emotion
    c. the dream is an abstract form of mental longhand that elaborates on a feeling or emotion
    d. the function of the dream is analogous to that of a cartoonist's picture
    e. there may be a role for the unconscious in dreaming

39. There is little evidence for all of the following assertions of psychoanalytic theory *except*:
    a. the existence of unconscious conflict
    b. the general theory of psychosexual development
    c. the central importance of biology in determining stages of emotional development
    d. personality is essentially fixed by the age of five or six
    e. the Oedipus complex

40. According to Horney, the vicious circle:
    a. results from neurotic conflict
    b. is more likely if there is more basic anxiety
    c. occurs in normal people
    d. all of the above
    e. none of the above

41. Repression is to deciding to ignore unpleasant news as:
    a. unconscious defense is to conscious defense
    b. inattention is to reaction formation
    c. coping is to ego psychology
    d. ego is to superego
    e. house is to bedroom

42. Coping is:
    a. like a conscious mechanism parallel to unconscious defense mechanisms
    b. somewhat consistent in style across decades in a given individual
    c. an unsuccessful way of dealing with problems
    d. all of the above
    e. a and b

43. The humanistic approach differs from both the behavioristic and psychoanalytic approaches in all but one of the following ways. Which of the choices below is *not* a difference between these approaches?
    a. emphasis on the positive side of human nature
    b. assumption of a hierarchy of needs
    c. acknowledgment of the existence of deficiency needs
    d. emphasis on self-actualization
    e. emphasis on free choice

44. In contrast to the behavioristic approach, the trait, psychoanalytic, and humanistic approaches all:
    a. emphasize internal causes of behavior
    b. focus on the conflict between biological and social needs
    c. posit a hierarchy of needs
    d. take a basically statistical approach to personality
    e. emphasize the role of the environment in shaping personality

45. Self-actualization is:
    a. at the top of the need hierarchy
    b. associated with a higher frequency of peak experiences
    c. dependent on satisfaction of lower-level needs
    d. all of the above
    e. a and b

46. Like the Romantic movement, the humanistic movement can be seen as a protest against:
    a. classical conditioning
    b. an overemphasis on culture
    c. a narrow and mechanical approach to human nature
    d. reliance on the scientific approach
    e. c and d

47. The sociocultural perspective differs from all other approaches considered in that only the sociocultural perspective:
    a. does not assume the individual is necessarily the basic unit
    b. considers the meaning of experience
    c. acknowledges a major role for environmental factors
    d. rejects a major role for biological factors
    e. b and c

48. The sociocultural approach compares parallel conditions in different cultures in order to:
    a. discover dimensions of human diversity
    b. extract common features of human nature across cultures
    c. test hypotheses, e.g., about the effect of early experience on later personality
    d. a and c
    e. all of the above

49. Collectivist cultures are *not* more concerned with:
    a. the nuclear family
    b. the extended family
    c. community
    d. in-groups
    e. a and b

50. Dimensions along which the self might vary in different cultures include:
    a. degree of belief in situational determinants of behavior
    b. degree of belief in personality traits
    c. permanence of personal names
    d. degree of interdependence with others
    e. all of the above

51. According to the parallel to drama, a rich portrayal of a unique and distinct character would correspond to the ____________ approach.
    a. trait
    b. humanistic
    c. behavioral-cognitive
    d. b and c
    e. none of the above

52. Overall, the five approaches to personality each:
    a. represent valid alternative perspectives
    b. present views that cannot, ultimately, coexist with all of the others
    c. overemphasize the importance of culture
    d. emphasize reason over feelings
    e. assign a different role to the function of drama

Answer Key for Self Test

1.	c p. 525	27.	b p. 533
2.	d pp. 526–27	28.	b p. 533
3.	b p. 527	29.	d pp. 533–34
4.	e p. 526	30.	b p. 534
5.	c p. 527	31.	a p. 534
6.	d p. 527	32.	c p. 536
7.	b p. 527	33.	b p. 536
8.	d p. 527	34.	e pp. 537–38
9.	b p. 527	35.	d p. 538
10.	d p. 528	36.	c pp. 539–40
11.	d p. 528	37.	b p. 541
12.	c p. 529	38.	c p. 542
13.	a p. 529	39.	a p. 543
14.	a p. 529	40.	d pp. 544–45
15.	b p. 530	41.	a p. 546
16.	c p. 530	42.	e p. 546
17.	e pp. 530–31	43.	c p. 548
18.	d p. 531	44.	a pp. 525, 548
19.	b p. 531	45.	d pp. 549–50
20.	a p. 531	46.	e p. 551
21.	a p. 531	47.	a p. 553
22.	b p. 531	48.	e p. 553
23.	b p. 531	49.	a pp. 555–56
24.	d p. 532	50.	e pp. 558–59
25.	b p. 532–33	51.	b p. 560
26.	c p. 533	52.	a p. 560

Investigating Psychological Phenomena

ANALYSIS OF DREAM CONTENT

Equipment: None
Number of subjects: One or more
Time per subject: Thirty minutes
Time for experimenter: Thirty minutes

The study and analysis of dream content has been of considerable concern to psychologists at least since the publication of Freud's classic work on dreams in 1900. A variety of hypotheses have been proposed to account for the content of dreams and for the way in which our past experiences and expectations about the future are frequently incorporated into our dreamwork.

Given the sparse evidence concerning dream content, there is still a good deal of controversy concerning the facts. One phenomenon of particular interest that is still controversial is whether present motivational states or expectations about the future (e.g., wish fulfillment) influence our dream content.

The present experiment further tests the hypothesis that dream content is influenced by present motivational state. The test is similar to the experiment of William Dement and Edward Wolpert cited in the Gleitman text, in which these investigators induced thirst in their subjects, then analyzed the subjects' dreams to determine whether there was evidence in the dream content for increased thirst.

You will be the subject in the present experiment. Starting on the next page, you will find eight pairs of dream reports. These are the reports of actual dreams from eight students enrolled in an introductory psychology course. One of the reports in each pair is the report of a dream from early in the term in which these students were enrolled in introductory psychology. The other report in each pair represents a dream that occurred on the night preceding a major midterm examination in the psychology course. The question we ask in this experiment is whether the specific issues involved in this examination or general anxiety about the examination was reflected in the dreams of these eight subjects.

In order to address the question, you should read each dream and try to decide which dream in each pair was the one that occurred prior to the examination. Be careful to consider the possibility, as Freud theorized, that conflicts or concerns may be either manifest or latent in dream content. That is, there may be direct or transformed reference to the event in question. For each dream pair, mark your answer sheet A or B according to which member of the pair you think was the dream that preceded the examination. In each case, think about the reason for your choice and assess your confidence in your decision. After listing your choices, check them with the answers given.

DREAM PAIRS

1A Someone was singing a rousing song about a coat. An audience of women, mostly of the type interviewed in commercials, was sitting on the floor of a large room. They were asked to describe how they had put together their outfits. Most were wearing the sweater-and-skirt sort of thing, but one woman in a peculiar-looking caftan told how she had bought the trim first and had then searched for something to use it on. The trim didn't look very good on the caftan.

1B A record store. The stuff that had been pasted up all over the walls (posters, clippings, etc.) had yellowed, creating an antique atmosphere. Some balloons. The store was giving away something for free—furniture I think. There was some argument. Something about a snake who liked a trollop. A young and quarrelsome married couple from a film I'd seen more or less reenacted their roles. I was in a strange room in a hotel or dormitory. There was, to my surprise, a small wrought-iron balcony. Night. From the balcony I could see the lights and reflections of the city gleaming white and yellow all around me. The lights began to go out, all at once—the restaurants and bars were closing. I was seeing into a little restaurant or ice cream parlor, very white and empty. Three people wearily got up and left as the place closed up for the night.

2A I was knocking at the door of my best friend's house. (Earlier in the dream I had seen her working on campus and spoken to her. [She lives in San Antonio, Texas.]) I covered the peephole to the front door, as is my custom, when she became very excited and yelled for her parents. She seemed to be very frightened. This is when the dream ended and I woke up.

2B Someone I didn't recognize was walking down Locust Walk wearing shoes exactly like some of mine, except for the color. Mine are red and blue. Hers were green and blue.

3A I dream I was sitting at a table with several people eating brownies with whipped cream and soap suds, fighting with one of my friends.

3B I dreamed that my kitten looked like a guinea pig. (I went home for the weekend and she had changed.) She wasn't tiger striped, she was only solid black and rust colored. Her ears were not pointed, they were small and flat. She had no tail and her legs were short.

4A I was going to go swimming. I sat on a bench on the side of the street waiting for a taxi or bus. With me were a girl and a German teacher. The man had a beach umbrella. He grew tired of waiting and left. I went to a different beach to look for the father from a foreign family I spent a year with.

4B I was with a boyfriend while he was making sandwiches for a party. Beaded strings were in the crevice between the wall and the ceiling. Another girl was there making coffee with a weird machine. Outside I played catch with a friend. First we used a ball, then an orange, and lastly a key. We almost lost the key in the snow. I was skiing with another girl and she kept complimenting Yamaha skis. I tried to park the car in front of my house but there were no spaces. Two guys who I didn't particularly like from high school were in one of the cars drinking. They were not my type. When they asked me to go drinking I declined. Finally I went to a party. A minister I know said grace. A guest commented that a girl's jewelry didn't match her clothes, yet it really did. A lot of people were talking and eating.

5A The dream opened with me having just had a baby, but for some reason the kid (a boy) was about the size of a year-old baby—maybe a couple of months younger. I didn't recall getting pregnant or delivering the kid. Somehow I knew that the kid (baby) had my boyfriend's nickname. I got extreme pleasure from hugging the baby and knowing he was mine, although I didn't know who the father was. Suddenly I realized that I was in high school and my mother would never let me keep the baby. So I had to give him up for adoption. I was very sad at handing him over to a stranger and the thought that I would never see him grow up was upsetting. This was a pleasurable dream until the last scene.

5B I went back to visit my prep school and I bumped into my favorite teacher there. She was terribly aged and frail, having had some sort of drastic operation. I kissed her hello on the cheek and she was very cold, as though I had misbehaved recently at school or something. I don't remember the rest of the dream clearly except that the teacher kept turning into my mother and back into the teacher, and evidently I had done something awful but no one would tell me what. It was a very anxious and unpleasant dream.

6A I was riding on a trolley coming home from high school. The driver asked me for my fare and I found out I didn't have any money. I ran to the back to try to get out. Then I woke up.

6B I dreamt I had a sexual affair with my psychology professor. He told me I was one of his best friends.

7A Dreamt about color vision. Repeatedly remembered seeing one page in the reading.

7B Dreamt that I woke up late for chemistry lab and that experiment failed.

8A I rode on a short train ride and on the return trip I met a very good friend who is coming to visit me for the weekend. However, the train departure is delayed so I sit down to lunch with my family and another three friends (I don't know where they came from). My family wants me to tell them about school, but I am more interested in seeing one of my friends—procuring tea bags and knives for my apartment (which I need). Another incident—I pass a stand with two older ladies selling homemade doughnuts (and cake) but I don't buy any, even though I see a girl sinking her teeth into one. Also, while I am walking toward the train station, the sidewalk is being paved (by males and females).

8B I have been waiting three weeks to see my boyfriend. Finally the weekend arrives and he comes to visit me. But, of course, we can't be alone since my best friend also drops in on me. Then I find out my grandmother has passed away (however, she is still among us when we all sit down to a mourning feast). When we finally get a chance to be alone again, my boyfriend and I are walking down a street. A car honks its horn and it turns out to be his old girlfriend asking for a ride home. During this same dream I remember buying a new bicycle and a pair of army boots.

Answer Sheet

Dream pair	Dream preceding examination (A or B)	Reason for choice
1.	________	______________________________
2.	________	______________________________
3.	________	______________________________
4.	________	______________________________
5.	________	______________________________
6.	________	______________________________
7.	________	______________________________
8.	________	______________________________

ANSWERS

1. B 2. A 3. A 4. B 5. B 6. B 7. A 8. B

QUESTIONS TO THINK ABOUT

1. Were you accurate? What does this suggest about the content of dreams and about how well they blend with life events?
2. Were there certain pairs where the choice seemed more obvious than for other pairs? Were you more accurate on these?
3. How might you improve on the experiment?

CHAPTER 18

Psychopathology

Learning Objectives

DIFFERENT CONCEPTIONS OF MADNESS

Psychopathology as demonic possession

1. Give examples from historical sources of the treatment of madness as demonic possession.

Psychopathology as a disease

2. Describe the history of the treatment of psychopathology as a disease.
3. Describe the somatogenic view of mental illness, referring to the example of general paresis.
4. Define psychogenic disorders, and explain the historical role of hysteria in clarifying the nature of these disorders.
5. Indicate the major features that define mental disorders, as developed in DSM-IV. What is the role of deviance, *per se*, in the definition?

THE UNDERLYING PATHOLOGY MODEL

6. Explain the underlying pathology model of mental illness.

Subcategories of the pathology model

7. Briefly describe the medical, psychoanalytic, and learning models as approaches to psychopathology.

Classifying mental disorders

8. Distinguish among symptoms, signs, and syndromes.
9. Describe the basic course of the diagnosis of mental disorders, including integration of information about symptoms, signs, course, and onset. What is the relation between the diagnosis and the prognosis and etiology?
10. Describe how psychiatrists used to distinguish between organic brain syndromes, neuroses, and psychoses. Indicate how mental illnesses are now classified, referring to the changes in the latest taxonomy, DSM-IV.

Explaining disorder: diathesis, stress, and pathology

11. Describe the diathesis-stress explanation of mental illness.
12. What does one have to know in order to explain fully a mental (or bodily) disorder?

SCHIZOPHRENIA

13. What is the incidence of schizophrenia?

Signs and symptoms

14. Describe the major symptoms of schizophrenia in the areas of thought, social relationships, motivation, and behavior.
15. Define restitutional symptoms, delusions, hallucinations, and ideas of reference.
16. What are the most salient symptoms of paranoid, catatonic, and disorganized schizophrenia?

The search for the underlying pathology

17. Show how the assumption of a disorder in focus of activity can explain many of the symptoms of schizophrenia.
18. Describe the dopamine hypothesis and indicate the types of evidence in favor of it. Suggest what types of experiments might prove it.
19. What is the mechanism of operation of antipsychotic drugs like Thorazine?
20. What is the anatomical deficit theory of schizophrenia? How are the anatomical and neurotransmitter theories related? Describe the two-syndrome hypothesis.

Ultimate causes of schizophrenia

21. Review the evidence for genetic factors in schizophrenia, and suggestions that schizophrenia is a neurodevelopmental disorder.
22. Describe the role of environmental effects in schizophrenia, including family pathology and prenatal stress.
23. Evaluate the alternative possibilities that the environmental correlates of schizophrenia are caused by or are causes of schizophrenia.

The pathology model and schizophrenia

24. Review the symptoms, underlying pathology, and remote causes of schizophrenia. Review the evidence for an organic basis for schizophrenia.
25. Apply the diathesis-stress model to schizophrenia.

MOOD DISORDERS

Bipolar and unipolar syndromes

26. Distinguish bipolar disorder from major depression. Compare and contrast mania and depression in terms of symptoms.
27. What is the relation between suicide and depression?
28. What is seasonal affective disorder?

Organic factors

29. Review the evidence for a genetic involvement in the causation of bipolar and unipolar disorders.
30. What is the biochemical hypothesis to explain depression?

Psychogenic factors

31. Review the evidence for psychogenic factors in depression.
32. Discuss whether mood or cognitive disorders come first in the causation of depression.
33. Describe Beck's cognitive theory of depression.
34. Describe the learned helplessness theory of depression, and summarize the evidence in favor of it that comes from both animal and human research.
35. Explain how the idea of despondent attributional style as a cause of depression grew out of the concept of learned helplessness, and review the evidence for this position.
36. Indicate the explanations for the higher incidence of depression in American females, as opposed to males.
37. Indicate the adequacy of each theory of depression to account for the range of symptoms.

Mood disorders and the diathesis-stress conception

38. Apply the diathesis-stress conception to mood disorders.

ANXIETY DISORDERS

39. What defines the anxiety disorders?

Phobias

40. Describe phobias, including social phobias, and explain how they can be accounted for in terms of conditioning.

Obsessive-compulsive disorder

41. Describe the symptoms of obsessive-compulsive disorders, and possible causes.

Generalized anxiety disorder

42. Describe generalized anxiety disorder, and both conditioning and psychoanalytic explanations for it.

Panic disorder

43. What is panic disorder, and how does it differ from generalized anxiety disorder? How does it relate to agoraphobia? What is a cognitive explanation of this disorder?

Post-traumatic stress disorder

44. What is post-traumatic stress disorder? How does dissociation fit into the development of this syndrome?

DISSOCIATIVE DISORDERS

45. Describe dissociative amnesia, dissociative fugue, and dissociative identity disorder. What do they have in common?

Factors underlying dissociative disorders

46. What is believed to be the psychological function of dissociative disorders?

Dissociative disorders and the diathesis-stress conception

47. What are the proposed diathesis and stress for dissociative disorders?

SOMATOFORM AND PSYCHOPHYSIOLOGICAL DISORDERS

Somatoform disorders

48. What are somatoform disorders, and what is the psychoanalytic explanation of them? How can their decline in recent decades be explained?

Psychophysiological disorders

49. Define psychophysiological disorders. What is the critical difference between psychophysiological and somatoform disorders?
50. Review the role of biological and psychological factors in the causation of coronary heart disease.
51. What is the Type A behavior pattern? What aspects of this behavior pattern seem most associated with coronary heart disease?

52. Apply the diathesis-stress model to psychophysiological disorders and to the issue of which type of disorder occurs in an individual.

A CATEGORIZING REVIEW

53. Explain how mental disorders can be classified according to the organic or mental basis of both the symptoms and the underlying pathology.

SOCIAL DEVIANCE

The sociopath

54. Discuss the distinctions between criminals and sociopaths.

55. Review the causes of sociopathy (antisocial personality disorder).

Sociopathy and the disorder concept

56. Discuss the advantages and disadvantages of making no legal distinction between sociopaths and criminals.

THE SCOPE OF PSYCHOPATHOLOGY

57. Discuss the problem of defining psychopathology and uncovering common principles underlying it. What, if anything, do all disorders described in this chapter have in common?

Programmed Exercises

DIFFERENT CONCEPTIONS OF MADNESS

1. A dominant early social response to insanity, which resulted in practices as varied as trephining the skull or the burning of witches, was based on the conception of insanity as ____________ ____________.	demonic possession
2. Prior to the 19th century, people with severe mental illness were treated more or less as we currently deal with ____________.	criminals (or prisoners)
3. The disappearance of the psychotic symptoms of ____________ ____________ following administration of penicillin provides strong evidence for a view of mental illness as a disease.	general paresis (or syphilis)
4. Mental symptoms that can be directly explained by malfunction at the organic level are called ____________. Those, like hysteria, that are best explained at the psychological level are called ____________.	somatogenic psychogenic
5. A disorder that is characterized by symptoms that appear to be somatic but have no organic basis was once called ____________.	hysteria

THE UNDERLYING PATHOLOGY MODEL

6. The commonly accepted definition for mental disorders is presented in ____________. It does not require ____________ as a condition for the diagnosis of a disorder.	DSM-IV abnormality (deviance)
7. According to the ____________ ____________ ____________, a particular disease is considered as the underlying cause of specific mental symptoms.	underlying pathology model
8. According to the ____________ model, mental illness has an organic basis, to be treated with somatic therapies. According to the ____________ model, mental disorders are, in large part, the result of maladaptive learning. According to the ____________ model, mental illness results from psychogenic factors, of the sort described by Freud.	medical learning psychoanalytic
9. Practitioners who ascribe to the learning model and emphasize classical and instrumental conditioning as causes of disorder are called ____________ ____________.	behavior therapists

10. A variant of the learning model, called the ___________-___________ model, emphasizes faulty thinking habits. Practitioners of this model are called ___________ ___________. — cognitive-behavioral; cognitive therapists

11. In psychopathology, as in physical medicine, the diagnostic process begins with a ___________ ___________. This elicits a set of complaints, or ___________. — clinical interview; symptoms

12. The diagnostician also looks for ___________, that is, indications that are not complaints, but that are consistent with the symptoms. — signs

13. A ___________ is a pattern of symptoms that go together. — syndrome

14. In the course of the ___________ ___________, the diagnostician integrates information about ___________, ___________, ___________, and ___________ to arrive at a diagnosis. — clinical interview; symptoms, signs, course, onset

15. As a result of the diagnosis, one can often predict the ___________ (outcome) and ___________ (cause) of the disorder. — prognosis; etiology

16. In the most recent classification or taxonomy of mental illness, called ___________, more emphasis is placed on the description of disorders, rather than on ___________ about their cause. — DSM-IV; theories

17. In the older classification of mental illnesses, ___________ were considered to be anxiety-related disorders in which there is good contact with reality, in contrast to the more severe disorders called ___________. A third category was ___________ ___________ ___________. — neuroses; psychoses, organic brain syndromes

18. According to the ___________-___________ conception, mental illness results from the interaction between a predisposition and some set of environmental events. — diathesis-stress

19. The analysis of mental disorders in the medical model includes description of remote and immediate ___________, which lead to the ___________ of the disorder. — causes, symptoms

SCHIZOPHRENIA

20. The incidence of schizophrenia is about one American out of every __________. — hundred

21. Schizophrenic symptoms include disorders in thinking and selective __________. — attention

22. Schizophrenic persons often lose contact with other people as a result of social ___________. This may lead to progressively worse problems, because they have few opportunities for social ___________ ___________. — withdrawal; reality testing

23. Schizophrenic symptoms include elaboration of the private world, or ___________ symptoms, such as ___________ and hearing voices or other ___________. — restitutional; delusions; hallucinations

24. Schizophrenics typically show either ___________ or ___________ affect. — apathy, inappropriate

25. Some schizophrenics begin to believe that external events are specially related to them, personally. These beliefs are called __________ _______ __________, and may be elaborated into a ___________ ___________. — ideas of reference; delusional system

26. Delusions are typical symptoms in a common form of schizophrenia, ___________ schizophrenia. — paranoid

27. A schizophrenic with unusual motor reactions, such as remaining motionless for long periods, is classified as ____________. If the predominant symptoms are extreme incoherence in thought and inappropriateness in behavior, a person is classified as a ____________ schizophrenic.	catatonic disorganized
28. A cognitive theory of schizophrenia holds that many symptoms, especially the disturbances in language and thought, result from an inability to keep things in proper focus. This results in an inability to hold on to one ____________ of thought or action. Some believe this is the basic ____________ ____________ in schizophrenia.	line (train) psychological malfunction
29. One argument for an organic basis for schizophrenia is the effectiveness of a group of drugs called ____________ in treatment.	antipsychotics (major tranquilizers)
30. A current organic theory of schizophrenia holds that it results from too much brain activity caused by the catecholamine neurotransmitter ____________, which may cause the overstimulation characteristic of schizophrenia.	dopamine
31. In accord with the theory that holds that neurons in the schizophrenic's brain are oversensitive to dopamine, the ____________, which enhance dopamine activity, make schizophrenics worse and can induce a schizophrenic-like ____________ in normals.	amphetamines psychosis (syndrome)
32. Anatomical evidence indicates that brain ____________ is associated with schizophrenia.	atrophy (damage)
33. A more modern classification of schizophrenia contrasts abnormal behavior, or ____________ symptoms, with the absence of normal behaviors, or ____________ symptoms.	positive negative
34. According to the ____________-____________ hypothesis, both anatomical deficits and neurotransmitter excess are causes of schizophrenia. The anatomical deficits are thought to be associated with the ____________ symptoms and the neurotransmitter excess with the ____________ symptoms.	two-syndrome negative positive
35. Twin studies indicate that there is a significant ____________ factor in the causation of schizophrenia.	genetic (hereditary)
36. Identical twins show a ____________ of 55 percent for schizophrenia.	concordance
37. According to the view of schizophrenia as a ____________ disorder, pathological genes cause brain abnormalities in the fetus, which eventually lead to schizophrenia.	neurodevelopmental
38. There is evidence that ____________ pathology may cause schizophrenia, but there is also evidence that it may be caused by schizophrenia.	family
39. In accord with the diathesis-stress model, the evidence for a genetic predisposition for schizophrenia corresponds to the ____________, while the demonstrated role of environment events corresponds to the ____________.	diathesis stress

MOOD DISORDERS

40. While schizophrenia can be regarded as essentially a disorder of thought, in the ____________ disorders, the dominant disturbance is one of affect or mood.	mood
41. The two major types of mood disorders are ____________ disorder and ____________ ____________.	bipolar major depression

42. ____________ is the opposite of depression, and is characterized, among other things, by endless talking and overabundance of energy. Mania

43. Depression is commonly associated with physical manifestations such as weakness, loss of appetite and interest in sex, and sleep disorders. These are called ____________ symptoms. vegetative

44. Depression is associated with a high rate of ____________. suicide

45. Depression associated with decreasing amounts of light as winter approaches is called ____________ ____________ ____________. seasonal affective disorder

46. Twin studies indicate a higher role for genetic factors in ____________ than in ____________ disorders. bipolar unipolar

47. There is evidence that abnormal levels of either of two neurotransmitters, ____________ and ____________, may account for mood disorders. At high levels, these neurotransmitters may lead to ____________, while at low levels, they may lead to ____________. serotonin, norepinephrine mania depression

48. According to a number of psychogenic approaches to depression, the primary disorder is ____________, which leads to changes in ____________. cognitive, mood

49. Beck asserts that depression results from a set of negative beliefs, and can be successfully treated with ____________ therapy. cognitive

50. According to the ____________ ____________ theory of depression, depression is caused by an expectation that one's actions will have no significant effects. learned helplessness

51. As a result of the difficulty in explaining symptoms such as self-blame in depression, emphasis on psychological causative factors has changed from learned helplessness to despondent ____________ ____________. attributional style

ANXIETY DISORDERS

52. An irrational and intense fear of an object or situation is called a ____________. phobia

53. According to a ____________ view, phobias expand by the process of generalization. conditioning

54. In ____________-____________ disorders, anxiety is produced by persistent internal events (thoughts or wishes). obsessive-compulsive

55. ____________ are persistent thoughts. ____________ are acts performed in an attempt to deal with these thoughts. Obsessions, Compulsions

56. In phobias, anxiety is focused on a particular object or situation. In ____________ ____________ disorders, it is all-pervasive. generalized anxiety

57. ____________ disorder is more acute than generalized anxiety disorder but, like generalized anxiety disorder, it doesn't focus on a particular object or situation. Panic

58. Fear of having panic attacks causes some people not to venture away from home, a condition called ____________. agoraphobia

59. Some have explained panic disorder as an overreaction to the bodily symptoms of ____________. fear

60. Recurrent nightmares and flashbacks about a traumatic event characterize ____________-____________ ____________ disorder. post-traumatic stress

61. Immediately after the trauma, people who will develop post-traumatic stress disorder often feel oddly unaffected by the event, or ____________. — dissociated

DISSOCIATIVE DISORDERS

62. In dissociative disorders, a whole set of mental events are removed from ordinary ____________. These disorders include ____________ and ____________ (cite two types). — consciousness, dissociative fugue, dissociative amnesia, or dissociative identity disorder

63. Many believe that dissociative disorders are a psychological ____________ against something the individual is unable to face. — defense

64. According to one formulation, the tendency to be able to be ____________ forms part of the diathesis for dissociative disorders, and ____________ ____________ is often the stress. — hypnotized; severe trauma (severe abuse, child abuse)

SOMATOFORM AND PSYCHOPHYSIOLOGICAL DISORDERS

65. In somatoform disorders, the principal symptom is a ____________ disorder, such as paralysis. — somatic (bodily)

66. The four different types of somatoform disorders include (list two): ____________ and ____________. — hypochondriasis, somatization disorder, somatoform pain disorder, conversion disorder

67. Conversion disorders are declining in incidence. This probably results from more ____________ child rearing and more general ____________ sophistication. — permissive, medical

68. In ____________ disorders, organic damage is caused by psychophysiological factors. — psychophysiological

69. The ____________ ____________ behavior pattern is associated with increased risk of coronary heart disease. The component of the personality most associated with coronary heart disease is ____________. — Type A; hostility

70. In the face of continued stress, some people get peptic ulcers, some get coronary heart disease, some get other psychophysiological disorders, and some show no obvious effects. These differences may be accounted for in terms of a preexisting somatic ____________. — diathesis (predisposition, susceptibility)

71. Psychophysiological disorders have primarily ____________ symptoms and primarily ____________ underlying pathology. — organic; mental

SOCIAL DEVIANCE

72. Someone who behaves antisocially without signs of remorse is called an antisocial personality, or ____________. — sociopath

73. Some explanations of sociopathy suggest that it may result from cortical ____________, or cortical ____________. — immaturity, underarousal

74. Another account of sociopathy holds that sociopaths have little ____________ for the consequences of their actions. — fear (concern)

75. The distinction between sociopathy and ____________ is often hard to maintain. — criminality

Self Test

1. Treatment of "mental disorders" in the past by such procedures as trephination or flogging is indicative of a conception of these disorders as caused by:
   a. microorganisms
   b. criminal impulses
   c. degeneration
   d. demonic possession
   e. medical malpractice

2. The discovery of a cure for general paresis gave support to the view of mental illness as:
   a. demonic possession
   b. akin to criminality
   c. a disease of society
   d. somatogenic
   e. resulting from medical malpractice

3. If a specific enzyme lack was pinned down as the cause of a previously poorly understood severe mental illness, it would change its classification from ___________ to ___________.
   a. psychosis, neurosis
   b. disease, pathology
   c. psychoanalytic, medical
   d. psychogenic, somatogenic
   e. minor, serious

4. According to the modern view, as expressed in DSM-IV, abnormality (deviance) is:
   a. part of the definition of mental disorders
   b. a frequent but not necessary feature of mental disorders
   c. unrelated to mental disorders
   d. directly linked to distress
   e. serious only when it is somatogenic

5. Both the medical model and the psychoanalytic model:
   a. emphasize somatogenic disorders
   b. fail to explain conversion disorders
   c. are limited versions of the pathology model
   d. emphasize psychogenic disorders
   e. emphasize the role of learning

6. It is probably true that most Swiss today are at least bilingual. Then a monolingual Swiss would be deviant or abnormal. Classification of such a person as suffering from a mental disorder would depend, according to the pathology model, on:
   a. the establishment of the deviance
   b. demonstration that monolingualism seriously impairs functioning in Switzerland
   c. description of some underlying pathology that caused monolingualism
   d. b or c
   e. none of the above

7. Which of the following goes along with symptoms, course, and onset in forming a mental disorder diagnosis?
   a. signs
   b. labeling
   c. deviance determination
   d. neurosis evaluation
   e. psychogenic evaluation

8. The diagnosis often leads to information about the:
   a. signs
   b. deviance
   c. prognosis
   d. etiology
   e. c and d

9. The fundamental difference between what was known as a psychosis and a neurosis was:
   a. the psychosis involves more detachment from reality
   b. the neurosis is easier to cure
   c. all psychoses have a known biological cause
   d. b and c
   e. a and c

10. Understanding of a disease includes knowledge of its symptoms, underlying pathology, remote causes, and:
    a. immediate causes
    b. psychogenicity
    c. psychoanalytic roots
    d. deviance
    e. a and c

11. Certain types of color blindness occur, invariably, if a person inherits a particular gene or pair of genes from his or her parents. This "disorder" does not fit the diathesis-stress model, because:
    a. there is no diathesis
    b. there is no stress
    c. both diathesis and stress are present, but either is sufficient for manifestation of the disorder
    d. both diathesis and stress are present, but they do not interact
    e. c or d

12. The general idea that schizophrenics have difficulty distinguishing between personal (internal) and external events can be used to explain some

of the symptoms of schizophrenia. Which of the following schizophrenic symptoms can be explained in this manner?
a. delusions
b. hallucinations
c. catatonic immobility
d. a and b
e. all of the above

13. Delusions differ from hallucinations in that:
a. delusions are restitutional symptoms
b. delusions are based on interpretations of real events
c. delusions are primarily visual while hallucinations are auditory
d. delusions are associated with apathy
e. delusions cause social withdrawal

14. Delusions in paranoid schizophrenics or bizarre behaviors in catatonic schizophrenics are examples of:
a. syndromes
b. diatheses
c. ideas of reference
d. negative symptoms
e. positive symptoms

15. The idea that the fundamental disorder in schizophrenia is a cognitive deficit having to do with failure to keep things in proper focus can explain all but one of the following. Which feature of schizophrenia *cannot* be easily explained?
a. disconnected thought
b. rhyming associations
c. social withdrawal (as a consequence of overstimulation)
d. apathy
e. c and d

16. Thorazine is a drug in the antipsychotic (major tranquilizer) family and is effective as therapy for schizophrenia. Antipsychotics are known to block the action of dopamine at the synapse. Dopamine is a neurotransmitter. Low levels of dopamine in animals lead to the neglect of stimulation. Taken together, these findings suggest:
a. that schizophrenia results from an excess of dopamine, leading to overstimulation or overload
b. that there is a strong, enzyme-based hereditary deficit in dopamine in schizophrenics
c. that schizophrenics have too little dopamine, leading to cognitive and affective symptoms
d. that there is probably no direct relation between dopamine levels and schizophrenia
e. that drugs should be given simpler names

17. Penicillin is to general paresis as __________ is (are) to schizophrenia.
a. dopamine
b. amphetamines
c. antipsychotics (major tranquilizers)
d. norepinephrine
e. genetics

18. According to the dopamine theory of schizophrenia, a drug that opposes the effect of amphetamines would:
a. be likely to reduce positive symptoms of schizophrenia
b. be likely to reduce negative symptoms of schizophrenia
c. cause schizophrenic symptoms in normal people
d. oppose the effect of antipsychotics
e. a and b

19. The two-syndrome hypothesis asserts that:
a. the positive and negative symptoms of schizophrenia have different causes
b. anatomical and neurotransmitter disorders produce different types of schizophrenia
c. there are two anatomical deficits underlying schizophrenia
d. amphetamines and dopamine are the two causes of schizophrenia
e. a and b

20. The concordance rate among identical twins for schizophrenia is 55 percent, while the comparable figure for fraternal twins is 9 percent. These results suggest that:
a. genetic factors predominate as causes of schizophrenia
b. there is a very weak genetic component in the causation of schizophrenia
c. schizophrenia is essentially caused by environmental factors
d. the primary cause of schizophrenia is probably lack of a neurotransmitter, rather than a genetic effect
e. both genetic and environmental factors play important roles in the causation of schizophrenia

21. There are some reports of poorer mental health in the *adoptive* parents of schizophrenics. This, along with studies of differences in the behaviors of mothers to their schizophrenic and normal children, suggests that:

a. pathological home environments cause schizophrenia
b. schizophrenic children can induce pathological behavior in parents
c. there is an organic basis for schizophrenia
d. there is a psychogenic basis for schizophrenia
e. a and d

22. The pathology model of schizophrenia presented in the text includes all but one of the following assumptions. Which assumption is *not* included?
a. Family pathology leads to deficits in the function of brain neurotransmitters.
b. Some genetic factors contribute to pathology in the function of certain brain neurotransmitters.
c. Neurotransmitter deficits can lead to inability to focus in time or space.
d. Inability to focus in time or space can lead to social withdrawal.
e. Inability to focus in space and time can lead to inappropriate emotions.

23. Manic disorders share with some forms of schizophrenia which of the following symptoms?
a. hallucinations
b. social withdrawal
c. shifting from one subject to another in conversation
d. blunted affect in response to stimuli that would normally elicit affective responses
e. enormous amounts of energy

24. A person shows little interest in the world around him. He shows little emotional response and has disconnected thoughts. On this basis, the most likely guess for a diagnosis would be:
a. mania
b. major depression
c. bipolar disorder
d. schizophrenia
e. a or c

25. There is evidence for a gene on the X chromosome that is associated with the occurrence of:
a. seasonal affective disorder
b. major depression
c. bipolar disorder
d. schizophrenia
e. none of the above

26. Parents with bipolar disorder tend to have children with bipolar disorder, and parents with unipolar disorder tend to have children with unipolar disorder. This suggests that:
a. parents are a stress
b. bipolar and unipolar disorders have a different basis
c. bipolar and unipolar disorders share a common cause
d. environmental events are the primary cause of mood disorders
e. bipolar disorder is more likely to be inherited than unipolar disorder

27. According to biochemical hypotheses, low levels of norepinephrine or serotonin are causative factors in:
a. mania
b. depression
c. schizophrenia
d. a and b
e. a and c

28. All but one of the following provide evidence in favor of the theory that low levels of norepinephrine in the brain lead to depression. Which of these findings does *not* support this theory?
a. Drugs that deplete norepinephrine cause depression in normals.
b. Helplessness training in animals depletes norepinephrine.
c. Drugs which increase the availability of norepinephrine are effective in therapy for depression.
d. Norepinephrine is involved with the systems in the brain that produce arousal and activation.
e. Dopamine, a neurotransmitter related to norepinephrine, is implicated in the causation of schizophrenia.

29. In terms of the biochemical hypothesis, which holds that high levels of norepinephrine (or serotonin) cause mania, which of the following should be an effective therapy for mania?
a. a drug that mimics norepinephrine
b. amphetamine
c. a drug that increases reuptake of norepinephrine by the presynaptic neuron
d. a drug that decreases the rate of breakdown of norepinephrine in the synaptic gap
e. a drug that increases the rate of synthesis of norepinephrine in the synaptic terminals

30. According to Seligman's helplessness views, the low affect of depression results from:
a. low levels of norepinephrine
b. negative cognitions that produce affective changes

c. a tendency towards suicidal thoughts
d. bipolar mood change
e. self-hatred

31. Which of the following symptoms of depression is particularly difficult to explain for both the biochemical and psychogenic (learned helplessness) theories?
a. negative affect
b. inactivity
c. responsiveness to antidepressant drugs
d. self-hatred
e. none of the above

32. According to the learned helplessness theory of depression, which of the following would be the most relevant diathesis for depression?
a. depletion of norepinephrine or serotonin
b. past experiences in which a person could not control his/her environment
c. genetic factors
d. parents who gave the person too much responsibility as a child
e. c or d

33. The advantage of the attributional style explanation of depression over learned helplessness is that the former can explain:
a. inactivity
b. suicidal thoughts
c. self-blame
d. global depression
e. low levels of norepinephrine

34. Which of the following hypothetical findings would oppose the attributional style explanation of a higher incidence of depression in adult females?
a. equal incidence in both sexes in preadolescence
b. equal incidence in both sexes in traditional cultures
c. lower levels of brain norepinephrine in females
d. lower levels of activity in adult females
e. a and b

35. Which of the following lists of disorders is arranged in order of *increasing* importance of psychogenic causative factors?
a. schizophrenia, depression, manic-depressive psychosis
b. schizophrenia, general paresis, phobias
c. phobias, depression, mental retardation
d. general paresis, depression, phobias
e. schizophrenia, phobias, general paresis

36. One effective treatment for specific phobias is to expose the phobic person to weak instances of the phobic object while the subject relaxes. The strength of the stimulus is gradually increased. Under these conditions, many phobias disappear, and no undesirable symptoms seem to replace them. This therapeutic success is an argument in favor of:
a. the conditioning view of phobias
b. a psychoanalytic account
c. a diathesis-stress model of phobias
d. a biological basis for phobias
e. none of the above

37. A disorder in which anxiety is handled by repetitive and ritualistic acts is called:
a. phobia
b. psychogenic fugue
c. obsessive-compulsive disorder
d. conversion disorder
e. generalized anxiety disorder

38. If phobias are often about objects, and obsessions are about thoughts, then panic disorder can be said to be about:
a. physiological symptoms
b. lack of ability to escape
c. sexual objects
d. denial of fear
e. sympathy

39. Post-traumatic stress disorder and specific phobias share:
a. a conditioning explanation
b. causation by a traumatic event
c. dissociation
d. low anxiety
e. ritualistic behaviors

40. Dissociative amnesia, dissociative fugue, and dissociative identity disorder are all examples of:
a. obsessive-compulsive disorders
b. psychoses
c. conversion disorders
d. dissociative disorders
e. none of the above

41. There has been a decline in the incidence of diagnosed conversion disorders in the United States. This might result from:
a. greater sophistication in making neurological diagnoses

b. increased medical sophistication of people
c. greater permissiveness in the upbringing of children
d. a and b
e. all of the above

42. The fundamental distinction between anxiety disorders and somatoform or dissociative disorders is that:
a. anxiety disorders are more generalized
b. anxiety is an explanation only for anxiety disorders
c. organic factors are much more heavily involved in anxiety disorders
d. only in anxiety disorders is anxiety expressed overtly
e. a and b

43. Obesity, smoking, and hostility have in common the fact that they are all:
a. components of the Type A behavior pattern
b. risk factors for coronary heart disease
c. associated with a competitive personality
d. a and b
e. all of the above

44. If a study found that, under the stress of threat of terrorism for a period of years, a group of 100 people developed a wide variety of psychophysiological disorders, including ulcers in some, hypertension in others, and asthma in still others, this would be evidence in favor of:
a. a diathesis factor
b. a stress factor
c. a role for neurotransmitters
d. an organic origin for psychophysiological disorders
e. therapeutic use of the antibiotic terrormycin

45. A fundamental difference between a somatoform disorder and a psychophysiological disorder is that:
a. treatment of the organic "complaint" is much more likely to be effective in psychophysiological disorders
b. psychophysiological disorders are much more likely to be accompanied by low levels of neurotransmitters
c. somatoform disorders are mental in origin
d. dissociation is involved only in psychophysiological disorders
e. psychophysiological disorders always involve the nervous system

46. In terms of the model of categorization of mental disorders in the text, diabetes is to psychophysiological disorders as schizophrenia is to ____________.
a. general paresis
b. bipolar disorders
c. asthma
d. sociopathy
e. pneumonia

47. A person is apprehended after committing a series of crimes. The question is whether he should be treated as a criminal or a sociopath. All but one of the following characteristics suggest that he is a sociopath. Indicate the characteristic that suggests a criminal, rather than sociopath, diagnosis:
a. he is a loner
b. he feels no guilt for the committed crimes
c. he is anxious
d. he is charming
e. he is intelligent

Answer Key for Self Test

1.	d	p. 566
2.	d	pp. 568–69
3.	d	pp. 568, 570
4.	b	p. 570
5.	c	p. 572
6.	d	p. 571
7.	a	pp. 572–73
8.	e	p. 573
9.	a	p. 573
10.	a	p. 574
11.	b	p. 574
12.	d	p. 577
13.	b	p. 577
14.	e	p. 580
15.	d	p. 580
16.	a	p. 579
17.	c	pp. 569, 579
18.	a	p. 579
19.	e	pp. 579–80
20.	e	pp. 580–81
21.	b	p. 582
22.	a	pp. 582–83
23.	c	pp. 576, 584
24.	d	p. 578
25.	c	p. 586
26.	b	p. 586
27.	b	p. 587
28.	e	p. 587
29.	c	p. 587
30.	b	p. 588
31.	d	p. 589
32.	b	p. 588
33.	c	p. 589
34.	e	pp. 589–90
35.	d	pp. 569, 587
36.	a	p. 591
37.	c	p. 592
38.	a	p. 593
39.	b	pp. 591, 594
40.	d	p. 595
41.	e	p. 598
42.	d	p. 598
43.	b	p. 599
44.	a	p. 600
45.	a	p. 599
46.	d	p. 601
47.	c	p. 602

Investigating Psychological Phenomena

DEPRESSION AND NEGATIVE EXPERIENCES

Equipment: Pencil, paper, and stopwatch or watch with second indicator
Number of subjects: One (yourself; you will need the cooperation of a friend to serve as a timer for about five minutes)
Time per subject: Twenty minutes
Time for experimenter: Twenty minutes

Depression is a very common disturbance. It can vary from almost universal "blue" moods to a serious, chronic, and incapacitating disorder. Because at least some of the characteristics of deep (psychotic) depression occur occasionally in most people, it is possible to study depression in a general population. In any population, there seems to be a more or less continuous distribution of people along a dimension running from depression to elation.

Severe depression is characterized by depressed mood, loss of interest in others and normally desirable things (such as food), feelings of hopelessness, helplessness, and worthlessness, and slowed down thought and motor activity. Many of these symptoms appear in mild forms in the general population. It is reasonable to expect that mildly depressed people will show some of the same bases or causes of their symptoms as severely depressed people.

A number of theories of depression are outlined in the text. These include biochemical explanations (e.g., depletion of norepinephrine), and psychological theories emphasizing hopelessness or learned helplessness. In this study we will explore a particularly simple additional theory: People are depressed because bad things happen to them. Clearly, some people get depressed in the face of success and others remain nondepressed following a series of adverse events. Nonetheless, it seems very reasonable that negative experiences would contribute to the causation of depression. We will test the hypothesis that people who are more depressed have had relatively more adverse experiences in the recent past.

A major purpose of this exercise is to illustrate some of the difficulties that arise in the scientific study of psychopathology. More than in previous studies in this study guide, we want to make you aware of the problem of making definitive measurements that clearly support a particular hypothesis. We want you to appreciate the difficulty of research and at the same time realize that progress can be made.

The first problem that we face is this: How do we measure depression? A basic issue that arises is the matter of "subjective" or "objective" measurement. In the case of a mood disorder, one might be inclined to subjective measurement, and indeed, much of the diagnosis of depression is concerned with what people say about how they feel. More objective measurements would involve observation of people (facial expression, level of activity) or having them report on their own activities (how many hours they sleep each night, for example). In this study we look at a totally subjective measure, the subject's rating of his or her own mood. Remember that we are dealing with the range of depression and elation seen in the general population, and not with people actually diagnosed as depressed. In the case of diagnosis, interview and observation by an experienced clinician is involved, sometimes along with administration of a question inventory. We will use only self-ratings of mood and will collect two such ratings: one for the subject's momentary mood (how depressed he or she feels now) and the other for how depressed he or she has felt, in general, over the past year.

The second problem is this: How do we develop a measure of the incidence of negative and positive events in the recent life of each subject? We will use as our measure the subject's recall of negative and positive events over the past year. There are many problems and alternative interpretations of the results of this procedure. We will discuss them after you have served as a subject in this study.

Fill out the two rating scales below and enter your self-ratings on the anwer sheet at the end of this section. Then continue to the recall task.

Rate what you judge to be your mood, right now. Circle the most appropriate number.

Extremely Depressed	Very Depressed	Moderately Depressed	Slightly Depressed	Neither Depressed Nor Happy
9	8	7	6	5
Slightly Happy	Moderately Happy	Very Happy	Extremely Happy	
4	3	2	1	

Rate what you judge to have been your mood, on the average, over the last twelve months.

Extremely Depressed	Very Depressed	Moderately Depressed	Slightly Depressed	Neither Depressed Nor Happy
9	8	7	6	5
Slightly Happy	Moderately Happy	Very Happy	Extremely Happy	
4	3	2	1	

RECALL OF NEGATIVE AND POSITIVE EVENTS

For this measure you will need the assistance of a friend who will time two separate two-minute intervals for you. No one but you will see what you write down.

You will go through two recall tasks, in order. Get a pen or pencil and sit at a table. When you are comfortable, ask a friend to say "Go" when the second hand of a watch crosses 12. When your friend says "go," turn to the next page, read the sentence at the top, and follow the instructions. Ask your friend to say "stop" when two minutes have elapsed. You should then stop the task.

The next time the second hand passes 12 (i.e., a minute after you complete the first part of the task), have your friend time another two minutes. When he says "go," turn to the page after the one you had just written on, read the instructions, and follow them for two minutes.

Do not read on until you have completed the above task.

You are asked to perform the following task for exactly two minutes.

Someone will time the two minutes. When he says "go" read the sentence below and follow the instructions. Continue until you hear "stop" at two minutes.

List below all of the negative things that have happened to you in the last twelve months.

You are asked to perform the following task for exactly two minutes, following the performance of the "bad events" task.

Someone will time the two minutes. When he says "go" read the sentence below and follow the instructions. Continue until you hear "stop" at two minutes.

List below all of the positive things that have happened to you in the last twelve months.

Add up the number of negative and the number of positive events that you remembered. Put these numbers on the answer sheet at the end of this section. Also enter the difference between the number of negative events and the number of positive events (# negative events minus # positive events), and the total number of events recalled (# negative events plus # positive events).

ANALYSIS OF DATA

We have obtained this same data (depression ratings and event scores) from sixty-four undergraduate students at the University of Michigan. We will present these data here. You will add your own results to theirs, and we will then discuss the results.

MEASURES OF DEPRESSION

We used two measures of depression: rated mood now and rated mood over the last twelve months. You might expect that momentary and long-term mood would be related but that the two could sometimes be different. That, in fact, is just what our data show. Below is a scatter plot that presents the data from all sixty-four subjects (see the statistical appendix to the text to learn more about scatter plots). Each point on the plot represents the two mood scores for one subject. Enter your own data point.

There is a positive relation between the two measures of depression. All relations described in these results will be expressed as correlation coefficients (see the statistical appendix). A value of +1.00 indicates a perfect positive correlation; a value of –1.00 a perfect negative correlation, and a value of 0.00 indicates no relation at all.

Our measure of "mood now" correlates +.46 with the measure of "mood over one year."

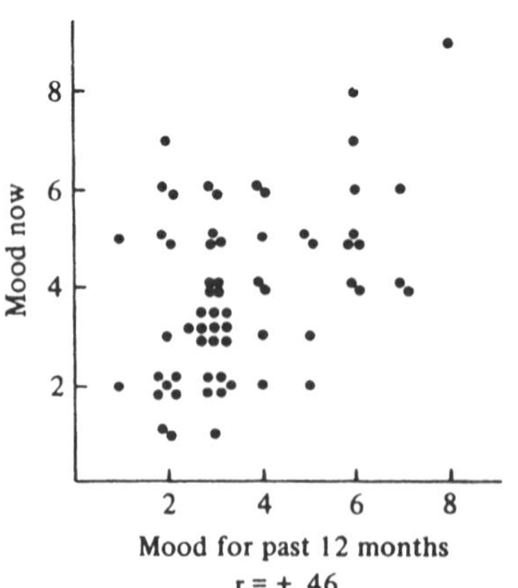

r = + .46

Looking at the scatter plot, you can see that there is some relation between the two mood measures. The general pattern of dots goes from lower left (happy on both scores) to upper right (depressed on both scores). But there are some exceptions. The correlation is positive, but far from perfect. Mark your point on the graph. Does your point fit in with the general pattern, or is it something of an exception? If an exception, can you explain this (e.g., it has been a very good year for you, but something unpleasant just happened to you)?

EVENT SCORES AND DEPRESSION

Before we test the major hypothesis (relatively more negative events in more depressed people), we can examine another prediction that can be made from the symptoms of seriously depressed people. Such people are characterized by a slowing down of action and thought. If this symptom also appears in milder form, in the low levels of depression in the student population, we would expect slowdown in memory search, along with other mental events. Therefore, we would expect that more depressed students would recall fewer events, positive or negative. (This type of finding would surely be true in a comparison of seriously depressed hospitalized patients versus "normal" subjects.) We can test for this possibility by computing the correlation between self-rated depression (mood now) and the total number of events recalled (positive plus negative events). Note that because high scores on the depression rating mean more depression and high scores also represent large numbers of events recalled, we would expect a negative correlation: High depression scores go with low event recall scores.

For our sixty-four subjects, the correlation between "mood now" and the total events is –.05: There is no evidence of any relation. Enter your score on these two measures in the scatter plot on the next page. You can see by examining the scatter plot that the two measures do not seem to be related. The relations between "mood over one year" and total events is also small. The correlation is +.14 (this is very small, but also in the direction opposite to the direction we predicted). There are two possible interpretations of our result. One is that our sample is not representative of the population, and that there actually is a negative depression–total event relation. Given the data we have, there is no reason to believe this. Another interpretation is that there is no relation, but that there might well be such a relation if we looked at severely depressed people as well: That is, the slowdown of

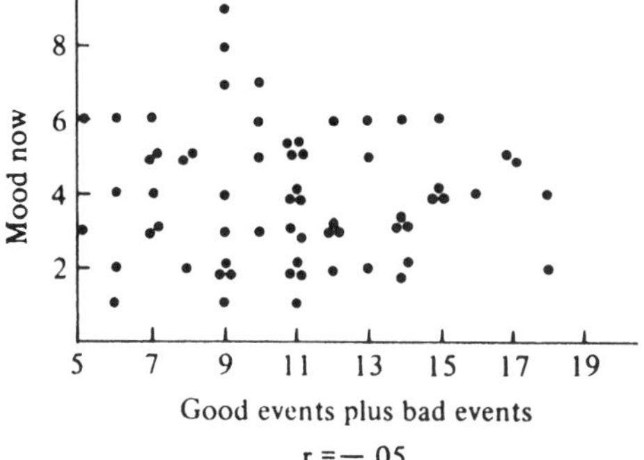

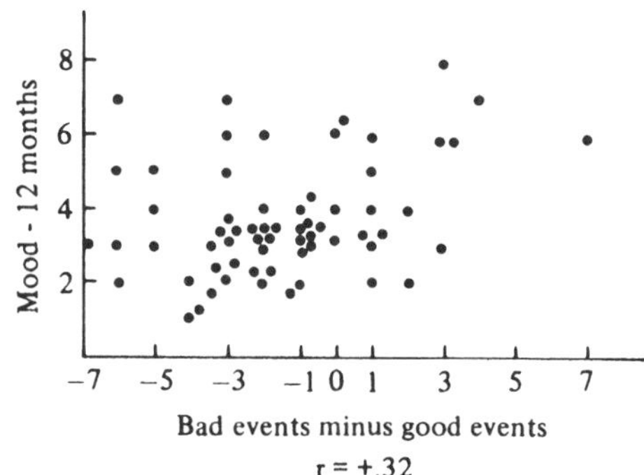

mental function may only be marked in severe depression.

We now ask whether increased depression goes with a higher relative incidence of negative events. If this was true, we would expect a positive correlation between either depression score and the difference between number of negative and number of positive events recalled. We present below the scatter plot for both depression scores. Enter your own points on each of these plots. Just by inspecting these scatter plots you should be able to see that there is a positive relation: Higher depression scores *tend* to go with higher negative minus positive event scores. In fact, the correlations are:

Mood now vs negative – positive events r = +.46
Mood over one year vs negative – positive events r = +.32

The relations are not overwhelming, but there is a clear relation. For example the .46 correlation is significant at more than the .001 level: This means that a correlation this high could come about less than one chance in 1000 if there was no relation between mood now and negative–positive events in the population (see the statistical appendix).

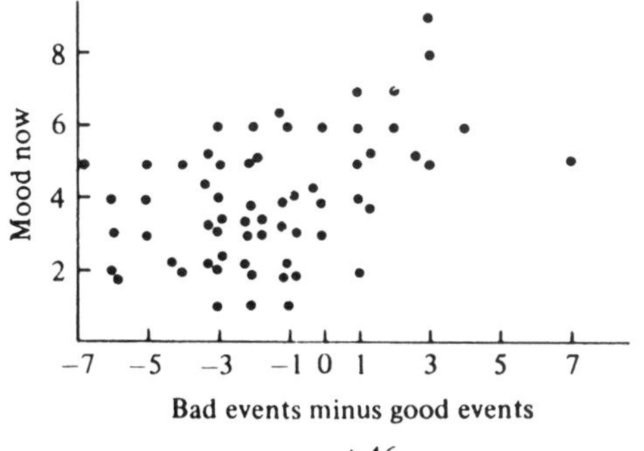

DISCUSSION AND COMMENTS

Our hypothesis that in college populations, depression as measured by self-rating is positively related to relative recall of recent negative events, has been confirmed. We will now discuss a few problems in interpreting these results, in order to make you more aware of the type of thinking that must go into research in general, and especially in this area.

First, our measure of events can be interpreted in a number of ways. We did not actually measure the number of positive and negative events that our subjects experienced. We measured their *recall* for these events. A predominance of negative events could mean either that the subject experienced more of them or that the subject selectively remembers them . . . presumably because she is depressed. Remember that correlations show relations, but not causes (see the statistical appendix). Our hypothesis was that negative events cause depression. But the results of our study could be taken to indicate that in a relatively depressed mood, a person is more likely to remember negative events. The fact that the correlation was bigger between negative minus positive events and mood now, as opposed to mood over the last year, suggests that current mood may well influence what one thinks about. Of course, it is also possible that both effects exist: Negative events lead to depression and depression leads to selective memory for negative events. There is some evidence in the literature for both of these effects. Under further activities, we will discuss ways of finding out whether both of these effects actually occur.

Second, even if more negative events do occur in more depressed people, the events may not be a cause of depression. By virtue of being depressed, more negative events may occur to a person. For example, a depressed student will be less active, less inclined to study, and will probably not perform as well as he could in school.

Third, the same event that is evaluated as negative by someone who is depressed may not be considered negative by that same person when he is in a good mood (or by another person in a better mood). Many events may be both positive and negative (e.g., receiving a B in a course when one hoped for an A but did very little work and actually worried about getting a C, or the break-up of a relationship which had been unsatisfactory for some years). Read through your own events and decide how many could be seen as positive or negative.

We have just begun to scratch the surface, but we hope that you can appreciate the fact that a study like this would be just a beginning and that many more studies would have to be done to clarify the relation between negative events and depression. It should also be clear that whatever that relation is, there are many factors that influence depression. After all, the correlations we do have between depression and events are significant, but they are not that high. We might improve the correlations by getting better measures of depression and negative and positive events. But we also know from other studies, including those dealing with levels of catecholamines in the brain and specific types of past experiences (e.g., helplessness), that other factors are involved.

FURTHER ACTIVITIES

Try to think of some ways in which you could pull apart the effects of actual negative experiences and selective recall of them. After you decide on a few methods, read our suggestions below.

One approach is to get a more objective measure of the actual negative and positive events that a person has experienced. It is not practical to follow them around for a year. But one could get a fair measure by giving them a checklist of rather objective events, that are clearly negative or positive. Thus you could ask someone whether, over the past year:

A close relative or friend died
A course was failed
A job was lost
A favorite team had a disappointing season
A close relationship was broken

and so on, and of course, a set of positive events.

One could then compare the negative minus positive recall score to the results of the checklist. What would you administer first to the subjects: the free recall or the checklist? Why? You could try to make up an appropriate checklist for college students. It isn't easy.

A second approach is to test whether depressed people selectively remember negative events. For example, you could write a story that included a number of negative and positive events. It could be read to subjects and one could measure their recall for the story, say one hour later. One could look at whether people who are more depressed remember relatively more of the negative events.

Answer Sheet

(If your instructor collects the data, fill out the report sheet in Appendix B.)

Self-rating of mood now (enter number) ____________

Self-rating of mood over last twelve months (enter number) ____________

Number of negative events recalled ____________

Number of positive events recalled ____________

Negative minus positive events ____________

Negative plus positive events ____________

CHAPTER 19

Treatment of Psychopathology

Learning Objectives

BIOLOGICAL THERAPIES

1. Describe some early precursors to therapy for psychological disorders.

Drug therapies

2. Discuss the effects of the antipsychotic medications, such as Thorazine, on schizophrenia. What symptoms do they affect and what symptoms do they leave largely untouched? What are side effects?
3. Discuss the effects of the monoamine oxidase inhibitors and the tricyclic antidepressants on the treatment of depression. How do the selective serotonin reuptake inhibitors differ from these? Why are they widely prescribed?
4. What is the effect of lithium salts?
5. What is the action of the anxiolytics and for what maladies are they prescribed?

Evaluating a medication

6. What are the drawbacks to using a before-and-after method to evaluate the effect of a therapy?
7. Describe placebo effects and discuss how they can have an impact in the evaluation of a drug therapy. What might cause placebo effects?
8. Discuss the double-blind technique and its usefulness in overcoming expectation effects.
9. Be aware of the limitations of pharmacotherapy and its impact on mental hospitals.

Psychosurgery

10. What has been the history of psychosurgery? When is it used today?

Convulsive treatments

11. What is electroconvulsive therapy used for, and how effective is it? What are its side effects?

PSYCHOTHERAPY

12. What are the five major types of psychotherapy, and what are the theoretical underpinnings of each?

Classical psychoanalysis

13. What is the theory underlying classical psychoanalysis? What investigative techniques are used in classical psychoanalysis?

Psychodynamic therapy

14. What are the modern variations on traditional psychoanalysis that have been made by neo-Freudians? How do they differ from Freud's techniques?

Behavior therapy

15. What basic assumptions are made by behavior therapists? How are these assumptions translated into treatment techniques?
16. Describe the basic assumptions underlying extinction, and explain why this technique is difficult to implement.
17. How does systematic desensitization use response incompatibility to eradicate phobias?
18. Describe aversion therapy and give examples of its use.

Cognitive therapy

19. How do cognitive therapies differ from traditional psychoanalysis? What are the major assumptions of cognitive therapy?

Humanistic therapy

20. How do humanistic therapists approach the topic of mental illness? Characterize Rogerian therapy.

Some common themes

21. What common themes underlie the various therapeutic schools? What are their major differences? How have the various schools of therapy become more eclectic?

Extensions of psychotherapy

22. Understand the reasons for the development of group therapy.
23. What are shared-problem groups? Give examples.
24. What are the advantages of therapy groups for the patients who join them?
25. Describe the goals and techniques of marital and family therapy. How are they related to the relationship rather than to the individual?
26. How has psychotherapy reached beyond the original goals envisioned by Freud?
27. Describe how knowledge of and sensitivity to the cultural background of a patient can enhance the course of therapy.

EVALUATING THERAPEUTIC OUTCOME

28. What extraneous factors might influence the perception of whether a therapy is effective?

Does psychotherapy work?

29. What is the evidence concerning the effectiveness of psychotherapy?

Comparing different therapies

30. Are there differences in the effectiveness of the various therapies? Describe the "Dodo bird verdict."
31. What factors do the various psychotherapies have in common? Are there specific effects of individual therapies that go beyond their common effects?
32. How has the implementation of psychotherapy been influenced by practical considerations of accountability?

A CENTURY OF THERAPY

33. What can be said about the effectiveness of psychotherapy? What beneficial effects are likely to be produced by this type of therapy?

Programmed Exercises

BIOLOGICAL THERAPIES

1. Until the Middle Ages, ____________, the removal of pieces of skull bone, was a popular treatment for mental disorders.	trephining
2. One of the first major successes of drug therapies was conquering general ____________, caused by a syphilitic infection.	paresis
3. ____________ are drugs that have an effect on mental illness, and the effectiveness of these was among the first lines of evidence of the biochemical basis of schizophrenia.	Antipsychotics
4. Effective drug treatments for schizophrenia include ____________ and ____________.	Thorazine Haldol
5. The advent of antipsychotic drugs led to the big movement in the 1960s to ____________ mental patients.	deinstitutionalize
6. An individual feels extremely depressed most of the time. We would expect one of two types of drugs to have an effect on her: the ____________ ____________ ____________ and the ____________ ____________.	monoamine oxidase inhibitors, tricyclic antidepressants
7. Recently, drugs such as Prozac have been developed for the specific treatment of depression. These drugs are called ____________ ____________ ____________ ____________.	selective serotonin reuptake inhibitors
8. Salts of ____________ have an effect on bipolar disorder, both in causing manic episodes to subside, and also in preventing depressive episodes.	lithium
9. Valium, Librium, and other ____________ have become commonplace in treating anxiety in that they increase the transmission of the inhibitory neurotransmitter GABA.	anxiolytics

10. The major weakness of using before-and-after assessment techniques to evaluate the effect of a drug treatment is that the patient may ___________ spontaneously. — improve

11. Sometimes merely giving a patient what he thinks is a drug will cause an improvement in his condition; this is called a ___________ effect. — placebo

12. It may be that ___________ effects are accounted for by the action of ___________, which are chemicals in the brain that act like opiates. — placebo, endorphins

13. It is hypothesized that a new drug will alleviate symptoms of air sickness. One hundred volunteers received an injection of this colorless liquid, while another 100 volunteers received an injection of saline solution (a colorless and totally inert liquid). All 200 subjects took part in a simulated flight. Both subjective and objective indices of discomfort were recorded. Neither patient nor experimenter knew who received which drug. This study used a(n) ___________-___________ technique to guard against any effects of expectations. — double-blind

14. The biggest cost associated with drug therapy is the likelihood of unpleasant ___________ ___________. — side effects

15. In a prefrontal lobotomy, the connections between the ___________ and the ___________ lobes are severed. — thalamus, frontal

16. Electroconvulsive shock treatment (ECT) is most effective in the treatment of ___________; however, repeated shocks may cause ___________ ___________ and ___________. — depression, brain damage, amnesia

PSYCHOTHERAPY

17. According to the ___________ school, neurotic ills stem from unconscious defenses against unacceptable urges. — psychoanalytic

18. A patient is asked to say whatever comes into his mind. This technique is known as ___________ ___________. — free association

19. During a therapy session involving free association a patient repeatedly changed the subject or forgot what she was about to say. This patient was displaying ___________, an indication that she was about to remember something that she had previously tried to forget. — resistance

20. The ___________-___________ view emphasizes interpersonal and cultural factors rather than psychosexual development. — neo-Freudian

21. Behavior therapists hold that the condition Freud called neurosis is caused by maladaptive ___________, which can be corrected through reeducation. — learning

22. A straightforward way to remove a classically conditioned response is through ___________. — extinction

23. The major goal of behavior therapists in treating phobias is to break the link between the ___________ stimulus and the ___________ response. — conditioned, fear

24. Sequential tensing and relaxing of the major muscles produces muscular relaxation, which is considered incompatible with fear response. Pairing the former with fear-evoking stimuli in order to eradicate phobias is part of the ___________ ___________ paradigm. — systematic desensitization

25. In order to break compulsive fingernail biters of their habit, we coat their nails with a harmless but extremely bitter liquid so that they experience an unpleasant taste each time they bite their nails. This is an example of ___________ therapy. — aversion

26. In contrast to behavior therapists, some therapists dispense with all conditioning techniques and, instead, help the patient acquire more appropriate ways of thinking. This is known as ____________ therapy. — cognitive

27. Unlike other forms of therapy, ____________ therapy deals with the individual at a global level. — humanistic

28. Rogers believes that people often dislike themselves. In his ____________-____________ therapy, an attempt is made to provide a situation in which personal growth can resume. — client-centered

29. Humanistic therapy is characterized by its ____________ nature, in which the therapist avoids advising or interpreting. — nondirective

30. The major focus of psychoanalysis is ____________; of behavior therapy, ____________; of cognitive therapy, ____________; and of humanistic therapy, ____________. — understanding doing, thinking feeling

31. A new trend in psychotherapy is ____________ ____________, doing whatever works. — technical eclecticism

32. One common element of all therapists is ____________ ____________, as the patient is encouraged to rid himself of intense and unrealistic fears. — emotional defusing

33. An important part of therapy helps show the patient how she reacts to others and is called ____________ ____________. — interpersonal learning

34. One of the important components of psychotherapy is ____________-____________, which may mean different things for different schools: For psychoanalysis, for example, it means insight into the patient's past. — self-knowledge

35. All the psychotherapeutic techniques recognize the ____________ nature of the therapeutic process. No progress is instantaneous. — gradual

36. There are various ____________ gains to be gotten from therapy, such as the development of a close relationship with the therapist, and the hope that one will improve one's condition. — nonspecific

37. In recent years, there has been a large shift in the delivery of therapeutic services from the one therapist-one patient model to ____________ therapy. — group

38. One example of ____________ therapy is the ____________-____________ group, in which a common affliction is present for all the patients. — group, shared-problem

39. A form of group therapy that concentrates on the relationship of the attendees rather than on them as individuals is ____________ therapy. — marital

40. An important issue in therapy is the recognition that the ____________ background of the patient may have an important effect on what techniques are likely to affect her. — cultural

EVALUATING THERAPEUTIC OUTCOME

41. The ____________ ____________ verdict is that all therapies are equivalent in their effects. — Dodo bird

42. ____________ refers to the trend to recommend particular therapies for particular maladies. — Prescriptionism

Self Test

1. Proposed remedies for mental disorders:
   a. are few in number
   b can be divided into biological and psychological intervention
   c. all have a high success rate
   d. all of the above

2. Antipsychotic drugs typically have effects on all of the following symptoms *except*:
   a. delusions
   b. hallucinations
   c. apathy
   d. none of the above

3. One of the important drawbacks to the antipsychotic drugs is that they:
   a. have serious side effects such as the production of apathy
   b. must be administered in a hospital setting only
   c. produce side effects that keep patients from taking them
   d. all of the above

4. All of the following are effective treatments for depression, either alone or in combination with manic episodes, except for:
   a. monoamine oxidase inhibitors
   b. tricyclic antidepressants
   c. lithium carbonate
   d. selective serotonin reuptake inhibitors
   e. all of the above

5. The action of Thorazine that makes it an effective drug for the treatment of schizophrenia is that it blocks dopamine receptors. This must mean that schizophrenia could be caused by:
   a. too much dopamine being taken up by receptors at synapses
   b. too little dopamine being taken up by receptors at synapses
   c. too little dopamine being produced at synapses
   d. too much dopamine being produced at synapses

6. Antipsychotic drugs (e.g., Thorazine) reduce many symptoms of schizophrenia. Below are characterizations of five patients suffering from some form of mental illness. Which patients would be expected to improve with Thorazine treatment?
   i. this patient suffers from bizarre thoughts and beliefs
   ii. this patient is withdrawn and noncommunicative
   iii this patient has frequent hallucinations
   iv. this patient is easily agitated
   v. this patient is deeply depressed
   a. all of the above
   b. i, ii, v
   c. i, ii, iii, iv
   d. ii, iv, v

7. It has been suggested that lithium carbonate may:
   a. be a general cure for forms of mental illness
   b. be useless, acting only as a placebo
   c. have a general activation and arousal effect rather than a specific treatment effect
   d. effectively treat bipolar disorder

8. Some drugs used to treat mental conditions have their action by increasing the amount of GABA that is released at synapses. This neurotransmitter is largely inhibitory in the nervous system, so one might assume that it reduces the amount of activity to the neurons with which it synapses. In view of this, which of the following drugs do you think have this action?
   a. Valium
   b. Librium
   c. anxiolytics
   d. all of the above

9. Which of the following sources would be convincing evidence that antidepressants do more than just produce euphoria to counteract the depression that they are meant to treat?
   a. if they did not produce euphoria in normal subjects
   b. if they acted on normal subjects to increase euphoria
   c. if they had specific action on neurotransmitters
   d. if they had an influence on other illnesses such as panic disorder

10. The main problem in using a before-after design to evaluate the effectiveness of a drug treatment is:
   a. the placebo effect
   b. the effect of expectation
   c. the effect of spontaneous recovery
   d. the Dodo bird effect

11. A researcher finds that after drinking nothing but milk for three months, three patients (out of nine) report that they no longer suffer from migraine headaches. The researcher proclaims the curative powers of milk. What critical questions cannot be answered due to the absence of a control group?
    a. What is the spontaneous recovery rate without treatment?
    b. How did the milk cure the headaches?
    c. Why were only one-third of the patients cured?
    d. Can this finding be repeated?

12. A motorist takes his car to the garage for a tune-up. Unbeknownst to him, the mechanic is dishonest and tells the motorist that he tuned the car when, in fact, he hadn't. The motorist feels that the car runs better. This is an example of:
    a. the placebo effect
    b. schizophrenia
    c. a double blind
    d. desensitization

13. A new drug is believed to alleviate the symptoms of bipolar disorder. The drug is tested in the following manner: One group of patients receives the drug in pill form, and another similar group receives a sugar pill. No patient knows which group he is in. A panel of psychiatrists evaluates each patient before and after the treatment period. The panel is not told whether a patient is getting the drug or the sugar pill. This is an example of:
    a. a placebo effect
    b. simultaneous control
    c. the double-blind technique
    d. transference

14. While drug therapy has produced a drastic decline in institutionalized patients, this has occurred at some cost. Patients on Thorazine, for example,
    a. experience varying side effects from their drugs
    b. make only marginal adjustments to the outside world
    c. must continue to take their drugs after release
    d. all of the above

15. The original idea behind psychosurgery was to "liberate the patient's thoughts from the pathological influence of his emotions." This required:
    a. localizing the area of the brain concerned with thought
    b. localizing the area of the brain concerned with emotion
    c. disconnecting the area of the brain concerned with thought from that concerned with emotion
    d. all of the above

16. A treatment which was designed to liberate the patient's thoughts from his pathological emotions, but which produced ambiguous results and which may impair foresight and attention is:
    a. electroconvulsive shock treatment (ECT)
    b. prefrontal lobotomy
    c. lithium treatment
    d. catharsis

17. ECT was originally used to treat schizophrenia but was later found to be more effective in treating:
    a. depression
    b. mania
    c. compulsive behavior
    d. it is still most effective in treating schizophrenia

18. Electroconvulsive shock treatment:
    a. is faster than many antidepressant drugs
    b. can produce severe memory impairment
    c. is generally used only after drug therapy has been tried
    d. all of the above

19. In contrast to pharmaceutical approaches to mental illness, psychotherapy:
    a. is much more effective
    b. involves interpersonal interaction
    c. is more relevant to the nature of psychopathology
    d. none of the above

20. Orthodox (classical) psychoanalysis:
    a. states that illness is a result of unconscious defenses against unconscious urges
    b. states that most problems date back to childhood
    c. was developed by Freud
    d. all of the above

21. The cure for mental illness can be achieved by ____________ according to the classical psychoanalysts.
    a. the victory of reason over passion
    b. a complete suppression of bad memories
    c. a reenactment of the cause of the problem
    d. none of the above

22. When a patient is asked to say whatever comes into his mind, it is believed that sooner or later the memory relevant to the disorder should appear. This technique is known as:
    a. resistance
    b. repression
    c. free association
    d. role playing

23. Modern day practitioners of psychoanalysis:
    a. emphasize interpersonal factors rather than sexual development
    b. subscribe to neo-Freudian views
    c. focus on the patient's present rather than his past
    d. all of the above

24. Behavior therapists argue that:
    a. the theoretical notions of psychoanalysis are untestable
    b. the therapeutic effectiveness of psychoanalysis is unclear
    c. neurosis is caused by maladaptive learning
    d. all of the above

25. The behavior therapist tends to emphasize:
    a. giving the patient insight into the origins of her problems
    b. righting improper behavior patterns without regard for underlying causes
    c. curing the patient by a variety of means, including free association
    d. enabling the patient to reach a full realization of her human potentialities

26. For behavior therapists, fear:
    a. is a classically conditioned response
    b. has its roots in early childhood
    c. is a manifestation of emotional traumas
    d. is an operantly conditioned response

27. Since behavior therapists believe that one of the causes of certain strong fears, such as that of heights, is early classical conditioning, their therapy rests on the principle of:
    a. second-order conditioning
    b. extinction
    c. reinforcement
    d. punishment

28. Systematic desensitization relies on which of the following principles?
    a. extinction
    b. operant conditioning
    c. counterconditioning
    d. none of the above

29. The pairing of an unpleasant stimulus with an undesirable behavior is known as:
    a. paired associate learning
    b. cognitive therapy
    c. response-produced anxiety
    d. none of the above

30. There is some question about the lasting effectiveness of aversion therapy because:
    a. it doesn't even seem to last while the patient is in the therapist's office
    b. the effects wear off even while the aversive stimulus is still applied after some time has passed
    c. without the aversive stimulus, the lasting effects seem to fade
    d. it has been shown to be an ineffective treatment for alcoholism

31. A therapist confronts a depressed patient with the irrationality of his belief that he cannot get a good job because he thinks he is incompetent despite evidence to the contrary. This therapist is most likely to be a proponent of:
    a. modeling
    b. cognitive therapy
    c. desensitization
    d. could be any of the above

32. Cognitive therapies:
    a. focus on the patient's beliefs and attitudes
    b. are not primarily concerned with the patient's history
    c. do not rely heavily on behavior modification
    d. all of the above

33. One of the features on which cognitive therapies concentrate is:
    a. the behaviors exhibited by patients
    b. the automatic thoughts that patients seem to have
    c. the irrationality of beliefs that patients have
    d. more than one of the above

34. In contrast to traditional psychoanalysis or behavior therapy, humanistic therapists:
    a. are interested in causes rather than effects
    b. deal with only one symptom at at time
    c. treat the individual at a global level
    d. believe that neuroses are a product of society

35. It seems as if the different forms of psychotherapy concentrate on different aspects of the problem. In particular,
    a. cognitive therapy concentrates on the patient's thoughts

b. psychoanalysis concentrates on the patient's understanding of her past
c. humanistic therapy concentrates on the patient's feelings
d. all of the above

36. Psychoanalysis can be summarized by the word "unconscious" in the same way that behavior therapy can be represented by "conditioning." What word best summarizes humanistic therapy?
a. cause
b. feeling
c. directive
d. rational

37. All of the following are common to the various therapeutic schools except:
a. interpersonal learning
b. self-knowledge
c. emotional defusing
d. therapy as an all-or-none process

38. A major difference between shared-problem groups and group therapy is:
a. that shared-problem groups involve more interpersonal interaction
b. that shared-problem groups work on a single problem that is common to the group members
c. that shared-problem groups incorporate a greater amount of self-knowledge of the problem in question
d. that shared-problem groups involve a more gradual therapeutic process

39. One of the differences between family therapy and classical psychoanalysis is:
a. family therapists deal with a group of individuals, not just one
b. family therapists concentrate on relationships, not individual mental health
c. family therapists don't concentrate on the developmental history of each individual
d. all of the above

40. If psychotherapy's only effect is nonspecific,
a. it may nevertheless have value in providing a shoulder to lean on
b. it will have proved largely an ineffective treatment course
c. it will then, by definition, be just a placebo effect
d. it will be more effective than if its effect had been specific

41. The notion that specific therapies may be most effective for particular mental maladies is called:
a. the Dodo bird verdict
b. prescriptionism
c. existentialism
d. none of the above

Answer Key for Self Test

1. b p. 607
2. c p. 609
3. c p. 609
4. e pp. 610–11
5. a p. 611
6. c p. 609
7. d p. 610
8. d p. 613
9. a p. 613
10. c p. 611
11. a p. 611
12. a p. 612
13. c p. 613
14. d pp. 609, 613
15. d p. 614
16. b p. 614
17. a p. 615
18. d pp. 615–16
19. b p. 616
20. d pp. 616–17
21. a p. 617
22. c p. 617
23. d p. 617
24. d p. 618
25. b p. 618
26. a p. 618
27. b p. 619
28. c p. 619
29. d p. 620
30. c p. 620
31. b p. 620
32. d pp. 620–21
33. d p. 621
34. c p. 621
35. d pp. 622–23
36. b p. 622
37. d p. 623
38. b p. 624
39. d p. 625
40. a p. 627
41. b p. 628

Investigating Psychological Phenomena

DEMONSTRATION OF ROLE PLAYING

Equipment: None
Number of subjects: Yourself and one other
Time per subject: Thirty minutes
Time for experimenter: Thirty minutes

Role playing is one technique used by therapists to educate their patients about various aspects of interpersonal relations. This technique requires at least two people to assume the roles of individuals other that themselves in a particular social situation. In so doing, the hope of the treatment is that the participating individuals will gain some insight about the feelings, emotions, and cognitions of the persons whose roles are being played.

Although the technique sounds simple enough in principle, in actual practice it is a bit risky. As the following quote illustrates, role playing participants frequently lapse back into their own personalities and have to be reminded about their role playing activities.

> [The therapist] says "Tom, do you really care for me?" Tom says "I would say to her that I do, but she'd complain." Therapist: "Don't tell me what you *would* do. I'm Jane. Talk to me. Tom, do you really care for me?" Tom (turning away, looking slightly disgusted): "Yes." Therapist (still as Jane): "You don't say it like you mean it." Tom: "Yeah, that's what she says, and I usually . . ." Therapist (interrupting): "You're again telling me *about* what you'd say. I'm Jane. Tom, you don't say it like you mean it." Tom: "It's very hard for me to answer her when she says that." Therapist: "OK, I'm Jane. Tell me how you feel." Tom: "Jane, when you do that it really turns me off. Maybe if you didn't ask me so often I'd be able to say it spontaneously without feeling like a puppet . . . (then, in a tone that indicates he is now talking to the therapist as therapist) Gee, I wonder what would happen if I really said that to her" (Wachtel, 1977, pp. 234–35).

You can try role playing on your own to discover some of its features. Solicit the participation of a fellow student of the opposite sex from your introductory psychology class and set up the following situation.

The two of you are married and have just graduated from college. Each of you has very well-defined career plans, and you have each been skillful and lucky enough to have been offered very attractive first jobs that fit precisely the career lines that you have planned. The problem is that your job offers are in cities 1,000 miles apart. How do you decide what to do?

You should go through two sessions: First, have a discussion about this problem with your partner with each of you playing yourselves. Write down each of your responses on paper. Second, switch roles and try having the discussion again. In each case, put yourselves in the other's situation. Again, write your responses on paper.

After you have finished playing both roles, talk about differences in the conversations that resulted from your playing the male versus the female role. Compare the transcripts of each session. Did this help you gain a different perspective on the problem?

At this point, you might want to try another role-playing exercise in which the two roles are quite different from one another. This will allow you to take two very different perspectives on a scene. Try out the following scene:

One of you should assume the role of an instructor for a course you are both taking (perhaps introductory psychology) while the other plays the role of a student. The issue is that the student has scored poorly on the midterm examination, but feels that at least part of the reason for his poor performance is that he was graded unfairly by the instructor. In addition, the student was faced with taking four midterm exams within three days, so his performance was bound to suffer. Now imagine that the student has come in to talk with the instructor about these issues. The person playing the role of the instructor should really try to assume the personality and attitudes of the real instructor in the course as much as possible. After you have acted out a scene, switch roles. This time, to add some variety, have the student role be one of a very aggressive student who is determined not to leave the instructor's office without a change of grade. Again, after each scene, write down your impressions so that you can later discuss and evaluate them.

Having finished this scenario, think about some of the following questions: Was it more difficult to assume the role of the instructor or student? Was it difficult to stay in character without lapses? What insights have you gained about instructor-student relationships? Would this be a useful exercise for students and instructors to try in general? How was this role-playing exercise different from the first one?

APPENDIX A

Statistics: The Collection, Organization, and Interpretation of Data

Learning Objectives

1. What is the topic of statistics about? When are statistical tests needed in psychological research?

DESCRIBING THE DATA

2. What is scaling? Why is it important to understand the types of number scales?

Categorical and ordinal scales

3. Understand what categorical and ordinal scales are. Be able to describe the arithmetic operations permitted with each. Give examples of these scales.

Interval scales

4. What is the important feature of an interval scale? Give examples.

Ratio scales

5. What defines a ratio scale? What are some examples of ratio scales?
6. How do interval and ratio scales differ? What arithmetic operation is permitted with ratio scales?

COLLECTING THE DATA

The experiment

7. What are the essential ingredients of an experiment?
8. What is the difference between independent and dependent variables?

The observational study

9. How do observational studies differ from experiments? How are they similar?
10. What are the advantages and disadvantages of observational studies?

The case study

11. What is the role of the case study in psychological research? When is it to be preferred over other methods?

SELECTING THE SUBJECTS

Sample and population

12. What is the difference between a sample and a population? When would you choose a sample?

Random and stratified samples

13. Understand some of the factors that must be taken into account in sampling.
14. What are the merits of random versus stratified sampling?

Sampling responses

15. Why must one be careful in sampling responses?

ORGANIZING THE DATA: DESCRIPTIVE STATISTICS

The frequency distribution

16. How is a frequency distribution created from the raw scores in an experiment? To get practice in constructing a frequency distribution, plot one for

the following heights (in inches) of males in a small class: 72, 72, 68, 66, 74, 73, 69, 69, 70, 67, 66, 73, 72.

Measures of central tendency

17. What is a measure of central tendency and why is it useful? Describe the three measures of central tendency that are commonly used. Calculate these three quantities for the scores given above.

Measures of variability

18. Describe what the range of a group of scores is, and describe why the range has limited utility. What is the range for the scores given in item 16 above?
19. What is the variance of a set of scores? Why is it a useful measure of variability? Calculate the variance and standard deviation of the scores given above.

Converting scores to compare them

20. How are percentile ranks calculated, and how do they permit comparison of scores obtained from different tasks?
21. What is a z-score? Why is it useful for comparing scores from two distributions?
22. How are z-scores and percentile ranks similar?

The normal distribution

23. What are the characteristics of a normal distribution?
24. Be able to convert a z-score into a rank for a variable that has a normal distribution.
25. Understand the principle that can explain when a variable will be distributed normally. To do this you should roughly understand how a repeated binomial event will approximate a normal distribution.

DESCRIBING THE RELATION BETWEEN TWO VARIABLES: CORRELATION

Positive and negative correlation

26. What is the meaning of positive and negative correlation?
27. How is a scatter plot constructed? What does it show? What does a line-of-best-fit have to do with a scatter plot?

The correlation coefficient

28. Understand what various values of r mean.
29. How is a correlation coefficient computed? Do you understand the logic of this computation?

Interpreting and misinterpreting correlations

30. Give examples of cases for which a correlation cannot be interpreted in terms of one variable causing changes in another. What is the danger in interpreting correlations in terms of cause-effect?

INTERPRETING DATA: INFERENTIAL STATISTICS

Accounting for variability

31. What does it mean to account for variance?
32. Understand how variance is accounted for in actual experiments, such as the examples given in the text.
33. How does one account for variance in correlational data?

Hypothesis testing

34. What are null and alternative hypotheses? How do critical ratios allow us to rule out one of these hypotheses?
35. What trade-off is involved in the decision about where to set the cutoff for the critical ratio?
36. Be able to describe how hypotheses about differences between means can be tested using a critical ratio.
37. What is the relationship between a sample mean and a population mean?
38. What is a standard error, and what role does it play in testing hypotheses about sample means?
39. Be sure to follow the statistical analysis of the imagery experiment presented in the text.
40. Explain what it means to be reasonably confident that the mean of the population will fall within a specified interval.

Some implications of statistical inference

41. Explain how statistical conclusions are probabilistic. How does this affect these conclusions both about population means, and about individuals?
42. Why should statistical conclusions be conservatively drawn?
43. Based on your knowledge of how to compute a critical ratio, describe how sample size affects a statistical conclusion. When may statistical and psychological significance differ?

Programmed Exercises

1. The collection, organization, and interpretation of numerical data comprise the topic of ____________. — statistics

DESCRIBING THE DATA

2. When all subjects in a group perform differently, or when the same subject performs differently on different occasions, we say that the data contain ____________. — variability
3. Differences among subjects ____________ groups and ____________ groups are the two sources of variability that are analyzed by statistical methods. — between, within
4. The assignment of numbers to events is called ____________. — scaling
5. The type of ____________ that numbers represent is defined by which arithmetic operations are permitted on those numbers. — scale
6. The assignment of students in a school to the 1st, 2nd, or 3rd of three kindergartens would involve the use of a(n) ____________ scale. — categorical (nominal)
7. If you ask someone to rank order four cola drinks from most to least preferred, you would be using a(n) ____________ scale. — ordinal
8. The Fahrenheit scale of temperature is a(n) ____________ scale as indicated by the fact that the difference between 30° and 35° equals the difference between 75° and 80°. — interval
9. The scale of length in feet is a(n) ____________ scale; thus, we can say that a board of 4 feet is twice as long as a board of 2 feet. — ratio

COLLECTING THE DATA

10. If an experimenter were interested in the effect of instructions-to-image on memory performance, she might run an experiment with a(n) ____________ group given imagery instructions, and a(n) ____________ group given standard memory instructions. — experimental, control
11. In the experiment referred to in question 10, the type of instruction is the ____________ variable, and a measure of recall performance is the ____________ variable. — independent, dependent
12. A(n) ____________ study of the effects of city versus suburban living on rates of schizophrenia would involve selecting schizophrenic patients who had lived in urban or suburban environments. — observational
13. The study of a particular aphasic subject intensively to reveal features of language behavior involves the use of a(n) ____________ study approach. — case

SELECTING THE SUBJECTS

14. Psychologists are interested in drawing conclusions about ____________ of subjects, but because it is frequently impractical to test large numbers of people, they tend to test ____________, then generalize their conclusions. — populations, samples
15. A ____________ sample is said to be unrepresentative of a population. — biased

16. A procedure for selecting subjects in which all individuals are equally likely to be selected is called a ____________ ____________. — random sample

17. ____________ ____________ is a technique for selecting subjects in which one tries to represent certain subgroups of a population in proportion to their size. — Stratified sampling

ORGANIZING THE DATA: DESCRIPTIVE STATISTICS

18. A ____________ ____________ of birthweight could be represented by a ____________, a graph of the numbers of people in a sample who are born at various weights in the range to be studied. — frequency distribution histogram

19. There are three major measures of central tendency, the ____________, ____________, and ____________. — mean median, mode

20. The distribution of reaction times in an experiment is likely to be ____________, since there will be none below 0, many short ones, and fewer and fewer long ones. — skewed

21. The ____________ is a measure of variation that is defined as the difference between the highest and lowest scores. — range

22. The ____________ is a measure of variation that takes account of each score's deviation from the mean. Its square root is called the ____________ ____________. — variance standard deviation

23. The ____________ ____________ of a score is the percentage of scores that lie below it. — percentile rank

24. A ____________-____________ expresses scores in terms of units of standard deviations from a mean. — z-score (standard score)

25. The heights of females in a population form a ____________ ____________, one in which there are equal frequencies of heights on both sides of the mean. — normal distribution

DESCRIBING THE RELATION BETWEEN TWO VARIABLES: CORRELATION

26. If two dependent variables are related to one another, they are said to be ____________. — correlated

27. If we ranked the top 10 runners in the world so that the top runner was ranked 1 and the 10th runner was ranked 10, and if we based these ranks on time to run the 1500 meter race, there would by definition be a ____________ correlation between rank and time. — positive

28. On the average, the faster one can complete each item on an aptitude test, the higher one's score, assuming that one doesn't sacrifice accuracy. There is thus a ____________ correlation between time per item and test score. — negative

29. Plotting two dependent variables, one on the abscissa and one on the ordinate, yields a graph that shows the relationship between the variables. This is called a ____________ ____________. — scatter plot

30. A line fit to the points of the graph described in question 29 is called a ____________-____________-____________-____________. — line-of-best-fit

31. A ____________ ____________ of −1 indicates that there is a perfect ____________ correlation between two variables. — correlation coefficient, negative

INTERPRETING DATA: INFERENTIAL STATISTICS

32. We say that we have ____________ variance when we can attribute some of the variability in a set of scores to a particular factor. — explained (accounted for)

33. Squaring a correlation coefficient yields a proportion of ____________ which is explained. — variance

34. For the experiment described in question 10, the ____________ hypothesis is that there is no difference between the groups, while the ____________ hypothesis is that the group with imagery instructions will recall more items. — null, alternative

35. The ____________ ____________ of a test statistic is usually set at 2 so that the probability of choosing the alternative hypothesis when the null hypothesis is, in fact, correct is quite small (one chance in twenty). — critical ratio

36. The standard deviation of a distribution of sample means is called the ____________ ____________. — standard error

37. The ____________ ____________ is the range within which we can be fairly confident the actual population mean will fall. — confidence interval

38. There are three important characteristics of statistical conclusions. They are affected by sample ____________, they are ____________, and they are ____________. — size, probabilistic, conservative

Self Test

1. If there are 100 questions on a test, with each question worth one point, then the set of scores from 0 to 100 constitutes:
   a. a nominal scale
   b. an ordinal scale
   c. an interval scale
   d. a ratio scale

2. If we wanted to investigate the effect of cigarette smoking by mothers on birth defects in their children, we would likely:
   a. perform an experiment
   b. use correlations
   c. perform an observational study
   d. use a case study approach

3. An experimenter is interested in determining the effects of caffeine on sleeping behavior. She selects two groups of subjects to test her hypothesis that caffeine causes sleeplessness. Group 1 drinks regular coffee before bedtime while group 2 drinks decaffeinated coffee. The experimenter then measures the amount of time it takes subjects to fall asleep (as measured by an electroencephalogram). In this experiment:
   a. amount of sleep is the dependent variable and caffeine is the independent variable
   b. amount of sleep is the independent variable and caffeine is the dependent variable
   c. both are independent variables
   d. both are dependent variables

4. In the description of question 3:
   a. group 1 is the control group; group 2 is the experimental group
   b. group 1 is the experimental group; group 2 is the control group
   c. both groups are experimental; the experimenter has failed to include a control
   d. neither group is experimental; this is an observational study

5. If we test a randomly selected group of college students and then generalize our results to all college students,
   a. we are using a stratified sampling procedure
   b. we are making inappropriate inferences
   c. we would need to correlate the results of our sample

d. we are testing a sample in order to draw conclusions about a population

6. Suppose we wanted to know the size of the memory span (how many items a subject could hold in short-term memory) for all students in a particular school. To do this, we place all the names of all the students in a hat and draw out 100 for testing. This procedure is known as:
   a. stratified sampling
   b. biased sampling
   c. random sampling
   d. skewed sampling

7. If, in question 6, we had sampled by grade in school, then we would have employed the technique of:
   a. stratified sampling
   b. biased sampling
   c. random sampling
   d. skewed sampling

8. The results of an examination are graphed so that each score is listed in order on the abscissa, and the number of students receiving that score is plotted on the ordinate. Such a graph:
   a. is a frequency distribution
   b. is a histogram of the scores
   c. is not a scattergram
   d. could be a normal distribution
   e. all of the above

9. Suppose the graph in question 8 turned out to look like the graph below. From this we could conclude that:

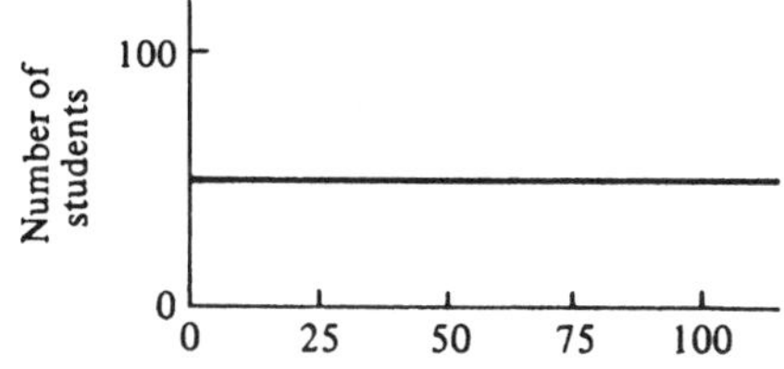

   a. the mean is greater than the median
   b. the mode is 50
   c. the variance is 0
   d. the test was statistically significant
   e. none of the above

10. Suppose the graph in question 8 turned out to look like the graph that follows. From this we could conclude that:

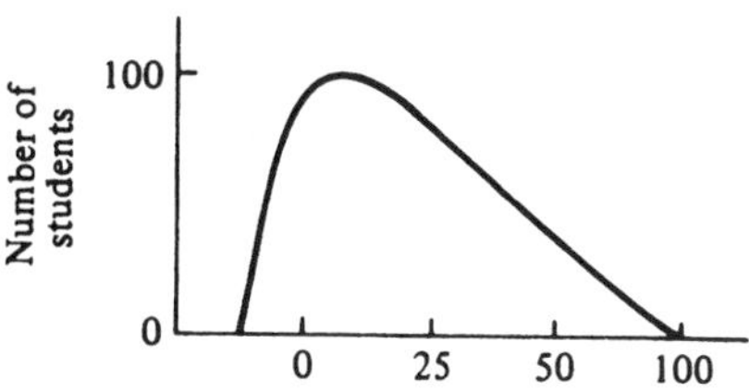

   a. the distribution is normal
   b. the median is lower than the mean
   c. the students with a score of 75 are in the 75th percentile
   d. the mode is 100
   e. none of the above

11. For the following five scores, 1, 2, 3, 4, 5:
   a. the median is 3
   b. the mean is 3
   c. the variance is 2
   d. all of the above
   e. a and b but not c

12. Variability is to central tendency as variance is to:
   a. correlation
   b. z-score
   c. mean
   d. standard deviation

13. All of the following could be measures of variation in a set of scores except:
   a. mean – median
   b. highest score – lowest score
   c. sum of (each score – mean)^2
   d. average of highest two scores – average of lowest two scores

14. Consider two examinations: On one, the mean is 50, the standard deviation is 5, and your score is 65. On the other, the mean is 50, the standard deviation is 2, and your score is 60. Which of the following is true?
   a. your percentile rank is higher on the second test
   b. your z-score is higher on the second test
   c. you can meaningfully compare your z-scores on the two tests
   d. you cannot meaningfully compare your raw scores on the two tests
   e. all of the above

15. If a set of scores on an exam has a mean of 75 and a standard deviation of 10, then:

a. the distribution must be normal
b. the distribution must be symmetric
c. a score of 50 corresponds to a z-score of −2.5
d. a z-score of 1.0 equals a test score of 75

16. If SAT scores have a mean of 500 and a standard deviation of 100, and if IQ scores have a mean of 100 and a standard deviation of 15, then with an SAT score of 650 and an IQ score of 115:
a. the z-score for IQ will be higher than the z-score for SAT
b. the percentile score for IQ will be higher than the percentile score for SAT
c. both of the above
d. the percentile score for IQ will be 84
e. the scores on the two tests will not be comparable since the tests differ

17. If we found a correlation coefficient of −.88 between reaction time and performance on a test of motor skill, we could conclude that:
a. a high score on the test of motor skill predicts a fast reaction time
b. a high score on the test of motor skill predicts a slow reaction time
c. motor skill causes people to have faster reaction times
d. reaction time and motor skill are largely unrelated

18. In the scatter plot shown below:

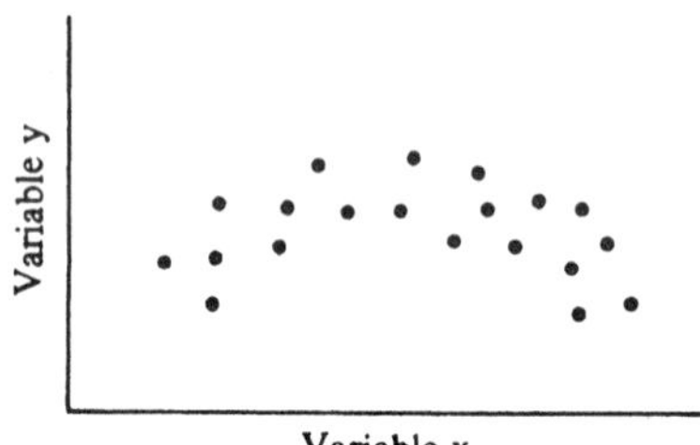

a. there is no relationship between x and y
b. the correlation coefficient is statistically significant
c. the correlation coefficient is close to 0
d. variable x is the independent variable

19. If a line-of-best-fit for a scatter plot were flat, then:
a. the correlation would be 1
b. the correlation would be 0
c. the correlation would not be significant
d. we know nothing about the correlation until we calculate it

20. Which of the following correlation coefficients shows the strongest inverse relationship between variables x and y?
a. .82
b. −.74
c. 0
d. −1.14

21. If the correlation between a parent's and his children's scores on a test of motor skills were .70, then we would know that:
a. seventy percent of the variability of the children's score is accounted for by the parents' scores
b. seventy percent of the variability of the parents' score is accounted for by the children's scores
c. children's motor skills are caused by the skills of their parents
d. none of the above

22. An experiment is performed to determine whether eating breakfast improves one's test performance. Two groups are given tests, one group after eating a good breakfast, one after no breakfast. Consider the following hypothesis. Eating breakfast has no effect on test performance. This hypothesis:
a. can be evaluated only probabilistically
b. is called the "alternative" hypothesis
c. cannot be evaluated in this experiment
d. is assessed by examining within-subject variability

23. In the experiment of question 22 which of the following would be necessary in order for us to believe that eating breakfast enhances test performance?
a. the sample must be normal
b. the sample must be statistically significant
c. the between-subject variance must be larger than the within-subject variance
d. all of the above
e. none of the above

24. Suppose you were to discover a hospital in which there were 8 new births each day, and you wished to test the hypothesis that this hospital had more births per day than the average hospital of its size. To do this we would need to know:
    a. the correlations among births at all the hospitals in question
    b. the mean, standard deviation, and number of hospitals in the comparison group
    c. only the standard error of the births in the comparison group
    d. none of the above

25. Two hospitals report 8 births per day average with a standard deviation of 10 births. For hospital A, this average was computed over 25 days; for hospital B, it was computed over 400 days. The standard errors of births in these hospitals:
    a. are equal
    b. are 2 in hospital A and .5 in hospital B
    c. are not comparable because of the difference in number of days
    d. none of the above

26. If a sample mean is 20, its standard deviation is 30, and the number of subjects in the sample is 9, then:
    a. you can be fairly confident that the sample is normal
    b. a subject with a score of 25 is in the fifth percentile
    c. a score of 17 would be equal to a z-score of 1
    d. you can be fairly sure that the population from which this sample was drawn has a mean greater than 0

27. Suppose you're trying to predict whether a Republican or Democratic candidate will win a particular senatorial race. You conduct a poll of the relevant voters and discover that 53% would vote for the Republican and 47% for the Democrat. Who do you think will win?
    a. You can be reasonably confident that the Republican will win.
    b. You can be reasonably confident that the Democrat will win.
    c. Given the polling data, it's not clear who will win.
    d. There isn't enough information to make a prediction one way or the other.

Answer Key for Self Test

1. d p. A3
2. c pp. A4–A5
3. a p. A4
4. b p. A4
5. d p. A6
6. c p. A6
7. a p. A6
8. e pp. A7–A13
9. e pp. A7–A11, A22
10. b p. A8
11. d p. A8
12. c pp. A9–A11
13. a pp. A9–A11
14. e pp. A11–A13
15. c pp. A11–A12
16. d p. A13
17. a pp. A16–A17
18. c pp. A15–A16
19. b p. A15
20. b pp. A16–A17
21. d pp. A17–A18
22. a p. A26
23. c p. A23
24. b pp. A22–A24
25. b pp. A22–A24
26. d p. A25
27. d pp. A26–A27

Investigating Psychological Phenomena

This exercise provides an opportunity for you to apply some of the statistical concepts described in the text. Reconsider the experiment described on p. A4 of the text in which subjects are tested for recall performance on lists of twenty words with and without instructions to form images. Imagine that twenty subjects had been run in this experiment—the ten described in the test plus ten others. The data of all these subjects are presented in Table 1 below. In the first column are the recall scores with imagery instructions; the second column contains recall scores when no imagery instructions were provided; the third column is the difference between the first two, the amount of improvement. Finally, the fourth column contains the results of a test of imagery ability that was given to each of the subjects in this hypothetical experiment (scores on this test could range from 0 to 40). Using the data in this table, perform the following tabulations and analyses.

TABLE 1

Subject	Score with imagery	Score without imagery	Improvement	Test of imagery ability
Alphonse	20	5	15	30
Betsy	24	9	15	26
Cheryl	20	5	15	27
Davis	18	9	9	21
Earl	22	6	16	33
Fred	19	11	8	26
Germaine	20	8	12	32
Hortense	19	11	8	38
Imogene	17	7	10	30
Jerry	21	9	12	27
Kerry	17	8	9	29
Linda	20	16	4	24
Moe	20	10	10	26
Nicolas	16	12	4	22
Orry	24	7	17	36
Penelope	22	9	13	32
Quarton	25	21	4	23
Ronald	21	14	7	26
Steven	19	12	7	24
Terry	23	13	10	28

1. Create frequency histograms for the recall data on the two unlabeled sets of axes below. The left graph is for the recall scores with imagery instructions, and the right is for recall scores without imagery instructions. Note that you must decide what specific values to place on each axis for each graph.

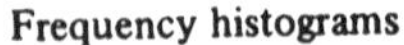

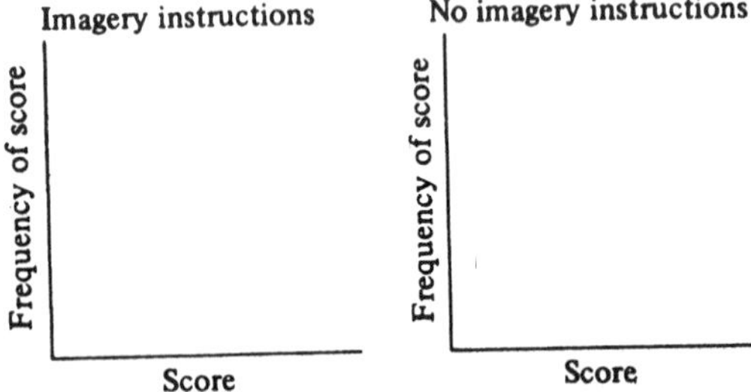

2. Calculate the mean, median, and mode of each of the distributions whose scores you have plotted above.

3. Calculate the range and standard deviation of each of these distributions.

4. Analyze the improvement scores to test the hypothesis that imagery instructions lead to better recall performance than no imagery instructions. To do this, you must compute a critical ratio that evaluates the sample mean of the improvement scores against the population mean for the null hypothesis (no improvement). Is this critical ratio larger than 2.0? If so, how do we interpret the improvement scores?

5. Examine the relationship between the improvement scores and performance on the test of imagery ability in two ways. First, create a scatter plot on the axes presented below. Second, compute a correlation coefficient between these sets of scores. Is there a relation between the variables? How would you interpret this relation psychologically?

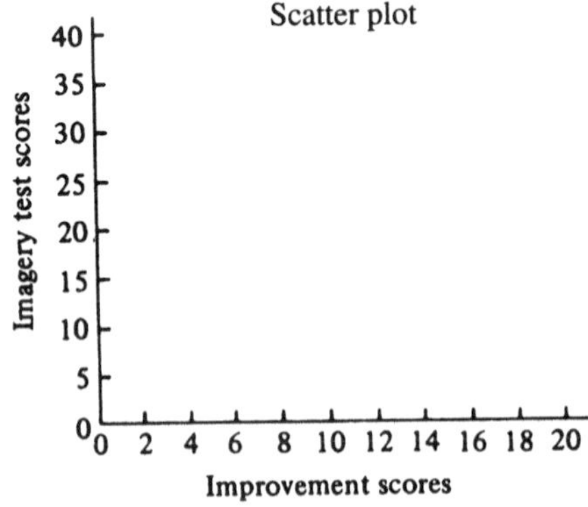

Now that you have completed your analyses, you should turn to the next page to examine the correct answers and compare them to your own answers.

Answers to Statistical Exercise

1.

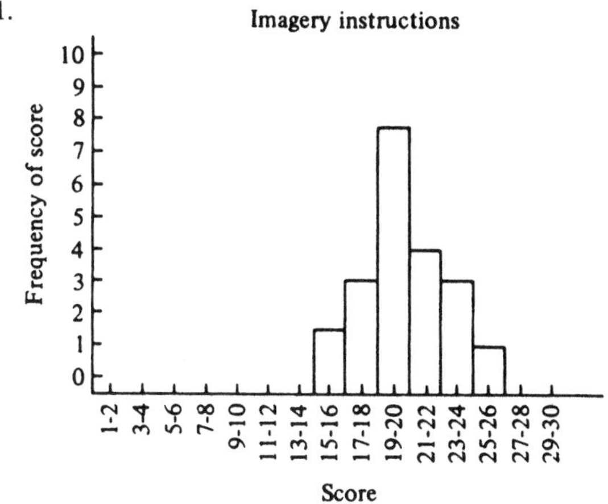

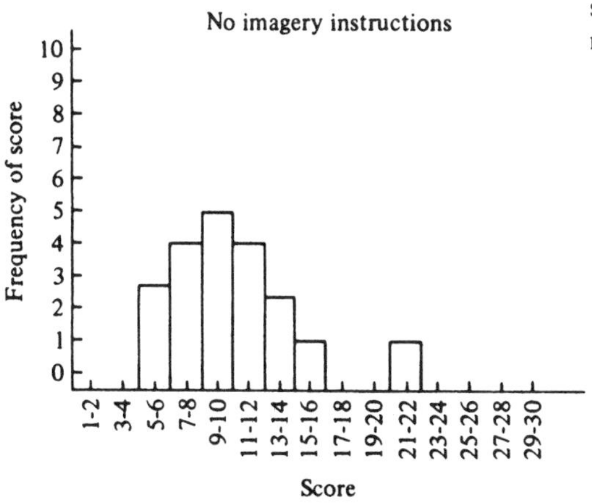

2. Imagery instructions
   - Mean = 20.35
   - Median = 20
   - Mode = 20

   No imagery instructions
   - Mean = 10.10
   - Median = 9
   - Mode = 9

3. Imagery instructions
   - Range = 9
   - Standard deviation = 2.46

   No imagery instructions
   - Range = 16
   - Standard deviation = 3.89

4. Critical ratio =

$$\frac{\text{sample mean} - \text{population mean by null hypothesis}}{\text{standard error of the mean}}$$

standard error of the mean

$$= \frac{\text{standard deviation}}{\sqrt{N}}$$

$$= \frac{4.05}{\sqrt{20}}$$

$$= .91$$

$$\text{critical ratio} = \frac{10.25 - 0}{.91} = 11.26$$

This critical ratio is much larger than 2.0; therefore we may conclude that there is a statistically significant improvement in recall scores comparing no imagery to imagery instructions.

5. Scatter plot

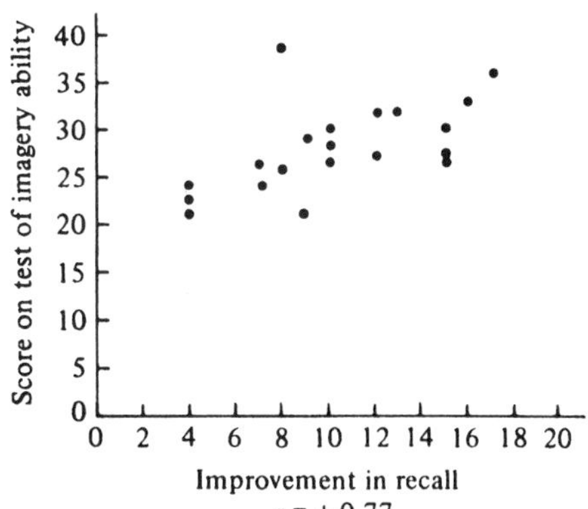

The correlation coefficient, r, is + 0.77.

Both the scatter plot and the correlation coefficient indicate that there is substantial relationship between the variables. We might propose the following hypothesis to account for this relationship. Subjects with a better imagery ability are better able to form mental images in the memory task, and thus perform better. Our hypothesis must remain tentative, however, since we are not permitted to draw cause-effect conclusions from correlational data.

APPENDIX B

On the following pages you will find the report sheets for several of the experiments in the preceding chapters. If your instructor wants to collect the data for these experiments, use these report sheets. You can cut them out and hand them in to your instructor.

Chapter 3

REPORT SHEET—HEART RATE

Data from Three Subjects (A, B, and C)

Instruction and time	A	B	C
"Begin and Relax"			
00:00–0:30			
0:45–1:15			
"Increase physical activity"			
1:30–2:00			
2:15–2:45			
"Relax"			
3:00–3:30			
3:45–4:15			
"Increase mental activity"			
4:30–5:00			
5:15–5:45			
"Relax"			
6:00–6:30			
6:45–7:15			

List for each subject the basic situation that they imagined in the "increase" minutes.

	Physical	Mental
A	______________	______________
B	______________	______________
C	______________	______________

Chapter 2

REPORT SHEET—NERVE IMPULSE

Practice Trial 1 ankle = Time in seconds*

Part I
Trial 1 ankle = ______________
Trial 2 ankle = ______________
Trial 3 ankle = ______________
Trial 4 ankle = ______________
Trial 5 ankle = ______________

Part II
Trial 1 upper arm = ______________
Trial 2 upper arm = ______________
Trial 3 upper arm = ______________
Trial 4 upper arm = ______________
Trial 5 upper arm = ______________

Test
Part III
Trial 1 ankle time = __________
÷ 25 = _________ (a)
Trial 2 upper arm time = __________
÷ 25 = _________ (b)
Trial 3 upper arm time = __________
÷ 25 = _________ (c)
Trial 4 ankle time = __________
÷ 25 = _________ (d)

$\frac{a + d}{2}$ = _____ (average ankle time)

$\frac{b + c}{2}$ = _____ (average upper arm time)

Average ankle time – average upper arm time = _____ (difference 1)

(1) Distance of ankle to base of neck (for third tallest person) = _____

(2) Distance of upper arm to base of neck (for third tallest person) = _____

Distance 1 – distance 2 = _____ (difference 2)

$\frac{\text{difference 2}}{\text{difference 1}}$ = (speed of nerve impulse)

*Record time accurate to .1 second.

Chapter 4

REPORT SHEET—LEARNED TASTE AVERSIONS

Number of subjects questioned ________

Number of subjects with aversions ________

Number of subjects who confirm Garcia's notions ________

Summarize the results from all of your subjects below. You decide which questions are relevant to each feature of learned taste aversion, and summarize your results with respect to each of the features listed below.

BELONGINGNESS Relevant questions (Nos.)

____

____

____

ONE-TRIAL LEARNING Relevant questions (Nos.)

____

____

____

LONG CS-US INTERVAL Relevant questions (Nos.)

____

____

____

NOVELTY EFFECT Relevant questions (Nos.)

____

____

____

"IRRATIONALITY" Relevant questions (Nos.)

____

____

____

OTHER INTERESTING RESULTS

____

____

____

Chapter 4

REPORT SHEET—MAZE LEARNING

Trial	Time	Number of of errors
1	________	________
2	________	________
3	________	________
4	________	________
5 (using paper with cut-out hole)	________	________

Chapter 5

REPORT SHEET—MEASURING BRIGHTNESS CONTRAST

Background values:	1	3	4	5	7	10
matching value 1:	________	________	________	________	________	________
matching value 2:	________	________	________	________	________	________
matching value 3:	________	________	________	________	________	________
Total matching value:	________	________	________	________	________	________
Average matching value:	________	________	________	________	________	________

Chapter 7

REPORT SHEET—IMAGERY INSTRUCTIONS

Answer sheet for list 1	Answer sheet for list 2
1. ________	1. ________
2. ________	2. ________
3. ________	3. ________
4. ________	4. ________
5. ________	5. ________
6. ________	6. ________
7. ________	7. ________
8. ________	8. ________
9. ________	9. ________
10. ________	10. ________
11. ________	11. ________
12. ________	12. ________
13. ________	13. ________
14. ________	14. ________
15. ________	15. ________
16. ________	16. ________
17. ________	17. ________
18. ________	18. ________
19. ________	19. ________
20. ________	20. ________

Chapter 9

REPORT SHEET—IMPLICIT LEARNING

1. ______	9. ______	17. ______
2. ______	10. ______	18. ______
3. ______	11. ______	19. ______
4. ______	12. ______	20. ______
5. ______	13. ______	21. ______
6. ______	14. ______	22. ______
7. ______	15. ______	23. ______
8. ______	16. ______	24. ______

Subject's statement of rule: ____________________

____

____

____

____

____

____

____

____

Number of correct responses out of 24: ________

Chapter 10

REPORT SHEET—PERSONAL SPACE

1 person elevator	Number of cases with subjects in predicted place (7 or 9)	________/15
2 person elevator	Number of cases with subjects in predicted place (7 or 9)	________/15
2 person elevator	Number of cases with subjects in noncontiguous squares	________/15

Chapter 8

REPORT SHEET—THE STROOP EFFECT

Experiment 1

Color patch list	Letter string list
List 1 ________ sec. ________ errors	List 2 ________ sec. ________ errors
List 3 ________ sec. ________ errors	List 4 ________ sec. ________ errors
List 5 ________ sec. ________ errors	List 6 ________ sec. ________ errors
List 7 ________ sec. ________ errors	List 8 ________ sec. ________ errors
List 9 ________ sec. ________ errors	List 10 ________ sec. ________ errors
Average = ________ sec.	Average = ________ sec.
Total errors = ________	Total errors = ________

Experiment 2

Neutral words	Color words
List 1 ________ sec. ________ errors	List 2 ________ sec. ________ errors
List 3 ________ sec. ________ errors	List 4 ________ sec. ________ errors
List 5 ________ sec. ________ errors	List 6 ________ sec. ________ errors
List 7 ________ sec. ________ errors	List 8 ________ sec. ________ errors
List 9 ________ sec. ________ errors	List 10 ________ sec. ________ errors
Average = ________ sec.	Average = ________ sec.
Total errors = ________	Total errors = ________

Experiment 3

Neutral words	Color referent words
List 1 ________ sec. ________ errors	List 2 ________ sec. ________ errors
List 3 ________ sec. ________ errors	List 4 ________ sec. ________ errors
List 5 ________ sec. ________ errors	List 6 ________ sec. ________ errors
List 7 ________ sec. ________ errors	List 8 ________ sec. ________ errors
List 9 ________ sec. ________ errors	List 10 ________ sec. ________ errors
Average = ________ sec.	Average = ________ sec.
Total errors = ________	Total errors = ________

Chapter 11

REPORT SHEET—IMPRESSIONS

Percent of subjects checking favorable adjective at left

	Asch's Data		Your Data	
Adjective Pair	group A (24 students)	group B (34 students)	group A (__ students)	group B (__ students)
generous	24	10		
wise	18	17		
happy	32	5		
good-natured	18	0		
humorous	52	21		
sociable	56	27		
popular	35	14		
reliable	84	91		
good-looking	74	35		
serious	97	100		
restrained	64	9		
honest	80	79		

Chapter 13

REPORT SHEET—CONSERVATION OF NUMBER

1. More blue _______
   More red _______
   Both equal _______
2. More blue _______
   More red _______
   Both equal _______
3. More blue _______
   More red _______
   Both equal _______
4. More blue _______
   More red _______
   Both equal _______
5. More blue _______
   More red _______
   Both equal _______
6. More blue _______
   More red _______
   Both equal _______
7. More blue _______
   More red _______
   Both equal _______
8. More blue _______
   More red _______
   Both equal _______

Chapter 18

REPORT SHEET—DEPRESSION

Self-rating of mood now (enter number) __________

Self-rating of mood over last twelve months (enter number) __________

Number of negative events recalled __________

Number of positive events recalled __________

Negative minus positive events __________

Negative plus positive events __________

Chapter 14

REPORT SHEET—SEX DIFFERENCES

Item	Your data* (combined with classmate's data)			
	Maless		Females	
	#	%	#	%
1. Killing cockroach	_____	_____	_____	_____
2. Queen Anne's lace (correct answer: flower)	_____	_____	_____	_____
3. Using word "shit" (less than 5 times)	_____	_____	_____	_____
4. Sew clothes	_____	_____	_____	_____
5. Intercourse only after spiritual love	_____	_____	_____	_____
6. Nude in locker room	_____	_____	_____	_____
7. Crying frequently (very often, often, or only with good reason)	_____	_____	_____	_____
8. Feel like smashing things	_____	_____	_____	_____
9. Chest measurement	_____	_____	_____	_____
10. Change tire	_____	_____	_____	_____
11. Playing radio	_____	_____	_____	_____
12. Prefer dominance in relationship	_____	_____	_____	_____
13. Overweight	_____	_____	_____	_____
14. Washing hair when depressed	_____	_____	_____	_____
15. Sleep in nude	_____	_____	_____	_____
16. Closest parent (mother)	_____	_____	_____	_____
17. Keep room neat	_____	_____	_____	_____

*Tabulate your results below in the following way. For the "yes" or "no" questions (e.g., item 1), add up the number of subjects who answered "yes." Then calculate what percentage answered "yes." For the "true" or "false" questions (e.g., item 8), record those who answer "true." For other items (e.g., item 2), add up the number of subjects whose answers are the same as those indicated in parentheses under "Item" (e.g., item 2—flower).

List the femalesness scores of all of your subjects:

Males: _____ _____ _____ _____ _____ _____ _____ _____ _____ _____

_____ _____ _____ _____ _____ _____ _____ _____ _____ _____

Females: _____ _____ _____ _____ _____ _____ _____ _____ _____ _____

_____ _____ _____ _____ _____ _____ _____ _____ _____ _____

Copyrights and Acknowledgments

Grateful acknowledgment is made to: F. Garb, A. Stunkard, and the *American Journal of Psychiatry* to adapt from Garb and Stunkard, "Taste aversions in man," *American Journal of Psychiatry* 131 (1974):1204–1207; W. Epstein, I. Rock, and the *American Journal of Psychology* to adapt from Epstein, W., and Rock, I., "Perceptual set as an artifact of recency," *American Journal of Psychology* 73 (1960):214–228; J. R. Stroop and the *Journal of Experimental Psychology* to adapt from J. R. Stroop, "Studies in interference in serial verbal reactions," *Journal of Experimental Psychology* 18 (1935): 643–662; A. S. Reber and the *Journal of Verbal Learning and Verbal Behavior* to adapt from A. S. Reber, "Implicit learning of artificial grammars," *Journal of Verbal Learning and Verbal Behavior* 6 (1967):858–863; S. E. Asch and the *Journal of Abnormal and Social Psychology* to adapt from S. E. Asch, "Forming impressions of personality," *Journal of Abnormal and Social Psychology* 41 (1946):258–290.

Illustrations

Page 2 Bugelski, B. R., and Alampay, D. A., "The role of frequency in developing perceptual sets," *Canadian Journal of Psychology* 15 (1961): 205–211. Adapted by permission of the Canadian Psychological Association.

Page 12 *bottom* and page 29 Keeton, W. T., *Biological science*, 4th edition. New York: W. W. Norton & Company, Inc., 1986. Copyright © 1986, 1980, 1979, 1972, 1967 by W. W. Norton & Company, Inc.

Pages 14 and 15 Hodgkin, A. L., and Huxley, A. F. "Action potentials recorded from inside nerve fibers," *Nature* 144 (1939):710–711. Adapted by permission.

Page 28 Nisbett, R. E., "Taste, deprivation and weight determinants of eating behavior," *Journal of Personality and Social Psychology* 10 (1968): 107–116. Copyright 1968 by the American Psychological Association. Reprinted by permission.

Page 40 Reproduced by permission of the publishers from Köhler, W., *The mentality of apes*, London, England: Routledge & Kegan Paul Ltd., 1976.

Page 41 *bottom* Pavlov, I. P., *Lectures on conditioned reflexes*, vol. 1. New York: International Publishers, Co., Inc. 1928. Adapted by permission of International Publishers Co., Inc.

Page 43 From Spooner, A., and Kellogg, W. N., "The backward conditioning curve," *American Journal of Psychology* 60 (1947):321–334. Copyright © 1947 by The University of Illinois Press. Reprinted by permission of the publisher.

Page 74 *left* From James J. Gibson, *The perception of the visible world*. Boston, Mass.: Houghton Mifflin Co., 1950.

Page 74 *right* Photograph by William Vandivert. From *Scientific American*, April 1960. Reprinted with permission of William Vandivert and *Scientific American*.

Pages 76 and 78 Boring, E. G., "A new ambiguous figure," *American Journal of Psychology* 42 (1930): 444–445; and Leeper, R. W., "A study of a neglected portion of the field of learning: The development of sensory organization," *Journal of Genetic Psychology* 46 (1935): 41–75.

Page 124 Reprinted from "Reproductive behaviors," by Etkin, E., in *Social behavior and organization among vertebrates* by Etkin, W., by permission of The University of Chicago Press. Copyright 1964 by The University of Chicago.

Page 138 Festinger, L., and Carlsmith, J. M., "Cognitive consequences of forced compliance," *Journal of Abnormal and Social Psychology* 58 (1959): 203–210. Copyright 1959 by the American Psychological Association. Reprinted by permission.

Page 163 Nilsson, Lennart, *Behold man*. Boston: Little, Brown, and Company, 1974.

Page 172 Copyright © Hallmark Cards, Inc., used with permission.